Charting Transnational Democracy

CHARTING TRANSNATIONAL DEMOCRACY

BEYOND GLOBAL ARROGANCE

Edited by

JANIE LEATHERMAN

and

JULIE WEBBER

First published in 2005 by
PALGRAVE MACMILLAN™
175 Fifth Avenue, New York, N.Y. 10010 and
Houndmills, Basingstoke, Hampshire, England RG21 6XS
Companies and representatives throughout the world.

PALGRAVE MACMILLAN is the global academic imprint of the Palgrave
Macmillan division of St. Martin's Press, LLC and of Palgrave Macmillan Ltd.
Macmillan® is a registered trademark in the United States, United Kingdom
and other countries. Palgrave is a registered trademark in the European
Union and other countries.

ISBN 1–4039–6952–3 (hc.)
ISBN 1–4039–6977–9 (pbk.)

Library of Congress Cataloging-in-Publication Data

    Charting transnational democracy : beyond global arrogance /
edited by Janie Leatherman and Julie Webber.
        p. cm.
    Includes bibliographical references and index.
    ISBN 1–4039–6952–3 (hc.)—ISBN 1–4039–6977–9 (pbk.)
        1. Hegemony. 2. Social movements—International cooperation.
    3. International relations. 4. Globalization. I. Leatherman, Janie, 1959–
    II. Webber, Julie A., 1972–

JZ1312.C53 2005
327.1—dc22   2004065482

A catalogue record for this book is available from the British Library.

Design by Newgen Imaging Systems (P) Ltd., Chennai, India.

First edition: August 2005

10 9 8 7 6 5 4 3 2 1

Printed in the United States of America.

To
Janie's brother John, and to Julie's kindred spirit, Deems

Contents

Glossary of Abbreviations

ACT UP	AIDS Coalition to Unleash Power
AFDC	Aid to Families with Dependent Children
AFL-CIO	American Federation of Labor-Congress of Industrial Organizations
AGO	Antigovernmental Organizations
AIDS	Auto Immune Deficiency Syndrome
ANSWER	Act Now to Stop War and End Racism
APL	Anti-Personnel Landmines
ARENA	Asian Regional Exchange for New Alternatives
ARMSCOR	Armaments Corporation of South Africa
ATTAC	Association for the Taxing of Financial Transactions for the Aid of Citizens (France)
BINGO	Business and Industry NGOs
BLSP	Business Leaders for Sensible Priorities
CBD	Convention on Biodiversity
CBJP	Brazilian Justice and Peace Commission
CCW	Convention on Conventional Weapons
CEH	Commission for Historical Information (Guatemala)
CIA	Central Intelligence Agency (U.S.)
CIVES	Associação Brasileira de Empresários pela Cidadania (Brazilian Business Association for Citizenship)
CUT	Central Única dos Trabalhadores (Central Trade Union Confederation)
CVR	Truth and Reconciliation Commission (Peru)
ECE	East Central Europe
ECOWAS	Economic Community of West African States
EEC	European Environment Center
EIA	Environmental Impact Assessment
ENDA	Environnement et Développement du Tiers-Monde (Environment and Development of the Third World)
EPIC	Electronic Privacy and Information Center
DONGO	Donor-Organized NGOs

FARC	Revolutionary Armed Forces of Columbia
FLAMINGO	Flashy Minded NGOs (representing rich countries)
FoE	Friends of the Earth
FTAA	Free Trade Area of the Americas
G-7	Group of Seven (world's powerful industrial states)
GATT	General Agreements on Tariffs and Trade
GEF	Global Environment Facility
GHG	Greenhouse Gas
GMO	Genetically Modified Organism
GONGO	Government-Organized NGOs
GRINGO	Government-Regulated and Initiated NGOs
GSM	Global Social Movements
HIV	Human Immunodeficiency Virus
IACHR	Inter American Commission of Human Rights
IBASE	Instituto Brasileiro de Análises Sociais e Econômicas (The Brazilian Institute of Social and Economic Analyses) (Brazil)
IC	International Council (of the World Social Forum)
ICBL	International Campaign to Ban Landmines
ICDS	Ibn Khaldun Center for Developmental Studies
ICT	Information Communication Technologies
ICRC	International Committee of the Red Cross
IGC	Institute for Global Communications
IMF	International Monetary Fund
INGO	International Nongovernmental Organization
ISP	Internet Service Provider
IUCN	International Union for the Conservation of Nature
KWRU	Kensington Welfare Rights Union
LIC	Low Intensity Conflict
MAI	Multilateral Agreement on Investment
MI	Medico International (Frankfurt, Federal Republic of Germany)
MST	Movimento dos Trabalhadores Rurais Sem Terra (Movement of Landless Rural Workers)
NAACP	National Association for the Advancement of Colored People
NIEO	New International Economic Order
NOW	National Organization for Women (U.S.)
NROS	Nadace rozvoje obcanske spolecnosti (Czech Civil Society Development Foundation)
NSA	National Security Archive
NSD	National Security Doctrine (Argentina)
OAS	Organization of American States

ODS	Občanská demokratická strana (Civic Democratic Party) (Czech Republic)
OECD	Organization for Economic Cooperation and Development
OPEC	Organization of Petroleum Exporting Countries
PM	Prime Minister
PMDB	Partido do Movimento Democrático Brasileiro (Brazilian Democratic Movement Party)
PPEHRC	Poor People's Economic Human Rights Campaign
PRWORA	Personal Responsibility and Work Opportunity Reconciliation Act (1996)
PT	Partido dos Trabalhadores (Workers Party, Brazil)
RAWA	Revolutionary Association of Women in Afghanistan
SADC	Southern Africa Development Community
SOA	School of the Americas
TRC	Truth and Reconciliation Commission
TRANGO	Transnational NGOs
TSMO	Transnational Social Movement Organizations
UNCED	United Nations Conference on Environment and Development
UNEP	United Nations Environmental Program
UNFCC	United Nations Framework Convention on Climate Change
UNITA	UniãoNacional pela Independêndcia Total de Angola (National Union for the Total Independence of Angola)
USIP	United States Institute for Peace
VVAF	Vietnam Veterans of America Foundation
WAND	Women's Action for New Directions
WEF	World Economic Forum
WMD	Weapons of Mass Destruction
WRI	World Resources Institute
WSF	World Social Forum
WSSD	World Summit on Sustainable Development
WWF	World Wildlife Fund
WTO	World Trade Organization

Notes on Contributors

David Cortright is president of the Fourth Freedom Forum in Goshen, Indiana and a research fellow at the Joan B. Kroc Institute for International Peace Studies at the University of Notre Dame. He has served as consultant or adviser to various agencies of the United Nations, the Carnegie Commission on Preventing Deadly Conflict, the International Peace Academy, and the John D. and Catherine T. MacArthur Foundation. He has written widely on nuclear disarmament, nonviolent social change, and the use of incentives and sanctions as tools of international peacemaking. He is the author or editor of twelve books, including *A Peaceful Superpower: The Movement Against War in Iraq* (2004), and two volumes released in 2002: *Smart Sanctions: Targeting Economic Statecraft*, and *Sanctions and the Search for Security: Challenges to UN Action*, both with George A. Lopez. His other books include: *The Sanctions Decade: Assessing UN Strategies in the 1990s* (2000), with George A. Lopez; *The Price of Peace: Incentives and International Conflict Prevention* (1997); and *Peace Works: The Citizen's Role in Ending the Cold War* (1993).

Lars K. Hallström is Associate Professor of Political Science and Canada Research Chair in Public Policy and Governance at St. Francis Xavier University in Antigonish, Canada. His research is broadly concerned with the intersections of environmental politics and policy, civil society, and political participation in systems of multilevel governance, but he has also published in the areas of IR theory and technology. Recent publications include "Gendering Governance? Civility and the Gender Gap in Poland" in *Canadian-American Slavic Studies*, "Eurocratising Enlargement? EU Elites and NGO Participation in European Environmental Policy" in *Environmental Politics* and "Support for European Federalism? An Elite View" in *Journal of European Integration*.

Krista Hunt is a SSHRC Postdoctoral Fellow at the Munk Centre for International Studies, University of Toronto. Her current research project examines the Bush administration's new "pro-women" foreign policy agenda; the impact of the war for women in targeted and coalition countries; and the transnational mobilization of women's rights activists in response to the war. Recent articles include "The Strategic Co-optation of Women's Rights Discourse in the War on Terrorism," in the *International Feminist Journal of Politics*. She is currently working on a coedited volume entitled *War Stories and Camouflage Politics: (En)Gendering the War on Terror*.

Jyl J. Josephson is associate professor of political science and Director of Women's Studies at Rutgers, The State University of New Jersey, Newark campus. She is the author of numerous articles on gender and public policy published in journals such as the *Journal of Poverty, New Political Science, Journal of Political Ideologies*, and *Women and Politics*. She is the author of *Gender, Families, and State: Child Support Policy in the United States* (Rowman and Littlefield, 1997) and coedited *Fundamental Differences: Feminists Talk Back to Social Conservatives* (Rowman and Littlefield, 2003) with Cynthia Burack. A second edition of *Gender and American Politics*, coedited with Sue Tolleson-Rinehart, will be published in 2005.

Janie Leatherman is full professor, Director of International Affairs, The College of Arts and Sciences, and codirector of Peace and Conflict Resolution Studies at Illinois State University. She has held appointments at the University of Notre Dame as a visiting fellow at the Joan B. Kroc Institute for International Peace Studies (1992–97), and Visiting Assistant Professor at Macalester College (1989–91), and Director of Brethren Colleges Abroad, University of Barcelona (1991–92). She received her Ph.D. from the University of Denver, Graduate School of International Studies in 1991. Dr. Leatherman's recent publications include *Breaking Cycles of Violence: Conflict Prevention in Intrastate Crises* (Kumarian 1999), coauthored with Raimo Väyrynen, William DeMars, and Patrick Gaffney, and also published in Indonesian in 2004 by Gadjah Mada University Press; and *From Cold War to Democratic Peace: Third Parties, Peaceful Change and the OSCE* (Syracuse University Press, 2003), and many book chapters, articles, and grants on the OSCE, conflict early warning and prevention, and foreign policy and transnational politics. She has served as a consultant to numerous organizations, including the United Nations University, UNIFEM, Catholic Relief Services, Search for Common Ground, the Brookings Institution, and the Council on Foreign Relations (New York). She is presently working on a volume on *Discipline and Punishment in Global Politics*.

Jim L. Nelson is an independent researcher and activist living in Jersey City, New Jersey, and project coordinator for the United Nations Association—USA New Jersey Division. He is former Assistant Director for Student Affairs with the Adlai Stevenson Center for Community and

Economic Development at Illinois State University, and he has participated in the International Campaign to Ban Landmines conferences in Oslo and Ottawa in 1997. He has taught in northeastern Namibia, bordering the landmine-affected parts of Angola.

Kate O'Neill is an assistant professor in the Department of Environmental Science, Policy and Management at the University of California at Berkeley. Her research concerns transboundary transfer of risk and dangerous products, and global governance. She is the author of *Waste Trading Among Rich Nations: Building a New Theory of Environmental Regulation* (MIT Press, 2000) and has recently published in *Global Environmental Politics, Public Understanding of Science, International Studies Review* and the *Annual Review of Political Science*. She is currently working on two books, one a review of international environmental politics, for Cambridge University Press, and the second, on the comparative politics of transnational diseases.

Carlos A. Parodi is associate professor and teaches in the Department of Politics and Government of Illinois State University since 1990. In the 1970s and mid-1980s he obtained economic degrees from Peruvian universities and worked for Peruvian research institutes publishing several books and articles on the subject of the relationship between the state and transnational corporations. He currently teaches courses in international political economy, U.S.–Latin American relations, and human rights. His most recent book is *The Politics of South American Boundaries* (Praeger, 2001), and he currently is working on a book manuscript about the politics of truth commissions in Latin America.

Marlyn Tadros, Ph.D. is the Founder and Executive Director of Virtual Activism, a nonprofit organization that provides ICT training to NGOs across the globe. She was a Visiting Scholar at the Women's Department, Northeastern University from 2001–03. Prior to that, Dr. Tadros had been a Visiting Fellow at the Human Rights Program, Law School, Harvard University. She also served as Deputy director of the Legal Research and Resource Center for Human Rights in Cairo, Egypt, and was Executive Director of the National Steering Committee of the United Nations International Conference on Population and Development, Cairo, 1994. Dr. Tadros has several publications and articles, and has been featured in several documentaries dealing with the Middle East. Currently, Dr. Tadros teaches computer and Internet Technologies at the Arts Institute of New England in Boston, and Northeastern University.

Teivo Teivainen is Director of the Program on Democracy and Global Transformation at the San Marcos University in Lima, Peru, and the

International Political Economy Section Chair of the International Studies Association. His newest books are *Enter Economism, Exit Politics: Experts, Economic Policy and the Damage to Democracy* (Zed 2002, winner of the Terence K. Hopkins Award of the American Sociological Association), *Pedagogía del poder mundial. Relaciones internacionales y lecciones del desarrollo en América Latina* (CEDEP 2003), *A Possible World: Democratic Transformation of Global Institutions* (Zed 2004, coauthored with Heikki Patomäki) and *Dilemmas of Democratization in the World Social Forum* (Routledge, forthcoming in 2005).

Stacy D. VanDeveer is the 2003–06 Ronald H. O'Neal Associate Professor in the University of New Hampshire's Department of Political Science. His research interests include international environmental policymaking and its domestic impacts, the connections between environmental and security issues, and the role of expertise in policy making. Before taking a faculty position, he spent two years as a post-doctoral research fellow in the Belfer Center for Science and International Affairs at John F. Kennedy School of Government at Harvard University. He has received research funding from, among others, the (U.S.) National Science Foundation and the Swedish Foundation for Strategic Environmental Research (MISTRA). In addition to authoring and coauthoring a number of articles, book chapters, working papers, and reports, he coedited *EU Enlargement and the Environment: Institutional Change and Environmental Policy in Central and Eastern Europe* (Routledge, 2005), *Saving The Seas: Values, Science And International Governance* (Maryland Sea Grant Press, College Park, Md., 1997) and *Protecting Regional Seas: Developing Capacity and Fostering Environmental Cooperation In Europe* (Woodrow Wilson International Center, Washington, D.C., 1999).

Julie A. Webber is Assistant Professor of Politics and Government at Illinois State University. She is the author of "Why Can't We Be Deweyan Citizens?" an article in the John Dewey Society Publication *Educational Theory*, a chapter in the edited volume *Education as Enforcement* (New York: Routledge, 2003), as well as a recently published book on violence in democratic institutions and societies, *Failure to Hold: The Politics of School Violence.* (Lanhan, Md.: Rowman & Littlefield, 2003), an edited volume: *Curriculum Dis\positions*: with William Reynolds (LEA Press, 2004) and a book chapter in E. Wayne Ross and David Gabbard (eds.) *Defending Public Schools* (New York: Praeger, 2004) entitled, "Schooling and the Security State." Dr. Webber's primary research and teaching areas are international political theory, educational theory, and theories of violence and women's studies. She is currently working on her second book *Virtual Violence and Western Values.*

Diana Zoelle is the author of *Globalizing Concern for Women's Human Rights* (St. Martin' Press, 2000), and other articles and reviews on gender and international human rights. She has taught political theory at Bloomsburg University since 1997. She received her A.A.S. from Butler County (Pennsylvania) Community College, her B.S. from Slippery Rock University; an M.P.A. from the University of Missouri and her M.A. and Ph.D. in politics and government from the University of Maryland.

Preface

This study has a long and more immediate history. Janie Leatherman began working on "global awareness" at Macalester College in 1990 with support of a Mellon grant to develop a gateway course to an International Studies major. That course was designed around the concept of transnational social movements and their emancipatory efforts under globalization to catalyze peaceful change on issues of global violence and injustice. This early work was informed also by feedback to presentations in Santiago, Chile, and a course she taught at the University of Barcelona on global awareness in the early 1990s. At the Kroc Institute for International Peace Studies at the University of Notre Dame, Janie continued this work with a stimulating project on transnational social movements with Jackie Smith and Ron Pagnucco under a 1993 Social Science Research Council grant that supported a 1994 workshop. At Illinois State, Janie brought these perspectives to bear on graduate courses in International Relations theory organized around the concept of global arrogance, U.S. hegemony, and transnational social movements in courses she instructed in 2000–02. Those fruitful seminars prompted this volume, which collaboration she initiated with Julie Webber in the fall of 2002. Janie wishes to express her gratitude for the support for developing this volume she received from Illinois State University's summer research fellowships, and a sabbatical in 2003.

As events in the world, and the recent election of George W. Bush signaled remarkable (and regrettable) changes to global order—this in the midst of the social and economic upheaval of the phenomenon long labeled "globalization"—Janie and Julie began to think about the continuing (and lasting) effects of "arrogance" for democratic change and progressive emancipatory projects. One initial conclusion was the world was quickly spinning out of control, but as too simple, sad, and arrogant a proposition that was, we decided to think about *which* agents might be challenging this arrogance and how successful they could be. As we embarked on this project, we challenged ourselves to be aware of arrogance in the ways our own lives were connected from local to global settings. We began to see the problem as less about specific actors/identities and more an attitude developed out of willful ignorance and a culture of superiority.

One special issue was the Internet; we knew that social movements had for a decade or so been radically altered in regard to the kinds of tactics they could deploy and that mass mobilization had been promoted by Internet organizing and information exchange. We also knew that this arrogance could no longer be labeled exclusively nationalism (the term under which arrogance had been subsumed for most of the Cold War, and as far back as the nineteenth-century power balancing experiments). As most scholars contend, "the process of globalization has created a third world within the first world as well as a first world within a third world" (Bilgin 2003, 214). This means that arrogance has changed its mode of appearance while maintaining anonymity before those people its actions harm. So, we wrote an International Studies Workshop grant proposal, and it was graciously funded and supported under a program spearheaded by John Vasquez to support projects that question the "state of the discipline" of international relations. The title of our project, "Confronting Global Arrogance: Transnational Movements and Global Democracy," allowed us to gather a group of nine scholars (five junior and four mid-career) from the United States and other countries of origin (including Canada, Ecuador, Egypt, and Finland) to author an edited volume on the "Politics of Global Arrogance."

In support of this goal, we held a workshop in conjunction with the 2003 ISA Conference in Portland, Oregon, and a second workshop at Illinois State that spring. At Portland, we also presented drafts of several papers to a very receptive and critical audience on the panel "The Politics of Global Arrogance and the Role of Nonviolent Emancipatory Movements." The exchange of ideas and the work by all panelists and presenters were crucial to forming the core of this project. We met with contributors again in the fall of 2003 on a panel at the Midwest International Studies Association Conference, and later in 2004 at the International Studies Association meeting in Montreal, Quebec. Discussants, audience members, and contributors all helped to consolidate the ideas in the volume we are presenting here, for which we are most grateful.

The editors wish to thank many people who gave us feedback on the volume and the ideas contained in it, including graduate students in the International Relations seminars spring 2000–02. We are also grateful to graduate students in a topics seminar summer 2003 that Janie instructed on "Global Arrogance," who heard presentations from a number of the volume's contributors and wrote incisive critiques of all the draft chapters of the volume, which feedback we shared with the contributors.

Illinois State University administrative faculty also helped in a number of ways. We wish to thank Jamal Nassar for generously contributing additional travel funds for the International Studies Association meeting in 2003 in Portland in support of the workshop, as well as other travel-related and publishing funds. Also, Roberta Seelinger Trites, in her capacity as acting dean, vigorously supported the project and whose tenure included encouragement of faculty research collaboration and teaching. The department of Women's Studies at ISU and its faculty were also helpful along with our colleague in Sociology, Maria Schmeeckle, who invited the editors to present ideas to their classrooms and gave feedback in public presentations on campus.

Finally we would like to thank our research assistants during the last couple years whose efforts have facilitated the development of this study, including Christine Wolf, Veronica Panizzi, Sienna Crawford and especially Layla Johnston, who assisted in the preparation of the manuscript and index. We would like to extend special thanks to Jan Aart Scholte, Maher Bages, Deems D. Morrione, and Diane S. Rubenstein for their support, feedback, and comments on chapters in the volume, including Julie's theory chapter. We save special recognition for two anonymous reviewers of the manuscript. They offered us many incisive critiques and suggestions for improvements. We have endeavored to take their advice to heart, and benefited greatly from their thoughtful and informed reading of the text. Their voice is thus part of the dialogue that unfolds throughout the book. We also extend our hearty thanks to all our authors, who have given us a wonderful learning experience, and to Anthony Wahl, our editor at Palgrave Macmillan, for his good cheer and very able direction of this volume. Janie expresses deep gratitude to her brother, John Leatherman, for his critical reading of her chapters, constructive comments, and many conversations about global arrogance that were part of our efforts to keep the violence, suffering, and injustices in our own local ambits in perspective with the global context. We thank all these individuals for their contributions to this study, and assume responsibility ourselves for any of its shortcomings.

CITATION

Bilgin, Pinar. 2003. "Individual and Societal Dimensions of Security." *International Studies Review* 5: 203–22.

Part 1

Escaping the Entrapment of Global Arrogance

Chapter 1

Global Arrogance and the Crisis of Hegemony

Janie Leatherman

In an era of wealth and opportunity, a simple fact demands our attention; most of the world's people lack basic human needs. Their daily struggle is a stark contrast to the privileged lives that a global minority take for granted. The chasm between these two worlds is growing. In his Nobel Peace Prize address, former U.S. President Jimmy Carter has called this "the most serious and universal problem," a disparity that we can trace to "the root causes of most of the world's unresolved problems, including starvation, illiteracy, environmental degradation, violent conflict, and unnecessary illnesses that range from guinea worm to HIV and AIDS." Carter calls on us to share with others "an appreciable part of our excessive wealth," but notes we seem to lack "understanding or concern about those who are enduring lives of despair and hopelessness" (2002, 3–4).

Instead of global awareness, we indulge in willful ignorance to avoid critical thought and action. *This* veil of ignorance serves *not* to discern justice as John Rawls has called for (1971, 12), but to escape from our responsibilities for justice.[1] We deploy this veil of ignorance not to alleviate, but to erase the suffering of a neighbor, the homeless, the local ghetto, the rural poor, or the unknown victims of violence and disasters faraway. When the news brings their lives into our homes, we shut them out. It is easy to do; we throw out the newspaper or click off the television remote control. Such arrogance of power is found anywhere from the local to the global. So we speak collectively of *global arrogance*. But it has not gone unanswered. Social movements have organized to challenge it, and bring empowerment and democracy back into political life. They have begun a dialogue spanning communities from small neighborhoods to transnational networks. *The democratic challenge social movements pose to global arrogance is one of the most profound political developments of our day.* This volume is devoted to understanding the kind of democratic change they are shaping, and the causes and principles which animate it.

Despite the explosion of nongovernmental organizations (NGOs) and social movements since the 1980s (Karns and Mingst 2004, 11), their role in promoting democracy from local to global levels remains undertheorized. The old models of world federalism or world government never materialized as expected. Instead, we have seen the emergence of multifaceted, multi-layered, and complex systems of cooperation. This kind of governance has no democratic base or accountability (Hettne and Odén 2002). Key institutions such as the United Nations Security Council, the World Trade Organization (WTO), or the International Monetary Fund (IMF) lack transparency in decision-making, and democratic rules of participation (Aksu and Camilleri 2002).

We find the United States in the topdog position of this system, but experiencing a crisis of hegemony. This is apparent in the changing nature of U.S. leadership—shifting from a reliance on consensual forms of power to coercion and force. In response, we see a renewed activism that seeks to escape the entrapments of global arrogance and build democratic alternatives locally, transnationally, and in the institutions of global governance. A recent United Nations panel on UN—Civil Society Relations recognizes these emergent relationships, and calls for measures to systematize them within the main UN organs and family of institutions (*We the Peoples* 2004).

Our project on transnational democracy and social movements shares the concerns of the UN—Civil Society Panel Report. But we have come at this project from the perspective of the democratic deficits of global governance, and the crisis of hegemony. We are asking: What is being done? How do movements challenge global arrogance? Are they hitting their heads with futility against the hard walls of hegemony? Or have social movements turned away from contesting the hegemon to develop their own democratic projects? Is an alternative order in the making? How can we put our finger on the pulse of changes that are opening up new democratic possibilities and spaces for action?

Conventional analysis places social movements in global civil society, typically situating them as secondary or subordinate to states and international organizations. Here NGOs can be critiqued as playing more of a supporting role to the hegemon, rather than challenging it (Barfield 2001). Other studies place NGOs and new social movements in the role of contesting the oppressive structures and politics we call global arrogance

(Risse et al., eds. 1999; Vandenberg 2000; Guidry et al., eds. 2000; O'Brien et al. 2000, Smith and Johnston, eds. 2002). A major project on global civil society at the London School of Economics recognizes the complexity of defining global civil society. They argue the actors of global civil society take many different organizational forms, and have many different objectives ranging from charities, vitual associations, humanitarian groups, single to multiple-issue campaigns, democratically run groups to autocratic sects, to philanthropic foundations, and so on (Anheier and Themudo 2002, 191). Karns and Mingst (2004, 18 Figure 1.5) also emphasize the variety of NGO types, citing a host of colorful acronyms such as GONGO (government-organized), GRINGO (government-regulated and initiated), BINGO (business and industry), or FLAMINGO (flashy minded NGOs representing rich countries).

This alphabet soup points to the difficulty of conceptualizing the actors of civil society, and how they are organized. The field of international relations employs the concept of NGOs. Sociologists, particularly those interested in the transnational aspects of social movements, have brought to us the concept of transnational social movement organizations, or TSMOs—highlighting both the social movement component of NGO activity, and the organizational forms they take within states and across their borders (Smith et al. 1997; Leatherman et al. 1994). Keck and Sikkink emphasize networking. They define transnational advocacy networks as encompassing "nonstate actors that interact with each other, with states and international organizations," which are "distinguishable largely by the centrality of principled ideas or values in motivating their formation" (1998, 1).

These different conceptual approaches of social movement and network scholars are not mutually exclusive. As Smith and Johnston point out, looking at transnational ties and networks also helps us discover "two related processes that are largely overlooked in the literature: (1) how transnational mobilization influences identity formation by bringing together activists with different political experiences; and (2) how mobilizing ideologies are worked and reworked by diffusion and innovation via transnational activist contact" (2002, 5–6). Our project shares with them concern over the "the extent to which [transnational ties] reflect or challenge predominant power relations in the global system" (6). In this volume we speak of transnational social movements, much in the sociological tradition in which Smith and her colleague are situated, yet also focus on NGOs and examine how these actors are networked to advocate for principled action on such social issues as the global movement to ban landmines. We ask whether, and if so how, social movements are working for change in the system of global governance, and also in their *own* arenas of action.

Significance of Study

Conceptualizing Global Arrogance

What is distinctive about our approach? First, it is centered on the concept of *global arrogance*. We speak of *global* arrogance because structural injustice and violence have long histories with local effects that are entangled in global networks of profit and power. We also speak of global arrogance because as politics has become globalized, traditional democratic institutions do not match up to new challenges. People are disempowered from the hollowing out of democracy at the nation-state level and the lack of democracy at the international level (Tehranian 2002, 71). People are also disempowered as the global supercedes the local. Therefore, local perspectives, wisdom, and resources are at risk of being lost, while global or outside (Western, northern) expertise and interests are privileged.

Historical Origins

Why should we use the term *arrogance*? The Social Sciences—even psychology—has not used it widely. Yet, the United States has faced accusations of arrogance historically, and increasingly since the 2003 invasion of Iraq. One of the most important statements comes from William Fulbright, who as chairman of the U.S. Senate Foreign Relations Committee during the U.S. war in Vietnam, warned that "the attitude above all others which I feel sure is no longer valid is the arrogance of power, the tendency of great nations to equate power with virtue and major responsibilities with a universal mission" (1966, 9). Criticism has come from outside the United States too, when Iranian students first decried the United States as "the Capital of Global Arrogance."[2] Iran continues to celebrate the anniversary of the 1979 take over of the U.S. embassy in Tehran as the "National Day of Campaign against Global Arrogance."[3]

At the core of the current debate over U.S. bellicosity, lack of empathy and generosity are charges of imperial overreach and decline, and the dangers of hard power undermining soft power (Nye 2004). We find calls for the exercise of U.S. power without arrogance from all sides of the U.S. political spectrum. For example, in his second presidential debate with Al Gore, George W. Bush said, "Our nation stands alone right now in the world in terms of power . . . . If we're an arrogant nation, they'll resent us. If we're a humble nation, but strong, they'll welcome us" (as quoted in Rubin 2001, 1). Similarly, National Security Advisor Condoleezza Rice claimed in a 2000 *Foreign Affairs* essay that under a Republican administration, "America can exercise power without arrogance and pursue its interests without hectoring and bluster" (63). However, some are more blunt. Johnson (2004, 1) argues "Theodore Roosevelt, an excellent role model of President Bush in these troubled times, came up with a good saying in 1903: 'Envy and arrogance are the two opposite sides of the same black crystal' "— Johnson's analogy of EU-U.S. relations today.

Fluidity of Global Arrogance

We do not limit our attention to U.S. arrogance. Instead, we examine the full range of elite, or "topdogs" of the global political and economic system. They are situated in different networks and layers of the system of global governance—ranging from its key institutions such as the World Bank, the IMF, the WTO, the G-7, and the leading states, to the big northern NGOs of global civil society, and all the way to local elites. However, global arrogance, like power, shifts and flows throughout this system. Thus, the source of arrogance can be hard to pin down. Just when a problem seems to center on the arrogance of the leadership of institutions of global governance, it may shift to the government of a state. Likewise NGOs in the global north may be found acting arrogantly in relation to their partners in the global south. We think of global arrogance as a nested problem like the proverbial set of stacked boxes. We can find arrogance inside of arrogance. As Krista Hunt demonstrates in her chapter in this volume on the global feminist movement, Northern feminists have been accused by women from the global South for their own brand of arrogant, neocolonialism.

Democratic Challenge

A second distinctive feature of this volume is our effort to understand the transformation of the social contract in an era of a hollowed-out nation-state, and runaway globalization. As Webber explains in chapter 2, in the struggle between reactionary and progressive forces, carried out through the virtual spaces of the Internet as well as in the street, we see the outlines of a *generic will*. Progressive forces are toiling to keep space open for ideas and interests to be democratically worked through. In the process, they are "holding the very *idea* of the world in place while it reorganizes itself." While this dialogue may not lead to consensus, it is educational.

Thus, a third distinctive feature of our study is the focus on dialogue as democratic instruction. Democracy is never finished. But dialoguing and joining others working for justice, peace, equality, inclusion, openness, truthtelling, and so on, puts democracy into action in a participatory and a dynamic way. We do not have in mind here a cosmopolitan process—rather something more ordinary. As dialogue is transnationalized and becomes more open, it crosses class and cultural lines and nation-states and reshapes our understanding of democratic forms of governance and the possibilities of transnational community. Democratic instruction is the future-oriented approach to challenging global arrogance.

Key Questions Guiding Study

First, we ask how global arrogance is being disrupted by the democratic challenge of social movements. Second, we question how governance by nation-states is being displaced by the rise of actors claiming democratic space in a transnational context. That is, how are social movements transforming the way we think about the politics of inclusion/exclusion, transnational solidarity, identity, and representation? What key values, principles, and goals are social movements drawing from as they create new democratic spaces? How are these goals pursued? How are these efforts organized from the local to the global? How does their impact vary? How often do they succeed? Do movements give up when they fail, or keep going? What keeps them going in the face of failures? How does the use of new communications technology facilitate or hinder their work, especially the Internet? Can new democratic spaces emerge in both the virtual and real? How are the two connected? And finally, how do movements deal with the dangers of replicating global arrogance?

This introductory chapter sets out the analytical approach that underpins the rest of the volume. First, I examine the nature of the crisis of hegemony, including runaway globalization, the flaws of global governance, and its democratic deficits. Second, I argue that as hegemony declines, its democratic deficits are masked by global arrogance. Third, I elaborate on the myths through which global arrogance is perpetuated, and the challenges to each of them sending them in decline. I conclude with an overview of democratic possibilities and the dangers of replicating global arrogance followed by a synopsis of the chapters in the volume.

Hegemony and Runaway Globalization

Since the end of World War II, the United States played the leading role in establishing the core institutions of the global capitalist and political system (Foot et al., eds. 2002). The mechanisms of U.S. hegemony have included the internationalization of the state and the forces of production

(Cox 1996, 107). The present hegemonic system is centered on the United States in the lead role, with other key industrial states, such as Japan or the European Union in supporting roles, along with key states in the semi-periphery, like many of the Asian or OPEC countries.

At its core, the global capitalist system rests on the outward projection of the national hegemony of the dominant social classes of the United States, and their protection through national security strategies. However, the resort to the use of force and various means of coercion, signal the ruling class's loss of legitimacy. As Hershberg and Moore note, "the events of September 11 graphically demonstrate that the U.S. position as the world's sole superpower hardly rests upon the consent of all the world's countries and populations" (2002, 4). We also see signs of such failings by the reliance of the Bush administration on coercion and the use of force to achieve many of its key foreign policy objectives. For example, in 2002, the United States stationed armed forces in some 100 countries, and publicly embraced a policy of replacing governments by force. The U.S.-led pre-emptive strike against Saddam Hussein put this policy into action.

Global arrogance is thus the mark of a crisis of hegemony. As Gramsci argues, "if the ruling class has lost its consensus, i.e. is no longer 'leading,' but only 'dominant,' exercising coercive force alone, this means precisely that the great masses have become detached from their traditional ideologies, and no longer believe what they used to believe" (1971). Thus, two key signs of the erosion of hegemonic power are: (1) the withdrawal of consent of the governed; and (2) the resort to the use of force by the hegemon to impose its will. I focus the analysis below on the first of these two sets of variables; the erosion of consent. Gramsci argued that "to the extent that the consensual aspect of power is in the forefront, hegemony prevails. Coercion is always latent but is only applied in marginal, deviant cases. Hegemony is enough to ensure conformity of behavior in most people most of the time" (as quoted by Cox 1996, 127). Social myths help to keep in place this hegemony, and also to legitimize the exercise of force when reliance on the consensual aspect of power begins to fail. However, we might expect to find these social myths more in question in the periphery than the core, since "hegemony is more intense and consistent at the core and more laden with contradictions at the periphery" (137).

Global Chasm between Rich and Poor

The runaway effects of globalization are most acute in the periphery, providing an important source of challenge to the contradictions of U.S. hegemonic leadership. According to the 2001 *Human Development Report*, globalization both fuels and facilitates legal trade as well as cross-border crime, with the illegal drug trade in 1995 estimated at $400 billion. At the same time, an estimated 1.8 million women and girls were victims of illegal trafficking (and as many as 4 million people were trafficked in 1998—see Sassen 2002, 4). Conflicts leave their human toll; there are 12 million refugees and 5 million internally displaced people. AIDS hits hardest among the world's poorest, with life expectancy dropping in more than 20 countries of sub-Saharan Africa between 1985–90, and 1995–2000. By the end of 2000, about 36 million people were living with HIV/AIDS— 95 percent of them in developing countries and 70 percent in sub-Saharan Africa (2001, 13).

Runaway globalization also fuels income disparities. While there is a reduction in relative differences between countries, absolute gaps in per capita income have increased. For example, the *Human Development Report* (2001, 19), citing a study by Branko Milanovic, finds that "the richest 10 percent of the U.S. population (around 25 million) had a combined income greater than that of the poorest 43 percent of the world's people (around 2 billion). Around 25 percent of the world's people received 75 percent of the world's income." Scholte notes that "as of the mid-1990s, the value of the assets of 358 billionaires exceeded the combined annual incomes of countries with 2.3 billion inhabitants, or the poorest 45 percent of the world's population" (2000, 239). The global patterns of inequality also have gendered effects. The global trade regime disadvantages women, leaving them vulnerable to exploitative labor practices (sweat shops, sex trade), while the effects of global economic restructuring (reduction of public services) falls hardest on women and children as well (Scholte 2000, 30).

While globalization facilitates global flows of capital, goods, information, and business people, it also unleashes other "entanglements." As Sassen observes, the debt crisis and immigration are two related issues which challenge the myth of inclusion and the current global governance structure. "There are now about 50 countries recognized as hyper indebted and unable to redress the situation" (2002, 3). For the global North, one challenge is to see the interconnectedness of the debt crisis and other manifestations of violence. September 11 illustrates the double edged sword of globalization; it can connect people to act for both good and ill. Migration here is critical. Migration will increase because debt, poverty, unemployment, and the closing of traditional economic sectors propel the illegal trade in people. At the same time, as rich countries get richer, they are more desirable, and global communication flows help to advertise this. So, as the rich raise walls to keep immigrants and refugees out, they fuel illegal trade in people (Sassen 2002, 4). We see how some officials in the North distance themselves from the tragedies that accompany such migratory pressures when a U.S. Border Patrol agent writes: "it is really of no importance what someone like me feels when they come across a dead body. I'm not the one dead. I've not suffered a tragedy" (Michelini 2002, 17). The issue of immigration comes face to face with the exclusionary character of citizenship. The question of who counts as a citizen is at stake. As Linklater notes,

> citizenship has been central to the politics of inclusion and exclusion in modern states. Efforts to restrict citizenship have been a key weapon in the exercise of monopolizing social privileges and opportunities, and struggles to extend citizenship rights have been crucial elements in the politics of challenging the uneven distribution of social entitlements. (1998, 189)

Globalization also changes what it means to be a member of a society, making it more difficult for states to mobilize separate and coherent nations (Urry 2000, 65). Moreover, the growth of cultural globalization, the UN, the EU, the European Court of Human Rights, the world refugee problem, aboriginal rights, and so on, all suggest that the "nation-state is not necessarily the most suitable political framework for housing citizenship rights" (p. 67). To address these issues of citizenship is also to raise questions about democracy in an era of globalization (Vandenberg 2000).

Democratic Deficit

Runaway globalization undermines democracy in several ways. First, it means that:

> the locus of effective political power can no longer be assumed to be national governments—effective power is shared and bartered by diverse forces and agencies at national, regional and international levels. Second, the idea of a political community of fate—of a self-determining collectivity which forms its own agenda and life conditions—can no longer meaningfully be located within the boundaries of a single nation-state alone. (Held 1998, 21)

The assumption that the authoritative allocation of values should be based on the consent of the political community affected has been contradicted in practice by the loss of the control by the state over its internal (and many external) affairs. This is most acute among the poorest states in the global South. As Bienen, Rittberger, and Wagner note, "the fundamental concept of democracy, the congruence between rulers and ruled, ceases to exist."

States can no longer be fully democratic in a nondemocratic international system. They suggest that the question of democracy at the global level is "crucial" at least under two assumptions: (1) that the nation-state cannot regain control of decision-making without undermining the outcomes that are sought; and (2) that "only democratic legitimacy will be accepted in international policy-making, at least in the long run." They stake the second claim on the need for institutions to be legitimate and effective, and that the norm for democracy has become a universal political value since World War II. Therefore, any institution, national or international, that makes substantive decisions now faces democratic expectations for its decision-making procedures (1998, 288–89).

The agents of global arrogance try to mask the democratic deficits of the current world order through discursive strategies that rely on myths. Myths serve a number of functions. They help the elite define the agenda of global politics, control the terms of debate, and discipline the participation of supporters and opponents. Myths obscure realities by diverting attention to the "right problems" or "right debate" on solutions to them and direct how the consent of the governed is controlled, rewarded, and punished.[4] Thus, myths seemingly depoliticize speech, but in fact they serve as a mechanism for exerting power, authority and claims to legitimacy (Barthes 1994). Georges Sorel, who influenced Gramsci's thinking, argued that social myth is a "powerful form of collective subjectivity" that works to block reform efforts (cited by Cox 1996, 131). The cumulative effect of such discourse is to normalize or naturalize unjust and violent social and political conditions. As Zoelle and Josephson's chapter shows, people living in poverty, along with their entire neighborhoods, become invisible to others (more secure, more wealthy) in society.

Myths of Global Arrogance and Their Decline

The discursive dimension of global arrogance can be captured through five types of myths: *the myth of protection, familiarity, inclusiveness, self-sacrifice, and the standard bearer.* However, the social movements challenging global arrogance exercise one type of speech that is *not* mythical—that is speech that remains political. They speak in order to "transform reality." Barthes argues "this is why revolutionary language proper cannot be mythical. Revolution is defined as a cathartic act meant to reveal the political load of the world" (1994, 146). The emergence of this kind of political speech is a sign that the myths of global arrogance are in decline. Below I illustrate the myths of global arrogance and their decline in the context of U.S. hegemonic leadership.

The Myth of Protection

The myth of protection casts safety in the language of threats, counter threats, military dominance, and the use of force (Tickner 2001, 45). Realists contend we are stuck with the security dilemma, and its binaries that juxtapose us/them, inside/outside, community/anarchy. Tickner argues that "war is a cultural construction that depends on myths of protection; it is not inevitable, as realists suggest" (51). The realist myth of protection does not allow for progressive change (46). This discourse focuses on the need of the United States to avert or contain interstate threats, and increasingly in the 1990s, on thwarting North–South threats. The effect is to project an image of the hegemon and its supporters under concerted threats, thus justifying a two-pronged approach: coercive and even preemptive action against its foes, if necessary (Tenet 2002, 3); and a protective policy for its friends, through military aid, stationing of troops, development of new bases and military agreements, and so on.

Security as it has been practiced under hegemonic leadership is more a form of discipline and control than it is protection. For example, youth are increasingly depicted as sources of threat (Webber 2003). Securitizing schools in response to school violence in the United States is but one manifestation of a larger, emerging demographic reality that pits a youthful, "aggressive" global South, against an aging North, which must rely on the high-tech capabilities of its "Golden Boys" (i.e., older power brokers) to contain the new global threat. The United States practices a containment policy on its own youth, and a war on terrorism against youth abroad. It is a struggle of brawn against wit (Tickner 2001, 60; see also Fukuyama 1998). As the former CIA Director George Tenet warns, "demographic trends tell us that the world's poorest and most politically unstable regions—which include parts of the Middle East and sub-Saharan Africa—will have the largest youth populations in the world over the next two decades and beyond. Most of these countries will lack the economic institutions or resources to effectively integrate these youth into society" (2002, 4).

The policy of new military humanitarianism introduced during the 1990s is another arena where the myth of protection is played out. Here it substitutes security policies and emergency responses for a deeper reflection on the failures of development policies over the last 50 years

(Duffield 2000; Chomsky 1999). Refugees are turned into security threats, rather than helped as people at risk. This security discourse has racial constructions, too. As Tickner explains, the "construction of national identities around the notion of a safe, or civilized space 'inside' depends on the construction of an 'outside' whose identity often appears strange or threatening" (Tickner 2001, 55–56). On the home front, the disciplining character of the hegemonic rule is evidenced in the prevalence of the war on drugs, war on crime, war on poverty, and so on, many of which also have overt racist connotations. The cumulative effect of the rhetoric is to desensitize the population to the real characteristics of war and racist attitudes that undergird foreign policy. As Susan Sontag writes (2002, A 31), "real wars are not metaphors." This security framework also has its gendered dimension, legitimizing hypermasculinity of supersized male action figures, superweaponized male movie stars of the 1980s and 1990s (Steans 1998; Hooper 2001), or more recently of George W. Bush's "topgun" landing on an aircraft carrier to proclaim (prematurely) "mission accomplished" in the Iraq war.

Myth of Familiarity

The myth of familiarity centers on hegemonic claims about what is best for the world, what the world needs, what its key problems and appropriate solutions are and the means for solving them. The hegemon controls the agenda of international relations and issues of debate. The power to name what is a problem is central to the exercise of hegemony (Edelman 1992, 263). Equally important, by defining some issues as problems while others remain unnamed, hegemonic discourse diverts attention to serve its own interests, rather than the problems that remain unnamed. Thus, knowledge claims are also claims to power (Foucault 1977). We can see the power of such discourse in claims that America is "the indispensable nation, the sole superpower, the lone conscience of the world" (Maynes 1998, 36–47).

Constructing and using social problems for political ends involves several hegemonic maneuvers. First, the process of constructing problems reduces the issue at hand to a certain origin. This excludes other perspectives and interpretations and thereby reinforces the dominant ideology and its justifications for certain courses of action or solutions (Edelman 1992, 265). Second, what is central to political life is not consensus—but the maintenance of rival claims, and the polarization of society so that advocates on both sides maintain support. As Edelman puts it, all the players "draw support from the evocation of a spectacle that shows their rivals as threats" (266). More important than solving the problem is sustaining contestation over it. This keeps movements busy and their attention where the regime wants it and not elsewhere. The U.S. Secretary of Defense under the George W. Bush administration, Donald Rumsfeld, uses this rhetorical strategy to such an extent that he regularly asks and then immediately answers his own questions. This also preempts any attempts by the press to put attention where the regime doesn't want it. This strategy has a third function: Edelman argues that the identification and origin of a problem "generates authority, status, profits, and financial support, while denying these benefits to competing claimants" (1992, 268).

Dominance is sustained by a fourth maneuver: solutions to problems can be used to perpetuate the problem (268). Thus, the World Bank defines problems with poverty in terms of structural adjustment—policies that only deepen the poverty and conditions of inequality (cf. Nandy 2002). Finally, Edelman argues "the terms 'problem' and 'crisis' are inducements to acquiesce in deprivations. For most people they awaken expectations that *others* will tolerate deprivations" (1992, 273). A poignant illustration is found in the collapse of the Cancún World Trade Organization talks on September 14, 2003 over agricultural subsidies and particularly cotton— which the global South found so disappointing. A delegate from Uganda lamented, "when it came down to negotiations, our daily problems were ignored" (Becker 2003, A4).

Fifth, it seems problems are chronic and crises are acute, but passing. However, Edelman refutes this popular logic, insisting that the distinction is arbitrary. Naming certain problems as a crisis is a political act—hence the dispute in the 2004 U.S. presidential election over the salience of the Iran or North Korean nuclear threat in contrast to the "crisis" over weapons of mass destruction in Iraq.

Myth of Inclusiveness

Opportunities for belonging, self-identifying, becoming a member of the club are presented as the myth of inclusiveness. "Join us" is the slogan. Move freely, speak freely, do as we do. The promotion of democracy is the centerpiece of the myth of inclusion. Democratizing national decision-making institutions is the means for both participation and equality, not just at home but in the global system (Fukuyama 2000). The collapse of communism with the fall of the Berlin Wall gave the project a boost; containment was replaced by democracy enlargement. With the consolidation of democracy came market reform (Mayall 2000, 61). As former Secretary of State Madeleine Albright explains (2000), "democracy is the hard rock upon which America's world leadership is built" (3). The U.S. identification with democracy is vital to the pursuit of its interests. The U.S. goal is to use "our assistance to foster vibrant civil societies, and economic reforms that reward the hardworking many, not just the privileged few" (5).

But the myth of inclusion is really a discourse of privilege for those who have rights, who have money, who have opportunity and choice and the freedom to move and do as they wish. The consumer is hero—what is in essence, economic citizenship. Thus, "the substantive conception of citizenship involves not only a political–legal conception, but also an economic idea. Full citizenship requires not only a claim of political rights and obligations, but access to and participation in a system of production and consumption" (Lipschutz 2000, 30, quoting Stephen Gill). The darker side of this reality is exclusion, marginalization, and oppression. Some scholars are less than optimistic about the likelihood of democracy to promote peace in the global South, where there are "poor, rising and dissatisfied states less wedded to the status quo and more sensitive to the resource scarcity and status hierarchies inherent in world politics" (Patrick 2002, 121). Other scholars object to the narrow conception of democracy that the United States promotes, with an emphasis on liberal democracy, to the exclusion of social and economic dimensions (Patrick 2002, 122; see also Boswell and Chase-Dunn 2000, 212). A more inclusive approach to democracy would also address gendered differences (Naples and Desai 2002; Bayes and Tohidi 2001).

Myth of Sacrifice

The myth of sacrifice is about the role of the United States, like the Lone Ranger, coming to the rescue of those at risk around the world (Jewett 1973). The myth calls for expressions of gratitude and loyalty. Rather than focus on the rescue per se, this myth focuses on the sacrifices that the United State has had to make to realize its historic mission, and the indebtedness of the world community to the United States for fulfilling these purposes. The myth of sacrifice asserts that the role of global cop has been thrust on the United States—it hardly sought out this responsibility. In his remarks to leaders gathered at the World Economic Forum in Davos, Switzerland, on January 26, 2003, Colin Powell, U.S. Secretary of State framed U.S. arguments for the war against Iraq much in this vein. Kagan (1998) even points to a sense of weariness among the political elite in the United States with these responsibilities (1998, 28), especially in light of growing hostility around the world to the U.S. government policies.

Speaking to these concerns, the Washington, D.C. Council on Foreign Relations issued a report in July 2002 underscoring the need to increase

U.S. popularity abroad. The study notes that "there is little doubt that stereotypes of the United States as arrogant, self-indulgent, hypocritical, inattentive, and unwilling or unable to engage in cross-cultural dialogue are pervasive and deeply rooted. . . . Also at the root of these negative attitudes is our perceived lack of empathy for other people's pain and hardship and the tragic plight throughout the developing world" (2002, 2). A public opinion poll conducted in 44 countries by the Pew Research Center also shows that the Bush administration's effort to "rebrand U.S. foreign policy" was not working (Scott 2003).

Myth of the Standard-Bearer

The last myth is about the role of the leading power setting the rules of the game; that is, the hegemon assumes special duties of enlightenment and forging normative consensus. The myth supposes that the hegemon subjects itself to the same rules it asks everyone else to play by. Woodrow Wilson brought U.S. leadership to the world stage during World War I invoking the principles of self-determination, and making the world safe for democracy (Dunne 2000, 3). The standard bearer presents its national interests as representing the great cause of humanity. But the myth of the standard bearer has its own contradictions, too. These encompass the selective application of norms and principles and a U.S. reluctance (and sometimes other leading powers) to implement their obligations or to enter into new commitments around which a global consensus is emerging (e.g., Kyoto Protocol, or the Ottawa Treaty to ban landmines).

The U.S. role as global cop also suffers from the contradictions of the standard bearer. For example, Brilmayer argues that "recognizing a right of moral intervention by the strongest powers tends to exacerbate the imbalance of power, because the version of morality that is imposed is the hegemon's version, complete with all the hegemon's mistaken judgments." Brilmayer aims her critique at the consequences of a system of global hegemony based on state consent to the prevailing normative arrangements, rather than a more inclusive, democratic, and diverse group of actors of the international community (1994, 159). Thus, the international community rescues Albanians from Serbian extreme nationalists but not Palestinians from Israeli occupation, nor the Tutsis from the radical Hutu in Rwanda, or the East Timorese from the Indonesian military, and so on.

Another problem is double standards; the hegemon can rule by its own set of rules, while it promotes (and disciplines) another standard for the rest of the world. In the case of Iraq, the United States raised the possibility of Iraqi acquisition and use of weapons of mass destruction to the level of a threat against the international community, but in preparing war plans to attack Iraq preemptively, the United States Strategic Command issued a "Theater Nuclear Planning Document" listing Iraqi targets for a *nuclear strike*. As Kristof argues (2003, A31), "by noisily weighing their options, [U.S.] officials are undermining the taboo against such arms."

Democratic Possibilities of Transnational Social Movements

The demand for global democracy emerges out of related developments; the crisis of global hegemony and runaway globalization, which eludes control of the world's most powerful states and actors. What kind of outcomes from this historic juncture might we envision? I follow Robert Cox, who in a seminal article, sketched a scenario of three possible outcomes for global order of the social forces generated by changing production processes. In the first scenario, he suggested the emergence of a new hegemony based on the global structure of social power generated by the internationalizing of production, with two corollary conditions: the continuing dominance of international over national capital within the major countries, and the continuing internationalization of the state. Along these lines, he suggested there would be a continuation of "monetarism as the orthodoxy of economic policy, emphasizing the stabilization of world economy (anti-inflationary policies and stable exchange rates) over the fulfillment of domestic sociopolitical demands (the reduction of unemployment and the maintenance of real-wage levels)" (1996, 113–14). In a second scenario, he suggested a non-hegemonic world order of conflicting power centers, opting out of the international capitalist system. A third, and less likely scenario centered on the emergence of a counter hegemony based on a Third World coalition against core country dominance, with two aims: to permit autonomous development and terminate center-periphery relations (114–15).

The first of these scenarios captures the nature of the dominant social forces behind the extension of U.S. hegemony since 1945. The project of resistance by a coalition of Third World states met with little success either in the context of the New International Economic Order or the New International Information Order promoted by the Group of 77 through the United Nations Conference on Development in the 1970s and 1980s. The end of communism meant a death-blow to the coalition of nonaligned states. Instead, democratization and global capitalism have become *the* political–economic game.

Nevertheless, we still might expect challenges to global arrogance to emerge from the global South. Hegemonic rule tends to have more contradictions in the periphery (137). Here "the capitalist world-system is most oppressive, and thus peripheral workers and peasants, the vast majority of the world proletariat, have the most to win and the least to lose" (Boswell and Chase-Dunn 2000, 221). However, the destitution of millions of people around the world living on a dollar a day or less means they are ill-equipped to mount an organized opposition.

Alternatively, change could emerge from the core. In the past, the workers in the developed North were not pitted in competition with workers in the global South. Indeed, low labor costs in the South meant lower costs for commodities and other goods imported to the North, so the arrangement was even beneficial to workers in the North. Now however, downsizing and outsourcing have meant that workers no longer enjoy job security; thus loyalty to firms has weakened, too. In addition, we see the emergence of new ties between workers in the global North and South, while struggles in the periphery over wages, sweatshop conditions, child labor, and so on, helps to shape the future of world labor-market competition (222–23).

Ultimately, what is important is whether and how the core and the periphery form new ties. In the global North, international competition and the weakening of the welfare state are bringing labor and new social movements together. But a solidarity approach among labor and new social movements reaching across the North–South divide, rather than solidifying only national ties, holds the greatest potential for democratizing global institutions and the market system (231). The formation of the EU and NAFTA also give the weakened national labor movements a "political locus for enforcing results of organizing that crosses state boundaries" (232). Such factors lead Boswell and Chase-Dunn to argue that "peripheral and semi peripheral workers in industrializing countries are the most motivated agents of global democratic relations; core labor has been the strongest political force opposing capital mobility that degrades labor standards" (13). If social movements of the nineteenth and twentieth centuries were mobilized to promote democracy at the state level, *then for the twenty-first-century movements, the challenge is to make democracy transnational, too.*

Approaches to Transnational Democracy

The rise of transnational social movements, encompassing movements from the global South as well as the North, raises new possibilities about the different values and theories of democracy that could be jointly developed as a global project. But first, we have to question assumptions about transnational democracy being the equivalent of the democratic state. Broadening the idea of democracy means asking questions about how substate actors and transnational actors, and international institutions are contributing to the articulation of new sites of democracy and new processes for promoting it (Laclau and Mouffe 1985). Second, we also have to raise new questions about identity separate from the state. Can people express their interests and define identities in democratic structures and processes that lie outside the state? Third, in what ways do these developments reinforce or curtail the democratization at the level of the state? Fourth, how are these developments redefining the source and definition of collective rights and the means for promoting them?

The chapters that follow examine social movements across many different issues and arenas of global politics. We see their involvement encompassing any of three strategies:

* working within the system to transform global arrogance;
* delegitimizing hegemony and global arrogance by standing in opposition to it—as antiglobalization movements do;
* moving beyond global arrogance by creating alternative, democratic spaces in self-conceieved arenas.

These strategies may not be mutually exclusive. Therefore, throughout the chapters that follow, the contributors have sought answers to questions about which strategies social movements pursue, in which fora, by which means, with what kinds barriers or internal struggles, and with what kind of support. A theme that runs through many of the chapters is the dangers of replicating global arrogance by the very actors who seek to criticize and move beyond it.

Part I of the volume, *Escaping the Entrapment of Global Arrogance*, consists of this introductory chapter and a theory chapter by Julie Webber. She plays on Rousseau to sketch out a postmodern understanding of a "generic will" to chart a global path toward transnational democratic arrangements. One of her key assumptions is that "responsibility is no longer the purview of governing structures, but is now put to the people." This theoretical point of departure is followed by a set of case studies in *Part II: Challenging Arrogance from the Local to the Global*. These chapters have in common the analysis of social movements challenging the arrogance of the United States or the European Union from local to regional and global perspectives. *Part III: Facing the Dangers of Replicating Global Arrogance* explores the dilemmas of replicating arrogance despite the intentions of social movements to get beyond it. In *Part IV: Creating Democratic Alternatives*, Teivainen examines close-up the experiment of the World Social Forum (WSF). Finally, in the concluding chapter, I draw out new findings about how democratic dialogue and participation are challenging global arrogance and opening up new democratic spaces.

Many of the contributors to the volume have been active participants in the movements they write about. They come from different parts of the world and disciplinary traditions. Therefore, our voices are as much a part of the dialogue and learning about global democracy as the research we have produced. The readers will find some different emphases in the use of the main concepts in the volume. Some authors direct their critique more toward the crisis of hegemony in general, than specific myths of global arrogance. For example, Parodi's chapter on truth commissions critiques U.S. hegemony, but ultimately he is interested in the way an emerging norm to the truth will help the oppressed escape the entrapments of global arrogance. Similarly, the chapters vary in the way the authors speak of the kind of transformation that moving beyond global arrogance entails. Thus we see some diversity in understanding and conceptualizing the central problematic of the volume; what kind of democratic challenge do social movements pose to global arrogance? In a post-structuralist framing and reading of the theoretical implications of the chapters that follow, Webber argues for liberation as a postmodern understanding of political change, rather than emancipation.

However, some of our contributors have stayed with the concept of emancipation, transformation or solidarity, while others speak of the search for a "third way," such as Hallström in his chapter on environmental movements in East Central Europe and their relationship to the EU, or Teivainen with the WSF. This plurality of terminology shows the diversity of perspectives the contributors to our volume have brought to our attempts to understand the possibilities of social movements opening new democratic space, and the means for describing these changes. Thus, just as Laclau and Mouffe (1985) argue for understanding democracy as a never completed project, we have described in this volume no final resting point, but many emergent forms of democratic dialogue, spaces, and avenues of participation.

The authors also have placed different emphases on the analysis of new communications technology. Its significance for creating new democratic space and dialogue has varied across the case studies. Zoelle and Josephson show that the Kensington Welfare Rights Union has used various media in creative and effective ways to raise awareness. For the global peace movement, as Cortright details in his chapter, the Internet played a crucial role in organizing protests simultaneously and in short time frames around the world, and raising money. But it was only a tool. What matters is how activists move from the virtual to action in the street. In Tadros' chapter on human rights and the Middle East, we see both how the Internet reproduces hegemony and arrogance, and provides means to resist it. In the conclusions, I draw out the strengths and limitations of new communications technology for democratic dialogue and instruction.

The volume also embodies a couple of ironic twists. Cortright, who writes about the global peace movement against the U.S. invasion of Iraq, and Nelson, who takes on the case of the global movement to ban landmines, bring to us a new superpower, but what they have in mind is not the United States, but a peaceful superpower of global social movements. A second ironic twist is found in our critique of hegemony. In this chapter, I have made the case that the hegemon manipulates problems and elevates them to crises as a maneuver to exercise authority and control. And yet, we must admit, that our own volume does this, too, as it reads the current global historical juncture as one of hegemonic crisis.[5]

This brings me to one of the most powerful findings that has emerged from our study; the danger of replicating global arrogance. In many of the case studies, critical intra-movement dialogue has been taking place over the last decade and especially between the global South and North. Thus, even as activists have challenged the arrogance of hegemonic powers, they found themselves reinventing arrogance in their own relationships with counterparts. *Part III* of the volume, therefore, brings together a set of case studies that alert us to the need for awareness and self-criticism along with dialogue and democratic instruction. In addition to Tadros' analysis of the human rights movement in the Middle East, Hunt brings these points home on the global feminist movement, O'Neill and VanDeveer on the global environmental movement, and Nelson on the global movement to ban landmines.

Conclusions

The United States and other leading powers can no longer ignore the fact that with globalization, the rest of the world knows how well a small part of it lives; and the rest are not satisfied with its unjust and often violent political, economic, social, cultural, or military manifestations. Global arrogance has come to define American dominance, and the projection of its power through the processes of globalization. For the have-nots, dealing with the inequalities of globalization as well as many other forms of insecurity are central features of their daily struggles.

How globalization is constructed, and how it is believed or challenged by people around the world will play an important role in shaping the future of world (dis)order. One of the most important tools of resistance and change is to redefine the terms of debate. By stepping outside of the traditional oppositional forms of contestation, advocates can articulate alternative futures, and do so in ways that confound the authority and control of elites. Thus, what we are interested in understanding in this project is whether and to what extent social movements are not just articulating antiglobalization ideologies and strategies, but creating new spaces for democracy in local and global contexts. Such strategies will not bring about a world government in the way world federalists long-ago imagined the direction of progressive change. Nor do we see transnational democracy as a comopolitan project. But by working from the ground up and through transnational networks, social movements can begin to define new avenues of participation and identity, and new democratic mechanisms for solving world problems to challenge hegemonic rule that privileges some but punishes many.

NOTES

1. Rawls speaks of the veil of ignorance in the sense of the original position, the state of nature, which he uses as a hypothetical situation to help us arrive at a conception of justice that we would all agree to, if we did not know yet what our own situation in life would be (economic, class, race, gender, genetic, geographic, generational, etc.). Thus he argues that "the principles of justice are chosen behind a *veil of ignorance*. This ensures that no one is advantaged or disadvantaged in the choice of principles by the outcome of natural chance or the contingency of social circumstances" (p. 12, emphasis added).
2. For example, see <http://www.middleeast.org/archives/1999_01_04.htm>. I am also grateful to Mohammad Tavakoli for bringing this to my attention.
3. See "Campaign against Global Arrogance." 2000. *RFE/RL Iran Report* 3, no.42 (November): 1–2.
4. Also drawing from Barthes (1994), Cynthia Webber in her 2001 textbook, *International Relations Theory*, offers an incisive critique of the function of myth (as well as culture and ideology) in the key theoretical approaches to the field. I also owe a special debt to Ann Tickner for her use of myths in *Gendering World Politics* (2001), which is closet to my approach in this volume.
5. I owe this point to one of our anonymous reviewers.

BIBLIOGRAPHY

Aksu, Esref and Joseph A. Camilleri, eds. 2002. *Democratizing Global Governance.* New York: Palgrave Macmillan.
Albright, Madeleine K. 2000. "Sustaining Democracy in the Twenty-First Century." The Roots Lecture Series, School of Advanced International Studies,

Johns Hopkins University, Washington, D.C., January 18. As Released by the Office of the Spokesman U.S. Department of State.

Anheir, Helmut and Nuno Themuod. 2002. "Organizational Forms of Global Civil Society: Implications of Going Global." Pp. 191–215 in *Global Civil Society*, ed. Marlies Glasius, Mary Kaldor, and Helmut Anheier. New York: Oxford University Press.

Barfield, Claude E. 2001. *Free Trade, Sovereignty, Democracy. The Future of the World Trade Organization*. Washington, D.C.: The AEI Press.

Barthes, Roland. 1994. *Mythologies*, trans. Annette Lavers. New York: Hill and Wang. 28th printing.

Bayes, Jane H. and Nayereh Tohidi, ed. 2001. *Globalization, Gender and Religion*. New York: Palgrave.

Becker, Elizabeth. 2003. "Delegates From Poorer Nations Walk out of World Trade Talks." *The New York Times*, September 15: A1, A4.

Bienen, Derek, Volker Rittberger, and Wolfgang Wagner. 1998. "Democracy in the United Nations System: Cosmopolitan and Communitarian Principles." Pp. 287–380 in *Re-Imagining Political Community*, ed. Daniel Archibuigi, David Held, and Martin Köhler, Stanford, Calif.: Stanford University Press.

Boswell, Terry and Christopher Chase-Dunn. 2000. *The Spiral of Capitalism and Socialism: Toward Global Democracy*. Boulder, Colo.: Lynne Rienner.

Brilmayer, Lea. 1994. *American Hegemony*. New Haven: Yale University Press.

Carter, Jimmy. 2002. Carter Nobel Peace Prize Speech. December 10. Transcript accessed September 15, 2004 <http://cnn.worldnews.printthis.com>.

Chomsky, Noam. 1999. *The New Military Humanism*. Monroe, Maine: Common Courage Press.

Council on Foreign Relations. 2002. *Public Diplomacy: A Strategy for Reform*. A Report of an Independent Task Force on Public Diplomacy Sponsored by the Council on Foreign Relations, Washington, D.C. <http://www.cfr.org/public/PublicDiplomacy_TF.html>.

Cox, Robert. 1996. *Approaches to World Order*. Cambridge, U.K.: Cambridge University Press.

Duffield, Mark. 2001. *Global Governance and the New Wars*. London: Zed Books.

Dunne, Michael. 2000. "U.S. Foreign Relations in the Twentieth Century: From World Power to Global Hegemony." *International Affairs* 76, no.1: 25–40.

Edelman, Murray. 1992. "The Construction and Uses of Social Problems." Pp. 263–80 in *Jean Baudrillard: The Disappearance of Art and Politics*, ed. William Stearns and William Chaloupka. New York: St. Martin's Press.

Foot, Rosemary, S. Neil MacFarlane, and Michael Mastanduno. 2002. *U.S. Hegemony and International Organizations*. New York: Oxford University Press.

Foucault, Michel. 1977. *The Archeology of Knowledge*, trans. from the French by A. M. Sheridan Smith. New York: Pantheon Books.

Fukuyama, Francis. 2000. "The March of Equality." *Journal of Democracy* 11, no.1: 11–17.

———. 1998. "Women and the Evolution of World Politics." *Foreign Affairs* 77 no.5: 24–41.

Fulbright, J. William. 1966. *The Arrogance of Power*. New York: Random House.

Gramsci, Antonio. 1971. *Selections from the Prison Notebooks*, edited by Q. Hoare and G. Smith. New York: International Publishers.

Guidry, John A., Michael D. Kennedy, and Mayer N. Zald. 2000. *Globalizations and Social Movements*. Ann Arbor, Mich.: University of Michigan Press.

Held, David. 1998. "Democracy and Globalization." Pp. 11–27 in *Re-Imagining Political Community*, ed. Daniel Archibuigi, David Held, and Martin Köhler. Stanford: Stanford University Press.

Hershberg, Eric and Kevin Moore. 2002. "Introduction: Place, Perspective and Power: Interpreting September 11." Pp. 1–19 in *Critical Views of September 11*, ed. Eric Hershberg and Kevin Moore. Social Science Research Council <http://www.ssrc.org/sept11/toc11b.htm>.

Hettne, Björn and Bertil Odén, eds. 2002. *Global Governance in the 21st Century: Alternative Perspectives on World Order*. Expert Group on Development Issues 2002:2. Stockholm, Sweden: Almkvist and Wiksell International.

Hooper, Charlotte. 2001. *Manly States*. New York: Columbia University Press.

Human Development Report 2001. *Making New Technologies Work for Human Development*. United Nations Development Programme <http://www.undp.org/hdr2001/>.

Johnson, Paul. 2002. "European Envy, American Arrogance?" *Forbes* 169, no.9: 37.

Kagan, Robert. 1998. "The Benevolent Empire." *Foreign Policy* (Summer): 24–35.

Karns, Margaret P. and Karen A. Mingst. 2004. *International Organizations: The Politics and Processes of Global Governance*. Boulder, Colo.: Lynne Rienner.

Keck, Margaret E. and Kathryn Sikkink. 1998. *Activists Beyond Borders*. Ithaca, N.Y.: Cornell University Press.

Kristof, Nicholas D. 2003. "Flirting with Disaster." *The New York Times* February 14, p. A31.

Laclau, Ernesto and Chantal Mouffe. 1985. *Hegemony and Socialist Strategy*. N.Y.: Verso.

Leatherman, Janie, Jackie Smith, and Ron Pagnucco. 1994. "International Institutions and Transnational Social Movement Organizations: Global Politics as a Three Level Game." Paper presented at the SSRC-Kroc Institute joint sponsored workshop on: International Institutions and Transnational Social Movement Organizations. April 21–23.

Linklater, Andrew. 1998. *The Transformation of Political Community. Ethical Foundations of the Post-Westphalian Era*. Columbia, S.C.: University of South Carolina Press.

Lipschutz, Ronnie. 2000. *After Authority*. Albany, N.Y.: University of New York.

Mayall, James. 2000. "Democracy and International Society." *International Affairs* 76, no.1: 61–75.

Maynes, Charles William. 1998. "The Perils of (and for) an Imperial America." *Foreign Policy* 111: 36–48.

Michelini, Dennis. 2002. "Tracing Clues Along the Border." *The New York Times* August 23, p. A17.

Nandy, Ashis. 2002. "The Beautiful, Expanding Future of Poverty: Popular Economics as a Psychological Defense." *International Studies Review* 4, no. 2: 107–22.

Naples, Nancy A. and Manisha Desai, ed. 2002. *Women's Activism and Globalization*. New York: Routledge.

Nye, Joseph. 2004. "When Hard Power Undermines Soft Power." *New Perspectives Quarterly* 21, no. 3: 13–15.

O'Brien, Robert, Anne Marie Goetz, Jan Aart Scholte, and Marc Williams. *Contesting Global Governance*. New York: Cambridge University Press.

Patrick, Stewart. 2002. "More Power to You: Strategic Restraint, Democracy Promotion and American Primacy." *International Studies Review* 4, no.1: 117–28.

PIPA/Knowledge Networks Poll. 2003. Americans on America's Role in the World after the Iraq War. Accessed at <http://www.pipa.org/OnlineReports/WarIraq/report_April29.pdf>.

Powell, Colin L. 2003. "Remarks at the World Economic Forum." Davos, Switzerland, January 26. Accessed at <http://www.state.gov/secretary/rm/2003/16869pf.htm>.

Rawls, John. 1971. *A Theory of Justice*. Cambridge, Mass.: The Belknap Press of Harvard University Press.

Rice, Condoleezza. 2000. "Promoting the National Interest." *Foreign Affairs* 79, no. 1 (January/February): 45–63.

Risse, Thomas, Stephen Ropp, and Kathryn Sikkink, eds. 1999. *The Power of Human Rights: International Norms and Domestic Change*. New York: Cambridge University Press.

Rubin, Trudy. 2001. "Arrogance of Global Power Is Worrisome." *Milwaukee Journal Sentinel* April 29, accessed October 25, 2004 <http://jsonline.com/news/editorials/apr01/rubin29_g042701.asp>.

Sassen, Saskia. 2002. "Governance Hotspots: Challenges We Must Confront in the Post September 11 World." Social Science Research Council/After Sept. 11. Accessed at <http://www.ssrc.org/sept11/essays/sassen_text_only.htm.>.

Scholte, Jan Aart. 2000. *Globalization: A Critical Introduction*. New York: St. Martin's.

Scott, Catherine. 2003. "Americans Aren't Consumers who have to be sold on War." *The Atlanta Journal-Constitution* January 22.

Smith, Jackie, Charles Chatfield, and Ron Pagnucco, eds. *Transnational Social Movements and Global Politics: Solidarity Beyond the State*. Syracuse, N.Y.: Syracuse University Press.

Smith, Jackie and Johnston, eds. 2002. *Globalization and Resistance*. Lanham: Rowman and Littlefield.

Sontag, Susan. 2002. "Real Battles and Empty Metaphors." *The New York Times*, p. A31.

Steans, Jill. 1998. *Gender and International Relations*. New Brunswick, N.J.: Rutgers University.

Tehranian, Majid. 2002. "Democratizing Governance." Pp. 55–74 in *Democratizing Global Governance*, ed. Aksu, Esref and Joseph A. Camilleri. New York: Palgrave Macmillan.

Tenet, George J. 2002. "Worldwide Threat—Converging Dangers in a Post 9/11 World." Testimony of Director of Central Intelligence George J. Tenet before the Senate Armed Services Committee, March 19, 2002. Accessed at

<http://www.cia.gov/cia/public?affairs/speeches/senate_hearing_03192002.
html>.

Tickner, J. Ann. 2001. *Gendering World Politics*. New York: Columbia University
Press.

Urry, John. 2000. "Global Flows and Global Citizenship." Pp. 62–78 in *Citizenship
and Identity*, ed. Engin F. Isin and Patricia, Wood. Thousand Oaks, Calif.: Sage.

Vandenberg, Andrew, ed. 2000. *Citizenship and Democracy in a Global Era*.
New York: St. Martin's.

Weber, Cynthia. 2001. *International Relations Theory: A Critical Introduction*.
New York: Routledge.

Webber, Julie. 2003. *Failure to Hold*. Lanham, Md.: Rowman and Littlefield.

We the Peoples: Civil Society, the United Nations and Global Governance. 2004.
Report of the Panel of Eminent Persons on United Nations-Civil Society
Relations. A/58/817. Accessed at <http://www.un.org/News/briefings/docs/
2004/Cardoso062104.doc.htm>.

Chapter 2

Outline of a Generic Will: Global Arrogance, Social Movements, and the Net

Julie A. Webber

I'm very pleased to be here as the secretary of state of a relatively new country on the face of the earth. But I think I can take some credit sitting here as being the representative of the oldest democracy that is assembled here around this table.

—Colin Powell, address to the Security Council, February 14, 2003

Undoing (what has been done): Psychological mechanism whereby the subject makes an attempt to cause past thoughts, words, gestures or actions not to have occurred; to this end he makes use of thought or behavior having the opposite meaning.

—Laplanche and Pontalis 1967, 477

The future can always be imported.

—Pico Iyer, "Abandoning the Past, Mired in the Moment"

Introduction

Two major events have led to the devilish exposure of Uncle Sam's dishonesty in recent years, and, in turn led to Powell's speech falling on deaf ears: one is September 11 which like an earthquake cracked the thinly spread coating holding world order and the great power system together, the other has been the slow, steady rise of social movements that oppose— *in public*—the very same order that September 11 cracked wide open. While the United States used to get away with this strategy of undoing, it is clear that now it will have to back down or explain history. Backing down seems the best option for a state that prides itself on not having a history (Baudrillard). Mavericks don't like to be "branded" because it leaves a trace.

In this chapter, I begin to outline what I think are the contours of world order or governance *that social movements respond to* when they propose new legislation, criticize world forums, treaty regimes and organizations, act out their middle-class alienation at venues like the World Social Forum (Teivainen, this volume) or even detail the egregious crimes committed by states and their minions (corporations, legal codes, courts, treaty regimes, police, armies/mercenaries, detention centers/prisons, etc.). Its purpose is to foreground, theoretically, the range of social and political positions described by contributors in this volume. I will end by noting a problem in social theory that is that we tend to organize/imagine resistance movements *in our heads* according to outdated models of power and governance that no longer exist empirically. This is an epistemological problem that is more complicated by media amplification of the specularity of events.

The failure of emancipation is not the fault of social movements (who are no doubt engaging in testing authority because they have no other options, no opportunity structures are in place for them to feel satiated by whatever scraps of power or control governments or corporations hand to them). The failure of emancipation is as an idea; responsibility for ensuring it is no longer the purview of governing structures, but is now put to the people, according to their cultural, gendered and needs-based assessments (Pasha 1996). The mechanism or thought process that lumps these misguided and outmoded ideas of emancipation together is their shared interest in outlining an Oedipal (representational) drama, or paternal metaphor (x is *like* Britain in the nineteenth century, y is *like* colonial resistance). The contributors to this volume seemingly disagree on many of the approaches taken by the social movements they study, and this dissonance demonstrates the plurality of approaches to arrogance; my purpose is to adumbrate the generic will of movements, not force them into agreement.

Protest Politics

One of the key problems with world politics (and we are finally witnessing "world politics" not unchecked hegemony) is that social movements often get separated from issues of governance and larger governing structures because they don't fall neatly into the social scientists dream schematic of a one-to-one correspondence between institution and individual.[1] That is, just because social movements do not produce tangible policy outcomes or monolithic institutions doesn't mean that they haven't produced change in the world; we are operating on a different terrain of power that no longer has a physical shape or temporal response to criticism, sabotage or humiliation. I do not believe that this is a problem that should fall on the social movements for failing to show Daddy his mistakes and make him properly accountable. What this demonstrates is precisely that Oedipal strategies are banal ones, and they don't go over well with structures thought to be accountable. Further, as international relations theorists we should be happy that the stranglehold the Neo's held over the 1990s has been knocked loose (in politics and academia), not by Wendtian constructivism or Giddens' "Third Way" but by grumbling from down below (and, of course, the spite of failed fathers) (Wendt 1992; Giddens 2000) that may *begin* to gesture toward global civil society (Kaldor 2003). We are "witnessing" world politics in the precise sense that these governing structures have lost their hold over movements and challenges to the world order system.

My second aim is to show an outmoded protest strategy continues to be pervasive in U.S. activist and popular culture. It mirrors the legacy of Emile Zola's effective criticism and public intellectualism as enshrined in activist thought as well as the effect of a literal protestantism (an ideology of protest; that is, it must occur in a particular way by particular individuals and have similar success value) that Roland Barthes has noted throughout history.[2] The problem is that we view protest against authority structures as the only effective means of changing them or reversing the effects of oppression. One of the central criticisms of social movements and NGOs/protestors is that they do not attract enough popular or media support, but clearly there is a problem with the very concept of global citizenship that follows from the world order accountability fallacy. Media conglomeration and censorship are challenges, but the real challenge to those who oppose media framing is to construct ways for people to get a global perspective, indeed even to maintain a global perspective on every aspect of their lives under globalization. Technology, like the Internet, the pervasive use of cell phones and telecommunications extensive reach do close some of the gaps between the haves and have nots in the world, but the medium itself does not transmit a progressive message: it can transmit any message without judging its political quality, negative, right wing or radical. So, while technology can aid global activism for local causes, it can also aid terrorists, right-wing presidents, or generals on the battlefield.

Part of the problem with the technology debate is that it's a nonstarter debate: the problem is the public that uses technology is not as enlightened as Kant would have wanted them to be (how can you treat a person as an "end in themselves" when the only sign of their existence that you have to cling to is electronic words or images of them in the media), or even as mature and aware of self-interest as Locke might have required. The idealism of those who cling to technology as a "good" object of modernity refuse to see that it is also assigned the status of "bad" object when it is used for malignant purposes. The proper problem is the lack of awareness on the part of the middle classes among the hegemonic states and upper classes in poorer ones toward those in the worst economic, social and militaristic situations, everywhere—throughout the entire world. Those people who have been empowered to criticize have adopted a provincial point of view while proclaiming the victory of globalization and free riding from its short-term gains. Here is the true democratic crisis and the *ground zero* of progressive politics: democracy can't spread if the people who possess its opportunity structures don't appreciate and use them.

This is a democratic problem that world politics and international relations have failed to acknowledge. We talk about the ways in which democracy fails in international politics but we only apply it to individual- ized nation-states, not to more pervasive movements of militarism, capital and labor that transgress national boundaries. We contain our democratic imaginary to models of the nation-state instead of applying it to the global spaces in need of democratic criticism, where narrow interests of world leaders determine the fate of populations. Carlos Parodi's chapter in this volume clearly demonstrates that the limits of Truth Commissions reside not only in state-centric international law, but also in the tricky way that they foreclose and surround issues of national reconciliation and contain them to national spaces.

The Generic Will of Social Movements

In social movements, we begin to see the outline of a "generic will" that charts a global path toward transnational democratic arrangements. These could very well break down in the near future, but for now they challenge the entire system of power relations because they are forced to operate against ideas and material realities, not exclusive institutions. Troping on Rousseau's "general will" as an expression of all people's rational sentiments toward a political trend or institution to which Rousseau said must be an expression of each person's desire, I have suggested we view social movements, peace rallies and even Internet polls against hegemonic structures as a "generic will" that exceeds the narrow boundaries of nationalism and even the narrowness of issue-specific causes. It is generic in the sense that it has no brand name or trademark attached to it; one can see this in the literature on social movements that details the disparate groups and historically adversarial movements that band together to protest global governance structures. It is a will in the sense that it is *the only sign of criticism* against global governance structures. As (Barthes 1986) reminds us over and over again, to criticize means to "call into crisis" and should not be read with the negative inflection that the media has attached to it so successfully in the last decades. I return to the generic will and the obstacles that it must overcome toward the end of the chapter, but first I would like to outline the contemporary options for political participation that structures the means of dissent.

First, we have a few important questions before us to normatively structure the way we read these essays from the volume.

What do social movements described in this volume constitute?
1. a permanent "anti-Enlightenment" modernist project (Lavine 1998);
2. a temporary emotional upheaval against brute force with no discernible political philosophy behind its machinations, demonstrating the dearth of collective political will in late modernity, the direct confrontation of capital and labor through material "resistance?"
3. the incoherent mass uprising against (arrogance's) representation in the form of U.S. hegemony?

The options for structuring our interpretations of the movements get thinner on the scale of normative or cognitive agency as we move from one to three.

First Option: Anti-Everything

The first option indicates that there is no nation to liberate. If we believe oppressive, violent governance structures when they make the claim for liberation then we are fools. As Galtung has outlined, we know that we are in the presence of a structure of violence when it enlists the help of repression to effect liberation using "as concomitants of other types of violence: detention, meaning locking people *in* (prisons, concentration camps), and expulsion, meaning locking people *out* (banishing them abroad or to distant parts of the country" (Galtung 1990, 293). If we are on the territory of liberation, then why are people locked in and out of a "nation?" Because there is no such thing as national liberation and this is the first critique of nationalism leveled by any "anti-Enlightenment" modernist project. It continually demonstrates the failures of governing structures in regards to what they have set out to accomplish, it proliferates these failures, documents them and questions their grand narrative structures.

This option also eschews the naming of leaders and heroes for its causes. Where a people finds itself angry at a group claiming to represent the views of that population, there is criticism of the representation, not the group's leaders or heroes. Since we are past the modern, we are past the need for recognition by authors of movements. This is how social movements function after ontology; this is to say that as the world becomes organized under increasing bureaucratic authority, it is less likely that we will see the rise of an individual to respond to questions of arrogance, or an individual to question arrogance, around which followers will emerge.

This is consistent in a virtual age where the presence of the body and sound of the voice of leaders is less and less effective at maintaining social allegiances; however, the look of a web page or the accessibility of it may shape an organization's success at garnering support. This discussion is not meant to deify "psychological individuals" as martyred figures or saviors, any more than it is meant to hold the fractal subject up as a proto-identity. On the contrary, we are already fragmented, the point is to acknowledge it and develop social practices that match this identity. When faced with fascisms everywhere, the lure of the fractal subjectivity is strong if only because it leaves the seeds of doubt in one's own position. To distinguish these subjectivities from previous ones in other eras is important; the identity is appropriate for the structure of the social and world politics in the present era. Whereas Martin Luther King, Jr. was a prophet for a generation living under the shadow of the Cold War and bipolar relations, he could triangulate the collective desire for freedom and channel it into a progressive agenda for civil rights legislation (Dudziak 2000). We are not faced with this option today, and while it important to remember King's legacy it is futile to wait for another figure that resembles him in any way to come to our aid against hegemonic structures.

Similarly, people are busy looking for fascism in the symbols of past eras: red and black clothing, swastikas and bunker groups whereas it is unclear that historical examples of fascism went undetected because they had never been witnessed before. Fascism will have to look different if it is to be effective. Swastikas and tanks, the fascisms we will undoubtedly face in the coming era will look nothing like them; or will have different meanings attached to them. As Hebdige (1977) has shown in his analysis of subcultures, style is a means of performing alienation and absence when social opportunity declines, and people adopt objects and invest them with new meanings or parodies of old values and traditions. While this may not be formal "resistance," it is a kind of performance of an absence, as he says following Barthes and Genet, but it is meant to "shock and awe" received opinion and confuse the dominant culture about its messages.

Second Option: Getting Projection Right

All the criticism of social movements in the present era is a criticism of failed organization, but what if we were to view organization of this sort as a form of dictatorship? Indeed, Lenin called it a "dictatorship of the proletariat" and this dictatorship, as Winnicott has underscored in a psychoanalytic way, is "the domination of good over bad, but the definition of good and bad belongs to the dictator and is not a matter for discussion among the individuals that compose the group" and not subject to revision by them. The other failed aspect of this will to organize a total emancipation, in addition to its manipulation of acute affect, is that, as Winnicott notes, it eventually becomes boring and the dictatorship breaks down, "To some extent it could be said that the dictatorship breaks down because the fixed meaning of good and bad becomes boring, and people become willing to risk their lives in the cause of spontaneity and originality" (Winnicott 1986, 225). I like this critique because it shows that no matter how hard dictators think about controlling populations, even in their name, they will eventually be outdone by the boredom of the very people they are attempting to control in the name of emancipation from a hated (and constructed) enemy.

There are elements of this projection in every movement, but the "managing projection" option that revolutionary Marxism (or anarchism or fascism or evangelicism) provides is dangerous and infectious. It is inherently undemocratic because the exploited are asked to believe an enemy that is largely the creation of the dictatorship's imagination (as in delusions of persecution and fantasies of total control) and for a while, Winnicott notes, this line or wall may satisfy the impulse to actual violence in societies, but it is constructed and whole populations are dragged into it for the sake of saving a few individuals the pain of experiencing their own personal depression or breakdown. The point is that it doesn't make sense to criticize social movements for a lack of effective organization; if people are doing it at a natural, even pace and making the challenges they need to make to oppression in a microcosmic (versus grand) sense, then they are not veering toward domination, and this is a good development, and, we might add, very democratic.

Third Option: Populism, Conservatively Speaking

Instead of calling this the "right wing" rendition of social movements, let's call it philosophically conservative. We have elements of the first two versions in this one: first, borrowing from the "anti-Enlightenment" perspective, the characterization of social movements as emotional upheavals with little to no forethought or principled reasoning behind them is guided by firm conservative belief that most people need to be governed by a select group of people born with this capacity. It is conservative because it shares the disbelief in grand projects with the anti-Enlightenment folks; except its perspective is premodern and it bases its claims on an unchanging conception of human nature. Don't get yourself into a mess, says this option, that the select few will have to get you out of when you get ensnared in messy thoughts about peace and harmony. Just do things the way they have always been done and believe the same way, because traditional social patterns with their stasis and ahistorical quality, make governing easier and people less temperamental. The difference is that whereas the anti-Enlightenment folks don't want the big project because they fear it gives the people who think they have been selected an opportunity for more control, the conservatives seize upon and exploit these failures to discredit any social action that is not in their interests. Further, they use these failures to justify their rule.

Pat Buchanan's view of immigration is one way of describing this option. He argues that immigration (which is social movement in its most elemental form) is detrimental to states because it causes an "overflow" of diversity in a society that can only tolerate a certain, limited amount of change, and has finite emotional and material resources to accommodate life. Playing upon people's fears of the unknown and their knowledge of the finite resources available to workers (after all none of these three options would argue that people are not exploited—there is no longer any critique of social movements from the perspective of plentitude and individual failure that is, no one says the world is *full* of opportunity any more). For example, this view was given even more strength after September 11, when it became perfectly acceptable to argue (not actually follow through with) that the borders of the United States should be closed to immigrants without judicious review of the consequences (Buchanan 1998). It became acceptable to ask questions about world politics that no one had ever bothered with before September 11. The perfect rhetorical question for this conservative sentiment is precisely this: why do they hate us? If a people cannot figure out how oppressed people living elsewhere (and even inside their own country) could possibly hate them for flaunting their wealth and invading other countries for their own gain, then they don't deserve to ask that question. The very fact that it is asked at all is arrogant to an infuriating degree.

As we can see with Diana Zoelle and Jyl Josephson's chapter, there are few limits to the arrogance of the American government and people when it comes to the poor and disenfranchised in the United States. The KWRU purposefully exploits this ignorance/arrogance binary in its performances and show trials. So, the argument is that social movements are problematic because they mess with the natural order of things, which is massive exploitation and social and political unevenness in all societies and worldwide. What the KRWU performs, then, is the absence of plenitude, and forces the attention of the generalized global culture and local political elites to look at the bareness created, the holes in progress (urban decay, neglect) that persist, despite the narratives of arrogance and market optimism that attempt to contain the populations subjected to localized austerity.

For the philosophically conservative narrative on social movements then, they are simply a means for alienated populations to act out their misery instead of buying into the false promises of globalization. The philosophically conservative narrative on social movements would suspect that they are not accomplishing anything because they do not topple governments, or make systematic critiques of world capitalism and governing structures. In other words, the philosophically conservative critic of social movements sets them up for failure by depicting them as isolated movements with no direction or indication of what they want and ignores the fact that there is no governing structure to appeal to after authority (Lipschutz 2000). This is ideology in the present era: most audiences assume that there is a modern solution to political problems, that governing structures will respond if populations word their pleas or construct their violent hostage-taking strategies in the appropriate way, the right way. Rather with the pace at which information is spread, the message is instantaneously lost in the merging of image, affect, and language on the screen when it is not transformed into something else.

There are alternatives to this all or nothing way of thinking about political action. The three options are not meant to exhaust the range of possible explanations for what social movements do and whom they might challenge. It may be that they do not challenge governing structures at all but instead gesture toward their uselessness and give the world a glimpse of future forms of political organization that are more reflective of politics in the future. Following the introductory chapter, we might say that social movements we are looking at in this volume do challenge the myths of global arrogance by locating their chauvinism, exploiting their irresponsibility and making it known. The existence of a widespread effort on the Left to "de-authorize" political acts from whole populations: Not In My Name as the signature line for a letter to an editor, or an article in a magazine convey to the reader that we are living in time period where the architects of globalization are acting outside the interests and beliefs of the people they are claiming to defend, in their name.

These are a few of the questions that this chapter has attempted to sketch out for the sake of understanding how effective or ineffective current social movements, movements that primarily use advanced technology to spread their messages, are at transforming public discourses on global problems. As is well known, interdependence, when narrowly indicated through market activity, has achieved unprecedented levels globally. That boundaries of authority have moved outside the realm of the nation-state is well known and intuitively felt whether one is "middle class" in the United States or super-exploited in the DRC. Social movements and theorizations about them have a long history that will not be recounted here. Instead, this following section outlines the contours of social movements that use technology to "circulate" information about dominant power arrangements and oppressive situations around the globe, and ask some normative and strategic questions about them.

Reaction Formations

One warning: this *circulation of information* may be seen as problematic. For example, recently in Nigeria, a court ordered a woman accused of having a child outside of marriage to be stoned to death once she had finished weaning the child *her* extramarital coupling had produced (the man is rarely mentioned). An Internet feminist group began circulating this information in an attempt to convince other more influential world leaders to step in and try to stay the execution of this woman. The court's response to this E-mail campaign was feared by local feminist groups within Nigeria, who have claimed that this act of arrogance by "Western feminists" who know nothing of the culture of Northern Nigeria (which is distinct in some ways from other areas) may only serve to irritate the court and speed up the community's feelings of revenge toward the woman and bring the execution forward swiftly. From the standpoint of strategy, the groups within Nigeria are correct as we are circulating information in a global economy with little or no forethought as to how the messages will be received (this is a major problem with Internet communication as it takes the body and cultural meanings out of the medium and it is impossible to control how the receiver will interpret them). Under the modern, information was not circulated, but transmitted from above to those down below, who had no access to information or education (it was assumed). Under globalization, information is circulated without any trepidation, and ideas of all kinds are to be found on the Internet without a stable interpreter (teacher) or manager of information (politician, media journalist). And yet, in the absence of authority or responsible governing or educational structures, communities have formed on the Net to challenge the actions in real time of governments, courts and militaries around the globe.

These "communities" exist in a virtual space outside of our traditionally modern concepts of territory, sovereignty, means of production, ethical or self-selected communities of like-minded individuals, or even the "streets." While they do meet in real time and on real spaces—eventually—they use virtual technologies to meet in cyberspace. They exist in a spatiotemporal continuum of "telepresence" in order to eradicate major distances between each other and save time in the race to outdo oppressive structures and the stable meanings they attempt to convey that will portray them as responsible and democratic. They have little control over how their messages are received by outside parties (those not belonging to the self-same communities they have formed). As Rose puts it,

> Such virtual communities are "diasporic": they exist only to the extent that their constituents are linked together through identifications constructed in the non-geographic spaces of activist discourses, cultural products and media images. And, while the language of community often locates discrete communities within a larger collectivity—a nation, a society, the planet itself, the nature of this superordinate allegiance is now most frequently posed as a problem. (Rose 1996, 333)

What newly wired communities are fighting is precisely this fragmentation of locality in favor of community choice on the Net. Their responses vary according to the futures they envision: where the courts in Nigeria are attempting to move backward against the future of globalization blaming the effects of economic austerity and imperialism (in a word: arrogance) on the figure of the adulterous woman, the women's movements in Nigeria, aware of the intricacies of the political battles they are fighting for themselves and women, are acting as a stopgap on the universalizing tendencies of Western feminists who export their own imaginaries about politics onto local Nigerian cultures. Each link in this fragile digital chain acts to maintain a momentum of women's movements, not into a future of a U.S. version of liberal feminism, but a hybrid, localized version that forestalls the backward movements of patriarchies within while correcting for the lofty (and dangerous) and yes, arrogant, aspirations of those without. As Krista Hunt's chapter in this volume clearly demonstrates, RAWA (Revolutionary Association of Women in Afghanistan) has been accepted as the voice of Afghan feminism by the global media, but this characterization has come out of its own arrogant vehicle and is challenged by women on the Net who know better.

In all, social movements on the Net that respond to global arrogance are attempting to keep alive the idea that there is "no turning back" (Freedman 2002) and to forestall the regressive thinking of local elites and global elites about uses of politics. As Rose points out, the decline of the social security state that was managed by governments in return for Cold War spending and military security has ended as governments have distanced themselves from whole populations that demand welfare subsidies, instead preferring to privatize all the previous means that they used to offset the damaging policies of militarization and uneven capitalist productivity. Now that the "social" is over, we have elites who are both dropping the ball on finding ways to absorb contradictions and blaming the populations trying to withstand their assault with imaginary, socially conservative policies that make security the responsibility of a social that does not exist, except in isolated, socially truncated and conflicting "communities." In extreme examples we might refer to the Hindu community and current political parties in India or in a reformist example we can look to Hunt's chapter and the way that RAWA stands in for the community of women in Afghanistan, who are by no means exhaustively represented by them on the Internet. With the end of a social space confined to the nation, we also witness the end of national solutions to common everyday problems experienced under globalization—the dream of emancipation has been eclipsed by the arrogance of elites at the end of the nation-state. See Lars Hallström's chapter in this volume.

Whither Emancipation?

We began this project with a question about emancipation. Some contributors of the volume wanted to continue to use this term, but only because we lacked a pristine concept with which to apprehend global social movement goals. Emancipation is a *modern* category; that is, it imagines people and the means of production as items to be released from oppression by a responsible identifiable agent. Emancipation moving away from something hegemonic and oppressive, but as we know from radical social thought since the end of structuralism, there is no end to ideology, only the means we construct in human societies to live with it or transform it to enhance the lives of the oppressed. They have been replaced by structures of domination that have anticipated their concerns, legislated against them, loaned capital on the promise that they will not be mentioned (e.g., IMF, World Bank). As Hardt and Negri state, in their post-Marxist analysis of *Empire*,

> Emancipation is the entry of new nations and peoples into the imperial society of control, with its new hierarchies and segmentations; liberation, in contrast, means the destruction of boundaries and patterns of forced migration, the re-appropriation of space, and the power of the multitude to determine the global circulation and mixture of individuals and populations. (Hardt and Negri 2000, 363)

This distinction between "liberation" and "emancipation" demonstrates the stakes involved in any political project aimed at fighting the hegemony of global arrogance, from narrow political elites who work together with the media to obfuscate the opinion of the democratic electorate in the world's only superpower (Nye 2002) to the educational systems and international organizations that channel the modern desire for progress and a "good life" into IMF rescheduling and the "discrete" technical problems each state must confront as a necessary step toward the ever just out of reach goal of "development" (Sen 1999; Nussbaum 1999; Escobar 1995; Duffield 2001). There is no such thing as perfect emancipation (Pasha 1996), and there is the co-optation of "liberation" by elites such as the current administration, but there are other means of liberation conceived of as any human ingenuity that can divert state power into human needs and security, or hide pleasure from disciplinary codes created by neoliberal power elites to forestall the question of "what next?" after a long hard day at work producing the hybrid forms of control that endlessly shape the limits of the possible in a world where nature is imaginary and inexhaustible and people are resource material for global capital. Liberation does not come from above but from below.

"Truth" in this global framework of arrogance is the mere ability to speak to power in a way that can heal wounds (Truth Commissions), repair injustices, material and corporeal, emotional and historical or take back spaces of democratic deliberation (KWRU) that have been stolen, destroyed, ignored or become decrepit. Our normative framework is constrained by the constant battery of injustices proliferating throughout the globe by movements of capital trying to increase rates of profit (small arms, explosives, drugs, prostitution, exploitation of resources) in the face of a massive unequal distribution of wealth, not only between North and South but also between the islands of the gated rich and oceans of poor, everywhere. Where there is a global movement to ban landmines there is the horrible truth that the same companies that produced the mines that hinder the movement of people's in their own territories, are also the ones bidding on the more expensive contracts to remove them. There is also the arrogance of the campaigns when they are high jacked by celebrity images and icons and show the ignorance of populations who can only be enticed to do the right thing if a popular person takes the first step, as Jim Nelson's chapter in this volume demonstrates.

"Justice" is no longer a matter of having exactly what those in power have (envy), it is also a matter of life and death (Foucault 1977, 135–59), dignity (Nussbaum 1999) and freedom of movement (de Certeau 1984, 91–130), and of forcing not just governments but their advisors to realize the dream that the defenders of capitalism made people believe: standards of/for living, literally. This is a sign that the modern project is over, and we are either forced to deal with constructing and studying the powerful machinations of the postmodern project or to view this period in time as a retrograde act on the part of governments everywhere who have fallen down on the job and allowed the dream of progress to die.

The Social Aspect of Movements

After the fall of the Berlin Wall in East Germany, and the subsequent fall of communism as an ideology throughout the world, global persons were confronted with a situation labeled "pan capitalism" to which no alternative ideology or way of life could juxtapose itself to show the contradictions (social, emotional, revolutionary, etc.) of capitalism (Kroker and Weinstein 1994). Ironic as it may sound, capitalism no longer had its adversary to drive it forward in competition and continue its moves toward progress to the point where many charged that the United States had to fight communism to have it, implying that it was too good of an idea to destroy completely. In social movements now, we witness the nostalgia for a security state, or for social welfare orientations that governments are not prepared to construct. Instead, by the mid-1990s many thought that unending prosperity and the march toward consumer efficiency would complete the idea of democracy, led by the now coalition of willing that was the entire world and its United States.

This particular version of the social in the United States is a major barrier to ending what we have called "global arrogance" because if you cannot find justice in the most ardent defender of democracy and capitalism (for its own people) then it is most definitely not to be found in U.S. exports. Nikolas Rose has defined the social in this way:

> The social, that is to say [sic], does not represent an eternal existential sphere of human sociality. Rather, within a limited geographical and temporal field, it set the terms for the way in which human intellectual, political and moral authorities, in certain places and context, thought about and acted upon their collective experience. This novel plane of territorialization existed within, across, in tension with other spatializations: blood and territory; race and religion; town, region and nation . . . .Simultaneously, political forces would now articulate their demand upon the State *in the name of the social*: the nation must be governed in the interest of social protection, social justice, social rights and social solidarity. (Rose 1996, 329)

But, as Rose goes on to argue, following Baudrillard and Foucault, the social seemingly ended when the social security regime that made its deal with Cold War politics died. What happened at the time, in conjunction with advertising hegemony, was the birth of community, another term to replace the social and set up islands of groups of people who had decided to cast their fate together, outside that of the nation-state. So, all types of communities can command different allegiances and form the "hybrid" subjectivity of which Hardt and Negri speak. The critical difference is that now the communities are varied and can be chosen by the subject on-line. People can choose their allegiance to the rapidly proliferating communities on the Net, and, while they do this they can abandon previous ties to the nation and forge new ties in hybrid forms based on other interests, identities and allegiances. This is the critical "choice" that subjects under globalization now have to make without the imposition of a hierarchy of values and transferring agents to mold or shape (reproduce) relations of production and nationalism.

    If we want to discuss how community and the social have been transformed then we should go back to the original source for community and choice: Jean Jacques Rousseau. Here I will discuss the "choice" that people have with respect to politics. Rose notes that community, which under Rousseau's conception, is a choice that people make: contrary to Hobbes, Rousseau argued that people choose to live in association with one another, not out of fear, but out of a mutual desire for association. Rousseau is further helpful because he attends to the specific ways in which people make their choices about the communities that are formed; they can choose good or bad communities. We could say the same exact thing about the Net, and that people who are disenfranchised by the "end of the social"

(Baudrillard 1994; Rose 1996) and the "insecurity dilemma" (Lipschutz 2000) have gone online to choose both good and bad ways (e.g., progressive Enlightenment ways, or regressive premodern ways; neither of which are wholly desirable) of recovering that original need for association and shared responsibility.

Since we are past the modern epoch, and Rousseau, as the first critic of the Enlightenment—the first to call it into crisis—was himself thoroughly modern for inhabiting the space of the social. We are witnessing the crisis of social contracts. He invented the contract that would eventually come to encapsulate popular demand in direct relation to the state through a social contract. He also implied responsibility on both sides. Now, we must try to imagine what the social looks like when moved outside the boundaries of the nation-state and into the virtual space of the Net. Between the reactionary narratives of philosophical conservatives and local elites, social movements on the Net and in the street, and the bodiless ideas and circulation of information in telepresence (Kac 1997) is the space where we find a generic will expressed, especially in our cases here in this volume, that the progress narratives of the Enlightenment, when not considered "grand" emancipatory projects, cannot be allowed to regress backward into the nostalgic memories of groups organizing their participation in the social around *fear*. Since they are really "temporal" holding spaces, these social domains are where ideas and interests are hashed out. They have a strategic geography to them: holding history and ideas in place to let the future catch up to politics, as the Iyer quote at the start of this chapter indicates, the future may even need to be "imported," perhaps based on ideas from the past with new realities in mind.

The Geography of Social Movements

> The critical aspect of the old system is *interpretation*, i.e., the operation by which one assigns to a set of confused or even contradictory appearance a unitary structure, a deep meaning, a 'veritable' explanation. Hence, interpretation must gradually give way to a new discourse, whose goal is not the revelation of a unique and 'true' structure but the establishment of an interplay of multiple structures: an establishment itself *written* i.e., uncoupled from the truth of speech; more precisely, it is the relations which organize these concomitant structures, subject to still unknown rules, which must constitute the object of a new theory.
>
> —Barthes 1986, 154

With the death of progress on a grand scale and the rebirth of accumulation (through new market hegemony), social movements have many major tasks set out before them. We are in a period of political regression and rollback, where progress cannot take place because governance structures are unable to remove barriers and obstacles put into place by arrogant power holders who wish to use this opportunity to increase the accumulation of capital and resources for narrow, selfish interests. In fact, it is often global governance structures that are used to justify the maintenance of these *barriers and obstacles*.

Since the founding of the (modern) sovereign nation-state, world politics, when it has occurred, has been marked by the logic of anarchy and narrated through the discourse of group fantasy: us versus them, the infidels and the believers, the enemy and the friend. Those people's movements that found themselves outside of this logic throughout history, such as civil rights demonstrators, the nonaligned movements, movements against colonial rule and mastery, have found temporary spaces outside of this logic which last for a time, endure in institutions, amendments to constitutions and civil codes and are reproduced in the teachings of activists and university professors, when they are not in danger of being destroyed. Nostalgia and memory begin to make and remake the strength and constitute the witness potential of these movements. But our central concern is that they *always reappear at crucial moments in time to open up spaces for a different kind of discourse and thought on the exploitative practices* of the day.

Baudrillard has called this reappearance an effect of the "promiscuity of values" in contemporary politics. As the Barthes quote above indicates, it is no longer satisfactory to simply interpret power moves and exploitation as a function of a stable signifying regime; social movements respond in real time or at least attempt to close the gap between the exploitative behavior and the response time of activists. Without borders, "activists" are already responding to a world communication system in which there is no benefit of response or criticism that is leveled at an institution or governmental structure because their meanings shift too quickly. According to Barthes and other social theorists, we no longer have the luxury of assuming that an author has control over the way in which images proliferating from her/his discourse will be received or rechanneled into other pursuits or causes. Events can be interpreted any way one likes, so the best bet is to be convincing in interpretation and to network the conveyance of meaning and information in such a way as to block or slow the *obstacles* in the path of the movements' goals.

Social Movement Barriers and Obstacles

These obstacles are the most important element for understanding the success of social movements, or reading the world as a site of democratic instruction or as Teivainen has suggested, seeing the world itself as a "school." They are the symptoms of the illness that global governance structures are suffering whether they admit to their maladies or not. These obstacles are emotional, as in the manipulation of affect on media presentations for both left and right causes; political and resource-based in terms of monetary support and military capabilities; epistemological in that the social movements must continually respond to the rewriting of history by the media, establishment and administration/managerial groups as well as the erasure of history by the actions of war combined with the ultimate emotional obstacle: bad historical analogies. The barriers are also material by design as in the architecture of the buildings where global elites meet to decide the outcome of events in secret, or arrange for barricades or "well-meaning" separate but supposedly equal spaces for NGOs to congregate outside of international forums. More material barriers include the simple enclosure of people's movement (in immigration, labor flows, urban implosion, imprisonment) after capital and resources to pursue a simple existence.

By far the least noticed, but in the long term the most important barrier, are the governmental blockages placed on civil liberties and freedoms that prevent activists and people's from organizing to protest all the other barriers. The hostage taking that Baudrillard has been describing since Watergate by politicians of publics is key: scandal has no effect in the virtual world of technologies and infinite speed and proliferation of meaning. Everyone is a war criminal, everyone a potential terrorist, everyone a thief—this is the "promiscuity of values," not the promiscuity of individual people held out as distracters and public examples, as the architects of global arrogance are trying so desperately to get the world to believe (Baudrillard 2001).

We witness this in the current fascination of pseudo-public intellectuals in the United States like Robert D. Kaplan, who echoing Fareed Zakaria almost a decade ago in less perilous times, told the readers of the *New York Times*, that "democracies take liberties" but do not use them effectively if they do not have the anchoring institutions (rule of law, etc.) (Zakaria 1996; Kaplan 2002). In other words, elections may take place but there is nothing that assures us that they are a real expression of the people's will, because the people's will has not been effectively shaped and informed by something called a genuine "civil society." And, for Rousseau, we should note, a society is civil if it is not solely based on survival and base instincts; that is, if people only act out of fear and scarcity (Rousseau [1782] 1987, 150–51).

This is tricky because as theorists know, Marx himself charged that "civil society does not exist" and is a tool of the powerful against the weak in the age of democracy and capitalism. Following Marx's lead, Gramsci derived a theory of civil society across national boundaries, claiming that the bourgeois class interests are reflecting this civil imperative. Louis Althusser took it further to pronounce that no politics were possible under ideological state apparatuses that produce the *idea fixée* of civil society. To use Rousseau's language, civil society is a "convention" that is either believed or not believed in by the people on whose behalf it is advanced as an idea. And yet the Rousseauian project of constructing civil society has been attempted and become a kind of communitarian sediment, locked forever in a certain generation's ideas about freedom from state power: free love, free of power, freedom to conform. This "counter Enlightenment thought style" is mired in a romantic conception of community, ignorant of the realities of power and manipulation, even in its own discourses. There is also the enduring effect of the *image* of American democracy (Dudziak 2000) that acts as a major stumbling block for social movements that have charged into the global social scene. Perched on the edge of Empire, Americans have shown the global communities on the Net exactly what they do not want from American hegemony to filter into their own social spaces. The response to the United States' unabashedly imperialist foray into Iraq provides the critical distance that social movements needed to figure out the future. The U.S. hegemony is an obvious starting point for any social movement in the present era to figure out exactly what they don't want the emerging social to imitate.

U.S. Hegemony: The Main (but not only) Example

He prevented his subjects from ever becoming what they could have been by persuading them they were something that they were not.

—Rousseau [1782] 1987, 166

Can a nation that began in rebellion against empire end by turning itself into an empire? Perhaps it can, but not if it wishes to remain a republic.

—Schell 2003, 45

We could certainly never claim that the outpouring of peaceful sentiment against war on February 15, 2003 was anything resembling a general will, but we can safely assume that it approximates a general outline of a will. I should like to call it a "generic" will instead of a general will. The generic will is formed through Internet technologies that make contact between subjects in the world more efficient and possible. It is not the same as a general will in that it is not formed by people who realize they are in a community that is unified under the nation-state, but precisely because people realize that they have been abandoned by their respective states (morally, politically, economically) and seek out a like-minded cohort of activists in global spaces that emerge on the Internet. As (Rose 1996) has argued, the Net becomes "a new territory of government" by the people; like the streets where protestors collect to voice their demands and opposition to wars, unjust policies, unjust elections, and unjust economic impositions. Political purchase rests in subjectivity; subjectivity is increasingly constituted in the media.

In some ways, we are in search of the American political imaginary when we are looking for answers to current forms of arrogance, and answers as to why the public votes against its "interests." Dewey was in search of the "phantom public" and believed that it was constrained by its own (though he would say) facile approach to enjoyment, "Man takes his enjoyment neat," he wrote, and "at as short a distance as possible" (Dewey 1958, 53). This is a continuous *telos* throughout Deweyan thought; he borrowed from everyone: Locke on the social construction of human "nature"; and Rousseau on the ill effects of the social in shaping what Dewey called "inferiority complexes." But Dewey's specific attention to the American people and its problems in forming a public that would confront the ever elusive "state" (which he claimed did not exist as an institution, but only as a phantom [following Walter Lippman] that comes into existence when necessary), is a valid contribution to thought even to this day. Dewey's insight is eerily Foucauldian, and he never used the word "power" for pristine theoretical reasons: you cannot discuss the power of a people that has never self-actualized to the point where it would recognize, *then grasp* power when it presented itself. People, as Rousseau has said, are not what their leaders tell them to be, even if they act as though they are; they may lose their purpose as a people, and flounder onto their ruin, but they were meant to be *something*, in accordance with their liberty. Those who follow their own rules, self-made rules, are exercising their liberty.

Americans are not the militaristic people (though they are *militarized*) that the world believes them to be, at least not in the calculating manner that they are described in newspaper and media accounts by their own leaders, public intellectuals, and media personnel. They are a people that have always been led, even in the moment of their inception at the American Revolution: by the military, their leaders, the media and their own proscribed notions of family. While they represent Enlightenment acts, they do not uphold enlightened ideals with any degree of consistency.

Now, as the model of an empire social movements can oppose, the U.S. continues in its contradictions and fails to correct for its arrogance, which always operates as if world opinion did not exist. Again: "why do they hate us?" This arrogance will provide the source for the outline of this "generic will" that is represented by social movements that challenge any narrative of progress or retrograde thought to keep alive the idea of a future. They are not perfect, but perfection was discarded with emancipation.

However incoherent, what we confront in antiwar protests like the ones inspired by MoveOn.org (the merger between Eli Pariser's group September 11 in Boston and MoveOn.org in San Francisco) are a direct challenge to authority (of global capital, the Bush Administration, the idea of limited war); the three-quarters of a million people that rallied against Tony Blair's support for U.S.-led intervention in Iraq, and the tens of thousands of demonstrators that turned out in every major city in the world to protest the intervention, despite their government's support for the action. The confrontation with authority is a sign of testing boundaries, learning how power properly works, what it will listen to and what it won't, finding the boundaries and hierarchies in a society (especially in the United States) that are usually compromised and occluded by ideologies of consumerism and so-called equal economic opportunity—essentially, the arrogance of U.S. hegemony that has reached global proportions. Marlyn Tadros's chapter in this volume very clearly demonstrates how entrenched boundaries and values are tested by the Net (from the overt sexual, moral and political boundaries of Egyptian society to the deeply unconscious boundaries of the American political imaginary and their phantasmatic images playing with ingrained attitudes that are racial, sexual and class-based). Now, we are learning the new boundaries of the world.

We might call these "island of civility" on the Net, adapting one of Mary Kaldor's depictions of the flight from war into a kind of quasi-settled existence outside the fog of war and insecurity generated by those people who aggressively confront the fear introduced worldwide by globalization and the decline of the nation-state (Kaldor 1997, 120–24). Mass publics and social movements share one thing: they no longer care about the end of the state as such, but about the end of the means of reproduction of culture, of communication of shared responsibility that are implied in it as a form of world organization; in a word, responsibility. They represent a generic will to keep the very idea of civility alive by constantly questioning the reactionary elements worldwide that keep the future foreclosed from active construction, and peace on the margins of war; they are holding the very *idea* of the world in place while it reorganizes itself.

Notes

1. I refer here to Louis Althusser's structuralism and the impact of "misrecognition" and "overdetermination" (Althusser 1971, 1996). The problem with the structural accounts that dominated international relations theorizing for quite some time (even in the Gramscian variety of thought) is that they are ahistorical and cannot account for shifts in thought and discourse over time. Any material change in the environment, which has priority over ideational ones in the Marxian tradition, is a minor factor for understanding the entire structure which will simply adjust itself to accommodate or form a compromise with these contradictions, leaving no room for agency and change. However, structuralism was a necessary step in the history of thought because it challenged modern assumptions about agency as belonging to a particular individual or even the distinct class formation in all their moral or intellectual superiority, thereby adding to thought the important claim that thoughts detached from individuals or introduced by accident were perhaps even more important than those celebrated by humanism as exclusive to the exemplary individual. Post-structuralism introduced a great amount of uncertainty as to sources of agency, change, and control into thought and was perhaps considered one of the most intellectual trends for this very reason. For ongoing work introducing uncertainty to constructivism via poststructuralist analysis, see Zehfuss (2002).

2. Barthes further elaborates that "anti-intellectualism" is a petite bourgeois mythical invention that is on the fascist side of power. As he writes, "what would become of a society which gave up seeing itself in perspective?" (Barthes, 1986, 344). One could easily say this about the United States and most members of social movements do, however, this has not convinced the public to see itself in any perspective other than that afforded by hastily formed inconsistent matrices of interest when pushed on an event. Social movements attempt to fight the anti-intellectualism (to force clarity or purpose on power) demonstrated by a widespread refusal to see a society in perspectives outside the ones the power structure and media provides. This is why it is important to note that the media has minimized the message of a great number of people who support these protests and social movements. See Cortright's chapter in this volume.

Bibliography

Althusser, Louis. 1971. *Lenin and Philosophy and Other Essays*, trans. Ben Brewster. London: Verso.

Ames, Paul. 2003. "Chirac Decries E. Europe's Stance on U.S." *Associated Press.* February 17.

Barthes, Roland. 1986. "Writing the Event." *The Rustle of Language*, trans. Richard Howard. Berkeley, Calif.: University of California Press.

Baudrillard, Jean. 1994. *Simulacra and Simulation*, trans. Chris Turner. University of Michigan Press.

————. 2001. *Impossible Exchange*, trans. Chris Turner. London. Verso.

Buchanan, Patrick J. 1998. *The Great Betrayal*. Boston: Little Brown.

"Bush Enlists Allies Domestic and Foreign to Lobby for U.N. Resolution on Iraq." 2003. *The New York Times* February 26, 2003, A-1, A8.

Copjec, Joan. 2003. *Imagine There's No Woman: Ethics and Sublimation*. Boston, Mass.: MIT Press.

Crawford, Neta C. 2002. *Belief and Change in World Politics*. London: Cambridge University Press.

De Certeau, Michel. 1986. *The Practice of Everyday Life*, trans. Steven Randall. Berkeley, Calif.: University of California Press.

Der Derian, James. 2001. *Virtuous War*. Boulder, Colo.: Westview.

Dewey, John. 1958. *Experience and Nature*. New York: Dover.

Dudziak, Mary. 2000. *Cold War Civil Rights: Race and the Image of American Democracy*. Princeton.

Duffield, Mark. 2001. *Global Governance and the New Wars*. London: Zed.

Escobar, Arturo. 1995. *Encountering Development*. New Jersey: Princeton University Press.

Foucault, Michel. 1977. *The History of Sexuality. Vol One*, trans. Robert Hurley. New York: Vintage.

Freedman, Estelle B. 2002. *No Turning Back: The History of Feminism and the Future of Women*. New York: Ballantine.

Galtung, Johan. 1990. "Cultural Violence." *Journal of Peace Research* 27, no. 3: 291–305.

Hardt, Michael and Antonio Negri. 2000. *Empire*. Cambridge: Harvard University Press.

Hebdige, Dick. 1977. *Subculture: The Meaning of Style*. New York: New Left Books.

Iyer, Pico. 2003. "Abandoning the Post, Mired in the Moment." *The Los Angeles Times*. Friday, July 4.

Kac, Eduardo. 1997. "Telepresence: A New Communicative Experience." *Epipháneia* no. 2 (March).

Kaldor, Mary. 2003. *Global Civil Society: An Answer to War*. London: Blackwell.

————. 1998. *Old and New Wars*. Berkeley, Calif.: University of California Press.

Kaplan, Robert D. 2002. *Warrior Politics*. New York: Random House.

Keck, Margaret E. and Kathryn Sikkink. 1998. *Activists Beyond Borders: Advocacy Networks in International Politics*. Ithaca, N.Y.: Cornell University Press.

Kroker, Arthur and Michael A. Weinstein. 1994. *Data Trash: The Theory of the Virtual Class*. New York: St. Martin's Press.

Lapham, Lewis. 2001. "The American Rome." *Harper's* 303, no. 1815: 31–39.

Laplanche, J. and J-B Pontalis. 1967. *The Language of Psycho-Analysis*. New York: W.W. Norton.

Lavine, Thelma, Z. 1998. *Reading Dewey: Interpretations for a Postmodern Generation*. Bloomington: Indiana University Press.

Lippman, Walter. [1925] 1930. *Phantom Public*. New York: MacMillan.

Lipschutz, Ronnie D. 2000. *After Authority*. New York: SUNY Press.

————. 1996. *For Marx*, trans. Ben Brewster. New York: Verso.

MacCannell, Juliet F. 1992. *The Regime of the Brother*. New York: Routledge.

Nussbaum, Martha. 1999. *Sex and Social Justice*. New York: Oxford University Press.

Nye, Joseph S. 2002. "The American National Interest and Global Public Goods." *International Affairs* 78, no. 2: 233–44.

Ortega y Gasset, José. 1932. *The Revolt of the Masses*, trans. Willard Trask. New York: W.W. Norton.

Pasha, Mustapha Kamal. 1996. "Security as Hegemony." *Alternatives* 21: 283–302.

Ramazani, Vaheed. 2001. "September 11: Masculinity, Justice, and the Politics of Empathy." *Comparative Studies of South Asia, Africa and the Middle East* 21, nos. 1/2: 118–24.

Rose, Nikolas. 1996. "The Death of the Social? Refiguring the Territory of Government." *Economy and Society* 25, no. 3: 333.

Rousseau, Jean Jacques. [1782] 1985. "On the Social Contract." *Rousseau, The Basic Political Writings*, trans. Donald A. Cress. Indianapolis: Hackett.

Schell, Jonathan. 2003. "No More Unto the Breach: Why War is Futile, Part I." *Harper's*. March 306, no. 1834: 33–46.

———. 2003. "No More Unto the Breach: The Unconquerable World, Part II." *Harper's*. April 306, no. 1935: 41–55.

Sen, Amartya. 1999. *Development as Freedom*. New York: Anchor Books.

Wendt, Alexander. 1992. "Anarchy Is What States Make of It." *International Organization* 46, no. 2 (Spring): 391–425.

White, Stephen K. 2000. *Sustaining Affirmation*. Princeton, N.J.: Princeton University Press.

Winnicott, D. W. 1986. *Home Is Where We Start From*. New York: W.W. Norton.

Zakaria, Fareed. 1996. "Democracies That Take Liberties." *The New York Times* August.

Zehfuss, Maja. 2002. *The Politics of Reality*. London: Cambridge University Press.

Part 2

Challenging Arrogance from the Local to the Global

Chapter 3

Making Democratic Space for Poor People: The Kensington Welfare Rights Union

Diana Zoelle and Jyl J. Josephson

The opposite of love is not hate, it's indifference.

—Elie Wiesel

In north Philadelphia in the summer of 1995, a multiracial group of welfare mothers, members of the Kensington Welfare Rights Union, set up a tent city on the lot of a Quaker Lace factory that had recently been the victim of arson. This event was the culmination of a series of events that can be seen as part of the U.S. context of the consequences of economic globalization. As journalist David Zucchino put it:

> In many ways, the arrival of welfare mothers at Quaker Lace was a fitting coda for the old factory and everything it represented about North Philadelphia's ongoing industrial decline. The collapse of manufacturing and the evapora- tion of blue-collar jobs had helped give rise to the illegal drug trade. Those who sold drugs had torched the Quaker Lace ruins, which in turn had provided a new home for another unfortunate byproduct of the area's economic collapse—welfare recipients. It was like a forest fire that cleared out old growth and made way for new vegetation. (Zucchino 1997, 59)

This process, however, was not—as Zucchino suggests by analogy—the scene of an unavoidable natural disaster. Rather, it was very much a matter of human decisions, individually and collectively, shaping the events that led to the tent city. The idea that humans—and in particular, U.S. policy-makers—could choose differently, so that, for example, low-income women have housing, food, and clothing for their children, is at the heart of the organizing done by the Kensington Welfare Rights Union.

One of the early uses of technology by the Kensington Welfare Rights Union (KWRU) was the documentary regarding their activities, produced by Skylight Pictures, entitled *Poverty Outlaw*. The film documents the situation of low-income people, primarily women and children, in Philadelphia in the 1990s. It shows the lack of investment and abandoned housing in the Kensington section of Philadelphia, and it documents how changes in welfare policy at the local, state, and national level are causing further hardships for these families.

We have shown this film in a number of undergraduate courses in American politics and public policy. Each time, many students' basic reaction has been to denigrate the women's efforts to organize. A number of students say, "Why do they spend all this time protesting? Why don't they just get a job?" This reaction reflects, we believe, not only the negative images of low income people that have been emphasized relentlessly both by public officials and by media and popular culture, but also the deep desire in the United States that "those people"—the poor—would just disappear. There is a desire to keep poverty hidden, and to see the problems of low-income people (regardless of how widespread and systemic those problems are) as problems of individual pathology.

Students do not come to these conclusions of their own accord. In the United States, a great deal of political and intellectual energy has gone into the creation of a conception of poverty that attributes the situation of poor people to individual pathology, not structural inequalities. While there is a long history of dividing the poor into the "deserving" and the "undeserving," (Abramovitz 1988; tenBroek 1964–65), in the latter half of the twentieth century the creation of the ideas of a "culture of poverty" and an urban "underclass" has powerfully influenced policy-making. While Lucinda Williams (1997) traces the role of right-wing think tanks in shaping the discourse regarding poverty beginning in the late 1960s, Alice O'Connor, in *Poverty Knowledge*, traces the idea of the "culture of poverty" back further. O'Connor argues that this notion was a product of Cold War ideology and imperialism. Federally funded studies of poverty in the "underdeveloped" "Third World" by anthropologists such as Oscar Lewis, articulated an explanation of poverty in individualist and psychological terms (Briggs 2002). These arguments could then be used to explain poverty in the United States in these same terms (O'Connor 2001, ch. 4). During the Cold War, U.S.-based scholars did not describe poverty as a byproduct of capitalism—this could too easily be dismissed as Marxist—but rather as a result of the "underdevelopment" of certain individual virtues in the poor, and in particular to the pathological familial and sexual behavior of women of color (Briggs 2002). Thus, poverty could be attributed to individual or group pathology, and not to the structure of the political economy or as a feature of market systems. This is also more comfortable for members of the middle class in industrialized democracies: under this conception, poverty cannot touch the "virtuous," nor can it threaten their ideology regarding the political/economic system of the United States. In this conception, citizenship is a matter of the formal political rights of voting, and social and economic inequalities raise no troubling questions regarding the practice of democracy.

Of course, another aspect of this reaction—why are they protesting instead of working—is also deeply antidemocratic and reflects a very privatized and formalized notion of political participation. Part of the arrogance of U.S. foreign policy reflects this privatized notion of democratic citizenship and political participation and rights. "Good" people channel their political concerns through voting and paying lobbyists to represent them, not through the more raucous and disruptive mechanism of a tent city. When KWRU took their tent city to a site across from the Liberty Bell, they created a political spectacle that is just beyond the pale of respectable political representation. David Zucchino noted the comments of some of the tourists who were visiting the Liberty Bell at the time:

> Not all the tourists seemed receptive. Many, in fact, were repulsed by the rickety tent and the scattered piles of blankets and bottles. 'Looks like a goddamned rock concert,' said a man from South Carolina. . . . A woman from Lancaster County said the homeless people might get a better reception if they cleaned themselves up and wore nicer clothes. (Zucchino 1997, 99)

As documented in this volume, political mobilization on the part of the poor is an international phenomenon. Nevertheless, most of this activism is focused locally, and the locus of political engagement is usually specific material gains (Webster and Engberg-Pedersen 2002, 257). Clearly, the potential scope of political activism and engagement by poor people is deeply constrained by national political conditions and the limits of state power as well as by the relative lack of political power that accompanies poverty. Thus, a movement such as KWRU that seeks to engage more broadly with institutional structures that create the conditions of poverty is in itself an interesting phenomenon.

In light of the collapsing of democratic spaces brought about by the expanding power of capital and the lack of effective democratic representation in both national governments and in global governance structures, the "breaking through" of sites of democratic voice and political protest by those not often heard represents a 'site of democracy' (Alperovitz, Williamson, and Imbroscio 2002). As Chantal Mouffe has argued, democracy is never a finished project, and one verification that democracy has not entirely collapsed is when conflict or opposition becomes visible. One way of seeing the activism of the KWRU is as an effort to take sites of oppression and turn them into sites of democracy. As Mouffe argues, "the prime task of democratic politics is not to eliminate passions from the sphere of the public, in order to render a rational consensus possible, but to mobilize those passions towards democratic designs" (Mouffe 2000, 103).

Seeing poor people in a symbolic, venerate site of democratic history may make tourists uncomfortable, but this in part was the point that KWRU wanted to make. They wanted to arouse the passions of citizens, both the tourists present at the Liberty Bell and those who would see the news coverage or the films. Our students' gesture is fundamentally antidemocratic; what they are really saying is why don't they take their political concerns and channel them into private life, just like we do? The activism of KWRU thus constitutes a site of democracy in Mouffe's sense.

This chapter is in three sections: First, we question the possibility of practicing democracy within the context of a neoliberal restructuring of values, then provide background information on the formation and political practices of KWRU. The second section discusses the use of technology by the group to get its message out to both public officials and to the public. The final section discusses the impact and potential of KWRU with respect to the practice of democracy in response to global arrogance.

Contextual Realities

Democracy and Neoliberal Restructuring

The failure of neoliberal restructuring is evident in the failings of the U.S. welfare state. And the failure of U.S. social policy to address problems of the poor is evidence of the inadequacy of neoliberal market mechanisms to serve the interests of all people, and in turn to serve the interests of democracy. KWRU, through its public statements and the issues around which it is organizing, has articulated an argument regarding the role of economic subsistence in any adequate notion of democratic citizenship. Seeing food, clothing, and shelter as basic human rights is an extension of the kinds of economic and social rights articulated in UN documents, but is contradicted by U.S. social policy toward the poor. Early in the emerging discussion of globalization, academics whose focus had primarily been on international human rights may have been quite naïve about the implications of the process, thinking it would encourage recognition of human similarities, concern for the common good, and promotion of justice and equity, as well as peace and security. Activists had no such delusions. When the reality of "market fundamentalism" in the form of neoliberal expansion of the nineteenth-century market utopia came to dominate the rhetoric—particularly in the North and West, the multidimensionality, and, thus, complexity, of the process came into focus (Soros 1998, xx). This case study of KWRU serves to highlight the pathology of unreflective reliance on the rationality of neoliberal economic systems in a globalizing world.

The lack of commitment on the part of the United States to rights of basic subsistence needs, whether for its own residents or in international economic policy, is abundantly clear and has been well documented by human rights scholars as well as feminist scholars of comparative welfare state policy. A decade before the fall of the Berlin Wall, Henry Shue (1980, ix), in the preface to *Basic Rights: Subsistence, Affluence, and US Foreign Policy* said, very simply, "this book is about the moral minimum—about the lower limits on tolerable human conduct, individual and institutional. It concerns the least that every person can demand and the least that every person, every government, and every corporation must be made to do." This assertion sets the stage for his thoroughly balanced argument for reintegration of rights to subsistence, security, and liberty. He does not make the argument that subsistence rights take absolute priority over rights to security and liberty, but makes the compelling argument that all of these rights are indivisible with regard to the responsibilities of the state, and thus represent an undifferentiated whole. Yet, he says, despite powerful rhetoric to the contrary, the State Department "cannot be said to be taking the rights to the fulfillment of basic economic needs very seriously" (7). While Shue's focus was on U.S. foreign policy, the same lack of concern has marked U.S. domestic social policy as well.

In the year 2000, Mosler and Catley, positing the tragic consequences of "imposing liberalism on a recalcitrant world" conclude that "peace in the next millennium will at least be partly contingent on the United States coming to terms with the global problems of increasing population, hunger, disease, and the uneven distribution of capital and technology, [but] . . . a liberal world order may not be designed to address these problems, just as a liberal state is not designed to address distributional issues" (Mosler and Catley 2000, 188). Consequently, despite the defensive maneuvers that neoliberals have made in the wake of opposition to the WTO, the IMF, and the World Bank, serious concern regarding disparities in wealth and well-being, whether domestic or international, is lacking. The demonstrations in Seattle and elsewhere, and the increasing use of remote and easily policed locations for WTO meetings, also clearly indicates a crisis in the functioning of the democratic process. The conflict between structures of democratic accountability and the bodies that control economic globalization is clear in mechanisms such as the World Social Forum (see Teivainen, this volume).

The failure of democracy was also painfully in evidence during the buildup to the recent war in Iraq. Those who had access to both mass media broadcasts and the technology that provided spontaneous organizational sites such as moveon.org, experienced the substantial disconnect between the official stance of the United States government and the "coalition of the willing" and the unofficial, yet burgeoning, resistance evident in the technological sites of democratic protest around the world. One is left with a very disturbing clarity concerning democracy in the United States and Great Britain, in particular. But the situation also made clear the unity and substantial agreement of many people throughout the world in reaction to U.S. hegemonic power. The questions then become: What (or who) is driving these policy decisions? How will this test of state power play out? How are decision-makers to be held to their commitments to the people? In other words, if globalization is the result of unrelated forces of science, technology, economy, and politics that move us toward a more connected international community, how, for example, in the face of the challenge of nonelected elites making decisions about the lives of the peoples of the world, is it possible to retain some semblance of control by "the people?" Who are "the people?"

In many ways, the existence and the character of globalization are irrelevant; the arguments we make as to whether it is a good or bad thing are a waste of precious time. For those committed to economic human rights and some form of democratic accountability within nation-states as well as in international decision-making bodies, the conditions of global arrogance constitute deep challenges to these commitments. Samir Amin poses the question that is central to the ability to deal with conditions as they exist for the poor:

> why in circumstances where capital is becoming increasingly internationalized, are the peoples of the world not responding to this by internationalizing themselves, that is, by affirming their class allegiance across national boundaries? Why, instead of asserting itself, is class consciousness giving way to self-identification by "race," "ethnic group" or religion? (Amin 56)

Some scholars, such as Robert Reich, in *The Work of Nations: Preparing Ourselves for 21st Century Capitalism* (1992), claim that globalism moves the locus of control out of the reach of localities, thus, further disempowering the people. Yet, it is the experience of organizations like KWRU that organizing locally and availing oneself of the technology at hand has the potential of reducing the impact of national decisions. Thus, in contrast to Reich, many urban scholars argue that cities in particular have become central, and more important, hubs as a result of economic globalization. Thus, Clarke and Gaile (1998, 3) reject "the conventional wisdom on cities—that they are obsolete relics of an earlier era—and [the authors] sketch a new geography of the twenty-first century. This new geography is rooted in a seeming paradox: globalization may mean that regions and localities become more important decision arenas." Thus, one of the phenomena of the recent global era is that localities are becoming the sites of activity and decision-making while national responsibility seems to be that of enabler rather than regulator (3). With regard to economic and technological changes, they argue that "the process is one of hollowing out of the nation-state as the locus of economic and political power is shifting *upward* to supranational institutions, *outward* to transnational networks of cities, *downward* to subnational scales" (7). It is certainly true that this "hollowing out of the nation-state" creates the decline in democratic accountability of economic institutions that protests against the WTO, World Bank, and the IMF are intended to highlight. But it has also created the opportunity for new forms of democratic activism and mobilization. Whether by foresight or good fortune, KWRU has developed strategies, taken advantage of technologies, and engaged supranational arbiters that are at the edge of twenty-first-century organizing.

The city of Philadelphia did not prosecute KWRU for the Tent City during the entire summer of 1995 at the site of the Queen Lace factory in the Kensington neighborhood of north Philadelphia. But when the group set up a two-day Tent City at Independence Park, the leaders of KWRU were prosecuted and convicted for failure to disperse (Zucchino 1997). Clearly, it is much more embarrassing to public officials when poverty is on display in a prominent public site such as the Liberty Bell than when it is in evidence in poor neighborhoods. Poverty on display, but out of sight of the nonpoor, is not nearly as disturbing as poverty and homelessness made visible in a prominent site of democracy. The very fact of making poverty visible, placing poverty in the public eye, is a form of resistance and an effort to democratize public policy-making in the arena of social policy. KWRU continues to use tent cities, as well as other tactics, to make poverty visible.

Background on KWRU

The initial organizing conducted by KWRU was in response to local conditions of neighborhood disinvestment, job loss, and poverty. Philadelphia is a classic rust belt city; job losses in manufacturing began in the 1960s. By the 1980s, formerly flourishing working class neighborhoods had become sites of concentrated poverty, with abandoned factories interspersed with abandoned housing. Then, in the state budget crisis of the early 1990s, many states, including Pennsylvania, cut social services for low-income people (Josephson 2000). The city of Philadelphia's housing and welfare services were also deeply affected by state and local budget cuts of the 1980s and 1990s. As KWRU describes it: "KWRU was started by a group of poor women in April 1991. We came together out of necessity—our communities and the survival of our families were threatened by Governor Casey's welfare cuts" (KWRU: Frequently Asked Questions). David Zucchino describes some of the initial civil disobedience actions of KWRU. At the conclusion of the tent city summer in 1995, the group moved into an abandoned Catholic Church in the neighborhood (Zucchino 1997, 159ff). Then, in December of 1995, each family took over a HUD house in North Philadelphia (Zucchino 1997, 286ff).

In 1996, protesting state cuts in Medicaid, KWRU held a "March for Our Lives" to the state capital in Harrisburg. They took over the capitol rotunda and set up a tent city outside the capitol building. Up to this point, all of KWRU's protest activities had been directed at local and state policy-makers. However, in 1996, Congress passed and President Clinton signed the Personal Responsibility and Work Opportunity Reconciliation Act (PRWORA). This law ended the AFDC program and the entitlement status of benefits, established work requirements, and time limits (Josephson 2000). This change helped to inspire KWRU to launch more national activities, and to see welfare policy in the United States as not only mean-spirited, but also as violating the human rights of low income people. In the wake of the 1996 federal welfare law, KWRU began to turn to the international arena, making human rights claims before the United Nations beginning with a June 1997 march to protest state and federal welfare laws, stating:

> These laws violate the human rights of all Americans, especially poor and homeless people in the United States. With the end of the entitlement to welfare, residents of the United States are no longer guaranteed the right to feed, clothe, and house ourselves and our children in this, the richest country in the world. In a time of high and rising unemployment, our government tells its people to "just get a job" without guaranteeing enough jobs at living wages. (KWRU Press Release, May 26, 1997)

KWRU held a second "March for Our Lives" in 1997 from Philadelphia to the United Nations; this event was a launching of the Economic Human Rights Campaign, a partnership with multiple other advocacy organizations. Subsequently, the KWRU has developed an Economic Human Rights Campaign, first by conducting a bus tour of the United States to collect stories of economic human rights violations, documented in the film *Outriders*. At the end of this bus tour, KWRU held an Economic Human Rights Tribunal, to present testimony regarding violations of international human rights documents. The organization submitted a petition to the United Nations regarding human rights claims, and has also brought similar charges against the United States before the Organization of American States (OAS). In this latter claim, KWRU cites both the OAS American Declaration of the Rights and Duties of Man as well as UN agreements (Inter-American Commission on Human Rights Petition, October 1, 1999). In August of 2004, the Poor People's Economic Human Rights Campaign (PPEHRC), the human rights project initiated by KWRU that now involves many organizations, again filed a formal request for a hearing before the Inter-American Commission of the OAS to investigate the poverty policies of the U.S. government (KWRU Press Release August 24, 2004).

With growing recognition of the effects of globalization on the economic conditions of the poor in the United States, KWRU has formed further coalitions with international movements of poor people in the Americas, and with other groups such as the Labor Party, and the Working Families Party. KWRU is a member organization of the National Welfare Rights Union. Other partners in various projects and activities have included the Temple University School of Social Work, poverty law groups and human rights lawyers, and student groups. Activities have included:

- In October of 1998, KWRU, along with the North-South Dialogue, held a "Poor People's Summit" at the Temple University School of Social Work. The summit brought together faculty and students from sixty schools of social work with people from over one hundred poor people's organizations.
- In October 1999, KWRU cosponsored a "March of the Americas" from Washington D.C. to the United Nations in New York (KWRU March of the Americas 1999).
- Cheri Honkala, who was present at the WTO protests in Seattle in 1999, along with a colleague, attempted to serve Citizens Arrest Warrants to the trade ministers of the G-7 countries for crimes against humanity. They were arrested, though the charges were subsequently dropped (KWRU Press Release, March 2000).

- Members of KWRU attended the April 16, 2000 protests against the IMF and the World Bank.
- KWRU helped organize rallies protesting the Republican and Democratic conventions in Philadelphia and Los Angeles during the summer of 2000.
- KWRU attended the World Social Forum in Brazil in 2003 and gave a presentation on poverty and welfare reform in the United States.
- In April of 2003, KWRU, as part of the Poor People's Economic Human Rights Campaign, conducted a Tri-National Speaking Tour on "Lessons from NAFTA." There were two tours, one on the east coast of the United States and Canada, and one on the west coast of the United States with a stop in Ciudad Juarez, Mexico. The idea of this tour was to critique the results of NAFTA for citizens and workers in all three countries, as well as to build opposition to the Free Trade Area of the Americas (FTAA). Both tours included alliances with a wide range of social justice groups including labor unions, locally based social justice organizations, university-based programs and activist groups, and in some cases local affiliates of the Labor Party and the Green Party.
- During the summer of 2004, KWRU had a series of activities leading up to the Democratic and Republican Party conventions in Boston and New York, respectively. There were more activities related to the Republican Convention, including setting up a tent city, dubbed "Bushville" first in Jersey City, then in Central Park, and finally in a church parking lot in Brooklyn. Activities culminated in a rally and march on the opening day of the Republican Convention on August 30.

KWRU's Claims of U.S. Violation of International Human Rights Agreements

As noted above, KWRU has made use of global governance structures, although this use has not actually affected political change in U.S. policy. This has included the use of human rights litigation through international bodies, as well as the continuing collection of data regarding economic human rights violations. The litigation before the OAS (Organization of American States) is discussed below.

For example, the Economic Human Rights Tribunal held at the end of the 1999 bus tour outlined a number of specific human rights violations directly resulting from implementation of the 1996 Personal Responsibility and Work Opportunity Reconciliation Act (PRWORA). These violations included provisions of Articles 23, 25, and 26 of the Universal Declaration of Human Rights. At the Tribunal, documented on the film *Outriders*, testimony collected on the bus tour was read by KWRU members, and in some cases, presented by the individuals whose rights had been violated.

In one sense, the Tribunal was an act of political theatre: since no specific legally enforceable remedies were available for these violations, the testimonies were judged by a jury of experts from academia and from international organizations and advocacy groups. On the other hand, this project generated the Economic Human Rights Campaign, which now consists of thirty-five organizations (Weiss 2000). The set of human rights claims made by this campaign, as we discuss below, argues for a conception of citizenship that includes basic economic and material rights.

KWRU's Organization of American States Claims

The United Nations is not the only international body that addresses human rights issues and in which the U.S. participates. KWRU, along with other parties including the National Employment Law Project, the Urban Justice Center, and the Center for Constitutional Rights, have filed a petition with the Inter-American Commission on Human Rights of the OAS, claiming that the U.S. law under PRWORA violates human rights provisions of the OAS Charter and the OAS American Declaration of the Rights and Duties of Man, as well as the American Convention on Human Rights (Inter-American Commission on Human Rights Petition, October 1, 1999).

KWRU and the other petitioners claim that PRWORA constitutes a violation of specific rights laid out in these OAS documents, including rights to an adequate standard of living, to health, the protection of family relations, to work under reasonable conditions, to food, housing, social security, and nondiscrimination (Inter-American Commission on Human Rights Petition, October 1, 1999, #34). The petition lays out the specific ways in which PRWORA violates OAS human rights, providing evidence from studies of the effects of the 1996 law.

Of particular note are the connections drawn in this petition between civil and political rights and economic rights. Citing documents of the Inter-American Commission on Human Rights, the petition argues that civil, political, social, economic, and cultural rights are "indivisible and interdependent" (Inter-American Commission on Human Rights Petition, October 1, 1999, #49). The petitioners quote a report of the IACHR, which states,

> When the most vulnerable members are denied access to the basic needs for survival which would enable them to break out of their condition, it results

in [a violation of] the right to be free from discrimination; the right to the consequent principles of equality of access, equity, and distribution; and the general commitment to protect the vulnerable elements in society being willingly or complicitly contravened. Moreover, without satisfaction of these basic needs, an individual's survival is directly threatened. This obviously diminishes the individual's right to life, personal security, and . . . the right to participate in the political and economic processes. (Inter-American Commission on Human Rights Petition, October 1, 1999, #51)

Given this principle of indivisibility, the petition argues that a violation of economic, social, and cultural rights constitutes a violation of political rights (Inter-American Commission on Human Rights Petition, October 1, 1999, #53). KWRU and fellow petitioners argue that human rights remedies are necessary. Since the filing of this document, KWRU has been collecting documentation of economic human rights violations at all of their events. In August of 2004, KWRU requested a hearing before the Inter-American Commission (KWRU Press Release 2004).

Strategies and the Use of Technology

Traditional Civil Rights Strategies

One aspect of the strategies used by KWRU is familiar, in that they are traditional civil rights strategies. KWRU is a multiracial coalition of low-income people. They use some of the strategies developed by the welfare rights organizations of the 1960s and 1970s (Bussierre 1997; Davis 1993; West 1981). Indeed, Cheri Honkala was involved in a welfare rights organization in Minneapolis in the 1980s, before founding KWRU (Zucchino 1997, 217). The organization also is rooted in a particular locality and its issues are derived from the concerns of people in that locality. Yet it also has formed coalitions with multiple other organizations, including labor unions, international groups with similar interests, human rights organizations, the School of Social Work at Temple University, and undergraduate students interested in social justice issues. As noted above, much of the more recent work of the organization has involved forming international coalitions, while still working on issues of direct concern to low-income Philadelphians.

Strategies of civil disobedience have also been a prominent feature of KWRU political engagement. The group first gained public attention by an occupation of an abandoned house in the Kensington neighborhood.

Out of this initial project, the group was able to gain some concessions from the city, including the provision of a few abandoned homes for rehabilitation and occupation by some group members. Initially, these occupations also yielded housing vouchers for members of the group, permitting them to bypass the city's requirement that recipients of housing vouchers stay in the city's shelter system. After the first two years, however, the city no longer permitted this practice (Zucchino 1997, 50). This is when KWRU turned to the use of the tent cities discussed at the beginning of this essay. This strategy is a combination of political protest, and in the instance of the Liberty Bell tent and the first Bushville sites in 2004, civil disobedience, since it was illegal to protest at those sites.[1] KWRU has also used the civil rights strategy of litigation, not in the domestic context, but in international human rights bodies, as noted above. Interestingly, much of their recent protest activity has been coordinated with other progressive protests, such as the WTO protests in Seattle in 1999, and the protests against the Democratic and Republican Party conventions in 2000 and 2004. This provides a way to gain greater attention for their issues as well as greater participation in their protest activities.

The bus tours also are a civil rights strategy that is familiar, but KWRU is using them for a slightly different purpose. The bus tours are intended to raise awareness regarding problems of poverty and human rights, but also to collect information regarding economic human rights violations in the United States. This is partly to supplement the information the organization has already collected, but also to get more people engaged with the process of collecting rights violation data. And ultimately, the goal is to raise awareness and democratize discussion regarding poverty and human rights.

In addition, as David Zucchino documents, KWRU has from the beginning been very successful in its use of the media to bring attention to the group's activities. Zucchino sees Cheri Honkala as extremely successful in manipulating symbols and strategies that will appeal to the press and will attract media coverage. Takeovers of abandoned HUD housing, tent cities, occupying an abandoned Catholic Church, and the tent city at the Liberty Bell, as well as Honkala's confrontational approach to public officials all helped to garner media attention for the group's activities.

KWRU and the Use of Technology

One of the most interesting aspects of KWRU civil rights strategies is that the organization has combined these strategies for mobilization and *engagement* in local politics with masterful use of new technologies and new coalitions. The KWRU web site is an important resource for the organization and for raising both funds and people for involvement with organization activities. Thus, the web site constitutes one way that the organization uses technology for mobilization, publicity, and engagement.

One feature that has been on the web site from the beginning, and which remains on the site, is a virtual tour of the Kensington neighborhood. This "tour" takes the viewer to a number of the sites mentioned in the films and other publications regarding KWRU. The tour provides photos of sites in the neighborhood, as well as a narrative description of the significance of each site. Sites include the old welfare office, which marks the beginning of the organization: KWRU mothers took over the office space after the office was closed because they wanted a community center (KWRU, *Kensington Tour*). Other sites include the site of the 1995 tent city, St. Edward's Church, and the old Schmidt's Brewery Plant.

Why have a virtual tour? This helps to keep the focus of the organization's activities grounded in local conditions, and helps to demonstrate the reasons that political organizing (and not just for provision of more social services) is necessary. The economic disinvestment in the neighborhood is massive, and the virtual tour makes this clear. This does not mean that Kensington is unique: rather, it is indicative of the kinds of disinvestment occurring in cities all over the United States. The decline of wages and the movement of jobs not just out of cities but out of the United States, accompanied by social disinvestment, has created neighborhoods of discarded people. The virtual tour makes this clear.

Other items featured on the web site are chronologies, photos, and testimony from the bus tours. Obviously, the tours themselves had an impact on the people who went on the tour and on the people that they were able to contact during the tour. But the use of the web site magnifies this effect, making the tour accessible to web users. Visitors to the site can see photos from each day of the bus tour and read testimony collected during the tour. There are also links to the forms and instructions for collecting economic human rights complaints, and visitors are encouraged to do this at the site.

The KWRU web site also features extensive information on the human rights claims being made by the group, links to relevant international human rights agreements, and a link to the text of the KWRU complaint filed against the United States before the OAS. In addition, the site includes links to descriptions of recent activities of the organization, and information about upcoming events along with instructions for visitors as to how to get involved with the organization. For some events, such as the summer of 2003 bus tour, visitors can link to and print out a flyer advertising the event. The April 2003 tours were also advertised with lists of daily activities so that people around the country could locate the event in their area.

A fairly recent addition to the site is information for students on alternative spring breaks with KWRU, ways to engage in civil rights organizing, and ways to contribute to the organization. The site also provides links to and sometimes publicity for other allied groups. For example, the site recently highlighted a twenty-four hour radio show on homelessness and indicated where that show could be heard. The visuals on the web site are professional and powerful, and the site is constantly changing but easy to access. In addition, the Economic Human Rights Campaign site has provided KWRU with a way to permit partner organizations to utilize web resources as well (www.economicrights.org). Thus, KWRU has successfully used this technology for purposes of organizing and publicizing their activities, as well as building coalitions with other organizations.

Another significant use of media has been the partnership that KWRU has had with Skylight Pictures, which has produced two films about the organization's activities: *Poverty Outlaw* and *Outriders*. The first film documents the tent cities and the initial organizing by KWRU. *Outriders* documents the Freedom Bus Tour and the human rights tribunal including testimony of economic human rights violations. A third film, *Battle for Broad*, was a project of the Media College of KWRU's University of the Poor. *Battle for Broad* documents the protests during the summer of 2000 Republican convention in Philadelphia. All of these films are relatively inexpensive to purchase, which is clearly intended to make them more widely available. KWRU also produces a weekly television program, "Moving On," which, as they describe it, provides "issues from the perspective of the poor and struggling" <www.kwru.org/educat/educat. html>.

Impact of KWRU

Material and Policy Outcomes

A number of specific material outcomes, as well as broader outcomes in terms of democracy and building a social movement of the poor have resulted from the work of KWRU. First, one outcome which has resulted beginning in 1993 has been to get housing for some low-income families, and this continues to be an issue on which the organization engages in civil disobedience. As recently as March 2003, members of the organization were in court responding to charges related to occupation of an abandoned HUD house to provide housing for two homeless families in March 2002. On March 21, 2003 KWRU leader Cheri Honkala was found not guilty of the charges related to this housing takeover. Important to the judge's finding was the fact that the two families in question did not have access to the city's shelter system, one because the mother had previous drug convictions, the other because the city shelter system cannot accommodate single fathers with children (KWRU Not Guilty, March 21, 2003).

For a period of time in the early 1990s, KWRU had a Community Center as the result of a time-limited grant. This provided the impetus for much of the initial organizing work of the organization.

The lawsuit against the United States before the OAS is another significant outcome. The legal action filed by KWRU is clearly intended to embarrass the hegemon even if there are no tangible results from the suit. Indeed, because in this lawsuit KWRU is making arguments about expanding the conception of citizenship, the goal of the organization in bringing this litigation may not be linked specifically to the success that a legal victory might bring.[2] During the Cold War period, racism and poverty in the United States were an embarrassment to the United States in international politics; this helped even conservatives to be more supportive of redistributive policies. But with the end of the Cold War there is no more external check on how low the United States can go in treatment of the poor. On the other hand, it is now easier for advocates for the poor to make the connections between economic, social, and cultural rights and civil and political rights without fear of red-baiting. The arguments made by the KWRU before the OAS, as discussed above, argue for a conception of citizenship that includes economic as well as civil and political rights.

Education, Mobilization, and Democracy

Another clear outcome is education of both the poor and the nonpoor on issues related to human rights, poverty, and citizenship. As Neubeck and Cazenave discuss in *Welfare Racism*, the ideas discussed in the "University of the Poor" section of the KWRU web site clearly raise issues of racism and its relationship to poverty policy, and provide grounds for understanding welfare policy in the broader context of its relationship to democracy. Building a democratic movement of poor people is an explicit goal of KWRU:

> The FTAA means one thing—another law to make the rich richer and the poor poorer, to create more unemployed people, to lower our wages, to pit us against each other. But we have another choice: Economic Human Rights. Economic Human Rights means everyone having our basic human rights to what we need to live, rights that have been guaranteed to us by international law: A job at a living wage, health care, housing, heat, water, food, education, the right to organize to defend our rights. We can win these rights back: by educating ourselves, by getting organized, by uniting as poor people, as

workers, both employed and unemployed, across the United States and across the Americas, by refusing to let them divide us or make us invisible. (KWRU FTAA Press Release)

As noted above, KWRU has a location on their web site inviting people to submit cases of economic human rights violations, with instructions as to how to submit these complaints (KWRU, "We Need Your Help"). This document also notes that collecting this information is a form of human rights education: "Teaching people to see their struggles as part of a bigger fight for human rights rather than seeing only their individual faults and failings is an important part of the Campaign" (1). Ultimately, through education and organizing, KWRU hopes to reconceive what it means to be a citizen. Through organizing, local activism, coalition building, and the use of both traditional civil rights strategies and new technologies, KWRU seeks to build organizations of poor people locally, nationally, and internationally to end poverty.

Conclusions

The global arrogance of the United States is usually thought of in terms of foreign policy. But the domestic poverty policies of the United States have the clear marks of a failed hegemon, of a state incapable of providing the basic resources in terms of living wage jobs and adequate social services to large proportions of its inhabitants. To activists in the KWRU and in the campaign for economic human rights, the democratic deficit evidenced by U.S. poverty policy is clear: poor people are invisible, as persons and as citizens, and their voices and concerns are not heard in the political process. Thus KWRU has turned to the arena of international human rights, seeking remedies through international bodies that have been closed off to them through domestic policy-making processes.

Poverty policy in the United States and KWRU efforts to expose it for what it is also demonstrate that it is indeed possible for the United States as hegemon to fight a war on two fronts. Indeed, expenditures on the international "war on terror" are used to justify cuts in social spending at home. The failed hegemon—unable to make the world safer—has also failed at the domestic social contract. KWRU points out all of these contradictions.

Though KWRU has been criticized for engaging primarily in the outsider tactic of protest politics, its commitment to grassroots organizing among the poor, to coalition-building with other organizations, and to a multiracial membership are evidence of a commitment to grassroots democracy. KWRU offers an interesting example of a social movement organization that is challenging the global arrogance of U.S. domestic and foreign policy, and connecting local with international concerns.

Notes

1. The Park Service permits protests near the Liberty Bell, but at a location that is not visible to the tourists who visit the Liberty Bell. Obviously, protesting in the designated area would not have the desired effect. The first Bushville in 2004 was in Jersey City, but was quickly dismantled by the police. The second Bushville was in Central Park, and after publicity regarding this site, a church in Brooklyn offered their parking lot to the group.
2. Stacy VanDeveer's comments helped us to understand this point.

Bibliography

Abramovitz, Mimi. 1988. *Regulating the Lives of Women: Social Policy from Colonial Times to the Present*. Boston: South End Press.

Alperovitz, Gar, David Imbroscio, and Thad Williamson. 2002. *Making a Place for Community*. New York: Routledge.

Amin, Samir. 1997. *Capitalism in the Age of Globalism*. London /New York: Zed Books.

Briggs, Laura. 2002. "*La Vida*, Moynihan, and Other Libels: Migration, Social Science, and the Making of the Puerto Rican Welfare Queen." *Centro Journal* Spring 2002.

Bussiere, Elizabeth. 1997. *(Dis)Entitling the Poor: The Warren Court, Welfare Rights, and the American Political Tradition*. University Park: Penn State Press.

Clarke, Susan E. and Gary L. Gaile. 1998. *The Work of Cities*. Minneapolis, Minn.: University of Minnesota.

Davis, Martha F. 1993. *Brutal Need: Lawyers and the Welfare Rights Movement, 1960–1973*. New Haven, Conn.: Yale University Press.

Edelman, Peter. 1997. "The Worst Thing Bill Clinton Has Done." *The Atlantic Monthly* 279 no. 3: 43–58.

Inter-American Commission on Human Rights. 1999. *Poor People's Economic Human Rights campaign et al. v. The United States of America*. October 1.

Josephson, Jyl. 2000. "Gender and Social Policy." Pp. 133–159 in *Gender and American Politics: Women, Men and the Political Process*, ed. Sue Tolleson-Rinehart and Jyl Josephson. Armonk, N.Y.: M.E. Sharpe Publishers.

KWRU March of the Americas. 1999. "Day 32: The United Nations." <http://www.libertynet.org/kwru/ehrc/moa/dnov1.html> (accessed 5/30/00).

KWRU: Frequently Asked Questions. Philadelphia: KWRU web site <http://www.kwru.org/> (accessed May 30, 2003).

KWRU FTAA Press Release. 2003. "FTAA: Who Wins? Who Loses? Who Decides?" <http://www.kwru.org/ehrc/bustour/ftaa2.html> (Accessed June 13, 2003).

KWRU Kensington Tour. <http://www.kwru.org/kwru/tour> (accessed February 12, 2001).

KWRU Not Guilty. 2003. <http://www.kwru.org/updates/03-21-03.htm> March 21 (accessed June 13, 2003).

KWRU Press Release. 1997. "The Kensington Welfare Rights Union Announces Historic March for our Lives." May 26. <http://www.libertynet.org/kwru/ kwru/mpress.html> (accessed 12/15/99).

———. 2000. "Honkala and Morehouse Vindicated in Constitutional Rights Trial." March <http://www.libertynet.org/kwru/updates/cheritrial2.html> (accessed April 26, 2000).

———. 2004. "The Poor People's Economic Human Rights Campaign Accuses the United States Government of Human Rights Violations and Demands an Investigation." August 24 <http://www.kwru.org/mfol/ pressrelease8-24.htm> (accessed September 7, 2004).

KWRU Economic Human Rights Tribunal Transcript. 1998. July 1. <http://www. libertynet.org/kwru/ehrc/tribunal> (accessed December 15, 1999).

KWRU. nd. "We Need Your Help to Document Economic Human Rights Violations." <http://www.kwru.org/action/hrdoc1.html> (accessed January 31, 2002).

Lyon, Beth. 2000. "Efforts and Opportunities to Use International Law to Alleviate Poverty in the United States." *Human Rights Brief* 7, no. 3 (Winter 2000): 6–9.

Mosler, David and Bob Catley. 2000. *Global America: Imposing Liberalism on a Recalcitrant World*. Westport/London: Praeger.

Mouffe, Chantal. 2000. *The Democratic Paradox*. New York: Verso.

Neuback, Kenneth and Noel Cazenave. 2001. *Welfare Racism: Playing the Race Card Against America's Poor*. New York: Routledge.

O'Connor, Alice. 2000. "Poverty Research and Policy for the Post-Welfare Era." *Annual Review of Sociology* vol. 26: 547–62.

———. 2001. *Poverty Knowledge: Social Science, Social Policy, and the Poor in Twentieth-Century U.S. History*. Princeton, N.J.: Princeton University Press.

Pitcher, Abby. 2002. "Human Rights Violations in Welfare Legislation: Pushing Recipients Deeper Into Poverty." New York: Urban Justice Center Human Rights Project.

Piven, Francis Fox and Richard A. Cloward. 1977. *Poor People's Movements: Why They Succeed, How They Fail*. New York: Vintage Books.

Reich, Robert B. 1992. *The Work of Nations: Preparing Ourselves for 21st Century Capitalism*. New York: Random House.

Shue, Henry. 1980. *Basic Rights: Subsistence, Affluence, and U. S. Foreign Policy*. Princeton, N.J.: Princeton University Press.

tenBroek, Jacobus. 1964–65. "California's Dual System of Family Law: Its Origin, Development, and Present Status." Parts I, II, and III, *Stanford Law Review* 16 (March 1964): 257–317, 16 (July 1964): 900–81, 17 (April 1965): 614–82.

Webster, Neil and Lars Engberg-Pedersen, eds. 2002. *In The Name of the Poor: Contesting Political Space for Poverty Reduction*. London: Zed Books.

Weiss, Peter. 2000. "Economic and Social Rights Come of Age: United States Held to Account in IACHR." *Human Rights Brief* 7, no. 3 (Winter 2000): 3–5.

West, Guida. 1981. *The National Welfare Rights Movement: The Social Protest of Poor Women*. New York: Praeger.

Williams, Lucinda. 1997. "Decades of Distortion: The Right's Thirty-Year Assault on Welfare." Somerville, Mass.: Political Research Associates.

Zoelle, Diana. 2000. *Globalizing Concern for Women's Human Rights: The Failure of the American Model*. New York: St. Martin's Press.

Zucchino, David. 1997. *Myth of the Welfare Queen*. New York: Scribner.

Chapter 4

The Peaceful Superpower: The Movement against War in Iraq

David Cortright

On February 15, 2003 in hundreds of cities across the world an estimated 10 million people demonstrated against the looming U.S.-led invasion of Iraq. It was the largest single day of antiwar protest in human history. More than a million people jammed Hyde Park and the center of London in the largest demonstration ever held in that city. More than a million marched in Rome, and huge throngs paraded in Barcelona, Berlin, Madrid, Paris, Sydney, and dozens of other cities. An estimated 400,000 braved bitter cold in New York, and tens of thousands demonstrated in San Francisco.[1] The people of the globe spoke out as never before in one unified voice against the planned attack against Iraq. "The world says no to war," was the slogan and the reality.

The February 15 demonstrations were the high point of a vast and unprecedented mobilization of public opposition to war. The Iraq campaign "was the largest antiwar movement that has ever taken place," according to Barbara Epstein (2003, 109). In the course of just a few months, the antiwar movement reached levels of mobilization that, during the Vietnam era, took years to develop. The Iraq movement was more international in character than any previous antiwar movement. Opposition to war emerged not just in the United States but literally all over the world, as action campaigns were coordinated internationally and demonstrators understood themselves to be part of a truly global struggle (110). The movement represented a convergence of antiwar and global justice efforts into a common campaign against military-corporate domination

(Levine 2003). It was an expression of what Stephen Gill has called "new . . . forms of global political agency" (2003, 218). But the movement also emerged from more traditional peace and justice networks and relied extensively on the knowledge and resources of organizations and individuals with previous experience in antiwar action. The roots of the Iraq antiwar movement dated back to the movement against the first Gulf War, and even further to the nuclear freeze campaign, the Central American solidarity movement, the antiapartheid struggle, and the Vietnam antiwar movement. It engaged religious communities, trade unionists, students, feminists, environmentalists, academics, business executives, Hollywood artists, musicians, and many more. The movement was built largely through the Internet, which served as the primary tool for developing and communicating strategies and actions, and which accounted for its extraordinary capacity for organizing massive numbers of people on short notice with limited resources. The movement effectively utilized mass media communications. The war in Iraq and the international opposition to it were the dominant news story throughout the world for months, and antiwar activists found themselves in the unaccustomed position of being the center of media attention. For the first time in history, observed writer Rebecca Solnit, the peace movement was portrayed in the media as "diverse, legitimate and representative," which was a "watershed victory" for the movement's "representation and long-term prospects" (2003).

A few days after the February 15 demonstrations, a *New York Times* reporter conferred "super power" status on the antiwar movement. The huge antiwar demonstrations were indications, wrote Patrick Tyler, of "two super powers on the planet: the United States and world public opinion." The White House faced a "tenacious new adversary" which was generating massive opposition to the administration's war policy and had left the world's greatest power virtually alone in the international community (2003, A1). Antiwar commentators quickly adopted the phrase and proclaimed their movement "the other super-power." Jonathan Schell wrote in *The Nation* of the movement's "immense power" in winning the hearts and wills of the majority of the world's people (2003). Even UN Secretary-General Kofi Annan used the phrase in referring to antiwar opinion (Nunberg 2003, Section 4, 4). A new form of global social movement had emerged, an unprecedented expression of collective consciousness and action bound together through the worldwide web (Moore 2003).

How did this supposed super-power exert its influence? What, if any, impact did the antiwar movement have on the policies of the Bush administration? In this chapter I analyze the emergence of the Iraq antiwar movement and trace the extraordinary scale of its development in the months leading up to the March 2003 attack on Iraq. My analysis is confined to the period prior to the beginning of war. I write as an active participant, one who was intimately involved in many of the activities described here. Mine is hardly a disinterested view, although I strive to uphold scholarly standards. I provide an overview of the many different elements of the movement, concentrating on the Win Without War coalition, in which I was most actively involved. I give special attention to two key dimensions of the movement—the role of Internet-based organizing, and the movement's communications and message-framing strategies. I conclude with some reflections on the movement's overall impact.

Premonitions

The development of antiwar activism began in the immediate aftermath of September 11. Eli Pariser, a recent college graduate living near Boston, sent an E-mail message to a group of friends urging them to call for multilateral police action rather than war in response to the terrorist attacks (Packer 2003). Friends forwarded his message to others, and it began to spread exponentially. In the vernacular of the Internet it went viral. At the same time, a recent graduate of the University of Chicago, David Pickering, posted a similar message on a campus website. When Pariser saw it, he contacted Pickering, and the two joined forces on a new website, 9–11peace.org. Within a week, 120,000 people from 190 countries had signed their petition against war. By the first week of October more than half a million signed. Pariser and his colleagues had discovered what a *New York Times* reporter described as "an organizing tool of dazzling power" (Packer 2003). It was the beginning of Internet-based peace organizing. A few months later Pariser teamed up with Wes Boyd and Joan Blades, software entrepreneurs in California, who had created MoveOn in 1998 to stop the impeachment of Bill Clinton. With Pariser spearheading its international campaigns, MoveOn quickly emerged as the dominant organizational and financial power in the fledgling antiwar movement.

The September 11 attacks had an enormous impact on the global justice movement. The struggle against corporate globalization had burst dramatically onto the political stage with the huge protests and urban lockdowns in Seattle in November 1999, followed by similar actions in Washington, Prague, Quebec, and Genoa. Another action had been planned for September 2001 in Washington but was cancelled after the terrorist strikes. For a time the global justice movement suffered from a loss of direction. Ironically, the war drive of the Bush administration gave the movement a new sense of urgency and purpose. Thousands of activists in the

United States and around the world began to see, as one activist leader put it, that "militarization was just the other arm of the corporate agenda."[2] Global justice activists began to pour their energy and creativity into the emerging antiwar movement.

The response to the Bush administration's militarized policies also included traditional street protests. The leftist splinter group, Workers' World Party, formed a new coalition, Act Now to Stop War and End Racism (ANSWER), which called for a demonstration in Washington on September 29, 2001 to oppose the Bush administration's war plans. ANSWER also sponsored substantial mass rallies in Washington on April 20 and October 26, 2002, and January 18, 2003. Speakers at these rallies condemned the war in Afghanistan and plans for the invasion of Iraq, but they also supported a variety of other causes, from freedom for Mumia Abu-Jamal to support for Palestinian rights. Many independent activists participated in the ANSWER rallies because of a desire to be counted in opposition to the Bush administration's policies, but an increasing number began to chafe at the coalition's sectarianism. A number of commentators and organizers began to call for a more broadly based antiwar coalition that could unify around a simple demand of opposition to war and that would avoid domination by leftist fringe groups. Todd Gitlin decried the "old left" tenor of the antiwar movement to date, and called for a more "extensive, inclusive popular movement" against the policies of the Bush administration (2003). Others echoed these sentiments, as plans developed for creating a genuine national antiwar coalition.

United for Peace and Justice

On October 25, 2002, the day before the ANSWER-sponsored rally in Washington, representatives of more than 70 peace, religious, and social justice organizations gathered in Washington to address the increasingly serious threat of war and the need for a broadly based activist coalition. The meeting was cochaired by Leslie Cagan, a veteran organizer widely respected throughout the peace movement (Hedges 2003, Metro Section 2) and Bill Fletcher, the president of Trans-Africa. The breadth of participation in the meeting reflected the wide recognition that an effective antiwar coalition was urgently needed. Participants in the larger meeting included traditional peace organizations that had led previous antiwar efforts—including Peace Action, American Friends Service Committee, Women's Action for New Directions, Sojourners, War Resisters League, Fellowship of Reconciliation—along with representatives from the new Internet-based groups (MoveOn, True

Majority, Working Assets), the global justice movement (Global Exchange), and constituency groups such as the National Organization for Women (NOW), the National Rainbow Coalition, and the Center for Community Change. At the end of the session, the participants agreed to create a new antiwar coalition, taking its name, "United for Peace," from a web site of the same name created by Global Exchange. Cagan and Fletcher were asked to chair the new coalition, and an ad hoc committee was selected to work out the details of process and program that were left unresolved.

United for Peace and Justice was quintessentially a grassroots activist coalition, and its principal action strategy was to organize protest demonstrations. The coalition's first action was a call for nationally coordinated local actions on December 10, which was Human Rights Day. More than 130 events took place that day all over the United States, generating substantial local and regional press coverage for the growing antiwar movement. The December 10 actions were a significant success, according to Cagan, and "spoke to the real breadth of opposition to what the Bush administration was doing."[3] As the coalition discussed options for national protest, it had to contend with ANSWER, which had already obtained permits and issued a call for a demonstration in Washington on January 18, 2003, the weekend of the Martin Luther King Jr. national holiday. Rather than attempt to compete with the ANSWER rally in Washington, United for Peace called for demonstrations in New York and San Francisco on February 15. The date was selected to coincide with global antiwar protests proposed by activists at the European Social Forum in Florence, Italy in November (Levine 2003).

The call for a mass demonstration in New York in the middle of winter was risky. No one knew if the protests would be successful. Organizing for the rally did not even begin until the second week in January. The mobilizing effort combined traditional methods of activist recruitment with the innovative potential of the Internet. More than a million leaflets were distributed in New York and in nearby states, and announcements were sent via the Internet, as visits to the United for Peace web site soon reached two million a day. The outreach effort benefited from decades of experience among veterans like Cagan and her team of volunteers, and it also drew energy from a new, younger activist movement that had emerged in response to globalization challenges and September 11.[4] The gathering momentum of the planned rallies around the world added excitement and energy to the organizing effort in the United States. In the end the public moment turned out to be exactly right, as popular alarm over the Bush administration's war policies peaked in the United States and throughout the world, producing the historic mass demonstrations of February 15, 2003.

United for Peace and Justice continued to organize protest actions until and after the war began. One of the biggest actions came in New York on

March 22. The demonstration had been announced a couple of weeks before but came a few days after the war began. The crowd that day rivaled the turnout on February 15. An estimated 300,000 people poured onto Broadway north of 34th Street and marched down to Washington Square Park. At one point the crowd completely filled Broadway for the entire length of the march. It was an overwhelming turnout that stunned even the organizers. Cagan recalled thinking, "Where are all these people coming from? We're not that good." For many New Yorkers, she believed, the demonstration was a reaction to September 11, and the Bush administration's manipulation of the city's suffering. "For those of us who lived through 9/11, there was a sense that we never wanted to see that kind of horror visited on other people, whether by a small group of terrorists or by the state terrorism of a military invasion."[5]

Win Without War

The October 25, 2002 meeting that resulted in the formation of United for Peace and Justice also led to the creation of Win Without War. Impatient with the tedious process and lack of focus at the United for Peace meeting, and eager to create a more structured and focused antiwar coalition, several groups met for dinner that night and agreed to begin working together to create a mainstream committee of national organizations. The founding groups were MoveOn, Working Assets (a telecommunications company with hundreds of thousands of subscribers), True Majority (an Internet-based activist network created by ice cream entrepreneur Ben Cohen), Women's Action for New Directions (WAND), and Fourth Freedom Forum. The groups wanted a coalition that could attract not only traditional peace groups, but also major constituency organizations. They also wanted a quick and efficient decision-making process. They believed that the political message of the activist movement should emphasize alternative means of containing and disarming Saddam Hussein without war. They also agreed on the pressing need for an effective public relations and communications campaign to reach mainstream audiences. Other groups that agreed to come together on the basis of these understandings included the National Council of Churches, Sojourners, The United Methodist Church, Physicians for Social Responsibility, the Sierra Club, NOW, and the National Association for the Advancement of Colored People (NAACP). Forty organizations eventually joined the new national coalition, which was officially launched at a press conference in Washington in early December.

Virtual organizing became the métier of the coalition, as it mobilized the vast membership networks of its Internet-based groups and constituency organizations for coordinated lobbying and action campaigns. Its most ambitious effort was the "virtual march" on Washington on February 26, 2003. Citizens all over the United States phoned, faxed, or E-mailed their elected representatives to oppose the march to war. All across Capitol Hill on February 26, the phones and fax machines were jammed. Members of Congress reported receiving hundreds and even thousands of messages by early afternoon that day. It was impossible to calculate the exact number of messages, but Win Without War national director Tom Andrews estimated that more than one million calls, faxes, and E-mail messages were sent. It was the largest one-day lobbying event in U.S. political history. Coming just eleven days after the massive street demonstrations of February 15, the virtual march was further evidence of the vast scale of the movement against war.

In the final weeks before the outbreak of war, the Win Without War coalition maintained a frenetic pace of activity in a desperate attempt to prevent an increasingly inevitable military attack. Relying primarily on the rapidly expanding membership network of MoveOn and True Majority, Win Without War launched an international petition to the UN Security Council urging rejection of a United States and British draft resolution authorizing war. The response was overwhelming, the greatest of any MoveOn petition, and undoubtedly one of the most successful mass petitions in history. Within days, more than one million people signed the Security Council petition. It was delivered to UN representatives in New York at a Win Without War/MoveOn press conference on March 10. At the same time the coalition issued an international call for antiwar vigils the following weekend, March 15–16. Once again the response was overwhelming, as thousands of groups all over the world announced plans to hold candlelight and prayer vigils in their communities. More than 6,000 vigils took place in more than 100 countries that weekend. Once again the world said no to war, this time in a prayerful plea at the last hour before the onset of military hostilities. It was the most diverse and widespread wave of local peace action in human history, another powerful indication of the unprecedented scale of the global movement against war.

The Role of MoveOn

Much of the success of Win Without War and the antiwar movement in general can be ascribed to the powerful impact of Internet organizing, and the specific role of MoveOn. The Internet first emerged as a tool of political mobilization in the campaign against the impeachment of President Bill Clinton in 1998 and in the broader global justice movement that emerged in 1999. It was not until the Iraq antiwar movement, however, that the full range of possibilities for utilizing the Internet for social change organizing became evident. The global justice movement used the Internet effectively as a means of communication, coordination, and education among decentralized networks of organizers around the world. To these functions antiwar activists added new dimensions of Internet mobilization: the development of organized "membership" networks, the creation of "meeting tools" to facilitate coordinated local actions, and online fundraising. The result was an unprecedented capacity to raise consciousness and mobilize political action.

MoveOn was the pioneer and leading force in this Internet revolution. It was the lead group within Win Without War and served as the backbone of the movement's most important organizing and communication efforts. Prior to the Congressional vote in October on a resolution authorizing military force, MoveOn circulated an antiwar petition signed by hundreds of thousands of people. MoveOn continued to play a central role in all of the subsequent antiwar actions, including the "virtual march," the petition to the UN Security Council, and the worldwide antiwar vigils in March 2003. All of this action flowed from an organization with only a handful of staff—an organization with a powerful computer and sophisticated software system, but none of the usual accoutrements of traditional membership groups. In the six months leading up to the outbreak of war in March 2003, MoveOn's online membership, U.S. and international, grew from approximately 700,000 to approximately 2,000,000. Other electronically based networks also experienced extraordinary growth and activity during this period. True Majority was founded in June 2002 and grew rapidly as the antiwar movement emerged, reaching 100,000 members by the end of 2002 and 500,000 a year later. Working in close partnership with Business Leaders for Sensible Priorities (BLSP), True Majority specialized in producing graphic and visually attractive newspaper ads and Internet messages that helped to attract new supporters. True Majority also developed a partnership with the National Council of Churches, helping to reach and mobilize religious leaders and faith-based activists throughout the country. Working Assets represented a different kind of electronic activist network based on the company's customer/subscriber base. Working Assets mobilized its subscribers to engage in progressive action through action notices that were included with monthly phone bills. As the antiwar movement developed, Working Assets naturally became involved and developed web-based organizing tools.

When Internet organizing began, some skeptics questioned the value of a tool that kept activists glued to their computer screens. The very ease with which one could click and send off a message, sometimes to hundreds of recipients, seemed to cheapen the value of the effort. Lobbyists reported that the impact of an E-mail message as a form of political communication paled in comparison with the impact of other forms of communication, such as a personal letter, phone call, or personal visit. MoveOn and the other Internet-based activist groups recognized these limitations early on and devised methods of mobilization that significantly broadened the impact of E-mail activism. One significant innovation was the use of the Internet to organize coordinated local meetings. Activists were encouraged to get up from their computer screens and go out to meetings where they connected with other activists in their communities. MoveOn developed a meeting tool that Eli Pariser termed "action in a box." Action campaigns were programmed so that respondents could be led easily through a series of prompts offering various venues and functions for action. An E-mail message from MoveOn would contain the call to action, and by clicking the appropriate icons, the respondent could be connected to other activists and could volunteer for various tasks, ranging from attending a meeting and sending an E-mail to Congress, to more ambitious duties such as coordinating a meeting, speaking in public, and contributing funds. Working Assets developed a similar meeting tool, which gave subscribers options for participating in local activities. By segmenting lists according to location and interest, Internet organizers could use their membership base to sponsor highly particularized forms of action. Equally important in translating Internet communications into political power was the development and use of online fundraising. Just as online marketing has become increasingly significant in the commercial economy, Internet-based fundraising has rapidly become a vital source of income for social movements, nonprofit groups, and political campaigns. In the months preceding the war MoveOn raised more than $1 million for newspaper and television ads and associated public relations activities, thus turning its vast Internet network into a crucial source of financial support for the antiwar movement.

Resource mobilization theory emphasizes the importance of formal dues-paying membership networks as a means of providing a sustained and predictable base of income and activism, enabling an organization or movement to exert political influence. Traditional membership networks also provide a mechanism for participatory decision making, with individual members or chapters playing a role in determining organizational priorities and selecting leaders. The Internet-based networks of MoveOn and True Majority are less formal and more loosely structured. There are no annual dues or membership requirements, and indeed no fixed organizational structure at all. The "members" of MoveOn participate only to the extent that they feel motivated to respond to particular E-mail action alerts.

It is an approach, writes Andrew Boyd, that "embraces the permission-based culture of the Internet, and consumer culture itself" (2003, 14). Pariser described this as a "postmodern organizing model" (14).

Other organizations with more traditional membership bases also developed E-mail networks during the antiwar movement. The religiously based organization, Sojourners, saw its newly created Sojo list expand from 20,000 in the summer of 2002 to approximately 70,000 in March 2003. Peace Action, The Council for a Livable World, and many other organizations also developed E-mail listservs and experienced growth in electronic membership. All of these groups used the Internet as a mechanism for political communication and fundraising. The use of electronic organizing and the overall growth of antiwar activism led to membership increases in most of the established peace organizations. Women's Action for New Directions, Peace Action, and Physicians for Social Responsibility all reported 20 percent increases in membership during the antiwar campaign.[6] The movement against war in Iraq thus became an opportunity for traditional peace groups to grow organizationally and financially.

Religion

The religious community played a central role in the Iraq antiwar movement, as it has in many important movements for peace and social justice.[7] Faith-based activists were the core and largest component of the grassroots antiwar movement (Epstein 2003). Nearly every major mainline Christian denomination—from the U.S. Catholic Conference of Bishops to all the various Protestant denominations, with the exception of the Southern Baptists—issued public statements opposing war, and many leaders and members of local congregations participated in antiwar activities. Church-based opposition to war was broader in the case of Iraq than in any previous conflict in modern U.S. history. Faith-based activists were major players in the United for Peace and Justice and Win Without War coalitions. Bob Edgar of the National Council of Churches and Jim Wallis of Sojourners were leaders of Win Without War and played important roles in mobilizing the religious community. Religious peace groups—including the Catholic pacifist organization Pax Christi and groups within the Friends, Mennonite and Brethren communities—played a leadership role in raising awareness and organizing expressions of antiwar concern.

Just as the overall antiwar movement became internationalized to an unprecedented extent, so did its religious component. Never before in history did so many religious leaders and organizations from around the world speak so forcefully against war. The most important voice was that of the Vatican which repeatedly condemned the proposed invasion of Iraq and pleaded with world leaders to pursue diplomatic rather than military solutions. "War is always a defeat for humanity," Pope John Paul II told assembled diplomats during his New Year address in January. "War cannot be decided upon," he declared, "except as the very last option."[8] As the war began in March the Pope urged people to continue standing against war. "It is ever more urgent to proclaim that only peace is the road to follow to construct a more just and united society."[9] National conferences of Catholic bishops in North America, Europe, Asia, and Africa joined the Vatican in issuing statements against war. The deliberative bodies of many other religious communities around the world joined in this nearly universal faith-based outcry against war.

To help harness this international voice for peace, Bob Edgar of the National Council of Churches organized a series of religious delegation meetings with world leaders. In early February Edgar led a delegation that met with senior religious leaders in Germany and then joined with these leaders in a one-hour session with German Chancellor Gerhard Schroeder. The following week a National Council delegation visited Paris to confer with colleagues in the European Council of Churches and meet with aides to French President Jacques Chirac. The following weeks included similar visits to London for a 50-minute meeting with Prime Minister Blair, to Rome for meetings with Italian and Vatican officials, and to Moscow for sessions with Orthodox Church leaders and aides to President Vladimir Putin.[10]

Jim Wallis led the religious delegation that met with Blair in London in mid-February. That session led to the development of one of the most significant initiatives of the church-based antiwar movement, a six-point plan for preventing war. The plan called for the indictment of Saddam Hussein on war crimes charges, and urged a vigorous multinational effort to disarm and contain the Iraqi dictator. Sojourners published the six-point plan in full-page advertisements in all of the major London newspapers on the day of the final debate in Parliament. The six-point plan was a last-minute attempt to dissuade Blair and Bush from invading Iraq. It was also an attempt to influence public opinion by addressing ethical concerns about the crimes of Saddam Hussein and his Baathist government. The plan reflected Wallis' conviction that the antiwar movement needed to answer the "what about Saddam?" question. Blair was particularly vocal in making the case for war on the basis of the human rights atrocities committed by the Iraqi leader. For both ethical and practical reasons, Wallis believed, the movement had to take a tough stance toward Saddam. It was not enough simply to point to U.S. and U.K. complicity in previously supporting Saddam. That was true but insufficient as a moral and political argument. It was also necessary to acknowledge and condemn Saddam's brutal regime, and to urge his removal. Wallis and his colleagues in the church community were in effect agreeing with the need for regime change in Baghdad, while remaining true to their nonviolent witness. They argued that legal, multilateral, nonmilitary means were available for disarming Iraq and countering Saddam Hussein.

Labor

The labor movement played a major role in the antiwar movement. Traditionally trade unions in the United States supported U.S. military action abroad and rarely participated in antiwar campaigns. During the Vietnam era, the AFL-CIO endorsed the war, and some construction unions in New York famously attacked antiwar demonstrators. In the wake of the September 11 terrorist attacks, unions generally supported the so-called war on terror. The president of the International Association of Machinists, R. Thomas Buffenbarger, openly called for a military campaign of vengeance. As the debate over war in Iraq heated up, however, trade unions became decidedly skeptical about the proposed military overthrow of Saddam Hussein. A growing number of local unions and central labor councils adopted resolutions against war and began to speak out for alternative means of containing the Iraqi leader. An unprecedented U.S. antiwar labor movement emerged. Led by former Teamsters organizing director, Bob Muehlenkamp, and AFL-CIO official Gene Bruskin, union leaders came together in Chicago in January 2003 to form "U.S. Labor Against the War." In total more than 300 local unions and committees, 45 central labor councils, and seven national unions adopted resolutions against war.[11] The level of antiwar activity among trade unions far exceeded comparable opposition to any previous U.S. military action.

The executive council of the AFL-CIO passed a resolution on February 27, 2003, officially declaring labor's opposition to a preemptive war fought without UN support. "The threat posed by Saddam Hussein deserves multilateral resolve," the executive council statement asserted, "not unilateral action." The council declared: "The president has not fulfilled his responsibility to make a compelling and coherent explanation to the American people and the world about the need for military action against Iraq at this time." If war comes, the council stated, it should be "truly a last resort, supported by both our allies and nations united."[12] The statement was hardly a ringing indictment of war, but it was an extraordinary departure from the AFL-CIO's positions on previous conflicts, and was another sign of deepening opposition to White House policy.

Communities of Color

"The most glaring weakness of the movement against the war in Iraq," according to Barbara Epstein, "was the limited involvement of people of color, especially African-Americans" (2003, 111). People of color were the most strongly opposed to war, but they were under-represented among those who demonstrated against it. Opinion polls showed that blacks opposed the war in roughly the percentages that whites supported it. A *Time*/CNN poll of February 19–20 found 61 percent of blacks opposed to using military force against Saddam Hussein, compared with 35 percent among whites.[13] An ABC/*Washington Post* poll of February 26–March 2 found 62 percent of "nonwhites" in opposition to war, compared with 32 percent of whites.[14] Yet in most of the major national and regional protests the demonstrators were predominantly white. The one exception to this monochromatic pattern was the April 20, 2002 ANSWER-sponsored march in Washington, which attracted a substantial turnout of Muslim Americans.[15] ANSWER generally did better than other antiwar coalitions in mobilizing people of color. African Americans and Arab Americans were part of the coalition's leadership, and ANSWER's political agenda of opposing racism and advocating Palestinian rights appealed more directly to the immediate concerns of communities of color. United for Peace and Justice also developed a more racially diverse leadership, and in this regard was better than the mostly white leadership of the Win Without War coalition.

The problem of racial misrepresentation in the peace movement is a recurring one, and has been present in all the major campaigns in recent memory. The Vietnam antiwar movement, the Central American movement, the nuclear freeze campaign, the movement against the first Gulf War—all suffered from underrepresentation of communities of color. One of the dangers of this imbalance, as Epstein noted, is that activists may attempt to address this problem by "slinging charges of racism at each other" (2003, 112). This has been a problem in past movements and can have a corrosive effect on the morale and energy of activists. This was not a major problem in the Iraq antiwar movement, largely because the short amount of time available and the frenetic pace of activity did not provide much opportunity for self flagellation.

Although underrepresented at peace demonstrations, African American, Latino, and other communities of color were by no means silent on the war.

The Church of God in Christ, the Progressive National Baptists and other African American churches were among the first to register their opposition to war in Iraq. Many community leaders spoke out, including representative Barbara Lee (D-CA), who had cast the lone vote in Congress against the resolution authorizing the use of force in Afghanistan; representatives Charles Rangel (D-NY) and John Conyers (D-MI), who spoke at the major antiwar rallies in Washington; Rev. Jesse Jackson, Sr., who spoke at several rallies in the United States and at the historic February 15 protest in London; and actor Danny Glover, chair of Trans-Africa. In Congress African American and Latino legislators were the strongest opponents of war. Every member of the Hispanic Congressional Caucus voted against the October 2002 resolution in the House of Representatives authorizing the use of force. Most African American members of Congress also voted against the resolution.

Women for Peace

Women traditionally have been more opposed to war than men and have been at the heart of many peace movements. The Iraq antiwar campaign was no exception, and in countless localities in the United States and throughout the world women took the lead in speaking out and organizing actions for peace. Studies of public opinion have found evidence of a substantial gender gap on war and military-related issues, with women consistently showing a greater propensity to support peaceful, diplomatic solutions to international crises and greater reluctance to endorse the use of military force. Opinion surveys during the Iraq debate showed that men were significantly more likely to favor war than women. An ABC News/*Washington Post* poll of February 26 March 2002 found 67 percent of men in favor of "war to remove Saddam Hussein," compared with only 51 percent of women.[16] A *Time*/CNN poll of February 19–20 found 59 percent of men favoring the use of military force, compared with 50 percent of women.[17] A Zogby International poll of February 21 found 34 percent of men opposed to war, compared with 46 percent of women.[18] A March 3–8 poll commissioned by the Vietnam Veterans of America Foundation showed support for war at 53 percent among men but only 41 percent among women.[19]

Women were leaders of national and local antiwar coalitions, and they also formed specific women's organizations to articulate a unique feminist peace perspective. In November 2002 a group of veteran peace and justice organizers led by Medea Benjamin, Starhawk, and Jodie Evans created Code Pink, Women for Peace. The goal, according to Benjamin, was to introduce a new discourse into a national debate dominated by the Bush administration's "testosterone-poisoned rhetoric."[20] The formation of Code Pink was announced at a vigil in front of the White House that began on November 17, 2002 and continued daily through March 8, 2003, which was International Women's Day. On that day 10,000 demonstrators marched toward the White House to protest the impending war. Women's Day actions also occurred in more than fifty cities in the United States. Across the country some ninety Code Pink chapters were formed.

The women's peace movement introduced a creative, at times even humorous spirit into the antiwar debate. Liza Featherstone wrote in *The Nation* that Code Pink was "not an organization but a phenomenon: a sensibility reflecting feminist analysis and a campy playfulness influenced in style and philosophy both by ACT UP and the antiglobalization movement" (2003). Code Pink specialized in high-spirited, disruptive actions that directly challenged those responsible for making and selling the Bush administration's war policies. In November they interrupted Secretary of Defense Rumsfeld as he testified on the war before Congress. In December they disrupted a briefing by State Department public relations official Charlotte Beers, unfurling a banner that read, "Charlotte, stop selling war." One of their trademark actions was to deliver "You're fired" pink slips, presenting actual women's slips to officials who supported the war. Among those targeted for such treatment was New York Senator Hillary Rodham Clinton. The Code Pink actions were part of a rising tide of innovative feminist action against war. Early in January 2003 a group of women gathered on the beach in Point Reyes, California to spell out "Peace" with their nude bodies. The women explained that they were protesting the Bush administration's "naked aggression."

Another creative women's initiative was the Lysistrata Project. Organized by actresses and women involved in the theatre in New York and Los Angeles, the project sought to bring to light the powerful but mirthful message of the 2,400-year-old antiwar comedy by Aristophanes. The story of Lysistrata (literally "she who disbands armies") tells of Athenian and Spartan women who refused to sleep with their men until they ceased their warring ways. On March 3, 2003 an estimated 1,000 readings of the play took place in all 50 states and in 59 countries.[21] In New York and Los Angeles, prominent actresses and actors headlined star performances. In London hundreds of British actresses and actors gathered at 11:00 AM in Parliament Square to read the play in what they termed a mass Greek chorus of disapproval.

Media Communications

The Iraq antiwar movement featured the largest, most sophisticated and most successful media communications effort in the history of the peace movement. Antiwar movements traditionally have suffered from poor media relations. As Todd Gitlin and others have observed, peace activists have been slow to recognize the enormous significance of media communications for social change. During the Vietnam era the image of the peace movement was often that of a motley and anarchic rabble. The major coalitions involved were more interested in street protests than media communications, and little effort was made to hire professional media consultants or sponsor public relations and advertising campaigns. In recent decades, however, peace and justice activists have come to recognize the power and influence of the media. They have seen how communications strategies are becoming the dominant factor in shaping political discourse and swaying political opinion. When the debate over war in Iraq began, many activists were determined to mount an effective public relations and media communications campaign.

The February 15 demonstrations in the United States and around the world were enormously successful in attracting media coverage of the antiwar movement. The demonstrations that day were the lead story in practically every broadcast and print news source in the United States and in much of the world. Never before had the peace movement attracted so much press coverage. The image of the antiwar movement as a "superpower" was the direct result of those demonstrations and the resulting media coverage. The demonstrations conveyed a simple "no to war" message that was easily understood and resonated well with world opinion. Although much smaller in scale than the United for Peace and Justice demonstrations, the actions of Code Pink were also successful in generating favorable media coverage. The women activists were a nettlesome presence at appearances of war making officials, and thus became the subject of press coverage. By appropriating feminist language and symbols, and by employing disruptive theatrics, Code Pink activists attracted considerable press attention and helped to frame opposition to war as a special concern of women.

One of the most important dimensions of media strategy is the framing of messages. Every political contest is at its core a struggle over the meaning of words and ideas. Social change often hinges on the way in which messages are interpreted and packaged. The context in which a message is delivered is often more important than the specifics in that message. According to William Gamson, the images and metaphors activists convey are central to their prospects for political success (1990, 147). Ideas such as justice or peace do not exist in a vacuum, in some rarified form that everyone automatically accepts. Their meaning is shaped by the social and political context in which they are communicated. Activists increasingly understand that they must shape that context and offer compelling images, symbols, and metaphors that resonate with and capture public imagination. The contest over symbolic expression has become a crucial element of social movement struggle.

Win Without War was specifically created as a vehicle for media communications. The coalition placed a great deal of emphasis on the framing of its message and the maintenance of a sustained and disciplined press operation. From the outset Win Without War sought to portray itself as mainstream and patriotic. Its press releases and newspaper ads featured an American flag, and its mission statement began with "We are patriotic Americans . . ." By framing its message in patriotic terms, Win Without War sought to capture the flag and thereby inoculate itself against the usual charges of aiding the enemy. The coalition, and many others in the antiwar movement, explicitly condemned the policies and rule of Saddam Hussein, and supported vigorous inspections and containment as means of countering the Iraqi military threat. The coalition expressed full support for the international campaign against terrorism, although it was careful to avoid any specific reference to or support for the administration's "war on terror" (so as not to reinforce Bush's militarized metaphor and policies). Through the framing and delivery of these patriotic messages Win Without War sought to reach the political mainstream and effectively contest the Bush administration's case for war.

There was considerable, sometimes heated debate within the movement about the use of patriotic symbols and language. Some activists expressed discomfort with the traditional militaristic meaning of the flag and other patriotic symbols. As George Lakoff and other communications experts noted, right wing groups had "commandeered patriotic language" and appropriated the meaning of the flag and other nationalist emblems (as quoted in Salladay 2003). The leaders of Win Without War argued that a patriotic frame was necessary pragmatically to gain the acceptance and support of uncommitted and persuadable Americans. The peace movement should not concede patriotism to militarism, they insisted, but should struggle to win back and redefine the concept of loving one's country. The Win Without War coalition name was itself a form of message framing. The phrase was alliterative and easy to express. It conveyed a positive theme (everyone wants to "win") without the negativity of being "against" war or the military. Yet it was specific about seeking a solution "without war," thus marking a clear break with the position of the Bush administration. The title implied support for constructive alternatives to war, such as vigorous

UN weapons inspections and continued containment. It avoided the ambiguity and negative connotation that some people, still influenced by Cold War misconceptions, associate with the traditional "peace" movement. The Win Without War name projected a new, proactive image for the antiwar movement. It was both message and sound bite, and it became a brand that was the most widely communicated message of the antiwar movement.[22]

Artists Unite

The antiwar communications effort was greatly aided by the development of Artists United to Win Without War, which was announced in December 2002, and Musicians United to Win Without War, which emerged in February 2003. The artists committee was initiated by actor Mike Farrell and producer/director Robert Greenwald after a Los Angeles briefing/reception featuring former UN weapons inspector Scott Ritter in early October 2002. The artists committee was officially launched on December 10, 2002, with a full-page ad in the *New York Times* and a press event in Los Angeles attended by Anjelica Houston, Tony Shalhoub, Loretta Switt, Martin Sheen, and other actors. More than 100 entertainers signed the Artists United letter to President Bush, closely modeled on the Win Without War mission statement. The musicians committee was launched in similar fashion, with a full-page ad in the *New York Times* on February 27, 2003 and a New York press event attended by David Byrne, Russell Simmons, and other performers and producers. The musicians' statement, again modeled on the Win Without War appeal, was signed by fifty of the world's most successful and popular rap, hip-hop, and rock musicians, including Sheryl Crow, Eminem, Jay-Z, Dave Mathews, and REM. The announcements of the artists and musicians committees generated widespread broadcast and print news coverage. Stories appeared not only in hard news segments, but in entertainment and style programs also. Youth-oriented programs like MTV aired frequent stories about the celebrities and musicians, helping to generate widespread sympathy and support for the antiwar cause.

The use of celebrities to draw attention to the antiwar message met the criteria for "publicness" that social movement groups must establish to convey their message in the mass media. A famous face or well-known personality can help to overcome media disinterest and draw attention to the challengers' message. The use of celebrities is not without drawbacks, however, and some of these were evident during the Iraq antiwar campaign. Media commentators criticized artists for exploiting their celebrity to speak out on a complicated matter of national security. The artists would often have to spend time defending their right to speak as citizens. Fenton Communications attempted to pair artists with policy exerts, but talk show producers usually insisted on booking artists alone. Several of the most active artists—including Mike Farrell, Susan Sarandon, and Janeane Garofalo—appeared on numerous television and radio interview programs. They were well-read and informed about the issues and were effective in conveying the Win Without War message.

The Iraq antiwar movement was the most successful in history at media communications. Through the extensive use of the Internet, professional public relations services, paid newspaper and television advertising, and the participation of famous artists and musicians, the movement utilized the tools of mass communications to an unprecedented degree. More than a dozen full-page ads in the *New York Times*, hundreds of ads in local newspapers, hundreds of national and regional television ad placements, thousands of national and local television and radio interview program appearances, and thousands of articles in national and local newspapers—all brought visibility and credibility to the antiwar message. The Win Without War media effort generated hundreds of millions of viewer impressions. This vast media communications campaign did not sway the unlistening Bush administration, but it significantly influenced public opinion.

Reflections

Despite the unprecedented scale and scope of the Iraq antiwar movement—the largest antiwar demonstrations in history, a campaign of global dimensions, a sophisticated and wide-reaching media effort—the Bush administration ignored the pervasive opposition to war and rolled ahead with its planned invasion. Given the administration's determination to remove Saddam Hussein by force, the movement probably had little chance of halting the march to war. Nor did the movement have much time to organize, less than six months from the time the major coalitions began to take shape in October until the onset of war in March. The broad public opposition to war nonetheless had significant impacts. The administration's decision to take its case to the United Nations was a victory for the advocates of diplomacy in the United States and around the world. Hardliners in the administration preferred bypassing the Security Council and proceeding directly to military action, but the administration needed at least the appearance of seeking UN involvement to gain political legitimacy in Congress and elsewhere. Once the UN debate began, France, Russia, and other countries were successful in forcing substantial changes in the draft resolution submitted by the United States and the United Kingdom in October. The resulting resolution in November, Security Council Resolution 1441, lacked the explicit authorization for military action that Washington and London had sought. When the Bush administration returned to the Security Council in February to seek authority for war, it was decisively rebuffed. Not only France, Germany, and Russia, but six non-permanent members—Chile, Mexico, Cameroon, Guinea, Angola, and Pakistan—refused to support the U.S. proposal. The opposition of the non-permanent members was especially significant, given their political and economic dependence on the United States. Washington made determined efforts to twist their arms, including diplomatic missions to each country, but to no avail. As Phyllis Bennis noted, the strength of worldwide antiwar sentiment prevented the Bush administration from gaining UN support for its planned invasion and forced the administration to abandon efforts to win UN endorsement (2003). As a result the United States and Britain stood practically alone in their drive for war.

The administration's apparent haste to launch its invasion in March 2003 may have been motivated in part by a desire to launch the attack before antiwar sentiment became too strong. The administration had already made its best case for war (the president's state of the union address and the Powell presentation at the UN), which produced a bump in the polls as expected. But the short-term gain for the administration in the polls was trumped by the rising tide of antiwar action, particularly the February 15 rallies and the virtual march. In late February and early March polls showed a slight decline in support for war, with many opposed to an invasion without Security Council approval, and majority support for giving UN inspections more time. Antiwar momentum was building. Time seemed to be on the side of the opposition. Membership lists were growing rapidly at MoveOn, True Majority, Peace Action, and other groups. Plans were being laid for additional rallies, concerts, and television broadcasts. The best way to short-circuit the antiwar buildup was to send in the troops, thus robbing the movement of its principal purpose and sparking the inevitable rally 'round the flag effect that occurs when troops are engaged in combat.

The degree to which antiwar opposition weighed on the deliberations of the Bush administration is unknown, and may not be known until former officials write their memoirs. In the aftermath of the February 15 demonstrations the president professed to be unmoved by the massive protests, saying that he would not decide policy merely on the basis of a "focus group" (as quoted in Stevenson 2003, A1). Such denials of social movement influence are standard fare among political leaders who are the target of protest. During the Vietnam era, President Nixon dismissed the huge Moratorium rally at the Washington Monument on November 15, 1969, claiming that he ignored the protest and was watching football on television. As Daniel Ellsberg later observed, however, the memoirs of Nixon and of his top aide H. R. Halderman showed that the administration was deeply concerned about the Moratorium actions, and was forced to abandon its plans for a major military escalation against North Vietnam for fear of sparking even greater protests.[23] Ronald Reagan and his advisers dismissed the nuclear freeze demonstrations and referenda of the early 1980s as "all sponsored by a thing called the World Peace Council"[24] (a false and absurd attempt to redbait the movement). In fact, public pressure during the 1980s derailed the MX missile system, blocked civil defense planning, persuaded Congress to halt funding for nuclear tests, and forced the White House to begin negotiations with the Soviets that eventually led to significant arms reduction.[25]

One impact of the Iraq antiwar debate that has not been widely acknowledged was the strategic decision of the White House to justify its preplanned war by emphasizing the supposed threat from Iraqi weapons of mass destruction. In a moment of unscripted candor after the war, Deputy Defense Secretary Paul Wolfowitz, a principal proponent of attacking Iraq, acknowledged that the focus on weapons of mass destruction was politically motivated. During an interview with *Vanity Fair* magazine, Wolfowitz stated: "The truth is that for reasons that have a lot to do with U.S. government bureaucracy, we settled on the one issue that everyone could agree on, which was weapons of mass destruction as the core reason."[26] This was an admission that the administration could not make an honest case for war and win the debate. Because opposition to war was so great, it was necessary to manipulate and deceive public opinion. By choosing to emphasize the weapons threat—disingenuously invoking fears of a nuclear mushroom cloud and chemical or biological attack—the administration focused the debate on issues it knew would be effective in mobilizing public concern. The tactic was successful in the short term, convincing many Americans that Saddam Hussein had deadly weapons poised to strike. But the strategy backfired when White House claims were exposed as lies—in large part through the continuing efforts of antiwar groups.

It is too early to tell as of this writing how the crisis over the Bush administration's invasion and occupation of Iraq will unfold. The U.S. military easily defeated the depleted and dispirited Iraqi armed forces, but the challenge of occupying and controlling Iraq turned out to be far more difficult. Many of the arguments made by the movement prior to the war

were proven correct in its aftermath. The administration's deceit in justifying war set the context for the political problems the White House began
to face afterward. The antiwar movement's steady drumbeat of criticism
about the lack of justification for war—the absence of a verified weapons
threat in Iraq, the failure to demonstrate a link between Saddam Hussein
and al-Qaida—laid the groundwork for the subsequent political vulnerability of the Bush administration when in fact no weapons threat or terrorist connections were found. The postwar criticisms of faulty intelligence
and flawed assumptions undermined confidence in the administration's
foreign policy, especially its new doctrine of military preemption. The
growing perception that the White House misled the country into war
weakened the president's political standing and emboldened his opponents
in the Democratic Party. The antiwar movement thus continued to have
political influence even after the conflict was over.

The ways in which social movements influence policy are not always
readily apparent. They often emerge in unanticipated form, or in future
impacts. Movements can win even as they lose. While the antiwar movement did not succeed in preventing the invasion of Iraq, it helped to set the
terms of the debate and exerted considerable influence on public opinion.
The Bush administration rammed through its war policy, but it lost the
larger and more important struggle for hearts and minds. The war was lost
politically before it ever began militarily. The political legitimacy of
American leadership suffered grievous setbacks on the international level.[27]
Whether these developments translate into a long-term loss for U.S. militarism, and a concurrent increase in support for cooperative internationalism, is unknown. The answer will depend on whether the legacy of the
international movement against war in Iraq is sustained and deepened in
the years ahead.

NOTES

1. Estimates of the numbers of demonstrators and antiwar events are drawn from the
    web site of United for Peace and Justice, the largest grassroots peace coalition in
    the United States, available August 5, 2003 at: <http://www.unitedforpeace. org/
    feb15.html>. For newspaper accounts of the protests, see Angelique Chrisafis
    et al., "Threat of War: Millions Worldwide Rally for Peace," *Guardian*
    (London), February 17, 2003, 6; Glenn Frankel, "Millions Worldwide Protest
    Iraq War," *Washington Post*, February 16, 2003, A1; Alan Lowell, "1.5 Million
    Demonstrators in Cities Across Europe Oppose a War in Iraq," *New York Times*,
    February 16, 2003, Section 1, 20.
2. Interview, David Cortright with Leslie Cagan, August 26, 2003.
3. Ibid.

4. Van Gosse, "February 15, 2003 in New York: A Preliminary Assessment," available at http://www.historiansagainstwar.org/feb15van.html.
5. Interview, David Cortright with Leslie Cagan, August 26, 2003.
6. Based on personal conversations with the directors of the three organizations— Susan Shaer, Kevin Martin, and Bob Musil—September 2003.
7. For a view of churches in the nuclear freeze movement, see my chapter, "God Against the Bomb," in Cortright (1993, 40–60).
8. BBC News, January 13, 2003, available at <http://www.news.bbc.co.uk/z/hi/europe/2654109.stm>.
9. CBC News, March 22, 2003, available at <http://www.cbc.cn/stories/2003/03/22/popewar_030322>.
10. Telephone interview, David Cortright with Bob Edgar, August 27, 2003.
11. Remarks by Bob Muehlenkamp, co-convener, U.S. Labor Against War, April 26 meeting, Chicago, Illinois. Available September 16, 2003 at <www.uslaboragainstwar.org/index.php?SingleItemFlag=1&news_id=6827>.
12. AFL-CIO Executive Council, "Iraq," February 27, 2003, accessed September 16, 2003. Available online at the *AFL-CIO* <http://www.aflcio.org/aboutaflcio/ecouncil/ec02272003h.cfm>.
13. Polling Report, *Iraq* (p. 4). Conducted by Harris Interactive. Accessed August 28, 2003 <http://www.pollingreport.com/iraq4.htm>.
14. Polling Report, *Iraq* (p. 4). Fieldwork by TNS Intersearch. Accessed August 28, 2003 <http://www.pollingreport.com/iraq4.htm>.
15. Libero Della Piana, "War's Racial Edge," *ColorLines*, Spring 2003, 21.
16. Polling Report, *Iraq* (p. 4). Conducted by Harris Interactive. Accessed August 28, 2003 <http://www.pollingreport.com/iraq4.htm>.
17. Polling Report, *Iraq* (p. 4). Fieldwork by TNS Intersearch. Accessed August 28, 2003 <http://www.pollingreport.com/iraq4.html>.
18. "Aggregate Zogby America Pre War Support, 9/25/02 thru 3/17/03," Zogby International, special report to Fourth Freedom Forum, August 26, 2003.
19. Greenberg Quinlan Rosner Research Inc., *Public Supports Bush, Is More Divided over Iraq: Report on the First WorldView Survey for VVAF*, memorandum from Jeremy Rosner and William McInturff to Vietnam Veterans of America Foundation, March 14, 2003. *Greenberg Quinlan Rosner Research Inc.* Accessed August 28, 2003 <http://www.greenbergresearch.com/publications/reports/VVAF031403_m.pdf>.
20. Quoted in Ann Moline, "Women's E News," National Organization for Women, Washington, D.C., December 29, 2002, accessed August 11, 2003 <www.now.org/eNews/dec2002/122902peace.html>.
21. Figures from Lysistrata Project report, available August 19, 2003 at <http://www.pecosdesign.com/lys/archive.html>.
22. The phrase was derived from the report, *Winning without War: Sensible Security Options for Dealing with Iraq*, produced by the Fourth Freedom Forum and the Joan B. Kroc Institute for International Peace Studies, Notre Dame, Ind., October 2002.
23. See the account of Daniel Ellsberg, "Introduction: A Call to Mutiny," in Thompson and Smith (1981, xv–xvi).

24. Quoted in Talbott (1985, 81).
25. See my summary of these impacts in Cortright (1993, 243–48).
26. The transcript of the Wolfowitz interview, accessed August 19, 2003 from the Defense Link news service of the U.S. Department of Defense <http://www. defenselink.mil/transcripts/2003/tr20030509-depsecdef0223.html>.
27. Former president Jimmy Carter wrote in a *New York Times* editorial on March 9, 2003, that "increasingly unilateral and domineering policies have brought international trust in our country to the lowest level in memory."

BIBLIOGRAPHY

Bennis, Phyllis. 2003. "Bush Isolated, Launches Terrifying Attack." *War Times* April 2003, accessed July 24 <www.war-times.org/current/9art1.html>.
Boyd, Andrew. 2003. "The Web Rewires the Movement." *The Nation* 277, no. 4 (August 4/11, 2003): 14.
Cortright, David. 1993. *Peace Works: The Citizen's Role in Ending the Cold War.* Boulder, Colo.: Westview Press.
Ellsberg, Daniel. 1981. "Introduction: A Call to Mutiny." Pp. in *Protest and Survive*, ed. E. P. Thompson and Dan Smith. New York: Monthly Review Press.
Epstein, Barbara. 2003. "Notes on the Antiwar Movement." *Monthly Review* 55, no. 3 (July–August 2003): 109.
Featherstone, Liza. 2003. "Mighty in Pink." *The Nation* February 13.
Gamson, William. 1990. *The Strategy of Social Protest*, second edition. Belmont, Calif.: Wadsworth Publishing.
Gill, Stephen. 2003. *Power and Resistance in the New World Order.* London: Palgrave.
Gitlin, Todd. 2002. "Who Will Lead?" October 14, accessed August 19, 2003 <http://motherjones.com>.
Hedges, Chris. 2003. "A Long-time Antiwar Activist, Escalating the Peace." *New York Times* February 4, Metro Section, 2.
Levine, Mark. 2003. "The Peace Movement Plans for the Future," *Middle East Report*, July, accessed August 27, 2003 <http://www.merip.org/mero/interventions/levine_interv.html>.
Moore, James F. 2003. "The Second Super-power Rears its Beautiful Head." Berkman Center for Internet and Society, Harvard Law School, March 31.
Nunberg, Jeoffrey. 2003. "As Google Goes, So Goes the Nation." *New York Times* May 18, Section 4, 4.
Packer, George. 2003. "Smart-Mobbing the War." *New York Times Magazine* March 9.
Salladay, Robert. 2003. "Peace Activism: A Matter of Language," *San Francisco Chronicle* April 7.
Schell, Jonathan. 2003. "The Other Super-Power." *The Nation* April 14.
Solnit, Rebecca. 2003. "Acts of Hope: Challenging Empire on the World Stage." *Orion* May 20, accessed November 24, 2003 <http://www. oriononline.org/pages/oo/sidebars/Patriotism/index_SolnitPR.html>.

Stevenson, Richard W. 2003. "Antiwar Protests Fail to Sway Bush on Plans for Iraq." *New York Times* February 19, A1.

Tyler, Patrick E. 2003. "Threats and Responses: News Analysis; A New Power in the Streets." *New York Times* February 17, A1.

Talbott, Strobe. 1985. *Deadly Gambits: The Reagan Administration and the Stalemate in Nuclear Arms Control.* New York: Vintage Books.

Chapter 5

Truth Commissions and U.S. Hegemony

Carlos A. Parodi

Truth commissions are institutions created to find the truth about past human rights violations committed by national governments and other organized forces, and to use such truth to punish perpetrators, heal victims, and bring about national reconciliation. Recent examples of truth commissions include Argentina (1983), Chile (1991), El Salvador (1993), Guatemala (1995), South Africa (1998), and Peru (2001). They share such common purposes as closing the gap between government and citizens; integrating victims and perpetrators into the national body; preparing a plan of national reparations; and restoring national trust and justice. A common assumption is that truth commissions investigate *intra*national human rights violations, not *inter*national human rights violations, that is, national groups committed violations against each other and, thus, national groups need reconciliation. Argentines violated the rights of Argentines, Guatemalans of Guatemalans, and so forth.

What this framework overlooks is the role of external actors in the violation of human rights in other countries. Should truth commissions hold such parties responsible as well? Should countries that committed human rights violations in other states establish their own truth commissions? In this chapter, my focus is on the truth commissions in light of the role of the United States in the Cold War conflicts that led to atrocities across the world. Could a process similar to these truth commissions be also established for the United States? What would a U.S. truth commission investigate? We might think of violations of Americans against Americans: for example, human rights violations of American colonizers against American settlers, American slave owners against American slaves, the internment of Japanese Americans in World War II, and so on. Many groups in the United States would no doubt welcome a truth commission's call for national healing, justice, and reconciliation. However, it would not investigate the violation of human rights committed by the United States against other nations. Here lies the rub: the prevailing truth commission methodology has only been applied to the investigation and resolution of human rights violations committed between groups belonging to the same nation.

Is it a serious limitation that truth commissions are not set up in order to investigate *inter*national human rights violations? In this chapter I argue it is, but truth commissions can, nevertheless, overcome their nationalist framework and challenge U.S. hegemony. First, I present the thesis that respect for state sovereignty, a key principle of international law, poses a serious limitation when it comes to judging *inter*national human rights violations, in general, and violations of the United States against other nationalities, in particular. The extraordinary post–World War II growth of human rights legislation focused on *intra*national human rights violations. But because it overlooked human rights violations committed by one nation against other nations, it only partially questioned state sovereignty. Except for war crimes, international law is seriously limited when it comes to violations of human rights that states commit outside their own borders. Should the U.S. government, corporations and citizens be held responsible for human rights violations they have committed outside the United States? If so, what should be the procedure for investigating and resolving them? The challenge facing national truth commissions is to pool resources to build an institution where the United States is part of the process of truth and reconciliation with other nations.

In the second part of the chapter I discuss the responsibility of the United States for human rights violations committed in countries where truth commissions have been established, giving special attention to Latin American truth commissions. Although evidence of violations committed by the United States exists, and sometimes is explicitly mentioned in truth commission reports, truth commissions do not bring in the United States as an actor responsible for violations. However, some truth commissions are willing to bring in the United States as financial donor for a process of national reparation and reconciliation.

Third, I analyze the potential truth commissions have for challenging U.S. hegemony. The main thrust of this section is to make the case for an international coalition of truth commissions in order to establish a process of truth and reconciliation between the United States and other nations. For existing and future truth commissions implemented outside the

United States, a crucial question is What should be their *foreign policy*, especially toward the United States? Should each truth commission approach the United States to ask for financial support to fund a national plan of reparations, or should all get together and demand reparations from the United States? What should be the foreign policy of a U.S. truth commission toward victims of violations committed by Americans abroad? Are national apologics enough? In essence, the purpose of this chapter is to investigate whether truth commissions "are able to break free of the entrapments of global arrogance" (Leatherman chapter 1 in this volume).

International Human Rights Violations

The impetus for the globalization of the idea of human rights stems from 1948 when "the nations of the time" adopted the Universal Declaration of Human Rights, "a masterly blend of Western libertarianism and 'welfare' state principles" (Henkin 1979, 231).[1] Since then the United Nations has produced an amazing body of international human rights law. However, respect for state sovereignty limits the application of human rights principles to intranational relations. The extension of human rights principles to international relations leads us to question the nationalist framework of international law. International law is not universalist enough for human rights.

International law of human rights has been commonly interpreted as a development that challenged pre–World War II or Westphalian conceptions of state sovereignty (Henkin 1979, 1990; Donnelly 1999; Falk 1999).[2] In the words of Louis Henkin,

> The law of human rights contradicts the one deep-and-dear premises [sic] of the international system that how a state behaved toward its own citizens in its own territory was a matter of "domestic jurisdiction," i.e., not any one else's business and therefore not any business for international law. (1979, 228)

The international law of human rights has unquestionably opened to scrutiny "the way in which states treat their own citizens" but, at the same time, it has shielded *inter*national relations from the critical power of human rights' universalism (Donnelly 1999, 73). Defenders and critics agree that the normative power of human rights is concentrated in the internal aspects of state sovereignty. For supporters of human rights, the transformation of the domestic system of relations according to internationally agreed principles is the appropriate path of development. For critics, human rights violate the integrity of national identity. For both, the transformative power of human rights resides in their capacity to end violations committed *within* nations. Do human rights principles also have the potential for transforming relations between nations? The answer is yes. However, in order to appreciate such potential, it needs to be recognized that the international law of human rights is not universalist enough to question relations between nations.

At first, the above criticism of the international law of human rights may seem unfair because, one could argue, human rights is only one aspect of international law and there are other areas of international law specialized in disciplining *inter*national relations according to universal standards of morality. This seems obvious because the name itself, international law, means laws that regulate relations between nations. However, I argue that the principles underpinning such laws are not human rights principles.

The moral foundation of *inter*national law is at best one of "mutual restraint and toleration of diversity." According to Nardin, international law prescribes "restraint, toleration, and mutual accommodation according to authoritative common standards of international conduct," and makes it possible "for states pursuing different ends to coexist" (Nardin 1983, 5). Contemporary *inter*national law, including human rights law, is anchored in "communitarianism" not "cosmopolitanism" (Brown 1992). Communitarianism understands that state autonomy is the moral basis of international society. Certainly, communitarians can be morally demanding before granting sovereignty to any state. A communitarian can be a strong defender of human rights. In the words of Richard Falk, "plausibly, it would be the re-empowering of the state as associated with citizens and territory that provides the best hope in the near future for mitigating the current cruelties and inequities of economic globalization" (1999, 179). However, communitarians also believe that state autonomy means that justice is not possible in *inter*national relations, only *intra*national relations.

In sum, the development of post–World War II international law of human rights brought the spotlight to *intra*national human rights violations but remains weak in the *inter*national arena. Every major piece of international human rights legislation since the 1948 Universal Declaration has been dedicated to transforming *intra*national relations. Within this framework it is understandable that post–World War II efforts to end "genocidal politics" were restricted to "crimes of state" such as "ethnic cleansing in Bosnia," "genocidal politics in Cambodia during the period of Khmer Rouge," and "the events in Rwanda and Burundi" (Ignatieff 2002, 182–185). Mark Gibney and Erik Roxstrom also highlight this characteristic of international law in their study of the "status of state apologies." For these authors, in "the positivistic (or state-centered) conception of international law," the "responsibilities of states for conduct that occurs or has an effect beyond their borders remains unclear" (Gibney and Roxstrom 2001, 916). Within this framework, a "fundamental misunderstanding" has resulted: "we are led to believe that human rights are simply about the relationship between a citizen and his/her state" (916).

Extending the universalism of human rights principles to *inter*national relations implies a radical challenge to state sovereignty and one should expect the move to be resisted. Challenges to human rights universalism abound (Ignatieff 2001; Brown 1999; Chomsky 1998; Evans 2001). What follows highlights the challenge to human rights universalism posed by United States hegemony. Is the United States responsible for human rights violations committed outside the United States? If it is, what should be the procedure for investigating and resolving them? The challenge is to build an institution where the United States is part of a process of truth and reconciliation with other nations. The following section elaborates this point focusing on human rights violations in the group of Latin American countries where a truth commission has been established.

United States and Human Rights Violations

A common characteristic of Latin American truth commissions is their resistance to consider the United States as a *responsible actor* in human rights violations, in spite of the fact that their final reports provide solid information about U.S. participation in human rights violations. Even when a U.S. President—specifically, Bill Clinton—decided to recognize U.S. responsibility and apologize for its role in human rights violations in Guatemala, Guatemalans reacted in disbelief. They were not expecting an apology.

Of four Latin American truth commission reports, only the one published in March 1999 in Guatemala by the *Commission for Historical Clarification* (CEH, Spanish acronym) prompted an apology from the President of the United States, Bill Clinton. No U.S. apology was heard after the publication of truth commission reports in Argentina (1983), Chile (1991), and El Salvador (1993). U.S. media coverage of the historical event highlighted the unexpected nature of Clinton's apology and the overwhelming evidence demonstrating "the extent of U.S. complicity" in the killing of "200,000, predominantly Mayan Indian." In fact, a common interpretation of Clinton's apology among sympathetic observers was that, faced with the overwhelming evidence, including documents released by the U.S. State Department,

"Bill Clinton said the only thing that made any sense. He expressed infinite regret over what had happened" (McGrory 1999).

   Clinton's apology in Guatemala during his Central American tour was not his first. Nor was he the first U.S. president to apologize "to foreign governments for the policies of his predecessors" (Kagan and Kristol 1999). However, the personal and unofficial character of the U.S. president's apologies made them suspicious. What was Clinton apologizing for? Why was an apology extended for U.S. participation in human rights violations in Guatemala, but not in Argentina, Chile, or El Salvador? Should the United States be included in the processes of truth and reconciliation being implemented throughout Latin America, or should these processes be only of a "national" character?

What was Clinton Apologizing For?

On March 10, 1999, in the National Palace of Culture of Guatemala City, on the last day of a four-day visit to Central America, President Clinton said that the United States should not repeat the "mistake" of supporting "military forces or intelligence units which engaged in violent and widespread repression" of the kind described in the CEH Report (Clinton 1999). The official purpose of the presidential visit was to review the damage caused by Hurricane Mitch (October 26 to November 4, 1998) and the progress in democracy, market reforms, and human rights by the governments of the region (U.S. Department of State 1999).[3] The apology was not part of the official script. Although "Clinton's aides said the president had thought for some time about how to word his near-apology" (Babington 1999), he finally decided to apologize "reading from hand-written notes."[4] Clinton's words "startled and pleased nervous Latino politicians" (McGrory 1999).[5] Guatemalan President Alvaro Arzu was so surprised with Clinton's words that his press aides said "they were unsure whether he would comment" (Babington 1999).

   In the United States, President Clinton's apology stirred some controversy; in Central America, the apology almost passed unnoticed.[6] For our purposes, an analysis of the apology reveals important elements of the truth and reconciliation process. To start, let's review how Guatemala's CEH report explained the participation of the United States in human rights violations. In the section "Conclusions and Recommendations," Guatemala's CEH affirmed that the "the movement of Guatemala towards polarisation, militarization and civil war" should not be understood exclusively as "national history" but should also be seen as "the result of the Cold War." The anti-communism "promoted by the United States within the framework of its foreign policy . . . demonstrated that it was willing to provide support for strong military regimes in its strategic backyard." This was a key factor "which had significant bearing on human rights violations during the armed confrontation." Anti-communism became the corner-stone of the National Security Doctrine, "first expressed as anti-reformist, then anti-democratic policies, culminating in criminal counterinsurgency." One of the most devastating effects of this policy was that "state forces and related paramilitary groups were responsible for 93% of the violations documented" by the Commission.[7]

Let's compare the above with President Clinton's apology:

> I have profound respect for the victims and the families who had courage to testify and for the courage of a nation for coming to terms with its past and moving forward. For the United States, it is important that I state clearly that support for military forces or intelligence units which engaged in violent and widespread repression of the kind described in the report was wrong, and the United States must not repeat that mistake. We must, and we will, instead continue to support the peace and reconciliation process in Guatemala.[8]

There are two important points to highlight. First, while the CEH characterized the actions of the United States as part of the "framework of its foreign policy," Clinton referred to those actions as a "mistake," that is, something out of the ordinary rather than the result of a carefully designed plan. The fact that the systematic nature of the human rights violations was overlooked did not mean that Clinton did not understand the meaning of genocide, or that he was unaware of the Cold War as the framework within which violence took place. His visit to Africa the year before was revealing in both these aspects. In March 1998, at the Kisowera School in Mukono, Uganda, President Clinton, after listening "very carefully to what the president [Musoveni] said about the history of Africa," responded:

> It is as well not to dwell too much on the past, but I think it is worth point-ing out that the United States has not always done the right thing by Africa. In our own time, during the Cold War, when we were so concerned about being in competition with the Soviet Union, very often we dealt with coun-tries in Africa and in other parts of the world based more on how they stood in the struggle between the United States and the Soviet Union than how they stood in the struggle for their own people's aspirations to live up to the fullest of their God-given abilities.[9]

Later that same day at the airport in Kigali, Rwanda, in a ceremony "to pay the respects of my nation to all who suffered and all who perished in the Rwandan genocide," Clinton said that the killings "were not spontaneous or accidental" but "grew from a policy aimed at the systematic destruction of a people." Then he added:

> The international community, together with nations in Africa, must bear its share of responsibility for this tragedy, as well. We did not act quickly enough after the killing began. We should not have allowed the refugee camps to become safe haven for the killers. We did not immediately call these crimes by their rightful name: genocide. We cannot change the past. But we can and must do everything in our power to help you build a future without fear and full of hope.[10]

President Clinton could have acknowledged the *systematic* nature of the killings and the wrong-headedness of U.S. Cold War policy in Guatemala also, but chose not to.

A comparison of Clinton's apologies in Rwanda and Guatemala is illustrative. In both cases he framed genocide as *national* tragedies. In Rwanda, Clinton recognized genocide as systematic killing and apologized in the name of the international community for not acting "quickly enough," rather than acknowledge how its policies facilitated genocidal killing. In Guatemala, however, Clinton recognized that the United States was involved in the killing, and apologized for a "mistake," not for a systematic policy. In both cases the official interpretation of the United States was that genocide was committed for the most part between members of the same nation, an interpretation consistent with the nationalist framework prevailing in other truth commissions and international law.

Clinton's apologies in Uganda, Rwanda, and Guatemala certainly were not intended as the first steps of a process of critical reflection on the responsibility of the United States for Cold War policies that caused violence leading to massive human rights violations across the globe. Clinton's purpose was not to open up a full-blown investigation and start a truth commission for the United States. On the contrary, in his speeches in Uganda and Rwanda, Clinton clearly indicated his discomfort with facing the past. In Uganda he said, "it is as well not to dwell too much on the past."

However, how can an apology be sincere if it is not done with a full account of the past? In Uganda, Clinton said, "we cannot change the past" (Clinton 1998). However, the point is not about changing the past, but changing the present and the future through an examination of the truth about the past. "In sum, President Clinton's apology to the Guatemalan people says very little, it helps us to understand very little, and perhaps, it changes very little" (Gibney and Roxstrom 2001, 936).

For an international process of truth and reconciliation, the United States is not the only actor required to change its approach. Truth commissions also need to break away from their nationalist framework of interpretation of human rights violations. The truth commission framework resists making the United States accountable. This is a serious but not fatal limitation of truth commissions.

Argentina's truth commission recognized the role of the United States in the implementation of Argentina's National Security Doctrine (NSD). The 1983 decree ordering trials for the members of the Military Junta, stated "thousands were illegally stripped of their freedom, tortured or killed as the result of the implementation of fighting procedures inspired in the totalitarian National Security Doctrine."[11] Argentine generals trained by the United States in anti-subversive strategies implemented the NSD. These generals perceived communist totalitarianism as the major threat to the "Western and Christian system of life" (936).[12] The report quotes from President Kennedy's Defense Secretary, Robert MacNamara, who in 1963 said:

> probably the largest return of our investment in military aid comes from training selected officials and key specialists in our military schools and training centers in the United States and abroad. These students are carefully selected from their countries to become instructors when they return. They are the leaders of the future, the men who will have the know-how and will teach it to their armed forces.[13]

Although the report brings out the responsibility of the United States in causing human rights violations in Argentina, it calls for no remedy. This was a truth with no consequence. More significantly, the failure to initiate a course of action against the U.S. government was in contradiction with the idea that the innumerable and gruesome violations described in detail in the report had to be understood not as aberrations but as consequences of a well thought out strategy. Kidnapping, disappearance, torture, and killing were part of a repressive methodology. The members of the military *juntas* may not have been the torturers, but they certainly gave the orders. It is on the basis of this principle that the government of President Alfonsín ordered in 1985 that trials be initiated against members of the previous three military juntas. By logic, the same principle should have been applied to the participation of the United States, but the nationalist framework did not allow it.

Chile's truth commission also framed the participation of the United States within the context of the Cold War. According to the *National Commission on Truth and Reconciliation* "the 1973 crisis may be generally described as one of sharp polarization between government and opposition."[14] The origins of such polarization are traced back to the Cold War, especially after the Cuban Revolution. The document is equally critical of parties of the left who believed in the path of armed revolution as parties of the right who supported the use of weapons to impose their views. However, this dialectic was the local manifestation of a global ideological conflict. In response to the development of guerrilla *focos*, the United States started a counterinsurgency campaign in Latin America.

Just like the *focos*, such counterinsurgency was both local in nature in each country and centralized through a degree of coordination between all Latin American countries. The United States took charge of the overall coordination, and to that end it took advantage of the fact that generations of officers from the various Latin American countries were passing through its military training schools year after year.

Although the United States was prominently mentioned in the Chilean report, the Commission did not bring in the United States as a responsible actor into the process of truth and reconciliation. Human rights violations were conceived as fundamentally caused by *intra*national not *inter*national relations. "Because of this approach, we are led to believe that human rights are simply about the relationship between a citizen and his/her state. . . . One consequence of this approach is that international human rights law has tended to ignore the relationship between one state and citizens of other states. The Chilean report is explicit about the responsibility of the United States in human rights violations" (Gibney and Roxstrom 2001, 917).

The case of El Salvador reveals even more saliently the limitations of the nationalist framework used by truth commissions to explain human rights violations. The Report of the Commission for the Truth in El Salvador makes a very brief reference to the fact that "the nation was a pawn in the East–West conflict."[15] However, as Priscilla Hayner, a leading scholar in the comparative study of truth commissions explains, the 1993 commission report, *From Madness to Hope*, was "criticized for failing to fully report on certain important aspects of the violence, such as the operation of death squads, and on *the role of the United States* in supporting the government forces" (2002, 39–40 emphasis added). How important was the participation of the United States in human rights violations in El Salvador?

> The U.S. provided $6 billion in economic and military aid to El Salvador during the war. . . . It was U.S.-trained Salvadoran officers who perpetrated most of the war's most notorious acts: Nineteen of the twenty-seven officers implicated in the murders of the Jesuits were trained by the U.S.; the late Roberto d'Aubuisson, charged with the 1980 assassination of Archbishop Oscar Romero, studied at the International Police Academy, a Washington institution later shut down by Congress for teaching torture techniques; of the five officers cited for the 1980 murder of four U.S. church women, three were trained in the U.S.; and of the twelve officers accused of responsibility for the 1981 Mozote massacre, eight graduated from the U.S. Army School of the Americas at Fort Benning, Georgia.[16]

Limiting human rights violations to actions committed by Salvadorans against Salvadorans weakened the otherwise strong commitment of the Report to "the truth, the whole truth and nothing but the truth."[17] The self-imposed limitation of the Salvadoran truth commission went hand in hand with the triumphalist disregard with which Washington treated Salvadorans after the destruction caused by the October 1998 Hurricane Mitch. Oblivious to the responsibility of the United States in the civil war that engulfed El Salvador in the 1980s, and thus, of one of its major consequences: massive migration of Salvadorans to the United States, the U.S. Immigration and Naturalization Service determined in March 1999 that "approximately one thousand six hundred Salvadorans and three hundred Guatemalans faced immediate deportation."[18] This announcement was made at the time of President Clinton's visit to Central America that included his "apology" in Guatemala City.[19]

Truth Versus Power

Truth commissions' potential for challenging U.S. hegemony resides in the principle that truth is the best way to challenge relations of domination. Nowadays, however, it seems many of us are becoming acutely aware of the tension between truth and power. Recently, U.S. Senator Robert C. Byrd's speech "The Truth Will Emerge" was widely circulated through the Internet (2003). In the speech, the U.S. Senator basically said the U.S. government lied to the American people about Iraq, but "eventually the truth will emerge. And when it does, this house of cards, built of deceit will fall." Really? If the American public still does not know or does not *want* to know the truth of the involvement of the U.S. government and its officials in human rights violations as well as those of American corporations and other individuals acting on behalf of U.S. policy interests, why will this suddenly change? And even if the truth comes out, will it have any consequence?

These questions are not new. The tension between truth and power is ancient, and it is the task of every generation to face it. In our days the challenge is coming from what provisionally I would call the *truth movement*. The concept of "movement" is chosen to indicate that the agenda of the people involved is to challenge powerful opponents (Tarrow 1998). Truth movements use truth as their major resource to challenge power. Understanding the functions of truth is critical for these social movements. This is the spirit that inspires organizations such as *Amnesty International* and *Human Rights Watch* to report human rights violations in detail around the world. It is the spirit that animates the relatives of the disappeared to demand the right to know the truth about the whereabouts of their loved ones. It is the spirit with which millions around the world challenge impunity and form truth commissions.

Truth commissions have potential and limitations for challenging power structures. Truth commissions are formally defined as "official bodies set up to investigate a past period of human rights abuses or violations of international humanitarian law" (Hayner 1994, 599).[20] A more politically and historically sensitive approach defines a truth commission as "the approach adopted by regimes that lack either the will or the means to prosecute the perpetrators of political crimes, and where the policy of forgive and forget is not viable because of the depth of division and level of bitterness in society" (Ribgy 2001, 7). Truth commissions are controversial because they represent a middle ground between the Nuremberg Trials and Spain's post-Franco "pact of oblivion" (7). They acquired global notoriety in 1992 when the United Nations sponsored the creation of a truth commission as part of the peace agreements to end the civil war in El Salvador. Two important antecedents were the truth commissions in Argentina (1983) and Chile (1990). In these cases, truth commissions were part of the transition from military to democratic government. In 1995 South Africa also established the *Truth and Reconciliation Commission* as part of the transition from white minority rule to black majority rule. In every case, truth was conceived as a tool to contest power and as a means of healing individuals and social relations. After South Africa, truth commissions were created in Guatemala (1997), Sierra Leone (2000), and Peru (2001).

Internet technology has improved the transformative potential of the truth movement. For example, the *National Security Archive*, founded in 1985,

> is the world's largest non governmental library of declassified documents . . . designed to apply the latest in computerized indexing technology to the massive amount of material already released by the U.S. government on international affairs, make them accessible to researchers and the public, and go beyond that base to build comprehensive collections of documents on specific topics of greatest interest to scholars and the public.[21]

The National Security Archive provided U.S. documents to truth commissions in Guatemala and Peru. The NSA's Director of the Guatemala Project, Kate Doyle, expressed that "now that the Guatemalan commission has finished its work, the United States should establish its own truth commission to expose, investigate and analyze our sometimes scandalous role in Latin American during the Cold War."[22]

The website of the United States Institute of Peace (USIP) offers a truth commission digital collection with 24 cases with links to several national reports.[23] South Africa's and Peru's truth and reconciliation commissions have their own website updated regularly.[24] There are methodologies and courses on-line with toolkits to implement truth commissions.[25] Finally, the website *Virtual Truth Commission* welcomes visitors by cautioning that "human rights abuses implicating the United States find little place in the public forum. Where the truth is not faced, healing cannot take place. This site is committed to telling the truth for a better America."[26] One of its links gives "information on human rights abuses with involvement by U.S. based multinational corporations."

Certainly, not every truth commission is an example of "contentious collective action" (Tarrow 1998). Some commissions were also set up "by a government to manipulate the public perception of its own tarnished image" (Hayner 1994, 609). However, in most cases truth commissions have challenged existing *local* power holders. The question is whether truth commissions have the potential to challenge U.S. hegemony.

Ending the Cold War

> For whole groups of countries, what post-Cold War politics is mostly about is moving beyond earlier horrors, some arising from rule by the left, others from rule by the right.[27]

There is global consensus that the fall of the Berlin Wall and the dissolution of the Soviet Union marked the end of the Cold War. However, the mood with which the end of the Cold War was received varied around the world. One response was the attitude of triumphalism commonly identified with Francis Fukuyama's version of the "end of history." Triumphalists experience the end of the Cold War as the victory of the "good" over the "evil" empire. This mood is similar to what the allied forces experienced in the Nuremberg and Tokyo trials after the end of World War II. Both historical moments show how at the end of a war triumphalists exalt their virtues and condemn the principles and actions of the enemy.

The triumphalist mood can be found in the opening sentence of *The National Security Strategy of the United States* published in September 2002: "The great struggles of the twentieth century between liberty and totalitarianism ended with a decisive victory for the forces of freedom—and a single sustainable model for national success: freedom, democracy, and free enterprise" (Bush 2002, iii). Sustained by the "faith in the principles of liberty, and the value of a free society," the triumphalist

President George H. W. Bush could proclaim: "We will champion the cause of human dignity and oppose those who resist it" (Bush 2002, 1, 4). Post–Cold War triumphalism has no sense of self-criticism.

We find another example of post–Cold War triumphalism in the persona of Chile's General Augusto Pinochet. With the confidence of having done a great service to the world for defeating communism in Chile and success-fully implementing market reforms, General Pinochet decided in 1988 to gamble and call a plebiscite in which he proposed the continuation of his government. He was confident he was going to win, but miscalculated and lost. Elections were called for March 1990. General Pinochet did not run but remained commander-in-chief of the army, a position he retained until 1998 when he was officially sworn-in as Chile's first senator-for-life. General Pinochet and many more who adored him, believed he was a national hero. Imagine the shock he must have felt when in October 1998 the London police told him, while he was lying on a hospital bed, that he was being detained by request of a Spanish judge who wanted to interrogate him for crimes committed while he was head of state! The same sense of disbelief and irritation must have been shared by U.S. conservative leader Patrick J. Buchanan. For Buchanan, General Pinochet was detained because

> this man of the right inflicted a historic, crushing defeat on Marxism. Watching his country slide into the grip of a murderous pack of Leninists, Pinochet in 1973 ordered the military to save it. They did, ruthlessly, and Pinochet's rule left Chile free, prosperous and pro-American, a crime for which the left can never forgive him.[28]

Triumphalism can also be seen in the words of Argentine General Viola. When asked in 1981 about the need for a serious investigation about the disappeared, he explained:

> I believe you mean investigating the Security Forces, and that, definitely not. In this war there are victors, and we were the victors, and rest assured that if in the last world war the troops of the Reich had won, the trial would not have taken place in Nuremberg but in Virginia.[29]

The post–Cold War triumphalism of Bush, Pinochet, Buchanan, and Viola contrasts with the sense of relief, anger, and pain felt by the millions of Chileans who said NO! to the dictator in the 1988 plebiscite. For them, as for millions in Argentina, Guatemala, and El Salvador, the end of the Cold War was the end of a hot and bloody civil war. Thus, a widespread reaction in these countries to the end of the Cold War was more critical, less celebratory. Millions had been killed, tortured, or disappeared in the name of the Cold War. Under the guise of national security, governments violated human rights with impunity. People could get killed just for asking questions. Now, with the end of the Cold War, survivors and their families were no longer afraid to demand answers.

A comparison of the triumphalist and critical responses to the end of the Cold War is helpful for understanding current political strategies. A triumphalist believes that the Cold War ended because, with the United States in the lead, "freedom, democracy, and free enterprise" defeated total-itarianism, communism, and statism. The dissolution of the Soviet Union and its satellite communist regimes in Eastern Europe demonstrated that centralized economies do not work and the "only sustainable model" is "free enterprise." In this new world, "the United States enjoys a position of unparalleled military strength and great economic and political influence" and "welcomes [the] responsibility to lead" in the "great mission" of saving "freedom" from "war and terror" (Bush 2002, iii, 4).

Critics see the end of the Cold War not as the victory of right versus wrong, but as the end of a structural arrangement that justified the use of violence to attain political goals. From this perspective, ending the Cold War means overcoming principles, institutions, and practices that condone violence. For a triumphalist, the use of violence in the past against the enemy was justified, as much as it is today against the new enemies. Critics, on the contrary, call to an end of the cycles of violence. Ending the Cold War means defeating U.S. triumphalism and replacing rule by an arrogant, hegemonic state with rule by "universal standards" in which the law applies equally regardless of how much power or influence a person or state has.

The triumphalist and critical responses to the end of the Cold War differ in their attitude toward the past. Triumphalism is associated with the idea of forgetting the mistakes of the past. In the words of General Pinochet, "We must forget. And forgetting does not occur by opening cases, putting people in jail. . . . And for this to occur, both sides have to forget and continue working."[30] This attitude is in sharp contrast with the one expressed in the first paragraph of the decree law that created Chile's *Truth and Reconciliation Commission*: "the moral conscience of the nation demands that the truth about the grave violations of human rights committed in our country between September 11, 1973 and March 11, 1990 be brought to light."[31]

The triumphalist attitude is an obstacle to overcoming the principles, beliefs, institutions, and practices of the Cold War that condoned and continue condoning violence. A critical attitude, while questioning the functionality of violence, is also compatible with the acceptance that there is plenty to celebrate about the end of the Cold War. The difference is in what the celebration is about. The triumphalist is blind to his own mistakes and celebrates his own virtues by doing more of the same as he did in the past but with a new justification. For a triumphalist the exercise of "power without arrogance" has been "America's special role in the past, and it should be again as we enter the new century" (Rice 2000). In contrast, for a critic "the Cold War was a kind of tacit arrangement between the Soviet Union and the United States under which the U.S. conducted its wars against the Third World and controlled its allies in Europe, while the Soviet rulers kept an iron grip on their own internal empire and their satellites in Eastern Europe—each side using the other to justify repression and violence in its own domains" (Chomsky 1993). The dissolution of the Soviet Union did not make the use of force obsolete, but, on the contrary, gave the United States more freedom to use military force to protect its interest. "It should have surprised no one that George Bush celebrated the symbolic end of the Cold War, the fall of the Berlin Wall, by immediately invading Panama and announcing loud and clear that the United States would subvert Nicaragua's election by maintaining its economic stranglehold and military attack unless 'our side' won" (Chomsky 1993).

In the United States, post–Cold War triumphalism has gone hand in hand with efforts throughout society to ideologically construct another enemy in order to justify a military force that was designed to fight the communist threat. For example, first policy-makers in Washington constructed the typical new threat as the "failed regimes" of Africa.[32] For Pentagon officials the new threat was regional powers intent on acquiring weapons of mass destruction (WMD). For them the general model of a threat became the "rogue state" ruled by an "outlaw regime" (Klare 1995, 27–28). Increasingly, the threat of Islamism has replaced the threat of communism: the "green menace" instead of the "red menace."[33] Today, the enemy is terrorism.

The fabrication of enemies is compatible with triumphalism because it is an ideological activity that glorifies the self by negating the "other." Triumphalism is always about how the righteous "self" defeats the evil "other." For a triumphalist, the end of the Cold War was a one-time event (fall of the Berlin wall or dissolution of the Soviet Union). That chapter of history is closed; we won, they lost. In contrast, a critical attitude sees the historical events marking the end of the Cold War in a way analogous to the decision of an addict to stop using drugs. The decision is only the beginning of a long and painful process of withdrawal. Similarly, from a critical point of view, the end of the Cold War is a moment for self-criticism, introspection, an opportunity to face our fears and change our mentalities and views about the other. A critical attitude calls for structural reform through introspection and dialogue with the "other." This critical attitude inspired the creation of truth commissions across the globe.

However, a limitation of truth commissions is the nationalist framework within which they operate. Truth commissions investigate the national history of human rights violations committed by Argentines against Argentines, Chileans against Chileans, and so forth. The reconciliation sought by truth commissions is national reconciliation. However, the limitations of the framework are apparent when the direct and indirect participation of the United States in human rights violations is taken into account. Although final reports recognize more or less the participation of the United States in human rights violations, truth commissions so far have not been conceived in ways that the United States can be brought into the process of truth and reconciliation.

Truth commissions' nationalist framework reinforces post–Cold War triumphalism. By framing human rights violations within the boundaries of the nation, truth commissions end up silencing the responsibility of the United States. The nationalist framework allowed the U.S. ambassador to Guatemala to comment after the public announcement of the commission's report, "I believe that the report's focus is appropriate, that these were abuses committed by Guatemalans against other Guatemalans—the result of an internal conflict" (Navarro 1999). Notice that these statements were made in spite of the fact that the U.S. funding and training of the Guatemalan army was publicly acknowledged.

The same dilemma over apportioning responsibility arises in the most recent case of a truth and reconciliation commission created in 2001 in Peru. Peru's *Truth and Reconciliation Commission* (CVR) presented its *Final Report* in August 2003. Similarly to other truth commissions, Peru's CVR did not offer a systematic discussion of the responsibility of the United States in human rights violations. The *Final Report* offers valuable information about the United States's role in human rights violations in Peru, but stops short of treating it as a *responsible actor* in the violence. The *Final Report* presents information about the influence of "low intensity conflict" (LIC) strategies and training in the School of the Americas (SOA) on the implementation of counterinsurgency strategies, and "negotiations" between Peru and the United States. With this information, the CVR had enough evidence to bring in the United States as a *responsible actor* into the process of truth, justice, reparation, and reconciliation; but it did not.

Conclusions

Most people believe that we have entered a phase of history known as the post–Cold War. I would add that together with opening a new chapter in

history, the task of 'facing history' has only started. It is important to understand how truth commissions are helping to bury the past of the Cold War.
To fully enter into the post–Cold War world we have to close the books on
the Cold War–past. Can Peru's TRC contribute to the end of the Cold War?
In the final pages of the Introduction, the TRC's *Final Report* stated:[34]

> the Commission places its work within the framework of a world scenario
> that shows uncertain paths. Human rights culture and its supporting insti-
> tutions are fragile and based on the consensus of States. In certain moments,
> like at the beginning of this century, fear of violence may generate a spiral of
> reprisals that can affect international legality and reduce the possibilities of
> strengthening the rights of nations and citizens of the world.

The TRC was right in believing that "fear of violence" was going to "generate
a spiral of reprisals," but their statement is too abstract. The TRC did not
clearly indicate who are the actors in the "world scenario" responsible for
manipulating fear to justify violence.

The absence of the United States as a responsible actor in human rights
violations in Peru is a key point of reference for understanding the TRC. As
stated by the TRC, truth has two dimensions: ethical and scientific.[35] The
narrative not only has to explain the direct and indirect causes of violence,
but responsibilities need to be established, as well. Peru's TRC together
with other truth commissions have great potential for initiating a global
process of truth, justice, reparation, and reconciliation. A crucial step in
this process is to bring in the United States as a responsible actor. Progress
in the human rights agenda requires victims interpelating perpetrators as
actors with the obligation to repair the harm done. Asking the government
of the United States for "aid" to fund reparations programs goes against this
spirit. The participation of the United States in reparations programs has to
be conceptualized in terms of obligation, not as a favor.

Notes

1. Henkin indicates that the "Communist bloc, Saudi Arabia, and South Africa
   abstained" (1979, 231).
2. See also Henkin (1979) *How Nations Behave*, chapter 12.
3. See U.S. Department of State, Office of the Spokesman, *Press Statement*, March 9,
   1999 <http://secretary.state.gov/www/briefings/statements/1999/ps990309a.
   html>. "Secretary of State Madeleine K. Albright will travel to Antigua,
   Guatemala on March 10–11 to join President Clinton for the Central American
   Summit. At the March 11 summit, the President and the Secretary will confirm

U.S. commitment to continued support for relief efforts and the promotion of peace, democracy and economic development in the region."

4. See "Of Truth and Apologies. The Guatemalan Truth Commission & the U.S. Role," *Latin American Working Group*, March 1999. Accessed at <http://www.lawg.org/truth.htm>.

5. See also "En la búsqueda del perdón auténtico," *La Prensa Libre*, Guatemala, March 13, 1999.

6. For media coverage in the United States see: Robert Kagan and William Kristol, "Clinton's Sorry Excuse for a China Policy," *The Weekly Standard*, March 22, 1999 <http://www.seip.org/people/kagstan11.htm>. Michael Radu, "An Apology Instead of a Policy: U.S. Blunders in Latin America," *CNS Information Services*, March 23, 1999 <http://www.conservativenews.org/Politics/archive/199903/POL1999o323a.html>. "Of Truth and Apologies. The Guatemalan Truth Commission & the U.S. Role," *Latin American Working Group*, March 1999 <http://www.lawg.org/truth.htm>. Mary McGrory, "Apologies are U.S.," *Washington Post*, March 14, 1999; "En la búsqueda del perdón auténtico," *La Prensa Libre*, Guatemala, March 13, 1999. Andrew Reding, "A Genocide Tribunal for Guatemala," *Journal of Commerce*, March 18, 1999. Edward S. Herman, "The Godfather's New World Order," *ZMagazine*, March 1999 <http://www.zmag.org/Zmag/articles/may99herman.htm>. Bill Vann, "Clinton's Crocodile Tears for Central America," *World Socialist Website*, March 1999 <http://www.wsws.org.articles/1999/mar1999/clin-m12.shtml>. Bob Harris, "Guatemala: Clinton's Latest Damn-Near Apology," *Humanist*, May/June 1999. Jim Lobe, "Rights: Time for a US Truth Commission," *www.oneworld.org*, March 14, 1999. For media coverage in Central America see: "Clinton se marcha sin pena ni Gloria," *La Prensa Libre Guatemala*, March 12, 1999. "Donaciones y crédito financiero no son suficientes," *La Prensa Tegucigalpa*, Económicas, March 13, 1999. "Lo que la visita nos dejó," *La Prensa Managua*, March 13, 1999.

7. See *Guatemala: Memory of Silence. Report of the Commission for Historical Clarification. Conclusions and Recommendations* <http://shr.aaas.org/ guatemala/ceh/report/english/toc.html>.

8. See William J Clinton, "Remarks in a Roundtable Discussion on Peace Efforts in Guatemala City," *Weekly Compilation of Presidential Documents*, vol. 35, no. 10: 377–418. Accessed at <www.frwais.access.gpo.gov>.

9. See "Clinton Praises Uganda For Strides Made In Education," *The White House*, March 15, 1998.

10. See "President Clinton Apologizes," *The Associated Press*, March 15, 1998.

11. See *Nunca Más. Informe de la Comisión Nacional sobre la Desaparición de Personas* <http://www.desaparecidos.org/arg/conadep/nuncamas/nuncamas.html>, chapter V, "The Doctrinary Support of Represión." (Translation from English into Spanish by the author.)

12. The quote is from General Onganía, the man responsible for the 1966 military coup. See *Nunca Más*, chapter V.

13. *Nunca Más*, chapter V.

14. All quotes are from the *Report of the Chilean National Commission of Truth and Reconciliation*, Part Two, Chapter One, "The Political Context." Accessed at <http://www.usip.org>.

15. See *From Madness to Hope: The 12-Year War in El Salvador: Report of the Commission on the Truth for El Salvador*, Belisario Betancur (Chairman), Reinaldo Figueredo Planchart, and Thomas Buergenthal, Epilogue. Accessed at <http://www.usip.org/library/tc/doc/reports/el_salvador/tc_es_03151993_intro.html>.

16. See "Truth and its Consequences," *Commonweal* 120, no. 8 (April 23, 1993): 4–5.

17. See *From Madness to Hope: The 12-Year War in El Salvador: Report of the Commission on the Truth for El Salvador*, Belisario Betancur (Chairman), Reinaldo Figueredo Planchart, and Thomas Buergenthal, Introduction. Accessed at <http://www.usip.org/library/tc/doc/reports/el_salvador/tc_es_03151993_intro.html>.

18. See "Inmigración EE.UU por expulsar a guatemaltecos y salvadoreños ilegales," *Prensa Libre* Guatemala, March 10, 1999.

19. See "Deportaciones de ilegales empañan visita de Clinton a Centroamérica," *La Prensa*, Tegucigalpa, March 8, 1999.

20. The Conflict Resolution Consortium of the University of Colorado. Accessed at <http://www.colorado.edu/conflict/peace/treatment/truth_com.htm>.

21. The National Security Archive is available at: <http://www.gwu.edu/~nsarchiv/nsa/the_archive.html>.

22. See "With Clinton in Guatemala," *www.accuracy.org*, March 10, 1999.

23. The United States Institute of Peace's *Truth Commissions Digital Collection* is available at <http://www.usip.org/library/truth.html#tc>.

24. See <http://www.doj.gov.za/trc/index.html and http://www.cverdad.org.pe/>.

25. See University of Colorado, Conflict Research Consortium, "International Online Program on Intractable Conduct. Truth Commissions," <http://www.colorado.edu/conflict/peace/treatment/truth_com.htm>; Creative Associates International, Inc., Conflict Prevention Web, Tool Category F: Judicial/Legal Measures. 23. War Crimes Tribunals/Truth Commissions. See <http://www.caii-dc.com/ghai/toolbox23.htm>.

26. Virtual Truth Commission, available at <http://www.geocities.com/~virtualtruth/index.html>.

27. See "The Truth About Guatemala," *The Washington Post*, Editorial, March 1, 1999, p. A18.

28. See Patrick J. Buchanan, "Let Pinochet Go!" *Internet Brigade*, December 1, 1998 <http://www.buchanan.org/pa-98-1201.html>.

29. See *Nunca Más. Informe de la Comisión Nacional sobre la Desaparición de Personas* <http://www.desaparecidos.org/arg/conadep/nuncamas/nuncamas.html>, chapter V, "The Doctrinary Support of Repression." (Translation from English into Spanish by the author.)

30. This statement was made on September 13, 1995, two days after the 22nd anniversary of the military coup. See "The case of Pinochet. Prosecute & Punish? Or Forgive and Forget?" Available at <http://cyber.law.harvard.edu/evidence99/pinochet/PPFFTTF.htm>.

31. See the Executive Branch Ministry of Justice, Undersecretary of the Interior, Supreme Decree No. 355, "Creation of the Commissionon Truth and Reconciliation," Santiago, April 25, 1990.
32. Kaplan (1994).
33. Huntington (1993) became a classic of this ideological position.
34. Comisión de la Verdad (2003), Introduction, p. 45.
35. Ibid., 32.

BIBLIOGRAPHY

Babington, Charles. 1999. "Clinton: Support for Guatemala Was Wrong." *Washington Post* (11 March): A1.

Brown, Chris. 1992. *International Relations Theory. New Normative Approaches.* New York: Columbia University Press.

———. 1999. "Universal Human Rights: A Critique." Pp. 103–27 in *Human Rights in Global Politics*, ed. Tim Dunne and Nicholas J. Wheeler. Cambridge. Cambridge University Press.

Buchanan, Patrick J. 1998. "Let Pinochet Go!" *Internet Brigade*, December 1 <http://www.buchanan.org/pa-98/1201.html>.

Bush, George. 2002. *The National Security Strategy of the United States.* Washington D.C.: The White House (September).

Chomsky, Noam. 1998. "The United States and the 'Challenge of Relativity.'" *www.zmag.org*.

Clinton, William J. 1999. "Remarks in a Roundtable Discussion on Peace Efforts in Guatemala City." *Weekly Compilation of Presidential Documents*, vol. 35, no. 10 (frwais.access.gpo.gov): 377–418.

Comisión de la Verdad y Reconciliación. 2003. *Informe Final.* Lima.

Donnelly, Jack. 1999. "The Social Construction of International Human Rights." Pp. 71–102 in *Human Rights in Global Politics*, ed. Tim Dunne and Nicholas J. Wheeler. Cambridge: Cambridge University Press.

Evans, Tony. 2001. *The Politics of Human Rights. A Global Perspective.* Sterling, Virginia: Pluto Press.

Falk, Richard. 1999. "The Challenge of Genocide and genocidal Politics in an Era of Globalisation." Pp. 177–94 in *Human Rights in Global Politics*, ed. Tim Dunne and Nicholas J. Wheeler. Cambridge: Cambridge University Press.

Gibney, Mark and Erik Roxstrom. 2001. "The Status of State Apologies." *Human Rights Quarterly* 23, no. 4 (November): 911–39.

Gibney, Mark, Katarina Tomasevski, and Jens Vedsted-Hansen. 1999. "Transnational State Responsibility for Violations of Human Rights." *Harvard Human Rights Journal*, 12 (Spring): 267–95.

Godoy, Lina. 2003. "CVR buscará apoyo del Banco Mundial." *La República,* June 8 <www.larepublica.com.pe>.

Harris, Bob. 1999. "Guatemala: Clinton's Latest Damn-Near Apology." *Humanist* (May/June).

Hayner, Priscilla. 2002. *Unspeakable Truths. Facing the Challenge of Truth Commissions.* New York and London: Routledge.

Henkin, Louis. 1979. *How Nations Behave. Law and Foreign Policy,* second edition. New York: Columbia University Press.

———. 1990. *The Age of Rights.* New York: Columbia University Press.

Herman, Edward S. 1999. "The Godfather's New World Order." *ZMagazine* (March) <http://www.zmag.org/Zmag/articles/may99herman.htm>.

Huntington, Samuel. 1993. "The Clash of Civilizations." *Foreign Affairs* 72, no. 3 (Summer): 22–50.

Ignatieff, Michael. 2002. "Human Rights, the Laws of War, and Terrorism." *Social Research* 69, no. 4 (Winter): 1137–58.

———. 2001. "The Attack on Human Rights." *Foreign Affairs* 8, no. 6 (November/December): 102–16.

Kagan, Robert and William Kristol. 1999. "Clinton's Sorry Excuse for a China Policy." *The Weekly Standard,* March 22 <http://www.seip.org/people/ kagstan11.htm>.

Kaplan, Robert D. 1994. "The Coming Anarchy." *The Atlantic Monthly* 273, no. 2 (February): 44–76.

Klare, Michael T. 1995. *Rogue States and Nuclear Outlaws: America's Search for a New Foreign Policy.* Hill and Wang.

Latin American Working Group. 1999. "Of Truth and Apologies. The Guatemalan Truth Commission & the U.S. Role" (March) <http://www.lawg.org/truth. htm>.

Lobe, Jim. 1999. "Rights: Time for a US Truth Commission." *www.oneworld.org,* March 14.

McGrory, Mary. 1999. "Apologies are U.S." *Washington Post* (March 14).

Nardin, Terry. 1983. *Law, Morality, and the Relations of States.* Princeton: Princeton University Press.

Navarro, Mireya. 1999. "Guatemalan Army Waged 'Genocide,' New Report Finds." *New York Times* (February 26).

Radu, Michael. 1999. "An Apology Instead of a Policy: U.S. Blunders in Latin America." *CNS Information Services,* March 23 <http://www. conservativenews.org/Politics/archive/199903/POL1999o323a.html>.

Reding, Andrew. 1999. "A Genocide Tribunal for Guatemala." *Journal of Commerce,* March 18 <www.joc.com>.

Rice, Condoleezza. 2000. "Exercising Power Without Arrogance." *Chicago Tribune,* op-ed column (December 31).

U.S. Department of State, Office of the Spokesman. 1999. *Press Statement,* March 9 <http://secretary.state.gov/www/briefings/statements/1999/ps990309a.html>.

Vann, Bill. 1999. "Clinton's Crocodile Tears for Central America." *World Socialist Website* (March) <http://www.wsws.org.articles/1999/mar1999/clin-m12. shtml>.

Chapter 6

Environmental Movements in East Central Europe: Between Technocracy and the "Third Way"

Lars K. Hallström

Or did I think that the pollution would be blacker just because it has been recently more publicized?

—Eva Hoffman (1993)

The "widening" and "deepening" of a pan-European political entity, which proceeded at a startling pace during the 1990s and began the twenty-first century with a common currency (the Euro) and a membership of 27 member-states, has raised a series of both practical and theoretical questions. Initially a response to the tragedies of World War II and a way to limit any possible military aspirations in post-Fascist Germany, the European Union (EU) has become a case study in globalization. Characterized by multiple, often intersecting and overlapping levels of decision-making (see for example Hooghe and Marks 2001), transnational policy networking, and a reconfiguration of Westphalian sovereignty, the EU has been referred to, perhaps erroneously, as the first postmodern state. This "regulation of deregulation" above the nation-state in the EU has not only weakened or modified traditional locations of political authority, it has also coincided with processes of fragmentation, subnational and regional empowerment, and the decline of state-based authority.

While its final form remains to be seen (see for example the comments of Rainier Baubock in 2000 and the ongoing constitutional debate), the emerging polity creates demand for new models of governance that globalization itself is unlikely to generate (Telò 2002). Super-regionalism (Delamaide 1994), subregionalism, and other non-state oriented centralizing tendencies point to political coordination both beyond and within the nation-state, but the EU also provides an insight into the possibilities of world governance and administration. Despite a substantial institutional and sociopsychological democratic deficit, the EU provides a model for a third possibility of post-Westphalian governance, based on "a kind of new political economy of world capitalism demanding 'reregulation' at the global level, by reinforcing regionalized democratic governance. . . ." (Telò 2002, 13). The political evolution of the EU demonstrates that regional and supranational "reregulation" tends to reinforce, rather than restructure, the layers of multilevel governance. However, this reinforcement of structure can also shift the distribution of authority toward "public centrally coordinated governance" (13), presumably with new institutional and procedural designs to meet the democratic challenges of such a shift.

It is this presumption that forms the basis of this chapter, and its relevance to the concept of arrogance. More specifically, I am concerned with improving understandings of the integratory process in Europe during the 1990s as part of a larger political framework built upon technical expertise, positivist-scientific knowledge, and bureaucratic, rather than public or civil, authority. While the various treaties and agreements that have led to the EU have long contributed to both a technocratic and largely nonparticipatory policy-making environment, the political reforms demanded since 1993 to accommodate the postcommunist member-states have been marked by a particularly unique form of arrogance found within both the concept and practices of "Eurocratization." As significant (re)distributions of policy-making and political authority took place during the 1990s in order to bolster institutional democracy in both the EU and states of East Central Europe (ECE), the participatory or deliberative components of democratic policy-making did not keep pace with those changes. In fact, the relevance of arrogance for this chapter can be found in the Eurocratic project itself, and in particular the failure of the EU to capitalize on opportunities to foster a more public form of governance. Instead, the EU remained embedded within technocratic and nonpublic forms of governing, effectively limiting the opportunities for European publics to participate in the integration process.

This research, therefore, examines an under-explored area of the literature on the EU—the implications of further integration and the enlargement of the EU, as a component of global governance, on civil society. Economic and political integration have led to the harmonization of many public policies, regulations and standards, and a shift in legislative power to

Brussels in numerous policy domains. However, this shift has not been accompanied by a public legitimization of the European institutions. In fact, the opposite has proven true, as the 1990s saw the end of "permissive consensus" toward the EU. As a product of both a historical reliance on technical and administrative expertise and an institutional gap between citizens and European legislation, the EU has demonstrated a substantial "democratic deficit" that has been the subject of considerable analysis (Chryssoochou 1998; Andersen and Eliassen 1996; Weiler 1995). In this text, I wish to include in this concept what Chryssoochou (1998) refers to as the "sociopsychological" elements of democracy for those post-communist states that became full members of the EU in 2004. I do so by examining the ways that East Central European attitudes and engagement toward civil involvement in public policy have changed due to European integration.

Despite the installation of democratic constitutions, institutions, and procedures, citizens of the East Central European states must cope with new understandings of the relationships that can exist between citizens, citizen groups, and decision-making or administrative institutions (Rosenberg 1996). At the same time, these new understandings are complicated by the presence of the EU as a policy and decision-making body, which expands both the physical and policy-making context within which civil society must function. In conjunction with Articles A and B of the Treaty on European Union (which mandate the creation of an "ever closer union among the peoples of Europe . . ." and "promote economic and social progress . . . through the strengthening of economic and social cohesion") integration into the EU implies important civic and cultural elements that must be addressed. The institutions of the EU not only structure and participate in the integratory process in their own arrogant right, but also have cultural effects within both these institutions, and the larger policy regimes present in the member and applicant states (March and Olson 1984; Bulmer 1997; Mazey and Richardson 1996). Political integration is, therefore, engaged in a "reshaping" of decision-making and regulatory power, which includes the role(s) of nonprofit and citizen-based groups.

I present five general trends in environmental policy-making and participation that should be considered when contemplating the politics of European enlargement, governance and environmental policy. First, although the number of nongovernmental organizations (NGOs) has increased dramatically across ECE since 1990, there has been a shift away from public input, participation, and involvement in the environmental policy process. This has coincided with an increased role for the EU as it became the primary source of environmental policy, legislation, and concern. Second, national-level actors and institutions have mediated this shift, and have demonstrated the capacity to both increase and diminish the roles for environmental NGOs. Third, both environmental NGOs and the larger populations of the Czech Republic and Poland had similar responses to political change between 1990 and 1996. Fourth, both NGOs and policy makers in Poland showed greater openness and activity in policy-making in the latter half of the 1990s. Poland may, therefore, serve as a "front-runner" in dealing with the sociocultural elements of European integration. And fifth, transnational cooperation and activism, while present, remain a limited factor in East Central European environmentalism. This is the result of a number of factors, including European integration, that have pushed many environmental groups toward highly localized, small scale, and "nonpolitical" activities.

Based on these findings, I draw a less than positive conclusion about not only the democratic direction and effects of policy integration and the pending enlargement of the EU, but also about the emergence of a supranational or even global civil society. While Kaldor (2003, 77) points to dissident movements and "Third Way" in ECE as both a legitimating force for the concept of civil society and a factor in the establishment of "the engagement of social movements, NGOs and networks in the process of constructing global governance" the experiences of the environmental groups and organizations in Poland and the Czech Republic post-1989 illustrate that supra-state politics need not be moving toward a "whole new [political] space" that deepens the democratic process. In fact, the primary thrust of this research is that as a previously integral component of antipolitical civil society in ECE, environmental groups have been more than "tamed" (to use Kaldor's terminology). Indeed, rather than becoming "interlocutors on issues with which new social movements are concerned" and being able to "challenge the official experts" (Kaldor 2003, 89), with some exceptions the 1990s saw environmental organizations withdraw from their position as participatory opportunities in civil society. Although such groups are both voluntary and participatory, I use the experiences, perceptions, and opinions of ECE environmentalists to challenge the idea that supranational politics is becoming a new form of democratic politics.

Communism, Environmentalism, and the "Third Way"

One of the most devastating legacies of communist rule in ECE is the damage imposed on the environment. Although the environmental situation in the Accession Countries has improved in the past decade, it is important not to underestimate the severity of environmental damage in numerous regions of ECE. Similarly, while there have been substantial improvements in certain environmental sectors such as classic air pollutants (SO_2 and particulate emissions), other sectors such as transportation, climate protection, energy consumption, and the construction of European-standard infrastructure continue to pose significant environmental challenges (ÖGUT 2002).

Although recent improvements are impressive, they are not the sole result of new technologies or policy reforms. Many of the initial improvements in air and water quality were the direct result of closing communist-era industrial facilities due to inefficient production, high costs, and excessive energy intensity. Similarly, as industrial and transportation infrastructure improves, a new set of environmental problems emerges. Not only are there massive costs associated with cleaning up the environmental damages created prior to 1989, but there are also considerable segments of the East Central European population, particularly in rural areas, without access to sewage or water treatment plants. Additional concerns include the environmental costs of building and connecting autobahn-style highways to "the rest of Europe," and the environmental implications of increased automobile emissions, fuel consumption, and extremely high levels of energy intensity (Czech MoE 1999; ÖGUT 2002; Interview with member of Children of the Earth, 2000). The environmental problems in states such as the Czech Republic and Poland, and how they are dealt with, provide an opportunity to examine the implications of rapid increases in consumption. They also provide insight into the ways that business, political, and nongovernmental organizations are learning to interact in an emerging supranational policy environment.

Environmentalism provided one of the few legal opportunities for political participation, dissent, and the reinforcement of civil society in many Eastern European states. It therefore provides a key case study into both the emergence and withdrawal of East Central European populations from public life at a time of shifting regulatory and political power. Not only had environmental groups provided an organizational and intellectual background for many dissidents, but also as newly democratic regimes, addressing the environmental failures of the Communist Party was an important goal. Environmental policies could further the legitimacy of democratic politics via both effective problem-solving and participatory inclusion, but could also assist in reducing the health and safety concerns of both politicians and publics in Germany and Austria. As a result, immediately after the collapse of communism, environmental groups and variants of environmentalism briefly held a position of some influence in policy-making.

The combination of a participatory impetus and the release of pent-up political demand led to a number of short-lived attempts to foster the combination of environmentalism and civil society in ECE. This new sense of participatory opportunity was both a continuation of existing civil practices such as Solidarity in Poland, and an attempt to reach the possibilities of Havel's "non-political politics" (Stroehlein 1999, 2) and the Third Way—an alternative to both the representative democracies of the West and the state socialism of the Soviet Union. Building on the large-scale protests and existing organizations in ECE, the early years of the 1990s saw an explosion in the number of nongovernmental organizations in general, and over fifty percent of the environmental organizations in this region were created since that time. Such movements were to provide the direction and guidance for a new democratic politics, one that challenged the tyranny and mistrust of state socialism with high levels of political involvement, debate, participation, and interaction: a Third Way between the risks of unrestrained capitalism and the stifling control of communism.

The term "Third Way" has reemerged in Western political discourse, specifically in Germany, Blair's U.K., and the United States as variant of reform liberalism or "capitalism with a human face" (Barry 1999). However, in ECE the "Third Way" embodied the importance of civil society in a more participatory and ultimately democratic form of governance (Tucker et al. 2000). Drawing from dissident scholars in East Germany, Czechoslovakia, and Poland, the possibility of *obcanske iniciativy* (civic initiative or "parallel society") completely separate from the state was to play a large part in the ways these states could take advantage of their apparently unique position in 1990. This continued throughout the 1990s, with divisions hinging largely on how public participation could improve political life. Despite continued intellectual support, ultimately the views of neoliberals such as Vaclav Klaus won out, largely limiting transition to consolidation of the party system and privatization, and creating a clear emphasis on a top-down, Schumpeterian model of democratic politics.

This neoliberal dismissal of civil society and the democratic potentials that it holds stands in contrast to the findings of this and other authors (Fagin and Jehlicka 1998; Fric 1999; Pehe 1993). The 1990s saw a substantial public retreat from politics and a decline in confidence in both the newly democratic institutions and the political direction of postcommunism/ European integration. While it has become apparent that the realities of transition have fallen short of the hopes for a "Third Way" guided by civil society, the paths followed thus far by the Czech Republic and Poland as they moved to membership in the EU show the continued importance of public participation and a civil sphere.

Although Kaldor (2003, 108) argues that "through access, openness and debate, policy-makers are more likely to act as a Hegelian universal class, in the interests of the human community" the 1990s saw a continued supranational preference for technical and scientific knowledge, limited grassroots or participatory involvement in policymaking, and little potential for a democratic form of global governance. Indeed, although the EU has taken steps to include environmental NGOs in policy-making, the majority of environmental groups have become increasingly separated from politics beyond the local or municipal level. In turn, the decline in requisite "social networks in which relations of trust, reciprocity, and cultural learning are shared" (Tarrow 1996, 16) at national levels through the 1990s seriously limits the potential for effective activism at the transnational level, and points to the possibility of long-term political problems for both supranational and national-level European democracy.

The Czech Republic

Czech Environmental Policy and Nongovernmental Organizations

From a democratic perspective, environmental policy-making in the Czech Republic has been increasingly removed from public input through the 1990s, both in the perceptions of the public and in the day-to-day practice of politics. Many politicians and public officials are seen as corrupt and dishonest, and the bureaucracy is viewed by many as a source of problems, rather than solutions. The process of meeting the *acquis communitaire* continues to demand considerable time and resources, and while this process is recognized by many policy elites as unavoidable and necessary, it is underlined with a certain degree of resentment. From the perspective of environmental NGOs, their capacity to work with both citizens and the government is highly dependent on the agenda of that government. As a result, a number of NGOs feel that the Klaus years during the early-to-mid-1990s have an effect that is still being felt, and privatization and economic reforms have led to a public disenchantment with both the Czech state and enviro-political organizations.

The perception of a corrupt and dishonest set of politicians and public officials, motivated by the *Občanska demokratická strana* (Civic Democratic Party (ODS)) model of economics-first, politics-second reform points to a valid reason for concern from the general public, NGOs, and even the EU.

From a participatory and democratic perspective, the economic emphasis under the Klaus government since 1992 (in contrast to the more integrated and long-term approach under Pithart [Prime Minister 1990–92]) has resulted in a relatively strong central state and political parties. This approach has created only a limited role for those organizations that might impede the economic reform program, and particularly those of a civil or protest nature.

As Potucek (1999) writes, the development of public policy in realms not directly connected with economic reforms was of low priority from the onset of the first Klaus administration (1992–96). Czech reformers have emphasized those organizations consistent with the economic goals of neoliberalism and EU membership, but have suppressed "the development of NGOs, professional associations, and public or quasi-public sector organizations" (Orenstein and Desai 1997, 44). At the same time, when citizens have attempted to provide nonexpert input into policy decisions, the response from the administration has usually not been favorable or positive.

This has been the case in a wide range of policy issues, including education and public health reforms in the mid-1990s. Ministries are still developing, and as a result often have underdeveloped experiences with public partnership. There are two implications arising from this: (1) ministerial and bureaucratic staffs are embedded in a tradition of imposing policy requirements, rather than trying to develop policy in conjunction with public and expert input; (2) rather than being readily available to the public, policy information remains a commodity. Until the end of the 1990s, freedom of information (FOI) did not exist in any legal detail. This gave administrators no real reason to share research and their own functions with the public. This, combined with the bureaucratic practices of both Communist and pre-Communist Central Europe, has constrained the participatory options for an already reluctant and suspicious population.

Despite suspicions of the government and the state, the number of NGOs, environmental and otherwise, has expanded considerably since 1990. In fact, only 27 percent of all nonprofit organizations in the Czech Republic were established before 1990, and 66 percent of Czech organizations are completely new. Ecological and environmental organizations compose over nine percent of the nonprofit sector in the Czech Republic, and over half of these groups were created or gained independence after 1990 (Fric 1999).

Environmental NGOs are engaged in a wide range of activities across the Czech Republic. Some groups adopt a very hands-on approach to environmental protection, sending groups of volunteers to work in national parks and protected areas for weeklong periods during the summer (Interview with former member of Brontosaurus, May 13, 2000). Other groups focus on small, localized projects, such as the reintroduction of indigenous species to waterways, tree planting, small-scale cleanup projects, and weekly informational sessions (Interview with members of Czech Union for Nature Conservation, May 19, 2000). However, environmental groups in the Czech Republic have also been engaged in democratic and mobilizing activities. These include attempting to gather general public support via petitions, demonstrations, and other activities, but are usually protest-oriented. In the majority of cases, these protests were targeted against a specific decision or procedure of a ministry or government (Fric 1999).

At the same time, environmental groups see a number of barriers to developing further public support that lie within the public itself. By far the largest of these is the perception of a distinct lack of public knowledge. Fifty-four percent of environmental groups see this as a problem, followed by concern that the public actually distrusts their organization (29 percent). These are followed by concern over hostile attitudes, at a relatively small 15 percent. More recently, the Ministry of Environment survey (2000) found that 60 percent of Czechs believe environmental organizations to be useful. However, a full 25 percent of Czechs feel that environmental groups and organizations are actually harmful. This sentiment is particularly true for men, members of the older generation, people from small villages or towns, and those with low levels of education (Fric 1999; Sofres-Factum 2000). As might be expected, hostility toward groups is higher toward those that do try to engage and mobilize the public.

With such difficulties in trying to gain public support and volunteer workers, a number of environmental organizations have now shifted toward a more expertise-oriented role. While still engaged in local "clean-up" or environmental education activities, they increasingly draw on in-group expertise and education. For groups such as Children of the Earth and the Czech Union of Nature Conservation, the 1990s have seen a move toward a combination of decreasing environmental protest, increasing local activism, and participation as environmental experts in Environmental Impact Assessments (EIAs). Children of the Earth, for example, attempts to fight its battles on two fields. On the one hand, they are trying to lobby the Czech government to resist the building of highways and transportation infrastructure (itself part of becoming a member in the EU) on conservation grounds. On the other, members of this group also participate in the later stages of EIAs as public participants, and in the earlier stages as ecological experts.

From a democratic perspective, the emphasis on expert rather than public knowledge in this process has both obvious and hidden effects. Even though certain environmental groups may be invited or selected to participate as experts, they are not included in what many feel is their primary role: to express a public perspective on environmental policies and quality. There is currently little opportunity for citizens to express their thoughts in this capacity, and in many cases when environmental organizations are involved, they do not improve the number of such opportunities. EIAs in the Czech Republic are not required to interact or liaise with any of the communities involved, and in none of the interviews conducted in this study was this seen as an issue. In fact, a number of NGOs place themselves in an informational role between government and the public. Through the use of newsletters, E-mail, and websites, these groups often pass information downward, rather than collect information from the public and transmit it to the state.

Being contracted as an expert to assist in an EIA is more than a recognition of environmental knowledge for a Czech NGO. It is also a means of earning revenue, and a way to directly influence public policy in a legal manner. Revenue is important for two reasons. First, the idea of funding for such groups coming from the public, rather than the state, is still new. Almost all groups in the Czech third sector rely heavily on funding from either or both the EU and the Czech government, but it is also well recognized that such groups should become self-supporting (Interview in Prague, with *Nadace rozvoje obcanske spolecnosti*—(Czech) Civil Society Development Foundation [NROS], May 2000). Contract environmental work is therefore a viable means of supplementing what are by most accounts fairly meager membership fees. Second, earning revenue from government contracts or subcontracts is also a means of reducing any reliance on state and particularly foreign funding. In fact, it is conceivable that for many groups losing the revenue from EIAs imposes costs too great to consider adopting a more proactive approach toward including public participation and potentially alienating what limited government support exists. Not only does this participation contribute to the continued fiscal survival of the group, but it can also provide a channel of access to policy elites. In contrast to other forms of interaction between Ministry, bureaucrats, and environmental associations, working in EIAs may give certain environmental groups the only real opportunity to directly influence environmental policies and quality.

This is in part a reaction to the political climate in which environmental NGOs must function. The ability of even large groups to influence policymaking has declined considerably since the early 1990s, and relationships between the Ministry of the Environment and NGOs have been described as being "based on suspicion bordering on outbursts of hostility" (Fagin and Jehlicka 1998, 122). What little formal contact there is between environmental groups and government is often *ad hoc*, and particularly under the Klaus government met with little success. Continuing financial problems, often combined with disproportionate inflation, have further reduced the resources available to environmental groups in the Czech Republic. This has lessened their capacity to both attract a popular base of support and lobby the government. It has also affected the ability of larger associations to attract and remunerate staff and skilled employees. Due to this combination of factors, many of the larger environmental organizations have become increasingly professional in their approaches toward lobbying public policy actors, but have done so at the expense of popular support.

While there have been considerable steps toward the harmonization of environmental legislation, the environmental policy and planning system in the Czech Republic at the national level is hampered by a variety of factors. These include bureaucratic disabilities, a traditional administrative culture that is both top-down and still adapting to capitalist economies, and a limited role for nonbusiness participation in the environmental policy process. The Communist tendency toward centralization of decision-making has been overcome in many ways, providing local governments considerably more authority and autonomy over environmental planning. However, unless environmental groups have preestablished connections to municipal officials or mayoral offices, the opportunities for participation are also limited. Indeed, some environmentalists in the Czech Republic feel that, without explicitly pro-environment political connections, many of the localized efforts of environmental groups would be in vain (Interview with members of Czech Union on Nature Conservation, May 15, 2000).

As a result, Czech politicians and policy officials have also moved much of their attention away from the Czech public toward the EU in the guidance and implementation of environmental policy. This was particularly problematic under Klaus during the early- to mid-1990s, when EU-oriented privatization policies led to widespread corruption and public disenchantment. These issues are in turn compounded by a historical tendency toward top-down patterns of public administration, where private or organized participation by citizens is viewed with some concern. In total, Czech environmental politics have followed the lead of Western countries by moving toward a strong, state-oriented pattern of environmental policy. Membership in the EU requires a strong state and administration to manage the policy requirements of the *acquis*, and civil society has been expected to play a role largely in name only.

Czech environmental groups have for the most part recognized this shift, and have chosen to either adapt to a formalized, professional pattern of interaction with policy-makers, or to refocus at a small-scale, localized level. As a result, most environmental groups point to much better relations with local and regional officials than at the national level, and have had considerable success with small-scale, population-specific projects. However, the Czech Republic is still developing the pattern of relations between the EU, national government, and lower levels of Czech government. As a result, EU and national policies often override preexisting local efforts, and can undermine their democratic impetus (Fric 1999; Interview with member of Czech Ministry of Environment, May 24, 2000).

Poland

From an economic perspective, Poland has remained one of the strongest East Central European actors. This, combined with its size and strategic location, placed Poland in perhaps the strongest negotiating position of the ECE states with the EU. However, there is also an awareness that the integration process can be manipulated by politicians and bureaucrats. This is seen to be particularly problematic in terms of the Euroskepticism that is developing in Poland. While the Polish population has generally been in favor of membership in the EU, there is a trend toward decreasing public support. This "is mainly the fault of the government . . . sometimes the governmental officials try to create policies which are painful . . . but they say, this is the EU, it's not me . . ." (Interview with member of P.M.'s Office. Warsaw, June 1, 2000). Similarly, there is limited information in Poland regarding the EU, and public participation and input in the integration process has been marginal throughout the 1990s. This is the product of a limited freedom of information policy, a historically constrained role for public participation in policy, and a sociopolitical environment that is often conflicted and fragmented.

While a number of environmental organizations have embarked on a process of professionalization, maturation and participation with political and policy elites, in the early 1990s several withdrew from active participation in public policy and the transformations of Poland. A result of legal impediments, a tradition of protest-based opposition, and cultural factors, the dramatic expansion of participatory opportunities in Poland was met with a slow and cautious response. This combination of factors limited the early success of the Polish environmental movement as a whole, but it is also indicative of the slow growth of general political activity in Poland on the whole during the early 1990s (Kolarska-Bobinska 1994). Many environmental groups were faced with a double reconfiguration: the dramatic transformation of their very character from a protest basis to political actor, and making the shift to the new political and economic institutions adopted at the beginning of the 1990s (Hicks 1996).

Environmental movements expanded in number throughout the 1990s in Poland, but primarily as a product of group fragmentation. This created a combination of expressive protest groups, locally and nationally based NGOs with a range of funding, ecological expertise, staff, and volunteers, and issue-specific groups based primarily on volunteers. Environmental groups therefore could initially chose to continue the patterns of behavior established during the 1980s, make the shift to "Western-style" interest intermediation and participation in policy-making, or withdraw to a much smaller and localized level (Hicks 1996; Interview, Klon Offices, June 13, 2000). The development of environmental participation can therefore be viewed in two stages. The first stage, taking place during most of the 1990s, was one of expansion in terms of the number of groups functioning in the environmental sphere. It was also a period of separation or withdrawal from the Polish state. The second stage, which began in the very late 1990s and continues today, is characterized by a shift by many groups toward more civil patterns of interaction. While many environmental groups still prefer spontaneous and small-scale activities, many environmental organizations point to better interaction with Polish policy-makers and administrators, changes in the legal environment for NGOs, and support from both EU and national institutions. As a result, Polish NGOs generally point to improvements in civil life, and possibly hold the greatest potential for contributing to transnational or pan-European environmentalism.

One way in which this pattern of development may be understood lies in the increased costs of public participation in policy-making, particularly when compared with the pre-1989 period. While political protests under Communism in Eastern Europe were usually met with a firm hand, environmental protests were an "acceptable" means of political expression. They did not carry the same potential costs as other, more explicitly anti-Communist methods. After 1989, the appeal of such activities increased due to the decreased likelihood of repression, and such activities have remained popular, particularly for smaller, more localized groups. This, combined with a still-changing set of personal, social, and economic values, has caused many environmental activists to shy away from more "civil" forms of interaction with new decision-making structures and institutions. As a result, those environmental organizations that have not at least partially embraced the Western models of interest organization have withdrawn from the current institutional world of environmental policy (Kolarska-Bobinska 1994). Instead of participating as formal NGOs in policy-making, or functioning on a protest basis, these portions of the "new" Polish environmental movement have engaged in such activities as humor of the absurd, rejecting all forms of violence, and establishing a certain distance from reality. Such organizations were generally based on a very loose and informal sense of organization, and were often based on direct democratic decision-making, consensus building, and a high level of interaction among members (Glinski 1998).

Not only were such groups at odds with many of the larger or more successful environmental organizations, but this withdrawal from participation in the policy process is also indicative of a distinctly negative perception of both politics and public involvement during the early- to mid-1990s, particularly among the younger segments of the Polish population. As Millard (1994, 233) pointed out, the significant political gains of the early 1990s did little to democratize the relationships between citizens and the Polish state. He writes:

> Indeed, there emerged important indications of a new legitimation crisis. Trust in politicians evaporated . . . Grassroots activity remained very limited—indeed, the most active groups were those of the old regime, especially trade unions and pensioners' associations . . . Hopes of a regenerated, animated civil society proved premature. Political apathy, a sense of inefficacy and demobilization reigned.

In the same vein, survey data from 1992 showed that over 76 percent of Poles felt that those wishing to be involved in social or public causes were incapable of affecting any real change (Glinski 1998, 140) Skepticism about the effectiveness of environmental activism has also remained high across all levels of government during this time (Hicks 1996). Similarly, while there has been a dramatic increase in opinion supporting politics and public life since 1995, tolerance and social interaction all fell in the latter half of the 1990s (PGSS 1999).

The "Communist Legacy" also played a role in limiting public involvement at both general and environmental levels at this time. The years under Communist control left Poland without a stable set of values and norms other than anti-Communism, and at this time there was a return to previously established patterns of political behavior. Not only did the younger portions of the population at this time treat politics as a deceitful and unethical activity, where individual rather than public aspirations were satisfied, but there is a larger cultural phenomenon within short-term post-Communist societies (Glinski 1998, Interview, Warsaw, Klon Offices, June 13, 2000). Specifically, there was confusion over the role of the state, and concerns over social status also led to a nonparticipatory perspective among many members of the general public. Similarly, organizational disorder and traditions of "oppositionism" rather than cooperation compromised the ability of groups and citizens to participate in the new practice of governance.

Having found influencing national or voivod-level policies difficult, a number of environmental groups in both Poland and the Czech Republic have concentrated their efforts locally since the mid-1990s. Projects such as tree planting, roadside clean-up, or restocking local ponds with indigenous fish are small-scale, affordable, and often socially rewarding. However, such projects are also low-key, difficult to publicize, and as a result often not seen or noticed by the public at large. At the same time, such activities are a considerable step away from larger-scale, protest-oriented activities that generated both publicity and a certain sense of public involvement, and while they can carry negligible political costs, they require both a greater time and physical commitment. Additionally, the rewards of participating in localized "greening" activities are often not realized immediately, making it difficult to attract public attention.

Part of this low ecological profile also lies in the difficulty of both affecting policy change and publicizing it. In contrast to the Communist era, the Polish press through the 1990s was presented with a huge range of issues and topics. This led to the relegation of environmental concerns to secondary status, particularly as economic and political concerns drew public attention. Similarly, the relative weakness of the Ministry of Environmental Protection, combined with the issues of access and integration into the EU noted above made identifying and "hitting" policy targets successfully all the more difficult. As a result, a number of the environmental groups interviewed in 2000 are taking innovative steps toward creating a more public image. By documenting their activities and programs in an effort to attract new members, environmental NGOs in Poland continue to try to raise public awareness about environmental considerations, and improve public legitimacy.

The Changing Face of Polish Environmentalism

Having evolved from a largely protest-oriented base in the 1980s, the environmental movement in Poland of the 1990s saw growth from approximately 135 organizations in 1989 to seven hundred in 1995, and over one thousand by 1998 (Glinski 1998). Environmental organizations in Poland now cover a wide range of activities and ideological perspectives, ranging from the long-established Polish League for Nature Conservation (established in 1928) to "deep ecology" groups and specialist/expert groups composed of economists, lawyers, and policy specialists. With this expansion in both the accessibility and scope of environmental groups have come qualitative changes in the form, style and even structure of environmental groups.

While some groups still engage in strongly resistant or protest activities, there has been a slow yet identifiable shift toward more "civil" forms of interaction and attempts to influence decision-making bodies. The more radical environmental groups from the 1980s have either disappeared or remain protest-oriented, while the more neutral groups have made the initial move toward becoming professional "interests." In fact, as a member of a Polish flagship organization pointed out, many NGOs have little choice but to do so. Sentiment exists among NGOs that a nonprofessional approach can be used as an excuse by public administrators. "We don't talk with you because you're not professional . . ." (Interview, Klon Offices, June 13, 2000) is a phrase if not heard then assumed among NGOs in general, a phrase which places such groups in a difficult position. At the same time, attempts to install the leadership and structure necessary for professional activities in the environmental policy sphere have been met with resistance. Throughout much of the 1990s, many NGOs displayed antiorganizational and antihierarchical characteristics, as well as a distrust of governmental bodies and granting organizations that expected them to function as such. Environmental groups have also been forced to overcome their distrust of other organizations in order to develop strategies of cooperation, information-sharing, and alliances in order gain both decision-making and public support (Jancar-Webster 1998).

Despite the improved role for NGOs in general, there are still a number of issues facing such groups, including legal, economic, and cultural issues. With legal, constitutional, and informational issues still being resolved, environmental groups have an uncertain place in the policy-making process. Additionally, they face a public that is unsure of NGOs in general and is caught between trying to affect environmental change in both policies and society at a time when resistance to environmental concerns is high. Members of environmental NGOs attribute this primarily to economic concerns, and hope that the combination of membership in the EU and new legislation regarding nongovernmental groups will improve both the perception and role of NGOs in Poland (Interview with members of the Institute for Sustainable Development (INE), June 16, 2000; European Environment Centre (E.E.C.), June 16, 2000). Similarly, environmental groups are aware of the cultural issues still present in Poland. "People are hard to change . . . they're not used to certain things . . . it will be a challenge for Poland in the next five to ten years to implement [new] laws" (Interview with members of E.E.C., June 16, 2000). As a result, environmental NGOs express concern about not only their perceived place in the political system, but also the environmental challenges that economic restructuring and industrial development can bring.

On the whole, the environmental NGOs interviewed for this study, while aware of problems that limit their effectiveness and public support, are positive about their role in Polish governance, and the role of the EU. Despite the legal and transparency issues facing these groups, the role for NGOs in policy-making is perceived as improving. Environmental groups are now invited to participate with the Ministry of Environmental Protection, one of the few Ministries to formally do so, and through the establishment of new offices and programs have much more information about both European and Polish environmental policy agendas. However, environmental NGOs also recognize that a non-protest role in policy-making is still new for decision-makers, administrators, and the groups themselves. As a result, both groups and officials have only recently started to interact in an institutionalized and civil fashion. Representatives from both groups attribute these improvements, at least in part, to the influence of the EU and the drive for membership.

The emerging forms of environmental NGO activity in Poland are increasingly modeled on Western forms of interest intermediation. Rather than simply staging protests and interventions, many groups are now involved in trying to monitor those in power, attempting to influence policy formulation and implementation, suggesting alternative perspectives on environmental problem solving, and providing both formal and informal means of education to the general public. Such "professional" behavior is indicative of a maturing body of interests, with formal strategies, expert guidance, and both intergroup cooperation and communication becoming normal. These groups have learned, both on their own and with the assistance of Western parent organizations, to conduct environmental campaigns, administer and fundraise for educational and lobbying projects, and to understand the legal and political environments within which they must function (Glinski 1998).

At the same time, there is some resistance to such steps. Representatives of NGOs participating in regional and national forums throughout Poland have expressed their need for structural guidance and a more formal pattern of interaction, but in doing so, there is still a conflict with the more *ad hoc* and spontaneous aspects of traditional nongovernmental interaction. "On the one hand, people need leadership, they ask (*sic*) and demand leadership. On the other hand, if you try to make it structural, in the NGO world people don't like it . . ." (Interview, Klon Offices, June 13, 2000). This is characteristic of the environmental movement in Poland. The skills and behavioral patterns learned during the 1980s and 1990s are still present, and differing conceptions of what environmental groups are leads to debate (Glinski 1998).

Environmental NGOs and Supranational Governance

In addition to cooperating with national groups and institutions, environmental groups in Poland and the Czech Republic also interact, to widely varying degrees, with the EU. However, this takes place not with the EU as a policy actor and a target for lobbying, but as a source of funding, information, and communication (Interview with members of E.E.C., June 16, 2000). There is, therefore, considerable interaction between some environmental groups and both the European Commission and the EU Delegations. While the EU recognizes the importance of NGOs in general, and provides considerable funding to aid in the development and support of the nongovernmental sector, environmental groups in ECE typically see little role for themselves in the European context. Instead, they tend to emphasize the role of the EU in providing information and environmental data that is then to be disseminated to the public. For example, the E.E.C. provides translations of EU environmental materials and legislation in order to make these data more accessible to Poles (Interview, Warsaw, June 16, 2000).

None of the groups interviewed in this study saw much of a role for environmental NGOs at the European level beyond the purely informational, but a small number of Polish NGOs do provide input to the EU on environmental issues and enlargement of the EU. Since 1999, three Polish environmental NGOs have become much more involved with the European Commission by participating in regular meetings with representatives from the EU and 30 NGOs from across ECE. These meetings are intended to provide the EU with regional input from nongovernmental sources on regional issues, and how these issues may interact with enlargement (Interview with members of E.E.C., June 16, 2000). However, given the presence of over one thousand environmental groups in Poland alone, and several hundred in the Czech Republic, the inclusion of only three in these meetings points to a limited level of input.

This is particularly true for smaller and localized environmental groups, who usually find it more difficult to obtain the membership and resources necessary to even consider addressing European-level policy-making. Lacking these resources, such groups must rely on larger groups to interact with other organizations and policy officials in Brussels. At the same time, those EU officials, such as Commission Desk Officers, who do travel to the negotiating countries, also can find it difficult to create contact with the smaller groups. These problems are increased if groups are not located in a large city such as Krakow or Warsaw, as Desk Officer visits are usually brief and very busy (Interview, DG Environment, April 14, 2000). This creates a number of different yet related results. Naturally, such groups begin to recognize the limited role made available to them, and the causal relationships between their size, resources, location and input into environmental policy. They also begin to modify their behavior, focusing their energies on local activities that they have the personnel and resources to afford, and attempting to exert some sort of political influence on local and municipal politics, thus leaving the national and European scene to the larger groups.

This is consistent with what Glinski (1998, 145) calls a "richly differentiated structure of group interests," but it must be interpreted in two ways. In Poland, the development of an environmental movement that is diverse, multifunctional, and after a period of withdrawal from politics, increasingly active in mainstream environmental politics is generally considered a positive sign of civil recovery or reemergence. Environmental groups are strategically attempting to function at different levels, and even interact with groups in other European states. In the Czech Republic, the withdrawal is indicative of an acquiescence to the realities of integration. For many Czech environmental NGOs, nonexpert involvement in both Czech and EU-level policy is a receding possibility, and such groups have turned inward. Although transnational organizations such as Greenpeace or Children of the Earth do provide some cross-national linkages, for the majority of environmental groups the combination of economic concerns, new and remote policy actors, and domestic politics has reduced the participatory opportunities in postcommunist life.

There are, therefore, a number of elements at play in the changing face of public participation in environmental policy in ECE. First, the sheer number of environmental organizations and interests has increased dramatically, a product of political liberalization, increased availability of international funding, and the pursuit of multiple, often narrow interests. There is little doubt that the increase in the number of these groups means they must compete for publicity, membership, and access to policy-making. This issue will compound as the EU reduces funding for civil society programs (Interview with staff of NROS May 2000). Second, the legal and legislative elements of creating a more participatory form of policy-making are not yet completely in place. While environmental groups have been able to participate in certain policy activities since 1980, limitations remain on where participatory activities are allowed, and at which stage in the policy process. Third, traditional practices of public administration in Poland, the Czech Republic, and the EU do not view citizen or lay participation in public policy in a positive light. There are common misconceptions about the role and consequences of public input into policy, but these misconceptions are beginning to diminish. Fourth, public administration in both

Poland and the Czech Republic is being reformed, both internally and with the assistance of the EU. This includes the recent "export" of administrative expertise from EU member-states to a number of the negotiating countries, transferring both participatory and exclusionary practices of policy administration. Fifth, Polish and Czech populations are politically fragmented, however, Poles are recovering from the withdrawal from public life during the 1990s. From the environmental perspective, environmental organizations and groups were seen as neither efficacious nor particularly useful politically. Sixth, despite steps fostering civil society, social capital, and involvement in the public sphere, both populations during the 1990s became increasingly "uncivil," demonstrating private virtues such as distrust, dislike, and an inability to compromise. In line with this, public opinion and grassroots participation is often separate from political and policy decision-making.

This is an issue that is only marginally affected by the processes of policy transfer and integration. Both environmental interests and policy officials frame the development of the third sector in Poland within a domestic light. Unlike the Czech Republic, environmental groups and officials see each other, and the EU, in a positive light. The maturation of participation in environmental policy, and the subsequent effects on civil society, is attributed to both national activities and the "help" of the EU. From this perspective, while civil society in Poland is far from being fully realized, the environmental movement has recently started to make a positive addition to its development.

While the environmental movements of ECE have become increasingly diverse, the role of nongovernmental organizations and citizen groups as actors in politics and public policy must also overcome the larger social tendencies present following democratic transition. Specifically, as an enclave of civil society, environmental groups have the capacity to provide legitimacy to Polish and European policies, as well as contributing to more public or "citizenly" attitudes. This can take place through the creation of tolerance, negotiating skills with both government and other groups, and responsible social actions. In order to do so, however, the public at large must be willing to tolerate the presence of such groups and the skills they can provide. This chapter shows a trend toward an initial decline in public involvement during the early and mid-1990s. However, in Poland the latter years of the 1990s, and particularly 2000, show the beginnings of a return toward more civil politics that is consistent with the behavior and opinions of Polish environmental groups. As a result, it is possible that Poland is once again taking on the role of "front-runner" in adjusting to political life in the new Europe—what remains to be seen is how this political life will change, across ECE, after May 2004.

A Pan-European Environmentalism?

For states such as Poland and the Czech Republic, meeting the requirements of the EU membership and the environmental *acquis communitaire* requires not only huge amounts of investment and spending in technology, infrastructure and clean-up, but also coming to grips with the growing political phenomena associated with limited sovereignty (Agh 1999). There is an increasing sense among both the public and decision-makers that they have traded one master for another. While no one interviewed in the course of this research stated that life was better under the Communists, there is little doubt that there is (1) an increasing public awareness of policy transfer to the EU; (2) some dissatisfaction with that policy transfer; and (3) a gradually changing view on the appropriate role of the state and government (Vecernik 1999). The populations of the Czech Republic and Poland are not only still trying to come to terms with democratic institutions and the role they can, should and will play; they are doing so in a consistently changing policy environment. Processes such as the Twinning Programme, recent membership negotiations, and the harmonization of public policies with the EU mean that there are multiple influences on the shape of public policy from "above." These influences, in turn, compete with the administrative structure and practices of the ECE countries, national party agendas and politics, as well as the voice of public opinion, when and where it is expressed, in the formation, implementation and enforcement of public policy.

In step with the reconstitution of political authority to regulate globalizing processes, the emergence of transnational political and policy spaces creates new demands on not just the core concepts used in the social sciences (Coleman 2003, 2), but also on the ways in which governance functions. As borders, boundaries, and the locations of policy-making authority change in the creation of a "complex political structure" (Cox 1987, 255) that others (see for example Kuehls 1996) have even characterized as "rhizomatic," the democratic question becomes one of not just who participates in this space, but also who and what permits them to do so. Political space, particularly in the European context, is shifting toward multiple levels and locations of policy-making authority and autonomy in order to realize relevant trans, supra, and subnational outcomes, and it is important to recognize that this coalescence of political space need not coincide with the expansion of democratic governance.

Recently, Kaldor (2003) and Beck (2002) have drawn attention to the possibilities of a global civil society that moves away from territorially bounded meanings and the "war-making colonial state," and instead draws upon public engagement and conversation. This perspective is compatible with Ernest Gellner's conception of a civil society that "while not preventing the state from fulfilling its role as keeper of the peace and arbitrator between major interests, can nevertheless prevent it from dominating and atomizing the rest of society." (in Kaldor 2003, 45) In both cases, the emergence of a transnational civil society, while not yet a reality of European political life, would seem to be a natural outcome of the supranational political and policy impetus of the EU. Indeed, the presence of a European civil society, existing as a subset or more regionally based example of a postliberal civil society, may be one of the only solutions to the sociopsychological democratic deficit present in the EU, particularly as it enlarges in 2004. However, while new(er) conceptions of civil society are, as Kaldor writes (2003, 46) "both an aspiration and a description of a partial and emergent reality," the case of EU environmental policy and enlargement illustrates the difficulties of achieving this reality.

1989 was a profound year for global politics, marking the resurgence of civil society as a viable concept to both political practice and theory, and ultimately providing the trigger for renewed European integration. The "Third Way" promoted by the East European dissidents gave credence to the concept of civil society around the world, and theoretically permitted the "engagement of social movements, NGOs and networks in the process of constructing global governance" (Kaldor 2003, 77). The evidence presented here, however, demonstrates that this engagement, and indeed the tentative optimism of authors such as Kaldor and Beck, may be premature. Specifically, the experiences and opinions of both EU environmental policy elites (see Hallstrom 2004) and ECE environmental groups point to an emerging surpranational polity that has "tamed" some ECE groups into professionalism and institutionalized patterns of intermediation, but has largely pushed a previously integral element of civil society away from environmental policy and policy-relevant public communication.

In the Czech Republic, and to a lessor degree Poland, the shift from national to European loci of environmental policy-making has not corresponded to a rise in NGO and social involvement to create a transnational social movement that contributes to global civil society. Indeed, this very shift is one of the causes that has pushed environmentalism away from politics, and while there have been tentative steps toward dealing with European policies and institutions, the primary effect of European governance has been to trigger a withdrawal from civil involvement. Dalton and Rohrschneider (1999) point out that there are considerable asymmetries in the patterns of international environmental action, and for Europe this is manifested in an East/West environmental divide. Unlike the politically consolidated states such as Germany, France, or Belgium, countries in ECE have not yet, or are only just beginning to develop the apparatus of interest intermediation and public involvement in environmental policy. European integration has compounded this factor by adding another, still evolving level of actors, opportunity structures, and policy regimes to be learned. As a result, while becoming members of the EU may act as an initiative toward improving environmental regulations and quality, the role for public involvement and the development of both national and European civil societies is limited.

Ultimately, without significant changes in the process and style of European environmental policy, much of the democratic potential held by environmental groups in ECE will go untapped, and quite possibly diminish.

BIBLIOGRAPHY

Agh, Attila. 1999. "Processes of Democratization in the East Central European and Balkan States: Sovereignty Related Conflicts in the Context of Europeanization." *Communist and Post-Communist Studies* 32: 263–79.

Andersen, Svein. S. and Kjell Eliassen. A. 1996. *The European Union: How Democratic Is It?* London: SAGE.

Barry, Norman. "Germany and the Third Way." Accessed January 20, 2003 <http://www.libertyhaven.com/countriesandregions/germany/thirdway.shtml>.

Baubock, Ranier. 2000. Public lecture at the Austrian Permanent Representation at the European Union.

Beck, Ulrich. 2002. *Macht und Gegenmacht in globalen Zeitalter*. Frankfurt am Main: Suhrkamp Verlag.

Bulmer, Simon. 1997. "New Institutionalism, The Single Market and EU Governance." Accessed January 18, 2002 <http://www.arena.uio.no/ pulications/ wp97_25.htm>.

Chryssochoou, Dimitris. N. 1998. *Democracy in the European Union*. London: Tauris Academic Studies.

Coleman, William. 2003. *Globality and Transnational Policy-making in Agriculture: Complexity, Contradictions, and Conflict*. Institute on Globalization and the Human Condition Working Papers. No. 6.

Czech Ministry of Environment. 1999. *Report on the Environment in Czech Republic in 1998*. Prague: MoE.

———. 1999. *State Environmental Policy*. Prague: MoE.

Dalton, Russel J. and Robert Rohrschneider. 1999. "Transnational Environmentalism: Do Environmental Groups Cooperate Globally?" Centre for the Study of Democracy, University of California, Irvine. Research Papers.

Delamaide, Darrell. 1994. *The New Superregions of Europe*. New York: Penguin Books.

European Commission. 2002. "The Enlargement of the European Union on May 1, 2004." *EU Info*, 6, 1.

Fagin, Andrew and Petr Jehlicka. 1998. "Sustainable Development in the Czech Republic: A Doomed Process?" Pp. 113–28 in *Dilemmas of Transition: The Environment, Democracy and Economic Reform in East Central Europe*, ed. S. Baker and Petr Jehlicka. London: Frank Cass.

Fric, Pavel. 1999. *Activities and Needs of the Non-Profit Organizations in the Czech Republic*. Prague: ICN—Information Center for Foundations and Other Not-For-Profit Organizations.

Glinski, Piotr. 1998. "Polish Greens and Politics: A Social Movement in a Time of Transformation" Pp. 129–53 in *Environmental Protection in Transition: Economic, Legal and Socio-political Perspectives on Transition*, ed. Daniel H. Cole and John Clark. Aldershot: Ashgate.

Hallström, Lars. K. 2004. "Eurocratizing Enlargement? EU Elites and NGO Participation in European Environmental Policy" Pp. 175–93 in *EU Enlargement and the Environment: Institutional Change and Environmental Policy in Central and Eastern Europe*, ed. J. Carmin and Stacy Vandeveer. New York: Routledge.

Hicks, Barbara, E. 1996. *Environmental Politics in Poland: A Social Movement Between Regime and Opposition*. New York: Columbia University Press.

Hooghe, Liesbet and Gary Marks. 2001. "Types of Multi-level Governance." European Integration Online Papers, 5, no.11.

Institute for Social Studies, University of Warsaw. 1999. *Polish General Social Surveys*. Warsaw, Poland.

Jancar-Webster, Barbara. 1998. "Environmental Movement and Social Change in the Transition Countries." *Environmental Politics* 7, no.1: 69–92.

Kaldor, Mary. 2003. *Global Civil Society: An Answer to War*. London: Polity.

Kolarska-Bobinska, Lena. 1994. "Social Interests and Their Political Representation: Poland in Transition." *British Journal of Sociology* 45, no.1: 109–25.

Kuehls, Tom. 1996. *Beyond Sovereign Territory*. Minneapolis, Minn.: University of Minnesota Press.

March, James G. and Johan P. Olson. 1984. "The New Institutionalism: Organizational Factors in Political Life." *American Political Science Review* 78: 734–49.

Mazey, Sonya and Jeremy Richardson. 1993. *Lobbying in the European Community*. Oxford: Oxford University Press.

Millard, Frances. 1998. "Environmental Policy in Poland." *Environmental Politics*, 7, no.1 (Spring): 145–61.

ÖGUT (Austrian Society for Environment and Technology) 2002. *Environmental Policies, Strategies and Programmes of the EU Accession Countries in Central and Eastern Europe*. Austria: ÖGUT.

Orenstein, Mitchell and Raj M. Desai. 1997. "State Power and Interest Group Formation." *Problems of Post-Communism* 44, no. 6: 43–53.

Pehe, Jiri. 1993. "Waning Popularity of the Czech Parliament." *RFE/RL Research Reports* 2/45.

Potucek, Martin. 1999. *Not Only the Market: The Role of the Market, Government and Civic Sector in the Development of Postcommunist Societies*. Budapest: CEU Press.

Rosenberg, Tina. 1995. *The Haunted Land: Facing Europe's Ghost After Communism*. New York: Vintage Books.

Sofres-Factum, s. r. o. 2000. Prague: Sofres-Factum.

Tarrow, Sidney. 1998. "Fishnets, Internets and Catnets: Globalization and Transnational Collective Action." Pp. 228–44 in *Challenging Authority*, ed. Hanagan, M. Leslie Page Mooch and Wayne Brake Minneapolis, Minn.: University of Minnesota Press.

Telò, Mario. 2001. *European Union and New Regionalism: Regional Actors and Global Governance in a Post-Hegemonic Era.* Aldershot: Ashgate.

Tucker, Aviiezer, Karel Jakes, Marian Kiss, Ivana Kupcova, Ivo Losman, David Ondracka, Jan Outly, and Vera Styskalikova. 2000. "From Republican Virtue to Technology of Power: Three Episodes of Czech Nonpolitical Politics." *Political Science Quarterly* 115, no. 4: 421–45.

Vecernik, Jiri. 1999. "The Middle Class in the Czech Reforms: the Interplay between Policies and Social Stratification." *Communist and Post-Communist Studies* 32: 397–416.

Weber, Cynthia. 1995. *Simulating Sovereignty—Intervention, the State and Symbolic Exchange.* United Kingdom: Cambridge University Press.

Weiler, Joseph. 1995. "European Democracy and its Critique: Five Uneasy Pieces." *EUI Working Papers.*

Part 3

Facing the Dangers of Replicating Global Arrogance

Chapter 7

Challenging and Reinforcing Dominant Myths: Transnational Feminists Use the Internet to Contest the War on Terrorism

Krista Hunt

Since its use at the Fourth World Conference in Beijing in 1995, feminists have been discussing the Internet's potential to "link women worldwide" (Bautista 1995). Its ability to facilitate the speedy transfer of information across borders, circulate urgent calls for action, respond in "real time" to international events, and create links between activists in various countries make it an important tool for transnational feminism. Arguments that a global women's movement is impossible without the Internet, or that the Internet allows feminists to "work together in more cooperative, cross cultural ways than ever before" push feminists to examine more closely the potential of this technology for feminist politics (Whaley 1996). Since the Internet can provide the tools to foster solidarity, exchange information, build coalitions around global issues, and strengthen local organizing, it is a technology that can—in theory—weave a World Wide Web of feminists committed to addressing the effects of power on diverse groups of women. According to Jenny Radloff and Sonja Boezak, "the use of electronic spaces is an example of how women are stretching the boundaries and divides that allow them to network, organize and change the world" (Womenspace 2000). As such, the Internet provides important opportunities for transnational feminists to challenge the oppression of women.

In order to assess these claims about the potential of the Internet for feminist politics, this paper looks specifically at how the Revolutionary Association of the Women of Afghanistan (RAWA) and its allies abroad are using the Internet to raise awareness about the situation of Afghan women and to mobilize a transnational feminist response to the war on terrorism. From an examination of this particular case, I argue that the Internet provides the space to both challenge and reinforce dominant myths, leading to complex conclusions about the potential of this technology to fight the oppression of women.

In terms of challenging dominant myths, the Internet has provided a space for feminists to mobilize against the impact of the war on terrorism for women, especially those in Afghanistan. Through their connection to the Internet, feminists are disrupting the U.S. administration's "myths of sacrifice and protection" that frame the war as a necessary sacrifice undertaken to liberate Afghan women and vehicle to protect the rights and freedoms of women around the world. By challenging these myths, feminists vocalize their opposition to the war on terrorism and U.S. hegemony more generally.

This mobilization of feminists in response to the war on terrorism exemplifies the ways that feminists are challenging violence and domination through the Internet and using this space to envision alternatives. In particular, the Internet has facilitated feminist discussions about the effects of war on Afghan women, the cooptation of women's rights to justify the war, and the necessity of having Afghan women represented in government. The use of the Internet by RAWA and feminists opposed to the war on terrorism exemplifies the power of this technology to give voice to women who have in many different ways been silenced off-line. For RAWA, the Internet has been essential in providing them with a way to subvert the suppression of dissent by the Taliban and the invisibility of women. It has also been invaluable in raising the international community's awareness about the human rights abuses being committed against women in Afghanistan. For feminists outside Afghanistan, the Internet has enabled them to vocalize dissent for the war, which has been silenced in the mainstream media (Bunting 2002). In this way, the Internet has provided an essential space to contest the U.S. administration's myth making about the war.

However, use of this technology also reinforces dominant myths that have plagued global feminism, limiting the potential for transnational feminism to represent diverse groups of women and effectively mobilize against oppressive power. Global feminism has been critiqued for assuming women's oppression to be universal and ahistorical, in essence, for focusing on the similarities between women at the expense of their differences. As a result, global feminism has been accused of colonizing the voices and experiences of other (non-Western/racialized/poor) women (Alexander and Mohanty 1997, xix). In many ways, global feminism has served to alienate ever more groups of women from feminism, as global feminisms have often been elite/Western feminisms in disguise.

This tendency within global feminism is acute with respect to the Internet since most women fall on the wrong side of the digital divide. As Nancy Hafkin and Nancy Taggart report, only one percent of people in many developing countries have access to the Internet, which is structured by race, class, geographical, and cultural factors (Hafkin and Taggart 2001, 1, 27–32). As I argue, the visibility that connected feminists[1] have often translates into assumptions by themselves and others that they are able to represent and speak for particular groups of women. For instance, while RAWA's virtual activities have greatly contributed to increased international attention to the situation of women in Afghanistan, their political visions for the future of Afghanistan are not representative of all Afghan women. However, the international presence afforded by the Internet has led to assumptions that RAWA is the "authentic" voice of Afghan women since this is the voice that is most often heard in cyberspace. Western feminists have embraced RAWA as the native informant on Afghan women, not only because of their visibility, but also because of the convergence of their political visions with those of Western feminists. As a result, connected feminists are reproducing the "myth of gender inclusiveness" by assuming that these connected women are able to speak for all Afghan women. In essence, these connected feminists reproduce a kind of "global feminist arrogance." These tensions highlight the complex and contradictory ways that the Internet is simultaneously being used to fight against the domination and oppression women and reproduce it. As such, they complicate technotopic claims about the potential of building transnational feminist networks through cyberspace.

RAWA

The Revolutionary Association of the Women of Afghanistan was founded in 1977. RAWA founders were urban, university-educated women whose long-term objective was to "involve an increasing number of Afghan women in social and political activities aimed at acquiring women's human rights and contributing to the struggle for the establishment of a government based on democratic and secular values" (RAWA 2002a). To this end, RAWA became involved in creating clandestine schools for women and girls, providing health care, and creating income generating projects within

Afghanistan and the refugee camps in Pakistan. RAWA's work continues to be based on the belief that the only way to achieve a stable peace in Afghanistan is to establish freedom, democracy and social justice.

In 1996, RAWA became the first Afghan political group to "get connected" to the Internet (Howell 2000). However, getting connected was and continues to be no small task. The group learned how to use the Internet from scratch and still relies on donations from supporters to upgrade hardware, maintain their site, and pay for the domain name. RAWA members based in Pakistani refugee camps have depended on support from administrators in Pakistan in order to maintain their head-quarters in cyberspace (O'Connor 2002). As a result of the assassination of their leader by fundamentalists and the Afghan branch of the KGB (KHAD) in 1987, as well as continuous threats to other members, RAWA operates in secrecy (Richtel 2002). They have no official office, the location of their web-server is a secret, and their only headquarters are in cyberspace. RAWA's activities within and beyond cyberspace are extremely risky; during Taliban rule, RAWA members risked losing their hands for the information they posted on the web. Thus, RAWA has always struggled to maintain their virtual connections and, for security reasons, to remain virtual.

While RAWA members based in these refugee camps have managed to access the Internet, their members located within Afghanistan itself remain unconnected (BBC News 2001). Years of civil war have destroyed tele-phone infrastructure, in addition to the fact that new information tech-nologies are unaffordable for most Afghans. RAWA reports that only the UN, the Red Cross, and a few other NGOs have Internet access within Afghanistan (RAWA interview 2002). Therefore, RAWA members in Pakistan have to maintain their virtual connections to the outside world and post reports from members in Afghanistan (Symon 2001). In order to address the digital divide between its members, RAWA also downloads information from the Internet to print and distribute in refugee camps, as well as to members and supporters within Afghanistan (Tom 2000). Here, RAWA is the conduit for moving the "virtual" into the "real," thereby bridging the gap between connected and unconnected Afghan women.

Compounding these challenges, the Taliban monitored, and then in 2001 officially banned Afghans from using the Internet (Agence France-Presse 2001). Since most Afghans do not have access to the Internet, this ban was intended as a warning for groups such as RAWA who were using the Internet to expose the Taliban's abuses internationally. As RAWA members use the Internet from Pakistan, and are therefore not subject to this edict, the Taliban had to "get connected" in order to counteract the damage done by RAWA. Online, the Taliban issued a statement that "they are fully committed to the social, cultural and economic development of women in employment, education and other areas" (BBC News 2001). This response to RAWA's virtual activities shows that the political salience of the Internet for gaining international attention and support was not lost on the Taliban. The anonymity that RAWA has achieved through this space has provided them with a unique opportunity to reveal the abuses committed against Afghan women to the international community while maintaining their anonymity from those attempting to silence them.

RAWA's Internet activities attempt to bridge the gap between Afghan women and the international community by providing "the only alternative to state-controlled media" (Scheeres 2001). One RAWA member states that the reports on their website are unavailable anywhere else "because [RAWA receives] reliable and authentic reports directly from Afghanistan" (Howell 2000). During Taliban rule, freedom of the press was nonexistent, and RAWA's reports "provided the world with some of the only accounts of Taliban atrocities" (Price 2002). Since the overthrow of the Taliban, the current Afghan government has created a law guaranteeing freedom of the press (Voss 2002). However, the law includes a clause that "bans coverage of 'subjects that could offend Islam,' 'subjects that could dishonor the people' or 'subjects that could weaken the army of Afghanistan' " (Price 2002). There are fears that this clause will be applied to limit dissent, fears confirmed by reports from journalists that they have experienced censorship and intimidation from the government about what they write. Therefore, even in post-Taliban Afghanistan, RAWA's ability to provide independent news through the Internet about the situation in Afghanistan remains an important resource for the outside world.

Through their website, RAWA disseminates information about the group, their activities, and the status of women in Afghanistan. This virtual space allows them to represent the realities of life for Afghan women:

> The main reason for having a website is to make people around the world aware of the untold atrocities committed by Islamic fundamentalists in our country. . . . A great number of people from the outside world who did not know anything about the situation of Afghanistan got their first glance of the ugly reality through our website. (RAWA interview 2002)

Beyond highlighting the struggles faced by women in Afghanistan, the Internet serves as an international forum to expose the lack of support by international protectors of human rights (including the United Nations) and to lobby for international attention to the plight of women in Afghanistan. The website is used to raise money for their social programs, including clandestine schools for girls and mobile health care units, and to lobby the international community to actively work on behalf of Afghan women's rights. In essence, RAWA's virtual activities are an extension of their commitment to "act as witnesses and record what is going on inside the country" (Symon 2001).

Challenging Dominant Myths about the War on Terrorism

Pre–September 11, RAWA's virtual activities were most effective at gaining international attention from feminists who became aware of the condition of women in Taliban-ruled Afghanistan (Armstrong 2002). The Internet served to end the isolation of RAWA from the outside world, allowing them "unrestricted scope for looking around, finding, contacting, and getting to know other women's organizations and sharing our aims and objectives" (Howell 2001). It has also provided the tools for visibility and open communication—both of which have been severely restricted off-line. RAWA's website became their "face shown to the world"; a face that could not be revealed within Afghanistan (O'Connor 2000). The Internet opened a space for RAWA to expose the Taliban's oppression of women to the international community and network with women's groups from around the world. Most importantly, their virtual activities are a means to affecting change off-line, both in terms of raising money for their social programs and by gaining international support for their alternative vision of Afghanistan's future.

Since the events of September 11, RAWA's website has been bombarded by visitors trying to find out more about the situation of women in Afghanistan. In particular, RAWA's website has provided information to the international public which, until now, had largely been unaware of the situation in Afghanistan (Armstrong 2002, 161; Pollitt 2001). According to BBC correspondent Fiona Symon, "renewed media interest in Afghanistan in the wake of the bombings in Washington and New York has focused attention on RAWA" (Symon 2001). The increased demand for information on the Internet not only increased RAWA's audience, but also made it possible to raise awareness about the effects of the war on terrorism for Afghan women, the problems with U.S. support for the Northern Alliance, and their positions about how to achieve peace and security in Afghanistan. Through this space, RAWA was able to provide the connected world with a very different picture of Afghan women than that available through the news media. In contrast to dominant representations of Afghan women as faceless, voiceless, victims covered by the burqa, RAWA provides the international community with images of Afghan women risking their lives to actively struggle against misogyny and oppression.

Currently, RAWA's website is an important link in an expanding network of feminists who are fostering transnational opposition to U.S. imperialism and the gendered dimensions of the "war on terrorism."

Feminists from around the world have adopted RAWA's pioneering efforts at seizing the tools of the Internet in order to subvert the silencing of dissent in the news media that occurred post–September 11 (Jensen 2002; Tapper 2001). After the attacks, news reports and political commentary in the mainstream media were overwhelmingly supportive of U.S. President Bush's war on terrorism. Dissenting voices were in fact very few and far between. According to the *Artists Network*, whose members include Noam Chomsky, Eve Ensler, and Alice Walker, this was the result of a clear message from the Bush administration to withhold criticism in the name of patriotism (Artists Network). Indeed, White House spokesperson Ari Fleischer issued the following statement after TV personality Bill Maher criticized the government's handling of the war: "There are reminders to all Americans that they need to watch what they say, watch what they do, and this is not a time for remarks like that; there never is."[2] Echoing this, Bush's *Joint Address to the Senate and the House of Representatives*, in which he stated that "you are either with us or you are with the terrorists," sent the message to citizens and journalists alike that patriotism demanded solidarity and a united front. Even veteran Dan Rather admitted to the BBC that he was one of the journalists who put patriotism ahead of his professional responsibilities, and commented that "patriotism run amok" led journalists to censor themselves (Jensen 2002). Reacting to the concerted effort to close down debate and silence dissent in the news media, many dissenting voices moved onto the Internet. The redirection of dissent to the Internet facilitated an uncensored, more democratic debate about the war on terrorism than was possible in the mainstream media.

In response to this silencing of dissent, feminists began using this space to rally each other to resist the war on terrorism. The Canadian Association of Sexual Assault Centres and the Canadian Association of Elizabeth Fry Societies issued a statement via the Internet:

> It should come as no surprise that women's groups are among the first to call out in opposition to violent retaliation to the September 11 events. We wish for no more deaths in the flurry of international unrest. . . . We call on everyone in this country, individuals and organizations concerned about the struggle for equality, peace and justice, the right to free speech and participatory democracy, to link their voice with ours in this critical time. (CASAC 2001)

Canadian feminist Sunera Thobani reiterated this goal to mobilize transnational feminists against the war on terrorism. Online, Thobani argued "there will be no emancipation for women anywhere until Western domination of the planet is ended" (Thobani 2001a). She stated "in the current climate of escalating militarism, there will be precious little emancipation for women, either in the countries of the North or the South." These calls for action exposed the ways that this conflict affects women around the world and served to mobilize a feminist response to the war on terrorism.

Connected feminists have been extremely critical about the way the Taliban's oppression of Afghan women has been used to justify the war in Afghanistan. In particular, they have been vocal about the way that the media and politicians have appropriated the image of the burqa as the "totem of women's oppression." As Nelofer Pazira argues, "now television and newspapers use images of bewildered refugee children and women under the covering burka to justify one of the most unjust and unnecessary wars of our time" (Pazira 2001). They argue that this cooptation of women's rights has been nothing more than a media mobilization to gain the support of American women for the war (Ehrenreich 2001). For example, First Lady Laura Bush's radio address to the nation articulated America's opposition to the oppression of Afghan women and stated "the fight against terrorism is also a fight for the rights and dignity of women" (Flanders 2001). While the government and the media attempted to spin the war on terrorism as one that would champion women's rights and give Afghan women the freedoms that American women enjoy, many feminists were quick to reject this claim. Online, Laura Bush's address was criticized for jumping on the bandwagon of Afghan women's rights, in addition to being labeled paternalistic. As Sunera Thobani remarked, "if we listen to the voices of [Afghan] women, we will very quickly be disabused of the notion that U.S. military intervention is going to lead to the emancipation of women in Afghanistan" (Thobani 2001b). Feminist analyses point out the fact that the situation of Afghan women received little attention before September 11, with coverage of the destruction of Buddhist statues garnering more press coverage than the human rights abuses taking place under the Taliban regime (Pollitt 2001). The fact that violations against women's rights in Afghanistan have not been a pressing issue of international concern in the past belies the political motivations for publicizing these issues now.

They also point out that this sudden interest in the lives of Afghan women becomes even more suspect when one considers the violence that they have faced since the American attacks on Afghanistan began. While Bush declared in his State of the Union declaration that today, women in Afghanistan are free (Delphy 2002), Afghan women have been killed and wounded by U.S. bombs; caught in the crossfire of rival warlords; subjected to rapes, beatings, and abductions by the Northern Alliance; displaced from their homes and country; and have to contend with the worsening humanitarian crisis in Afghanistan. In contrast to media depictions of women shedding their burqas, Human Rights Watch reports that women in Afghanistan have been the victims of sexual violence by various armed factions and that they are limiting their movement outside of their homes and continuing to wear the burqa in order to protect themselves (Human Rights Watch 2002). RAWA argues that if the United States was genuinely concerned about women in Afghanistan, they would not be supporting the Northern Alliance. In their appeal to the UN and world community, RAWA states:

> Thousands of people who fled Kabul during the past two months were saying that they feared coming to power of the [Northern Alliance] in Kabul much more than being scared by the U.S bombing. . . . Though the [Northern Alliance] has learned how to pose sometimes before the West as "democratic" and even supporter of women's rights, but in fact they have not at all changed, as a leopard cannot change its spots. (RAWA 2001)

Even UN Secretary General Kofi Annan has warned that a culture of violence against women persists in post-Taliban Afghanistan (Associated Press 2002). Thus, First Lady Laura Bush's denunciations of the Taliban's treatment of women ring hollow considering the fact that the Northern Alliance is guilty of the same abuses. Through the Internet, RAWA and their allies contest U.S. myth making that the war is being fought in the name of Afghan women.

Connected feminists including RAWA are also using this space to present alternatives for the future government of Afghanistan. They argue that peace and democracy in Afghanistan and throughout the world are necessary conditions for improving the status of women. They contend that the empowerment of women is dependent on eradicating fundamentalism in all its guises. As Katha Pollitt states,

> Where women have education, healthcare and personal rights, where they have social and political and economic power—where they can choose what to wear, whom to marry, how to live—there's a powerful constituency for secularism, democracy and human rights. (Pollitt 2001)

Following the defeat of the Taliban, one of the most pressing issues for feminists has been the need to have women represented in the new Afghan government. Afghan women's rights advocates are demanding that women be included in the new government and are calling on feminists from around the world to help them achieve this.

To this end, the Internet is used to provide information and solicit participation for activities taking place off-line. Specifically, connected feminists are using the Internet as a tool in their efforts to ensure the inclusion of Afghan women in the political process. For instance, the Canadian Voice of Women for Peace (VOW) initiated an electronic letter writing campaign. The letter, which was sent to Jean Chretien, George W. Bush, Tony Blair, and Kofi Annan, stated:

> We call on those now involved in discussing post-Taliban Afghanistan to ensure prompt and effective action for the participation of Afghan women in government, in transitional and future arrangements, and in all stages of decision-making in other conflict resolution and peace processes. We reject absolutely that any complexities whatsoever in the Afghan situation can justify the exclusion of women from participation in these matters. (PAR-L listserve 2001)

VOW distributed their letter through the Internet and E-mail asking feminist organizations to lend their support in cosigning the letter. Using their virtual connections, the UN Division for the Advancement of Women sent out a call for information on Afghan women's groups in their efforts to have women represented at the Bonn meetings (Womenspace 2001). During the Bonn talks, the Feminist Majority Foundation updated connected feminists about the role of Afghan women in the new government (FMF 2001). At the end of the Afghan Women's Summit for Democracy in Brussels, which produced a list of demands including access to education, information, and the full participation of women in the reconstruction of Afghanistan, the proceedings were posted on the Internet (Afghan Women's Summit 2001). In the "Declaration of Solidarity," the Summit participants expressed their commitment to "mobilize a worldwide demand for the implementation of the Brussels Proclamation issued by the Afghan Women's Summit," something that has been facilitated through the use of electronic spaces. Through the Internet, feminists pressured the international community to put into practice their self-declared commitment to Afghan women's rights. In different parts of the world, feminists began linking their voices in support of Afghan women through efforts to lobby their respective governments to ensure the inclusion of Afghan women in the future of Afghanistan.

Following the establishment of the interim Afghan government, the Internet was used to discuss questions of women's representation in the new government. In response to the fact that after the first month of a six-month term Minister Sima Samar had yet to receive office space, staff, or funds to set up the Ministry of Women's Affairs, the International

Centre for Human Rights and Democratic Development initiated an Internet-based letter writing campaign urging Canadian Prime Minister Chretien and Foreign Affairs Minister Bill Graham to support the ministry (ICHRDD). Likewise, the Feminist Majority Foundation website posted an E-mail letter urging UN Secretary General Representative to Afghanistan, Lakhdar Brahimi, to provide adequate resources to the ministry. While Minister Samar remarked that having women in the interim government is a positive development, she also stated that in order to accomplish the work that is needed to improve the situation for women in Afghanistan, "[w]e will need a great deal of support and solidarity from women all over the world" (ICHRDD 2001).

The Internet has provided an essential, transnational space for RAWA to expose human rights abuses and build alliances within the international community regarding the situation of women in Afghanistan. Since September 11, the Internet has provided a space for critics of the war on terrorism to resist their silencing in the mainstream media, expose the strategic co-optation of women's rights discourse to legitimize the war, and call on world leaders to make good on their commitments to have Afghan women represented in government. Feminist responses to the war on terrorism have been facilitated by Internet technology, which has provided an alternative space for feminists to disseminate ideas that challenge the myths of the war on terrorism.

Reinforcing Dominant Myths about "Global" Feminism

Although the Internet has been an invaluable space through which to build transnational opposition to the war on terrorism and provide alternatives to violence and domination, its use has also reproduced a kind of "global feminist arrogance." Through the Internet, RAWA has become internationally recognized as the voice of Afghan women. However, in contrast to assumptions by RAWA and their supporters, the information posted on their website and their anti-fundamentalist, democratic political views are not representative of all Afghan women. The danger of considering RAWA to be "the face of Afghan women on the Internet" is that it homogenizes Afghan women's voices and political positions and sets RAWA up as the native informant for Western feminists, reproducing the global feminist myth of gender inclusion. These tensions complicate easy conclusions about the potential of this technology to create alternatives to "global arrogance."

Since September 11, those seeking information about women in Afghanistan have turned to RAWA. In the weeks following September 11, RAWA's website was flooded by visitors. In addition to this, they conducted over 500 interviews with international media, including the *Washington Post, The Los Angeles Times,* the BBC, and CNN (Beaumont 2001). For feminists in the West, RAWA has become "the voice of the people" and continues to be "the basis of much knowledge that Western groups . . . have about the atrocities in Afghanistan" (Miller 2002). Polly Toynbee points to RAWA as the group that could bring the lives of Afghan women into discussions about the war on terrorism (Toynbee 2001). Judy Rebick states that RAWA is "arguably the only credible voice of Afghan women" (Rebick 2001). Echoing this, Wani Muthiah comments that RAWA is "the most credible organization representing the voice of the Afghan masses at the moment" (Muthiah 2001). International observers turn to RAWA as the representatives of Afghan women and the legitimate source of information about the situation in Afghanistan. As Valentine Moghadam remarks, RAWA has become "the darling of the media and the feminists" (quoted in Thrupkaew 2002).

That RAWA is considered to be a reliable and representative source of information about Afghan women is not surprising. RAWA is a long established organization whose members continue to work in the trenches of Pakistan's refugee camps and throughout Afghanistan, risking their lives in order to educate girls, provide medical attention, document human rights abuses, and find ways for women to support themselves financially. Information about RAWA is also easily accessible to Western feminists—specifically because they are more likely than not to be connected to the Internet and because the site is in English. The fact that many Western feminists are turning to RAWA to ask how they can contribute, instead of taking up the cause of "saving Afghan women," is an attempt to avoid the colonial and hegemonic tendencies of Western attempts to speak for Afghan women or to presume to know what Afghan women need. Turning to RAWA is considered to be the best way to overcome the problems that have plagued global feminism, especially the tendency for Western feminists to embark on colonialist projects of saving objectified, helpless, third world women.

This acute awareness of and resistance to global feminist arrogance is exemplified in recent criticisms of the Feminist Majority Foundation (FMF). The FMF has initiated various campaigns in the name of Afghan women, including a fundraising drive that sold pieces of burqa-like cloth with the message: "Wear a symbol of remembrance for Afghan women." This particular campaign has been criticized by Sonali Kolhatkar, Vice President of the Afghan Women's Mission, for representing Afghan women as helpless victims rather than political actors (Kolhatkar 2002). Kolhatkar argues that approaching Afghan women as victims not only overlooks the work being done by activist groups such as RAWA, but also exhibits the tendency for Western feminists to act as the saviors of inferior, Southern women. Similarly, Elizabeth Miller condemns the FMF for embodying "hegemonic, U.S.-centric" feminism after an article profiling them was published in *Ms. Magazine* (which the FMF now owns) (Miller 2002). In the article, the Feminist Majority Foundation is credited for their part in "bringing an end to gender apartheid in Afghanistan" (Brown 2002). Miller criticizes the article for suggesting that:

> [the FMF], other Western women, and a handful of expatriate Afghan women have single-handedly freed the women of Afghanistan from an oppression that started and ended with the Taliban. What is missing from this telling of the "Feminist Majority Story" is any credit to the independent Afghan women who stayed in Afghanistan and Pakistan throughout the 23 year (and counting) crisis. . . . (Miller 2002)

In particular, Miller strongly denounces the FMF for not recognizing the work of groups such as RAWA. Once again, the FMF is criticized for representing themselves as the champion of passive, victimized Afghan women. This representation of Afghan women as victims, rather than activists, not only bolsters Bush's myth of protection about saving Afghan women, but also reinforces the imperialistic tendencies of Western feminism. As Gayatri Spivak states, "the most frightening thing about imperialism, its long-term toxic effect, what secures it, what cements it, is the benevolent self-representation of the imperialist as saviour" (Razack 2000, 39). In resistance to the myth of Western feminists as the saviors of Afghan women, Kolhatkar and Miller argue that attention must be focused on feminists within Afghanistan—namely RAWA.

However, looking to RAWA as the authentic voice for the women of Afghanistan is not a straightforward solution to issues of representation or the tendency of Western feminists to speak for other women. To begin with, RAWA is only one of many women's organizations working within Afghanistan and Pakistan. Although their connection to the Internet (something that virtually all other Afghan women's organizations lack) has made them the most internationally recognized Afghan organization, this does not make them the most representative.

Fundamental tensions exist between women's rights activists within Afghanistan. As Fariba Nawa reports,

> With little coordination among the various women's activists, the emergence of a unified, broad-based women's movement appears unlikely. While united

in their concern about the future of women's freedoms in Afghanistan and their frustration over their exclusion from the ongoing negotiations, Afghan women's groups are deeply divided on numerous other issues. (Nawa 2001)

There are stark divisions between those pushing for the radical transformation of Afghan society and those set on granting women rights and freedoms without dismantling traditional assumptions about gender. The existence of these divisions between Afghan women's rights activists indicates the vast differences between Afghan women about their visions of the future for women in Afghanistan.

RAWA's position that radical change is necessary in order to restore and protect women's rights in Afghanistan is one that differs from almost all other Afghan women's groups (Nawa 2001; Schuermann 2002). RAWA also stands apart from other activists in their demand that all fundamentalists including the Northern Alliance be excluded from present and future Afghan governments. They are one of the few women's groups working to transform the political situation in Afghanistan by establishing a secular, democratic government.[3] Their staunch calls for an anti-fundamentalist, democratic government has lead to critiques of the interim government. In particular, RAWA has criticized the two women appointed to the interim government because they are closely tied to fundamentalist parties. According to RAWA, "the existence of one or two showpiece women in the transitional administration . . . is more an insult to Afghan women than a symbol of the restoration of their status and legal rights" (RAWA 2002b). RAWA maintains that until there is a government that includes people committed to democracy and women's rights, the situation for women in Afghanistan will not improve.

As a result of their challenges to the political establishment in Afghanistan, RAWA has been accused of extremism. Sima Wali of the organization Refugee Women in Development argues that RAWA is a group on the extreme left of the political spectrum and that their activities and principles are very controversial (Schmidt 2001). RAWA is also accused of creating barriers to solidarity between Afghan women's groups, resulting from their harsh criticisms of other women activists in the country. According to Noy Thrupkaew, "RAWA has denounced numerous other Afghan women's groups as insufficiently critical of fundamentalism. It has also publicly attacked prominent Afghan women activists . . . ." (Thrupkaew 2002). As such, RAWA is not considered to be a group that can create connections to other Afghan women's rights groups. Wali argues that, "the ability to work with others, build coalitions and use tactics that are in keeping with the more moderate "Afghan norm". . . are crucial skills for making the transition from resistance to reconstruction—and they are skills that

RAWA seems to lack." As a result, many other activists are unwilling to work with RAWA and "most Afghan women [do not] feel that RAWA represents them."

While RAWA member Mariam Rawi admits that they are considered radicals, she maintains,

> but we are the voice of our people, especially the voice of our women. What they feel and what they say is much stronger than what RAWA says. If you go and interview an ordinary woman, whose son was killed by one of the factions, whose husband was killed, whose daughter was raped, who has lost everything, and then was not allowed to have a job, and had to become a prostitute or start begging in the street to survive, what she feels and says doesn't even compare to our position. (Coop 2001)

RAWA members believe that they can and do speak for Afghan women. According to Sahar Saba, RAWA "represent[s] half of the population of Afghanistan" (BBC Talking Point Forum 2001). She continues, "we believe that the goals we have—the objectives—which are women['s] rights, democracy and secularism is what our people and our women want." For RAWA, the capacity to represent the women of Afghanistan hinges on denouncing fundamentalism in all its forms and refusing to compromise with the warlords. Even though RAWA holds this revolutionary vision, which calls for the political, social, and economic transformation of society, they contend that they are the only group capable of representing the views of Afghan women.

These debates highlight the diversity of visions that Afghan women have regarding political change. Thus, to consider RAWA the voice of Afghan women silences the diversity of perspectives of Afghan women's rights advocates and the women that they represent. RAWA is differentiated from other Afghan women not only because of their virtual connections, but also because of the fact that this organization is made up of educated, internationally connected women calling for radical social and political changes. Although RAWA provides transnational feminists with information about the situation in Afghanistan that is otherwise unavailable, it is crucial to remember that women in Afghanistan do not all share their political objectives. Forging feminist networks in cyberspace to contest the war on terrorism "must reflect the differences not just between women in [the] North and South, but between women *within* the North and South" (Gabriel and Macdonald 1994, 561). As such, it reflects a global feminist arrogance to consider RAWA the "authentic" voice of Afghan women just because these are the voices that transnational feminists hear most often.

Beyond the fact that RAWA does not represent the voices of most Afghan women, it is necessary to further examine the reasons that feminists in the West have so readily embraced RAWA. I argue that it is not simply a result of their connection to the Internet that RAWA has garnered so much attention. Although their presence in cyberspace has granted them international visibility, this does not account for the political support that they have received by Western feminists who have vocally taken up their cause. In contrast to liberal discourse, getting connected to the Internet does not automatically translate into political power and international allies. A major factor that has determined RAWA's political connections through the Internet has been the convergence of RAWA's positions with those of their largely Western audience.

RAWA's voice has been heard in cyberspace, not because of the revolutionary power of the Internet, but because their voices were "the voice of difference this western audience longed to hear" (Minh-ha in Razack 2000, 44). For instance, RAWA's homepage states: "If you are freedom-loving and anti-fundamentalist, you are with RAWA" (RAWA homepage). They argue that peace, democracy, and the protection of human rights—achieved through the support of the international community—are the only way to defeat fundamentalism and terrorism. In their appeals to solidarity with transnational feminists, they continue, "as a battalion of the great army of women partisans of freedom around the world, the women of the world will find us at our posts" (RAWA 2002b). This anti-fundamentalist stance coupled with calls for democracy in Afghanistan is a position eagerly supported by many Western feminists because it confirms assumptions about the oppression that Muslim women face. As Michelle Lowry argues, "Muslim women are often understood by western society and western standards to be oppressed victims of their patriarchal culture and religion" (Lowry 2001, 122). Not only does RAWA's position confirm this assumption, but it also allows Western feminists to avoid making these critiques of Afghan culture, religion, and politics themselves. As a result, Western feminists are seen as simply supporting criticisms of Islamic fundamentalism made by Afghan women. By virtue of this, Western feminists are able to circumvent accusations of cultural imperialism—criticisms that have been leveled against them in the past.

The result is that RAWA has become the authentic native informant for their Western feminist audience. Sherene Razack defines the native informant as someone who represents or acts as a "stand-in" for "women of colour" (Razack 2000, 41). The Western feminist assumption that RAWA represents the voice of Afghan women, coupled with RAWA's eagerness to develop alliances through the Internet with the West, contributes to their status as the native informant. Razack states that the role of the native informant "is frequently to help the First World engage in a politics of saving the women of the Third World . . ." whereby Western feminism avoids looking imperialistic by "facilitating the retrieval of Third World women's voices for the sake of global feminism" (42). This is confirmed by the fact that RAWA has become the token Afghan voice in a largely Western feminist discussion about the situation of women in Afghanistan that has been taking place on the Internet. According to Radhika Gajjala, women and men from the South often use their connection to the Internet to become "ideal native informants for Northern audiences. In this sense, the Internet [becomes] a space for them to perform to the Northern audience and receive favors for appropriately westernized or sufficiently exoticized performances" (Mamidipudi and Gajjala). As such, the ability to build transnational feminist networks in cyberspace is clearly structured by issues of access and knowledge production, which serve to shape the sorts of feminist politics that are reproduced through the Internet. Western feminists are guilty of privileging RAWA at the expense of other Afghan women's rights activists. This is the context in which RAWA's voice is heard in cyberspace.

What is debatable is whether RAWA would have garnered as much support by Western feminists if they advocated less revolutionary ideas. Afghan women's rights activists Noy Thrupkaew and Sima Wali think not. Both argue that RAWA espouses a "very Westernized radical approach" that is particularly appealing to Western feminists (Thrupkaew 2002). According to Thrupkaew, "for many Western feminists, RAWA reflects a familiar yet glorified self-image: the fiery words, the clenched fists and protest signs, the type of guerrilla feminism that seems unflinchingly brave." As Thrupkaew continues, "RAWA reflects much of the Western feminist community's own values—a fact that has earned RAWA strong support in the West but few friends in a strongly Muslim country weary of political battles and bloodshed." As such, the characteristics that make RAWA so attractive to their Western allies are exactly what impede their ability to forge feminist coalitions within their own country.

This points to the serious disconnections that are being created between women in the South. In this case, privileged Afghan women with connections, not only to the Internet but also to an international coalition of feminists, speak for all Afghan women. This relationship between RAWA and Western feminists has caused further tensions between RAWA and the women that they attempt to represent. Afghan women have criticized RAWA for their close relationship with Western feminists. They have also criticized Western feminists for failing to listen to the voices of other Afghan women. In order to rectify this, Thrupkaew and Wali argue that "Western feminists need to support, fund and take their cues from the other 'moderate . . . diverse voices of Afghan women,' and keep the pressure on their own governments" (Thrupkaew 2002). While RAWA has gained solidarity from feminists around the world for their political positions, there is little consensus between Afghan women about what political changes are necessary to secure women's rights. As such, RAWA's Internet use both contests dominant myths about the war on terrorism, as well as reproduces the global feminist myth of gender inclusion. It is necessary to be extremely aware of the political effects of these cyber-connections. The success of the Internet in fighting against gender-based oppression depends on these networks bringing together feminists in cyberspace, as well as beyond. Cyberspace should only be seen as a virtual link to politics on the ground.

Conclusion

Exploring the potential of the Internet for transnational feminism necessitates an examination of both the tensions and possibilities related to using this space for feminist praxis. As this examination shows, the Internet's use to contest the war on terrorism has both challenged and reinforced dominant myths. With RAWA and the feminist response to the war on terrorism as the case study, I have argued that connected women are using the Internet to forge crucial transnational networks, to speak out against the cooptation of women's rights, and to organize against gender-based oppression. Most importantly, the virtual spaces that RAWA and their allies have claimed are beyond the reach of state powers that would silence their voices and limit their ability to contest dominant myths and oppressive power more generally. As a result, these feminists are using this space to not just resist oppressive power, but also to promote alternatives to war and create new visions for the future of Afghanistan. These connections have been essential in gaining international attention to the situation of Afghan women, getting feminists in other parts of the world to initiate campaigns against these human rights abuses, and to make connections with other people who oppose the war on terrorism.

However, the ability to gain a voice through the Internet translates into the power to produce knowledge and direct political action in ways that reflect the agenda and priorities of those with connection. Just as Western feminists have been accused of speaking for non-Western women, connected feminists must also confront the problems associated with presuming to represent the experiences and positions of all women. While the West's focus on RAWA has to do with their success at using the Internet to gain international attention to the abuses against women in Afghanistan, it is necessary to recognize that this technology promotes RAWA's particular political vision—one that does not represent the priorities of many Afghan women. That RAWA is privileged with the power of connection in a way that many feminist organizations in both the first and third worlds are not is particularly relevant when assessing the potential of the Internet for transnational feminism.

In complex and contradictory ways, the political positions that connected feminists vocalize through the Internet are both discourses of those silenced in the mainstream media and those privileged enough to "get connected." Yet there are additional power dynamics at work that relate to knowledge production between Western and non-Western women. RAWA has certainly gained a voice in cyberspace and the power to speak for all Afghan women, and as a result, is considered by feminists outside Afghanistan to be the authentic native informant. RAWA's role as the authentic voice of Afghan women is essential to legitimizing Western feminist involvement in political campaigns for Afghan women's rights. As seen in the example of the Feminist Majority Foundation, not including a voice of Afghan women—namely RAWA—results in accusations of practicing Western, imperialist feminism. As such, RAWA legitimates these transnational feminist networks as they stand in as the voice of difference. RAWA has not only taken it upon themselves to stand in as the representatives for all Afghan women, but they have also been encouraged by Western feminists to do so. That RAWA espouses a commitment to eradicating fundamentalism and calling for democracy in Afghanistan situates this group as, although "different," similar enough in their political beliefs to make alliances with Western feminists much easier to build. These particular tensions nuance conclusions that the Internet is simply a medium of Western feminism. At the same time, they highlight the ways that Western voices and perspectives—whether espoused by Westerners or not—are most easy to hear in cyberspace.

Notes

1. Connected feminists not only have access to the Internet but are also using this technology to make political connections to other women's rights activists around the world for the purposes of communication, collaboration, information sharing, and joint political actions. Connected feminists are most often western, middle-class, English speaking women or elite women from developing countries.

2. This comment was in response to Bill Maher's statement that "We have been the cowards lobbing cruise missiles from 2,000 miles away. That's cowardly." See The Anteroom Discussion Forum, "Saturday, September 19, 2001," <http://www.theanteroom.com/Greymatter/index.shtml> (August 7, 2002).

3. One of the key reasons that RAWA is able to take this stance is that they are one of only two women's organizations that are not affiliated with a political party.

BIBLIOGRAPHY

Afghan Women's Summit for Democracy. 2001. "The Brussels Proclamation." December 11, accessed July 15, 2004 <http://www.equalitynow.org/english/un/afghan_womens_summit/brussels_en.html>.

Agence France-Presse. 2001. "Internet banned in Afghanistan." *The Nando Times* August 26, accessed July 15, 2004 <http://www.totalobscurity.com/mind/news/2001/internet-banned.html>.

Alexander, M. Jacqui and Chandra T. Mohanty. 1997. "Introduction: Genealogies, Legacies, Movements." Pp. xiii–xlii in *Feminist Genealogies, Colonial Legacies, Democratic Futures*, ed. Jacqui M. Alexander and Chandra T. Mohanty. New York: Routledge.

Armstrong, Sally. 2002. *Veiled Threat: The Hidden Power of the Women of Afghanistan*. Toronto: Viking.

Artists Network. "Not in Our Name." Accessed July 10, 2002 <http://www.artistsnetwork.org/news4/news170.html>.

Associated Press. 2002. "Annan: Afghan Women May Still Suffer." February 20, accessed July 15, 2004 <http://rawa.org/annan-w.htm>.

Bautista, Rhona O. 1995. "Linking Women Worldwide." *Annual Report of Isis International*. Manila: Isis International. 12–13.

BBC News. 2001. "Afghan Feminists Go Online." *BBC News* March 23, accessed July 15, 2004 <http://www.rawa.org/bbc-rawa.htm>.

BBC Talking Point Forum. 2001. "Women and the Taliban." October 18, accessed July 15, 2004 <http://rawasongs.fancymarketing.net/bbc-forum.htm>.

Bean, Matt. 2001. "Risking Death to Expose the Taliban." *Court TV* September 27, accessed July 15, 2004 <http://rawasongs.fancymarketing.net/courttv.htm>.

Beaumont, Sally. 2001. "RAWA's Work Continues in the Midst of War." *Sch News of the World* November 16, accessed July 15, 2004 <http://www.schnews.org.uk/sotw/rawa-after-war.htm>.

Brown, Janelle. 2002. "A Coalition of Hope." *Ms. Magazine* 12, no. 2 (Spring): 65–76.

Bunting, Madeleine. 2001. "Women and War: Special Report: Terrorism in the U.S." *The Guardian*. September 20, accessed July 15, 2004 <http://www.guardian.co.uk/analysis/story/0,3604,554794,00.html>.

CASAC. 2001. "For Immediate Release." October 3, accessed July 15, 2004 <http://www.casac.ca/conference01/conference01_pr.htm>.

Coop, Stephanie. 2001. "Sowing the Seeds of Revolution." *The Japan Times* December 18, accessed July 15, 2004 <http://rawasongs.fancymarketing. net/japant.htm>.

Delphy, Christine. 2002. "Free to Die." *Le Monde diplomatique*. March, accessed July 15, 2004 <http://rawa.org/lemonde-d.htm>.

Ehrenreich, Barbara. 2001. "Veiled Threat: To Fully Grasp the Dangers of the Post-Sept. 11 World, We Have to Examine the Taliban's Hatred of Women." *Los Angeles Times*. November 4, accessed July 15, 2004 <http://www.commondreams.org/views01/1104-02.htm>.

Flanders, Laura. 2001. "Beyond The Burqa." *ZNet Commentary* December 14, accessed July 15, 2004 <http://www.zmag.org/sustainers/content/2001-12/14flanders.cfm>.

FMF. 2001. "Afghan Women's Participation in New Government Becoming More Defined." *Feminist Daily News Wire* December 3, accessed July 15, 2004 <http://www.feminist.org/news/newsbyte/uswirestory.asp?id=5996>.

Gabriel, Christina and Laura Macdonald. 1994. "NAFTA, Women and Organising in Canada and Mexico: Forging a 'Feminist Internationality.'" *Millennium: Journal of International Studies* 23, no. 3: 535–62.

Hafkin, Nancy and Nancy Taggart. 2001. *LearnLink Gender, Information Technology, and Developing Countries: An Analytic Study.* Washington: AED/LearnLink.

Howell, Donna. 2000. "Afghan Women on the Web—Q & A." *About.Com.* July 19, accessed July 15, 2004 <http://www.rawa.org/aboutcom.htm>.

Human Rights Watch. 2002. "Afghanistan: Women Still Under Threat." May 9, accessed July 15, 2004 <http://www.hrw.org/press/2002/05/burqa0509.htm>.

Hunt, Krista. 2002. "The Strategic Co-optation of Women's Rights Discourse in the War on Terrorism." *International Feminist Journal of Politics* 4, 1: 116–21.

ICHRDD. 2001. "Dr. Sima Samar Named to Transition Cabinet in Afghanistan." December 5, accessed July 15, 2004 <http://www.ichrdd.ca/english/commdoc/humphrey2001/simaSamarGovernmentAfghanistan.html>.

———. "Take Action Now." Accessed February 22, 2002 <http://www.ichrdd.ca/english/supportSamar.html>.

Jensen, Robert. 2002. "Journalist Should Never Yield to 'Patriotism.'" *Newsday* May 29, accessed July 15, 2004 <http://www.commondreams.org/views02/0529-02.htm>.

Kolhatkar, Sonali. 2002. "'Saving' Afghan Women." *Znet Gender Watch* May 9, accessed July 15, 2004 <http://www.zmag.org/content/Gender/kolhatkarwomen.cfm>.

Lowry, Michelle. 2001. "Rethinking Culture, Tradition, and Multiculturalism: Anti-Racism and the Politics of the Veil." Pp. 121–32 in *Feminism(s) on the Edge of the Millennium*, ed. Krista Hunt and Christine Saulnier. Toronto: Inanna Publications.

Mamidipudi, Annapurna and Radihika Gajjala. "Cyberfeminism and Development." Accessed March 30, 2001 <http://www.cyberdiva.org/erniestuff/cybergad.html>.

Miller, Elizabeth. 2002. "An Open Letter to the Editors of Ms. Magazine." April 20, accessed July 15, 2004 <http://www.pittstate.edu/isp/gobar/letter.html>.

Muthiah, Wani. 2001. "U.S. Contributed to Destruction of Afghanistan." *The StarMalaysia* October 15, accessed July 15, 2004 <http://rawa.org/the-star.htm>.

Nawa, Fariba. 2001. "Demanding to Be Heard: Advocates for Afghanistan's Women are Pushing to Ensure that Women's Freedoms are Protected under a Post-Taliban Government." *Mother Jones* November 14, accessed July 15, 2004 <http://www.motherjones.com/web_exclusives/features/news/afghan_women.html>.

O'Connor, Anne-Marie. 2000. "Internet Gives Voice to Afghan Women's Cause." *Los Angeles Times* July 8, accessed July 15, 2004 <http://rawa.fancymarketing.net/latimes.htm>.

PAR-L listserve. 2001. "Re: Urgent Call to Action to Get Women to Participate in the Recovery of Afghanistan." Accessed November 24, 2001, PAR-L@unb.ca.

Pazira, Nelofer. 2001. "Bombs and Bread." *Maclean's* October 29, accessed January 14, 2002 <http://www.macleans.ca/>.

Pollitt, Katha. 2001. "Where Are the Women?" *The Nation* October 22, accessed July 15, 2004 <http://www.thenation.com/doc.mhtml%3Fi=20011022&s=pollitt>.

Price, Niko. 2002. "Freedom of Press in Afghanistan?" *Associated Press via the Frontier Post* May 5, accessed July 15, 2004 <http://rawa.fancymarketing.net/press.htm>.

RAWA homepage. Accessed July 24, 2002 <http://rawasongs.fancymarketing.net/index.html>.

RAWA. 2001. "The People of Afghanistan Do Not Accept Domination of the Northern Alliance." November 13, accessed July 15, 2004 <http://rawa.false.net/na-appeal.htm>.

———. 2002a. "About RAWA. . . ." Accessed July 8, 2002 <http://rawa.fancymarketing.net/rawa.html>.

———. 2002b. "RAWA Statement." Accessed July 24, 2002 <http://rawa.false.net/ mar8-02en.htm>.

RAWA interview. 2002. "Re: Interview Request." Accessed February 3, rawa@rawa.org.

Razack, Sherene. 2000. "Your Place or Mine? Transnational Feminist Collaboration." Pp. 39–53 in *Anti-Racist Feminism*, ed. Agnes Calliste and George J. Sefa Dei. Halifax: Fernwood.

Rebick, Judy. 2001. "Re: Only Women Can Defend Women's Rights in Afghanistan." Accessed November 21, 2001 <http://www.rabble.ca>.

Richtel, Matt. 1999. "Crying for Justice from Kabul." *Yahoo! Internet Life Magazine*. March, accessed July 15, 2004 <http://rawa.org/yahoo.htm>.

Scheeres, Julia. 2001. "Risking All to Expose the Taliban." *Wired News* August 10, accessed July 15, 2004 <http://www.rawa.org/wired.htm>.

Schmidt, Susan. 2001. "Female Foes of Taliban Seeking Support Abroad." *The Washington Post* October 8, accessed July 15, 2004 <http://rawasongs.fancymarketing.net/wpost.htm>.

Schuermann, Julia. 2002. "They Want to Be the Light." *Frankfurter Allgemeine Zeitung* January 3, accessed July 15, 2004 <http://rawa.org/allgemeine.htm>.

Symon, Fiona. 2001. "Afghanistan's Clandestine Army." *BBC News* September 25, accessed July 15, 2004 <http://rawasongs.fancymarketing.net/bbc-rawa2.htm>.

Tapper, Jake. 2001. "Whitehouse Whitewashers." *Salon.com* September 27, August 7, 2002 <http://dir.salon.com/news/feature/2001/09/27/spin/index.html>.

Thobani, Sunera. 2001a. "You Cannot Slaughter People into Submission." October 1, accessed July 15, 2004 <http://www.wworld.org/archive/archive.asp?ID=90>.

———. 2001b. "War Frenzy." October 28, accessed July 15, 2004 <http://www.globalresearch.ca/articles/TOB110A.html>.

Thrupkaew, Noy. 2002. "What Do Afghan Women Want?" *The American Prospect* August 29, accessed July 15, 2004 <http://www.alternet.org/story/13980/>.

Tom, Allison. 2000. "Afghan Women Unite in Cyberspace against Taliban Repression." *CNN* July 14, accessed July 15, 2004 <http://rawa.org/cnn-rawa.htm>.

Toynbee, Polly. 2001. "Behind the Burka." *The Guardian* September 28, accessed July 15, 2004 <http://rawasongs.fancymarketing.net/guardian2.htm>.

Voss, Michael. 2002. "Afghanistan Gets New Press Law." *BBC News* February 9, accessed July 15, 2004 <http://news.bbc.co.uk/hi/english/world/south_asia/newsid_1810000/1810983.stm>.

Whaley, Patti. 1996. "The Public Forum: Potential Contributions of Information Technologies to Human Rights." *Women & Performance* 17, no. 9.1: 225–32.

Womenspace. 2000. "Fwd: Internet and Women, B+5." *Womenspace listserve* June 7, womenspace@yorku.ca.

———. 2001. "Afghan Women's Groups." *Womenspace listserve* June 20, womenspace@yorku.ca.

Chapter 8

Knowing the Promises, Facing the Challenges: The Role of the Internet in Development and Human Rights Campaigns and Movements in the Arab Middle East

Marlyn Tadros

Introduction

Over the last decade, there has been mounting interest in the uses of Information Communication Technologies—ICTs—(satellites, computers, telephones, faxes, and the Internet) in human rights and developmental movements and campaigns around the world. The Internet is the quintessence of this new ICT technology, with its speed, lack of centralization, and citizen-to-citizen connectivity. According to some analysts, the Internet has shifted power to access and present information from governments to people, which has given rise to the hope, and fuel to the claim, that it is indeed a possible democratizing force. While there is truth to those claims, one must not lose sight of the problems and challenges that impede such progress. After all, the Internet continues to be an elitist tool whose access, cost, and skills make it prohibitive to many in the Global South. It is specifically controversial in the area of development—should we use development in a much narrower sense—where the rate of illiteracy is high in some poor countries, not to mention the rate of computer literacy and technical skills.

This chapter deals mainly with the Internet as a communication medium, and its impact on human rights and development campaigns in the Arab Middle East. I argue that while it is too early to assess the impact of the Internet on the Arab Middle East, there is enough evidence to suggest that unlike other media, it has exceptional potential because of, among other things, its interactive nature. While it is true that to-date it has not been used effectively by civil society, given a comprehensive strategy, it could be a source of unimaginable strength and progress. I also claim that currently the obstacles that impede the democratic progress in the Arab Middle East are not easy to overcome, especially in the short run, and they will not be resolved through the Internet; however the Internet is one of the available tools and means of encouraging such progress and empowering civil society.

This chapter is divided into four sections. The first section provides a background on Internet usage in the Middle East and compares it with international trends and statistics. The second analyzes the human rights movement in the Middle East, and shows how the Internet has been used to-date by civil society. The third discusses the potential of the Internet in the Middle East as an enabling medium, and highlights the challenges facing such a potential, and is followed by some concluding assessments.

Internet Usage in the Arab Middle East

Egypt, the United Arab Emirates, and Kuwait had been at the forefront of Internet expansion in the Middle East. They began providing Internet services in the early 1990s, initially through universities and only to faculty and students. While other countries followed suit, some trailed behind significantly [including Syria, Sudan, Libya, Yemen, and Iraq], and others continue to this day to confine it to universities. This lag is attributed to political issues and freedom of speech, although governments continue to deny this and attribute it to culture and sexually explicit materials.

By the late 1990s, some Middle Eastern governments such as Egypt and Kuwait began approving Internet service providers (ISPs) outside university facilities and handed them over to the private sector and private enterprises. Privatization helped speed up the spread of the Internet throughout the Middle East and increased the number of Internet users and number of hosts. The importance of E-mail usage to businesses was one of the motivators of opening up the Internet and expanding the user base. While the move to privatization was primarily intended to encourage economic growth and to enable further access to a free market potential, it has been widely used for entertainment as well as for human rights and development causes. English language hegemony had been a detriment to the spreading of Internet usage; the development of Arabic language web browsers and computer software increased consumer demand and further helped the growth of the Internet in the region (NUSACC 1998).

It is perhaps surprising to know that a relative late-comer to the Internet world like Saudi Arabia currently has the single largest Internet community among all Arab countries with 1.6 million Internet users, even though Internet usage is confined to universities and medical facilities (Madar 2001). This is because some Saudis connect long distance with neighboring countries to access the Internet, bypassing their country's filters and restrictions. In 1999, Saudi Arabia permitted local ISPs to connect directly to the Internet but continued to be routed through a single, government-controlled server, giving the government a filtering and censoring capability.

Egypt and the United Arab Emirates follow Saudi Arabia in numbers, with 1.5 million and 900,000 users respectively (Madar Research Group 2001). There is no doubt that affluence tends to be a major factor in increasing Internet users in the region, within the same country, primarily because of prohibitive computer and software prices, as well as Internet access prices. The spread of Internet cafes has ameliorated some of the effects of this problem and has brought the Internet to mainstream Arabs. Many Arab countries have taken additional steps to further encourage Internet usage: Egypt began providing free Internet access as of 2003 and has encouraged the creation of Multi-Purpose Community Telecentres in different Egyptian governorates to help those who are furthest from urban areas to access the Internet. The United Arab Emirates created the Dubai Internet City, a huge free-trade zone initiative that aims at encouraging e-Commerce and encouraging technology-related education.

Having said that, it should be noted that the political factor continues to be a detriment to the spread of the Internet, curbing the natural increase in Internet usage numbers and Internet penetration. The number of Internet users in petro-affluent countries of the region is growing at a slower pace than less developed countries such as Egypt. Gulf State countries have financial strength and state-of-the-art information technologies, yet the number of Internet users is growing more slowly than other countries (The Estimate 1998). The primary reason behind this is the myriad political restrictions on access to information.

There is no doubt that the Arab Middle East has to overcome Herculean hurdles to access and penetration, especially when compared to international trends. The United Nations has created a framework of millennium indicators to assess progress toward development around the world. Target 18 states that in cooperation with the private sector, governments should make available the benefits of new technologies, especially information and communications, such as telephone lines and cellular subscribers, as well as personal computers in use and Internet users. While making considerable strides, the Middle East still lags behind other regions in the world. In 2000, the percentage of the population online in the United States was 47.95 while the online population of the Middle East was 0.7 percent in 2001.

The Human Rights Movement in the Arab Middle East

One segment of civil society using the Internet is the human rights movement which, itself, is a relatively new movement in the Middle East. Its birth came just a short time before the Internet came into widespread use across the Globe, and certainly in the Middle East. The Arab Organization for Human Rights, being the oldest human rights organization, is only 20 years old and was founded outside the Arab World when no Arab country would host it. Others began to form years later depending on degrees of permissions provided by different governments. The absence of such organizations in some countries, even to this day, is primarily because within the established political system in the Middle East, human rights are of secondary importance to political stability, national security, and economic development.

The role of individuals in Arab Middle Eastern societies is downplayed. People are unable to participate in public life because of an arsenal of laws and prohibitions that place unnecessary constraints on them. Most constitutions in the Arab Middle East, where existent, affirm political and civil rights as well as freedom of expression. However, they are applied "within the constraints" of the law, hence rendering the practice of these rights subject to the law of a given era. In addition, some countries, such as Egypt, Sudan, Algeria, and Syria have been living under emergency laws for several decades at a time, in effect rendering the constitution irrelevant. Once again, internal and national security issues are given priority over the pursuit of democracy, and it seems to be only increasing. The U.S. "war against terrorism" and its violations of civil rights in the United States has given gleeful justification by example to governments that had been practicing similar policies for decades.

Civil society had always been in a particularly precarious position in the Middle East, being the target of repeated governmental crackdowns. Political parties, where existent, syndicates, the media and the press, clubs, and, more significantly, nongovernmental organizations that deal with "controversial" developmental issues as well as, more recently, human rights issues, are all under the control of governments. Strict nongovernmental laws are in place ensuring the hegemony of the State, and they continue to be developed to obstruct the free expression of opinion and political participation. Such measures tend to further close the already fragile traditional methods of human rights activism. Nongovernmental organizations and civil society institutions are faced with the necessity of implementing new and creative strategies to continue to function.

A fundamental element of any government's hegemony is through controlling the flow of information which is a "necessary condition to ensure democratic decision making whether in a partial or a holistic scope." (Fergani 2002). This is because as Rheingold (2000) asserts, access to information is indeed a political process capable of altering the power structure between governments and people and within different communities:

> Access to alternate forms of information and, most important, the power to reach others with your own alternatives to the official view of events, are, by their nature, political phenomena. Changes in forms and degrees of access to information are indicators of changes in forms and degrees of power among different groups.

Not only is access to information an important political process, but it also implies "adequate guarantees for transparency of the information available" (Fergani 2002). There is, therefore, a close correlation between human development on the one hand, and both political freedom and democratic participation on the other, with the flow of information contributing to the democratic process. Participation in decision-making and political freedoms have an impact not only on social and political life, but also on society's economic development because it "allows people to influence directly or indirectly the process of economic policy-making so that it would be receptive to their needs" (Fergani 2002).

Typically in the Arab Middle East, information has long been restricted and one directional: from governments to people. Information was, and continues to be, the product of government-controlled media, through newspapers and television. Arabic media and newspapers "had long ago ceased to be readable by the early 1990s, and Arab television, for the most part, was a drab affair with fawning national news coverage and third-rate entertainment programming" (Alterman 2002). There is a complete absence of national debates on issues, and absence of space for self-expression is the norm. Censorship of the media has been and continues to be Arab governments' primary preoccupation.

Major changes in the last two decades have contributed to the forceful opening up of Arab countries to the world. The end of the Cold War on the one hand, and the explosion of communications technology on the other, during the 1980s and 1990s were harbingers of change (Alterman 2002). Photocopying machines came into use at a time when making copies of a petition or attempting to publish a report was considered a criminal offence. Additionally, "fax machines, videocassette recorders, telephones, satellite television and the Internet [began to be] within the reach of an increasingly broad spectrum of the world's population" (Alterman 2002), including the Middle East. Communication, especially with access to the Internet, became more interactive with decreasing governmental intrusion, thus opening up possibilities and space for civil society institutions.

Human rights organizations in particular have been some of the victims of the media in the Arab World. The terms "human rights" have been demonized in government-controlled media which in turn created a culture of resentment among the population to the terms and concepts of human rights. Human rights workers and activists have been portrayed as "spies" to the West, writing "reports" for the West, encouraging the dissipation of Arab culture at the expense of a foreign or "alien" culture and attempting to impose principles that are contrary to existent religious and traditional beliefs. On the other hand, human rights organizations have little access to the media to refute such claims or to present their own points of view and the principles upon which they stand. Organizations that have publications of their own have very limited distribution capabilities. In addition, television and radio are more powerful than publications because they reach a wider audience, including the larger illiterate population of the Middle East.

In conclusion, negotiated space for human rights activism, where existent in the Middle East, had been limited ever since the struggling human rights movement began in the late 1980s, and had been dwindling further following the September 11 attacks, under the guise of fighting terrorism and protecting national security. Some governments, such as the governments of Egypt and Tunisia, have changed laws, closed human rights organizations, and arrested human rights activists. Such measures require civil society to have new and creative strategies to continue to exist, as well as continue devising new tools and mechanisms for activism. The Internet provides such a potential, and this will be further discussed below.

The Potential and Challenges of the Internet in the Middle East

With nothing more than a computer and an Internet connection, a single person, in their living room or in a cyber café, can tell the whole world what they think. All they need to do is set up a web site, take part in a newsgroup or send email messages. This person can even freely denounce human rights violations or repression in their country, no matter how authoritarian and closed it is.

—Reporters without Borders 2002

This section discusses the potential of the Internet in the Middle East as an enabling medium, and how activists have used the Internet to date, and also discusses the challenges facing such a potential. It is important, however, to determine how we can assess the success or failure of their usage of the Internet, given that there have not been any in-depth studies of the issue, nor credible statistics of the impact of their work. In real life, campaigns are assessed by their impact on legislative change and the progress they make in changing and impacting policies and the decision making process. However one of the criteria that this paper has chosen to determine the success of the Internet as an enabling power in the Middle East is not the impact of online campaigns and activities on policy change, but rather the impact of a campaign on individual participation as a first step toward empowerment and awareness and toward democratic participation. Additionally, its success can be assessed by comparing it to similar actions and activities in the real world within the Middle East, rather than comparing it to international campaigns and their impact. This provides a much fairer assessment of whether the Internet is providing progress toward democracy or not.

There is no doubt that even with very limited physical space and resources, civil society institutions in the Middle East have been organizing diverse campaigns long before the Internet with varying degrees of successes and failures. What, therefore, is the importance of being out there on the Net as opposed to just doing their work locally without international or regional connection? Would their work be effective without it? The answer to the last question is yes, their work would continue to be limited but as effective without the Internet, and civil society institutions will continue to work within the space that has been provided to them, or the space that they will be able to carve for themselves, and will continue to try and create other spaces for themselves. The advantage of the Internet, however, is that it is an adaptable tool that strengthens and facilitates work, and that creates a venue and a space within which they can disseminate their information with speed and at minimal cost. The Internet is an additional tool that civil society institutions may use to strengthen their campaigns and to draw upon the information that is available on the Net to adapt to their work. Civil society institutions become no longer isolated, but have immediate and speedy connectivity and networking with like-minded organizations within the region and beyond it.

In the physical world, given the constraints on civil society in general and the human rights movement in particular, the latter was, and continues to be, isolated within the elitist intellectual community. It has not been very effective in reaching the grassroots, especially with the absence of access to means of communication. With the advent of the Internet, an alternative medium was created, but remains within the grasp of the educated elite, hence denying the majority of the population in the Arab World which continues to be illiterate, any access to it. It took some time for civil society to recognize that through this new medium traditional methods of censorship have been rendered almost useless and that it can be used as a powerful tool of communication. Anyone can publish anything at any time, and there is little that traditional gatekeeper governments can do to prevent or control using traditional control mechanisms.

While it is too early to make an accurate scientific assessment of the Internet's impact on both the NGOs and their audience, there is no doubt that it has already created a distinct community within the Arab World— a community of online activists, able to communicate with each other and capable of producing their own two-way information without direct government intervention. It may be even called a parallel community of activists, strengthened by the fact that individuals who normally would not be involved in activism are now "speaking out" and expressing themselves on the Internet. It has connected activists and non-involved individuals alike in discussion and dissemination of information that has generally been inaccessible prior to the Internet. Civil society organizations and in particular human rights organizations in the Middle East have been online quite early on and have been using the Internet in their work although not as efficiently as other sectors.

It should be noted also that most NGOs in the Arab World, and especially human rights NGOs, have no memberships in the first place because they are not full legal entities. In assessing how effective the Internet has been in bringing about interested members, one should compare it only to real life, and not to actual numbers. It is clear that a virtual existence has facilitated people's access to those NGOs, providing them information on their work and activities without necessarily compromising themselves. This access created an audience for the NGOs who access their website to get information but not to necessarily participate in activities nor in discussion foras. Yet it has also created a "curious" audience who ask questions and who demand more information, especially among the younger generation and the youths. The Internet presence of those NGOs has created an interest in the issues those NGOs try to present, and has helped security-shy students and individuals to receive this information with the click of a mouse. While this is not considered "membership" it is a first step toward awareness-raising and eventual active participation. It is important to note that most Internet users in the Arab World are the youth who are seeking an identity in an increasingly globalized world. It is through them that there is a hope for building transnational democracy, through a cumulative process of education and awareness-raising that will no doubt lead to more active participation and democratization.

The Internet has also reduced the isolation of human rights activists themselves in the Arab World by removing geographical boundaries and facilitating direct connectivity. Not only are they now connected to one another on a national and regional level, but they are also connected on an international level. Where regular mail was slow and uncertain, and where faxes were expensive and unaffordable, the Internet has provided a cheaper way of daily communication with each other and with the outer world. It has helped build bridges across these isolated communities, and has created an "information-inclusion" platform for them. They have succeeded in creating online networks that had been previously very difficult to follow prior to the Internet. One of the earlier individual sites that was created in the Middle East was the Arab Media Internet Network—AMIN. It is a collection and a directory of online newspapers in Arabic. Its creator, Daoud Kuttab, a Palestinian journalist, said that he created it because he saw that Arab press was free only when criticizing other Arab countries, and he therefore wanted to make all online newspapers available on the Internet accessible to Arabs everywhere.

Because of the speed by which information travels across the Internet, it has been an extremely effective tool in spreading information about human rights violations and other special human rights situations. NGOs have used E-mail alerts and sent out their regular reports using E-mail rather than paper and fax machines, hence cutting down substantially on costs. Online campaigns and petitions cross and recross the Globe several times, before governments could take action against them. A major benefit of having technology integrated into nonprofit organizations is the increased ease and flow of information: communication with coworkers and target audiences, the ability to coordinate their activities with other organizations and networks, the ability to create and join various coalitions, receive and act upon urgent action alerts and updates, and the ability to find news and conduct research.

The Internet has also provided campaigning and lobbying skills to isolated human rights activists across the globe and also in the Middle East and has facilitated the sharing of information and skills between organizations. It has given access to international instruments and documentation that was previously accessible only to a limited group of activists who knew how to get them. It has also given them the ability not only to be recipients of information, but also to act upon that information, even if by signing a simple petition or passing around a politically charged E-mail. Additionally, organizations and campaigns on the Internet seem to be larger than life even when they are lone individual campaigns, which has helped magnify the "smaller" voices and the smaller campaigns.

Participation requires active participation on the part of the users, which television does not provide. The Internet, on the other hand, provided a new opportunity for passive Middle East citizens to become active users. It has also provided anonymity in case individuals wanted to express opinions without being known for expressing them. Additionally, it provided a proliferation of discussion groups on diverse topics, and an opportunity for networking and coalition building. It therefore provided the means to circumvent traditional media and to create a new space for the users where they can feel more comfortable with participation.

The Internet also forged an identity for the Middle Eastern voice in an increasingly globalized world, providing alternatives to mainstream government-controlled media. It allowed active engagement with the West on an intellectual level, and almost on a par. The presence of Middle Easterners on the Internet is itself empowering and their influence is likely to increase because their very presence revived a national and a Pan-Arab debate. Additionally, through exposure to different opinions and perspectives, and in particular through their exposure to published scientific research, antireligious, and anti-Islamic material which has long been a taboo and a criminal offence in all Middle Eastern countries, and other culturally challenging information, the Internet has provided the opportunity of exposure to analytical thinking and forced the Middle East into strategies to counter such material using the same methods and other creative ones. Sites that attempt to disseminate information on Islam and an explanation of its content and principles abound on the Internet. Additionally, sites that attempt to respond to criticism of Islam and/or of "culturally sensitive" issues also abound on the Internet. Indeed it could be said that the Internet has not only altered the self-perception of the Middle East and pushed it into the twenty-first century, but has also created a constant challenge because of the stark exposure of the Middle East when placed on the same "intellectual" plane compared with other regions in the world, free of governmental intrusion.

Given the currently relatively small role of government on the Internet, it has significantly altered the relationship between individual and State and between civil society and the State. No longer is the individual dependent on information provided by their government, but Arab citizens could go on the Internet themselves and seek out the uncensored information they want. No longer are States able to manipulate the media into a propaganda machine that touts government accomplishments. The State found that it needed to upgrade its standard of information provision as well as significantly curb its censorship urges and become relatively more open to external ideas.

Because of the ability to publish anything at any time, and because of the flow of information from the West to the East, Middle Eastern political leaders are currently held more accountable than ever before. Information about them that was previously taboo and censored is currently on everyone's desktop. Opposing views have been brought forth into discussion, and criticism of leaders is no longer taboo, even if within the confines of cyberspace and through anonymity. Governments began to be questioned and reports flowed regarding corruption and other political issues that were never accessible to Middle Easterners. The increasing exposure of corruption had Arab governments scrambling not just to explain themselves to their Arab population but more importantly to "reassure their Western funding sources" that they are doing their best to fight corruption and to show transparency and accountability (Reporters without Borders 2003).

Among the many uses of the Internet in the Middle East, is that it continues to be used as an opposition/resistance tool. It is a means of challenging authority on a political as well as individual level. More time needs to be given to be able to assess the successes and failures of such models in order to build upon and replicate. Nevertheless such instances have been prevalent. In Algeria, opposition parties use the Internet to disseminate information about their activities. In Egypt, several political petitions were circulated in 2003 urging people to make statements on the need for constitutional, political, and legal reform in Egypt. Almost every opposition party from the Arab World, whether existing within the region or outside it, exists on the Internet with its newspaper and publications, the content of which is occasionally censored in real life. The Egyptian Islamist al-Shaab party and newspaper were banned from real life but continued to exist on the Internet as a publication. Newspapers shut down in Morocco re-posted their articles on the Net; in Tunisia, a journalist was denied the license to publish a newspaper and she took it to the Internet and published her paper there. Parties with little public outreach capabilities currently have discussion forums and e-Newsletters in Arabic as well as other Internet tools where Arabs from all over the world participate, subscribe to, and share ideas and voice their opinions.

Because media has been traditionally constrained in the Arab World, the Internet has provided a useful alternative. Some activists have used the Internet as an alternate information and media tool, not just to receive information but also to disseminate it. Daoud Kuttab created Ammannet in 2000, which provides radio broadcasting on political issues of the Arab World, including human rights violations as well as elections. The broadcast could also be heard on FM radio. This broke the taboo on private media ownership. While this is only one initiative based in Jordan and which primarily targets Jordanian citizens, it is replicable in other countries.

Given that Arab governments do not wish to undermine the strength and importance of the potential economic empowerment which the Internet provides, they have not been able to permanently ban the Internet. Nevertheless they are becoming increasingly concerned with the free flow of information and they are being educated on filtering strategies and technologies. In spite of such technologies, they realize that plain censorship is no longer a viable strategy and understand that they must devise other strategies for control and hegemony. Civil society should make use of the Internet and should be involved in policy-making regarding the communications and have a leading role in its development and promotion, before governments regulate it beyond recognition.

Obstacles and Threats

It should be noted that in spite of the optimism expressed in this chapter, there are shortcomings that hinder the use of the Internet in generating a political consciousness capable of activating people. Such shortcomings have to do with the structure and accessibility of the Internet itself, the political climate of the Middle East, and individual problems that still need to be addressed. Democratization is an accumulative process, and the purpose of this chapter is only to point out the Internet's potential as such, without understating the magnitude of the problems, obstacles, and threats that have yet to be overcome.

In terms of Internet structure, the Internet itself is a global economic, technological, and communication network dominated by the West. It is, by default, North/West centric. The issue of Internet governance itself is important. While it is decentralized in some aspects, Internet governance is still through the United States, creating a new model of power structure. This issue is relevant to the Middle East because it reinforces the idea of Western hegemony over the world and in particular over the Arab World.

Given that the Internet is a product of the American military, there is an overwhelming English language content where 68.4 percent of Internet content is in English. This hegemony constitutes a problem for non-English speakers, in terms not only of content, but even of mere access. In addition, the cost of both hardware and software, not to mention Arabized software, is prohibitive. Through language domination, the West is capable of disseminating a culture that is "foreign" to local and national values. It is perceived as a cultural invasion that increasingly affects the younger generation in particular who are more vulnerable yet more technologically capable and savvy, alienating them from their environment and society. After all, as Rheingold (2000) said: "Televisions, telephones, radios, and computer networks are potent political tools because their function is not to manufacture or transport physical goods but to influence human beliefs and perceptions." In diplomatic terms, such inventions are called "soft power," as opposed to military "hard power," because of their ability to influence without resorting to violence.

Clearly the Internet does not exist in a vacuum, just a virtual world that is apart and separate from the physical world. It is a technology that is part of the physical world and affects it and shapes it. It also has a culture that is shaped and affected by the physical life of those who provide input into it and those who access it. It therefore provides and transmits values across borders. Technology, to use the words of McMahon (2001), and especially the Internet, is "never value neutral; it always promotes certain social interests over others, and more specifically, certain institutional forms over others." This is one of the reasons for the wariness of Arab communities to embrace it.

Perhaps the quotation from Hassan Hanafi (1998), a prominent Arab Islamic scholar, is indicative of this wariness:

> Globalization is a fabricated concept, not a reality. It is an ideology in spite of the old myth, the end of ideology and the beginning of technology . . . In the name of the world as a global village, the information revolution, the Internet, the E-mail, the satellites and all modern means of communication and mass-media, all borders are dropped, between nations, peoples, cultures, customs, and manners called specificities, particularities, value-system, etc. The purpose is to pass the free market economy, the end of economic planning and the state economy after the fall of socialist regimes in 1991 proved that the free market economy is the most congruent to human activity. With multi-national corporations, economy is implemented on a world-wide scale.

The Internet is therefore viewed as a reflection of negative globalization, a reference solely to free trade and a free economy, and a tool for the elitist economic empowerment. It is perceived as an expression of "one sole course of history of a special historical consciousness, that of the West." It is colonialism and imperialism at their worst, where "the powerful was the global while the weak was the local. The global was the center while the local was the periphery" (Hanafi 1998). The Internet, together with other technologies, is hence perceived as an alienating tool, one that by default eventually appropriates a foreign and hence negative culture, aimed at alienating the younger generations from their heritage and origins for the benefit of the economic and militaristic security and supremacy of the West. It is an "all or none" concept that is repeated and prevalent in Arab discourse in general, and the Internet is the current principal tool for achieving this objective.

Another dimension of cultural adapting is language, and the Internet no doubt has English language hegemony. Encouraging the creation of Arabic language content will increase the participation of Arabs in communication with the world and regionally among themselves.

As was the case with the human rights movement, when the Internet was first introduced to the Middle East, there was an initial suspicion of its benefits. Among the majority of Middle Easterners, it was perceived as a cultural invasion, another part of a series of attempts at globalization, hegemony, and control by the West. It was portrayed in the media primarily as the producer of pornographic and antireligious material, a new extension of globalization, an attempt at dissolving cultural norms, traditions, and values, a producer of non-authentic culture, and a tangible manifestation of immorality. This view is particularly detrimental to the human rights movement, since now there is a combination of two aliens: human rights concepts on the one hand, and Internet technologies on the other that are inundating the Arab World with an alien culture. Yet while this view continues to be pervasive, it has nevertheless witnessed a dramatic change as more and more individuals began gaining access to the Internet, and began using it as a forum of open and free discussion even on otherwise taboo issues. Younger users in particular are undeterred in their desire for access to this new world. In fact, younger users take particular delight in shattering social taboos and traditions on the Internet, and in their ability and tech-savviness to circumvent their families' supervision and control.

By far the biggest hurdle to overcome, if not *the* primary one besides culture, is governmental control. The U.S. State Department's Annual Review of Human Rights (2002) claims that over 90 countries illegally monitor the communications of political opponents, human rights workers, journalists, and labor organizers. Telecommunications are generally government owned, and this enables government to control access to "sensitive" information. Arab governments are beginning to note the impact of the Internet and are creating means of monitoring and surveillance of activities. They are catching up quickly to the potentially "dangerous" usages of the Internet by human rights groups. In Jordan, for instance, security officers monitor telephone conversations and Internet communication, read private correspondence, and engage in surveillance of persons who are considered to pose a threat to the Government or national security. In Tunisia a "full corps of cyber-police went into operation to track down subversive websites to be blocked, intercept email or attempts to reach sites containing political or critical material, hunt for and neutralize proxy servers used to get round directly-blocked access to sites, and track down and arrest over-active Internet users—the cyber dissidents" (Reporters Without Borders 2003). Egypt began tightening its surveillance of the Internet in 2002 and went as far as setting up a government department to "investigate online crime." Internet users were "warned off taboo issues such as relations between Copts and Muslims, publicizing terrorist ideas, human rights violations, criticizing the president, his family and the army and promoting modern versions of Islam and told that too much outspokenness was unwelcome." The director of this new department, Ahmed Essmat, told an Egyptian newspaper that his staff monitored the Internet on a daily basis. This no doubt constitutes a serious threat to democracy and to the human rights movements in the Middle East.

Ironically, Middle Eastern governments, as do other totalitarian governments around the world, are getting their surveillance technology from the West, and in particular the United States which had been complaining of the lack of democracy in the Middle East not only verbally, but also on a yearly basis in its State Department's Annual Human Rights Reports. Just as Middle Eastern governments import Internet and computer technologies, they are also importing monitoring and filtering technologies. The Electronic Privacy and Information Center—EPIC, in its Annual Privacy and Human Rights Report (2001), echoed the concern of other human rights groups in the United States, that much of this technology is exported to developing countries that "lack adequate protections." The report explains that currently surveillance technology is indeed a huge industry second only to the arms industry, and that "governments of developing nations rely on First World countries to supply them with technologies of surveillance such as digital wiretapping equipment, deciphering equipment, scanners, bugs, tracking equipment and computer intercept systems."

Moreover, the EPIC 2001 Annual Report says that the then FBI Director Louis Freeh traveled extensively around the world promoting the use of wiretapping. It is encouraged in the name of preventing cyber crime and terrorism. The report also concludes that such technology can "exert a powerful chilling effect on those who might wish to take a dissenting view and few will risk exercising their right to democratic protest." It acknowledges that much of this technology is in fact used to "track the activities of dissidents, human rights activists, journalists, student leaders, minorities, trade union leaders, and political opponents." In short, it is used to target the activities of civil society.

Indeed this has been one of the primary criticisms of those critical of the concept of e-democracy, where they perceive the Internet as yet another tool that allows governments to violate the privacy of their citizens. Indisputably, Arab governments are making use of this technology. Once again Western hegemony as well as double standards are both at play, where the United States claims to be trying to export democracy while concurrently undermining budding democratic potential and supporting oppressive governments against their people. While it encourages governments to use such technologies, it has made it difficult for people to get access to existing anti-surveillance technologies such as encryption that could bypass government control. Privacy protection software and other counter-surveillance software are restricted export technology because of terrorism. The U.S.-based Human Rights Watch says that while such software could greatly benefit human rights activists and organizations, the U.S. government has prohibited, and in fact even pressured other countries as well to prohibit, the export of such technologies:

> contrary to the spirit of international norms that recognize privacy as a fundamental human right, governments continued to use export controls or other national laws limiting the public's access to encryption technologies and inhibiting the development of new encryption products. In December 1998, the Wassenaar Arrangement (a group of thirty-three states) announced, largely due to United States pressure, new guidelines that would authorize restrictions on the export of most commercial cryptography products above a fifty-six or sixty-four bit strength. (Human Rights Watch 2000)

In addition, since September 11, the United States has imposed additional restrictions to the acquiring of, and even training on, what it defines broadly as potential weapons of mass destruction technologies. Non-U.S. citizens, and in particular members of specific countries, are prohibited from studying such technologies in the United States nor on training on them in the name of security. In its Technology Alert List, the United States identifies such "sensitive" technologies, as those that include advanced computer and microelectronic technology; information security (technologies associated with cryptography and cryptographic systems to ensure secrecy for communications, video, data, and related software); robotics (technologies associated with artificial intelligence, automation, and computer-controlled machine tools, pattern recognition technologies).

Civil society, therefore, and in particular the human rights movement, are encountering an enormous hurdle in trying to use such technologies. They need to understand these issues and attempt to counter such policies within their own countries and beyond it. They also need to gain the necessary available skills and technologies by which they could protect themselves before it becomes impossible to do so. After all, their battle for human rights is not only with their government but also with their Western "allies."

Conclusion

The enthusiasm of young people in the Arab World to learn to use computers, to acquire the necessary skills, and to connect with the world is the main reason for optimism in the potential of the Internet in this region. Democracy is an accumulative process, and the current participation of Arab youths online is one form of self-expression and a desire to be a part of the "outside" world. It is important to remember that there was a significant demographic shift in the region since the early 1950s, where the young population under 25 years old constitute more than 60 percent of the region's overall population and the numbers are rising. This youth population are the ones who are seeking to find alternatives to the political, economic, and social frustrations already existing.

Access to information alone will not create democracy nor democratic participation, yet it is a powerful first step toward this goal. A belief that mere access to the Internet will create democracy is part of what Winner (1991) rightly called *mythinformation* and what Rheingold (2000) called *disinformocracy*. It is not a magical formula. Rheingold argued that connecting to the Internet alone without considering the hard work that needs to be done in real life to "harvest the fruits of that democratizing power" does the Internet a disservice. The Internet, as he emphasizes, is not a "utopian vision of the electronic agora, an Athens without slaves, made possible by telecommunications and cheap computers." The power of the Internet is currently the same as the power of the printing press when it first came out: it has "made a literate population possible, and literate populations, who are free to communicate among one another, came up with the idea that they could govern themselves. Radio and television each had effects on the public sphere" (Reingold 2000).

The strategic use of the Internet, which would aim at translating this flow of information into real knowledge and a serious application of this knowledge, is the means to achieving progress. Knowledge is only acquired through the manner with which the Internet's vast resource of information is sorted, managed, and processed (Fergani 2002).

While the argument on globalization and hegemony is indisputably true, the Internet, more so than television and other forms of technology, should be viewed in the light of "accommodation." There can be no doubt that like other tools, it does have its problems, but its benefits cannot be overlooked. One of the keys to overcoming this obstacle is redirecting and therefore accommodating globalization rather than opposing it. It lies in choices that the Arab World could make, acknowledging and preserving its culture, yet at the same time having a willingness to appropriate what it feels necessary for its progress, without feeling threatened. The Arab World needs to create strategies to deal with the complexities and challenges of globalization without isolating itself. This is one of the roles of civil society institutions.

Although the Internet is essential to the human rights movement in the Middle East, it should be stressed that online activism is not necessarily active and genuine participation and does not necessarily indicate a democratic change. If such a strategy is not followed up with on-the-ground support and follow up, it becomes insignificant. We must not undermine the power of involvement in signing a simple petition in the Arab world, where individuals are usually indifferent to political issues and have no hope of addressing their leaders. Signing petitions or joining a discussion forum or publishing a website are only first steps toward becoming actively engaged in politics. What is needed is a strategy to keep their interest and curiosity, to work toward their mobilization and, more importantly, to help them mobilize themselves around their own issues.

Human rights and social movement organizations need to plan such strategies at this early stage of Internet usage in the region. They need to be aware and significantly involved in the policy-making process regarding the Internet. Some of the basis of their strategies should take into consideration the following: what issues are more suitable for online campaigns? Who are being mobilized and why? What is expected of them? Are issues that have transnational values and concepts easier to mobilize around? Is the creation of a "new internationalism" more of a priority than very localized issues? Are there standard models that they can use and replicate?

With such a conscious and deliberate strategy, the Internet could indeed in the long run be a powerful democratizing tool in the Middle East. Given a comprehensive strategy which involves civil society, such a strategy could help the disempowered instead of further disempowering them.

Bibliography

Ahmed, Ashfaq. 2003. "Internet Chatting Is Becoming an Addiction." *Gulf News* July 29 <http://www.gulf-news.com/Articles/news.asp?ArticleID=93777>.
Alterman, Jon B. 2002. *The Effect of Satellite Television on Arab Domestic Politics.*

Al Thani, Sheikh Hamad bin Khalifa. 2003. Speech on the Eve of the Referendum for a Constitution, April 23 <http://www.al-bab.com/arab/docs/ qatar/ emir2003.htm>.

Amnesty International Report. 2002. *Jordan: Freedom of Expression at Risk*, 19/03.

Anderson, Jon. 2001. "Muslim Networks, Muslim Selves in Cyberspace: Islam in the Post-Modern Public Sphere." Working papers on new media and information technology in the Middle East. Georgetown University. <http:// nmit.georgetown.edu/paperes/jwanderson2.htm>.

Arab Advisors Group. 2002. *Bandwidth Increasing in Middle East in 2002*. <http:www.arabadvisors.com>.

Bush, George W. 2001. "Homeland Security Presidential Directive-2." *Combating Terrorism Through Immigration Policies*. October 29.

Clift, Steven. 2002. "E-Democracy: The Promise of the Future is a Reality Today." <http://www.publicus.net/articles/today.html>.

Committee to Protect Journalists. 2001. *Press Freedom Reports from Around the World*, October. Accessed at: <http://www.cpj.org/news/2001/ US04oct01na.html>.

Docherty, Alan. 1999. "Net Journalists Outwit Censors," in *Wired News* March 13.

Electronic Privacy and Information Center—EPIC. 2001. *Privacy and Human Rights*. <http://www.privacy.org/pi/survey/phr2001/>.

Emirates Internet & Multimedia. *Number of Internet Cafes in UAE Doubles*. <http://www.emirates.net.ae/>.

The Estimate. 1998. "The Internet in the Arab World: An Update as the Saudis Go Online." December Vol.X #26. <http://www.theestimate.com/public/ 121898.html>.

Fergani, Nader et al. 2002. *The Arab Human Development Report 2002*. UNDP. <http://www.undp.org/rbas/ahdr/english2003.html>.

Hamilton, Lee. 2003. "National Security and Science and Technology." In *Making the Nation Safer: The Role of Science and Technology in Countering Terrorism*. Washington, D.C.: Committee on Science and Technology for Countering Terrorism Division on Engineering and Physical Sciences. National Research Council, National Academy Press.

Hanafi, Hassan. 1998. "The Middle East, in Whose world?" The Fourth Nordic Conference on Middle Eastern Studies: *The Middle East in a Globalizing World*. Oslo, August 13–16 <http://www.hf.uib.no/smi/pao/hanafi.html>.

Human Rights Watch. 2000. *The Internet in the Middle East and North Africa: Free Expression and Censorship*. <http://www.hrw.org/advocacy/internet>.

Kraidy, Marwan. 2003. "Arab Satellite Television Between Regionalization and Globalization." *Global Media Journal* 2, no. 2 (Spring).

Kubursi, A. A. 1999. *Sustainable Human Development under Globalization: The Arab Challenge*. The United Nations Economic and Social Commission For Western Asia, August. <http://socserv.socsci.mcmaster.ca/kubursi/ebooks/ global.htm>.

Lee, Jennifer. 2001. "TECHNOLOGY; Companies Compete to Provide Internet Veil for the Saudis." *New York Times*, Late Edition—Final, Section C, Page 1, Column 2. November 19.

Madar Research Group. 2002. *Arab World Set To Get Online*. Accessed October 21, 2003, www.nua.com.

McMahon, Peter. 2001. "Technology and Globalization: An Overview" in *Prometheus* 19 no. 3 at: <http://www.tandf.co.uk/journals>.

Naughton, John. 2001. "Contested Space: the Internet and Global Civil Society," in *Global Civil Society*, ed. Helmut Anheier et al. London: Center for the Study of Global Governance.

NUSACC. 1998. "The Current Status of the Internet in the Arab World." Cornell University Library. <http://www.library.cornell.edu/colldev/mideast/nusacci.htm>.

Reporters without Borders. 2002. *The Internet on Probation: Anti-Terrorism Drive Threatens Internet Freedoms Worldwide.*

————. 2002. *20 Enemies of the Internet.*

————. 2003. *Annual Report 03.*

Rheingold, Howard. 1993 reprinted 2000. *The Virtual Community.* <http://www.rheingold.com/vc/book.html>.

Rodgers, Jayne. 2001. *Globalization and the Internet: Practices and Political Transformation.* Paper presented to the ISA Hong Kong Convention of International Studies, July 26–28.

U.S. Department of State, *Bureau of Consular Affairs Visa Services.* 2001. "Using the Technology Alert List (Update)" 10/18. <http://travel.state.gov/state147566.html>.

Winner, Langdom. 1991. "Mythinformation." In *Questioning Technology*, ed. John Zerzan and Alice Carnes. Penn: New Society Publishers.

Zineldin, Mosad. 1998. *Globalisation and Economic Integration among Arab Countries.* The fourth Nordic Conference on Middle Eastern Studies: The Middle East in Globalizing World. Oslo, August 13–16.

Chapter 9

Transnational Environmental Activism after Seattle: Between Emancipation and Arrogance

Kate O'Neill and Stacy D. VanDeveer

The protests in Seattle against the World Trade Organization Ministerial in 1999 were a pivotal moment for the transnational environmental movement. Seattle brought together a diverse range of environmental groups from around the world in a volatile, direct-action situation as opposed to the more "civilized" context of an international meeting. Present were not only the lobbying groups who have begun to make their mark on the international scene, but also more radical groups—opposing global capitalism, genetically modified organisms (GMOs) and a range of other issues, who were prepared to utilize tactics that the mainstream movement had previously not had to confront. We argue that Seattle and subsequent events helped crystallize a particular set of issues for the mainstream transnational environmental movement, forcing members to confront issues of organization and tactics that they had heretofore marginalized. These include explicitly linking environmental concerns to a global justice framework, and deliberately embracing tactics of nonviolence in order to distance themselves from the "saboteurs" who have captured so much media attention at international protests. These new emphases were particularly visible at the 2002 Johannesburg World Summit on Sustainable Development and recent campaigns around altering common practices within extractive industries. At the same time, by (re)opening their tactical repertoire to include street protest and Internet and E-mail organizing tactics, transnational environmental groups have opened an opportunity to widen their societal base, reaching a younger and more diverse audience. Lastly, the substance and participation patterns within transnational environmental debates are also expanding beyond their North American and Northern European origins.

How do these developments fit in with the global arrogance research agenda? For the most part, our story is one of a struggle between "arrogance" and "emancipation" among (and within) movement organizations themselves. Development theorist Wolfgang Sachs and others have argued that Western environmental groups in particular had developed an elitist, arrogant-agenda over the first 20 or so years of their involvement on the international scene (Sachs 1993, 1999). This is, of course, a generalization. However, it makes an important point. When a small and not very diverse group of people purports to speak for (or "represent") the earth and most humans, some charges of elitism and arrogance likely apply. Western NGOs were key in pushing what many saw as a northern environmental agenda, focusing on issues such as climate change and nature conservation, which many felt excluded the needs and concerns of poorer communities. North–South divides in turn have been important in formal interstate negotiations. For example, during negotiations over the Basel Convention on Hazardous Waste Trading, some viewed the position of Greenpeace, for instance, as overly patronizing to poorer countries, forbidding them to import hazardous wastes under any circumstances, rather than allowing them to make those decisions themselves. Finally, the main location of most international environmental NGO activity increasingly became the meeting halls of the UN and other bodies managing international negotiations. Certainly, these NGOs have honed their skills in affecting meeting agendas and outcomes, however, at the cost of losing some of their grassroots connections and identity.

In the same way the environmental justice movement challenged some of the basic assumptions about environmental protection in the United States, so has the sustainable development/global justice movement—with its focus on human emancipation—challenged mainstream NGOs working transnationally. Thus, this chapter examines how Northern (or Western) groups within the transnational environmental movement have begun to transform themselves, and reframe their positions in ways that attempt to speak to broader audiences, positioning environmental movements within broader social justice agendas. In other words, important actors within the transnational environmental movement are experiencing their own transformation, potentially moving away from their own kind of hegemonic dominance of the "global" environmental agenda. These organizations show a greater willingness to participate in, rather than seek to define, transnational spaces for environmental politics and debate. For example, one sees more effort to create spaces for debate among different actors in the transnational environmental movement, and advocacy of horizontal, rather than vertical, network organization. In turn, these developments may enhance the potential for transnational social movements to more effectively transform global political discourse.

First, this chapter outlines the emergence and forms of transnational environmentalism. It then focuses particularly on "Western" or "Northern" environmentalism, and its underlying principles. These principles have been strongly criticized by others, especially southern writers and groups, on the basis of arrogance. This arrogance is reflected in a tendency to define a specific agenda of global environmental politics, representing a set of concerns that did not necessarily represent the main concerns of poorer nations, prioritizing, for example, species protection or global commons issues far removed from the daily lives of the world's poor (or even moderately wealthy). It is also reflected in a "managerialist" tendency: that problems can be solved with the "right" science, technologies and management techniques. In this way, environmentalism subscribed to the "myth of familiarity," relying on the mantra that technology, and good management, will save the earth. This comforting story harkens back to modernization theory prevalent in the 1950s, and even to childhood beliefs that mankind (*sic*) can overcome any challenges through ingenuity—without paying attention to social and political factors underlying environmental degradation, and the different perspectives on environmental problems held by many (and not only between North and South).

The second part of the chapter describes how northern environmentalists have begun to move away from these earlier, more elitist approaches, strategically and substantively. In terms of strategies, Western NGOs are leaving the "boardroom" for the street, and in terms of content, reframing global environmental issues in terms of global justice, human rights and sustainable development. The protests in Seattle in 1999 were pivotal in this process, and led to groups explicitly embracing nonviolence, in order to distance themselves from more radical groups present at the protests. We assess this shift, in terms of enhancing the transformative capacities of the global environmental movement. While limits remain, and many of the initiatives we describe remain in their early stages, concrete examples, such as the agenda of the World Summit on Sustainable Development held in Johannesburg, September 2002, and the emergence of new groups and networks embracing global justice themes demonstrates the shift many mainstream, Western environmental groups are making.

Many transnational environmental organizations are beginning to
shift some aspects of their work, moving beyond challenging the "powers
that be" (e.g., states) toward creating separate arenas of social and political
action. Yet, Northern groups remain constrained—or embedded in—the
prevailing incrementalist and "anti-sacrifice" attitudes of Northern populations, cultures and governments.

Who (or What) Is the Transnational Environmental Movement?

Naturally, it is an oversimplification to talk about the transnational
environmental movement as if it were a unitary entity. However, at the
most general level, it is organized around groups who work internationally
or across national borders to help solve common environmental issues.
These may be global in scope (such as climate change), or transboundary
(such as river management), or local-cumulative—shared problems, such as
biodiversity protection or waste management.

Table 9.1 gives some illustrative examples of different types of transnational
environmental groups and organizations relevant to this chapter. We dif-
ferentiate them partly on the basis of self-definition, partly in terms of what
they do, who their base is, and who their main targets are. In the first category are international NGOs—more formal organizations whose main
activity regarding international environmental issues is to engage in lobbying national governments, international organizations, and delegates
engaged in international negotiations. They tend to be hierarchically organized, with headquarters and so on. They rely on membership dues as well
as foundation grants to underwrite their activities. We focus specifically on
how these groups have reoriented themselves in the years up to, and in the
wake of, the Seattle protests in 1999.

Second are direct-action oriented groups. These tend to be much looser,
even cell-based organizations who adopt a range of tactics from street protest
to crop sabotage. They are much less interested in engaging policy processes
or traditional sources of funding, and some veer toward the use of violence
in the interests of their cause. These groups have been frequent participants
in antiglobalization protests, and have tied their agenda to that cause. At the
same time, many groups opposed to or deeply skeptical of globalization
have actively sought to distance themselves from these groups, and to garner
more media attention for their more peaceful messages.

The third category—grass-roots organizations with international
concerns—include anti-mining and anti-dam groups, and indigenous land

Table 9.1   Examples of transnational environmental
organizations and groups

Policy oriented organizations
- Greenpeace International
- Third World Network
- Friends of the Earth
- Climate Action Network
- Basel Action Network
- Global Witness

Direct action-oriented groups
- Anti-GM groups: Genetix Snowball
- Environmental Liberation Front
- People for the Ethical Treatment of Animals
- Earth First!

Grassroots organizations
- Narmada Dam Movement
- U'wa Tribe based in Colombia
- U.S. Environmental Justice Movement

Networks and alliances
- Pesticide Action Network
- Rainforest Action Network
- Local Agenda 21
- International Rivers Network
- Project Underground

rights groups. Most frequently, such activists are engaged in struggles over ownership of and access to natural resources, particularly as livelihood issues, in the face of governmental or corporate power. They are, however, not solely "third world" organizations. For example, the U.S. environmental justice movement, which grew up in particular to combat the problem of toxics in minority and poor communities, also best fits into this category.

Fourth is a category that overlaps with INGOs and with grassroots organizations in many ways. As Keck and Sikkink (1998) point out, the "network" as an activist organizational form has become very prevalent in transnational relations. It refers to a horizontal form of organization, whereby individuals and groups engaged in similar struggles in different countries come together in a loose or a more tightly-knit, short-term or long-term coalition, to pool resources, move information and knowledge, diffuse norms and lobby different governments, multinational corporations, international financial institutions and other actors. For example, a group such as the Pesticide Action Network helps coordinate anti-pesticide action and education in various localities (e.g., California or Senegal), as well as playing a role in major negotiations (e.g., over persistent organic pollutants). The International Rivers Network coordinates groups involved in anti-dam activity around the world. Generally, each member group is responsible for its own fundraising and membership base, and international coordination is based more on communication and discussion rather than central planning. This set of organizations is at the vanguard of reshaping transnational environmental activism. Certainly, many of them are concerned with international negotiations and global problems, as well as lobbying government actors, but at the same time, they emphasize the importance of the civil sphere and local actors in addressing environmental problems, and working outside of official channels to achieve desired ends.

Framing the Globe I: Forms of Transnational Environmentalism

This section traces the emergence of a particular form of transnational environmentalism, sometimes referred to as "managerial," which is associated with mainstream, primarily Western, environmental groups and related actors. This discourse generated some powerful critiques: we enumerate them and examine how the mainstream has reacted to these critiques. We identify this tendency as the "arrogance" within the movement, compared with emancipatory trends, which are based on notions of a just *and* sustainable international society, necessarily incorporating an environmental component. Still, because of prevailing views early on that environmentalism ignored "human" concerns and focused on concerns of the wealthy, the movement has struggled to gain a place in the global justice movement. This larger movement, post-Seattle, has defined itself as a broad coalition of transnational actors dedicated less to the overthrow of globalization per se, than to a transformation of globalization into a process that incorporates the notions of human rights, sustainability, and distributional equity.

Environmentalism arose in many countries, and in the United States in particular, out of the twin concerns of wilderness (or historical landscape) preservation, and localized environmental degradation, as urban areas suffered severe episodes of smog, toxic chemicals proliferated and so on (Carson 1962). In the late 1960s and early 1970s, environmental concern began to take on a global dimension, as scientific studies began to reveal the extent of transboundary air pollution, the threat of ozone depletion, the near-extinction of whales, and rainforest destruction. Over the same period, images of the earth taken from space began to enter popular culture. This "Spaceship Earth" image became a powerful symbol for nascent transnational environmentalism, a visual illustration of our fragility and our ecological interdependence (Jasanoff 2001). Activists, politicians, and scientists began talking in terms of "protecting the planet" as a whole, and thinking and writing in terms of a global ecosystem, or "sustainability" (Jasanoff 2001).

The year 1972 marked the first meeting of the international environmental community under the auspices of the UN in Stockholm. This meeting took as its slogan "Only One Earth" (Jasanoff 2001). Although some multilateral environmental agreements predated this meeting, it essentially marks the genesis of global environmental protection as we understand it today, and set up a range of institutions, most notably the UN Environmental Program (UNEP) to manage identified environmental problems through international cooperation. The following years saw the solidification of a particular discourse of global environmental politics. This discourse first of all identified and prioritized the "global commons" (the atmosphere, oceans, biological diversity) as the primary arenas of cooperative action. Second, it worked on the basis of policy informed by good science and scientific consensus—of a particularly Western tradition. Third, it set up multilateral negotiation processes as the main form of activity: states would agree on common goals and policies aimed at implementing them, under regional and global institutions, as much as possible.

Over the next two decades—up to and after the UN Conference on Environment and Development (UNCED), held in Rio de Janeiro in 1992, progress was made in putting this discourse into practice. Other global institutions, such as the World Bank, got into the act, instituting environmental provisions into the projects it funded. The Global Environment Facility (GEF), a fund managed by UNEP, the World Bank, and UNDP specifically funded projects in less developed countries related to global commons issues (ozone depletion, climate change, biological diversity, and international waters). Environmental NGOs during this time period began to orient their activities toward influencing international negotiations: while unable to attain voting rights, still the province of states, they drew up draft conventions, lobbied delegations, suggested official language, and were active in international and domestic agenda setting and, in some cases, in the monitoring of international agreements. At the same time, the emergent discourse of sustainable development began to gain currency in the international arena. Initially cast as a "southern" response to northern environmental concerns, it too became caught up in the same managerialist tendency that afflicted the purely environmental discourse—a trend that became more noticeable as the two debates converged in the years prior to the 1992 Rio meeting (Sachs 1999; Chatterjee and Finger 1994).

Over the same time-frame, counter-discourses to global environmental managerialism were emerging and gaining favor, especially among policy-makers and activists in Southern countries, many of whom saw existing approaches as examples of Western, or Northern, arrogance based on a particular set of assumptions about what was important in environmental protection and the appropriate scale and means of action. A brief review of the related literature gives rise to a few particularly cogent critiques, which began to emerge in international negotiations as early as 1972, and have fundamentally altered the course of several international conventions.

First, Vandana Shiva has argued that the "local" is being erased in environmentalism, as "global" solutions are proposed, in turn further empowering Northern institutions, such as the World Bank, to set the policy agendas of poorer countries (Shiva 1993). Second, critics argue that the international community prioritized a particularly Northern set of issues, as witnessed by the issues funded by the GEF, which ignore the most important environmental problems in poorer countries: lack of safe drinking water, clean energy sources, desertification (Shiva 1993; Easterbrook 1994).

Third, this discourse more or less discounted Southern forms of environmentalism, based less on affluence or on post-material values than on physical survival and overcoming environmental pressures caused by pressures of poverty or overambitious development projects (Guha and Martinez-Alier 1997). Ramachandra Guha's essay, "Radical American Environmentalism and Wilderness Preservation: a Third World Critique" (Guha 1997) has become a classic in this area. In it, he critiques the biocentrism of American deep ecologists, and the extent to which they have inappropriately tried to apply it to, or relate it to, the Third World and its spiritual traditions: he refers to the international conservation movement as "an ecologically updated version of the White Man's Burden, where the biologist, rather than the civil servant or military official, knows that it is in the native's true interest to abandon his home and hearth and leave the field and forest clear for the new rulers of his domain" (Guha 1997, 104). Nancy Peluso (1993) points out the very real and violent impacts on local populations in the name of species preservation and forest protection in Kenya and Indonesia. Eduardo Gudynas (1993) develops the "fallacy of eco-messianism:" "within the environmental movement—especially some Northern groups—there are organizations or individuals who believe they have the knowledge and the human and financial resources which entitle them to lead the environmental movement, and hence all of society, on the only true road to Earth's salvation" (Gudynas 1993, 170).

Fourth, as environmental politics globalized, questions of representation became paramount. As many Northern environmentalists became concerned with environmental problems in the global South, they began lobbying their own governments and international organizations "on behalf" of people in the South (Fox and Brown 1998). Questions were raised not only by Southern groups, but also by organizations such as the World Bank and by Southern governments as to how representative these groups were of "on-the ground" concerns. In turn, this undermined the credibility of Northern groups with target organizations. Many Southern groups felt they needed to alter, or reframe their tactics and issues in order to "fit" with Northern concerns to be heard. For some, this meant, for instance, down-playing the social costs of the problem, or putting forward a face that was not truly representative of their constituencies (e.g., Baviskar 2001). Perhaps one of the best examples of the arrogance of these approaches was the enormous interest among Northern environmental groups and publics in the 1980s and early 1990s in saving tropical forests— without considering the welfare of existing forest communities, a project that often suited the ends of government officials (Hecht and Cockburn 1989; Peluso 1994).

Finally, Northern environmental groups have continually skirted an issue absolutely central to Southern groups—the nature and extent of consumption, especially in northern countries (Princen et al. 2002). Consumption is the "third rail" for many environmental groups, as directly confronting consumption patterns and consumer culture as political issues could well alienate their donor bases and the political allies (Princen et al. 2002). Instead, they have tended to frame consumption issues as ones of individual rather than collective responsibility: plant a tree or recycle, rather than actively change the consumerist base of Northern society (Maniates 2002). Ignoring Northern consumerism and the ecological and human violence at various stages of the global commodity chain of production also helps to perpetuate the myth that the aggregate human population—particularly that contributed by poorer parts of the globe—is among the chief drivers of global environmental degradation. Thus, Northern groups perpetuated the notion that Southern nations should alter the size of their families and related social values, while Northern consumers could continue apace.

Another set of critiques asks what sense it makes to speak of "the global environment" as a unitary system, and one that can be usefully modeled (Buttel et al. 1990; Taylor and Buttel 1992). Different human needs, perceptions, and priorities vary so widely that such "globalspeak" or global science runs the risk of ignoring humans and equity. Sheila Jasanoff's perceptive essay on images of the globe and global environmental consciousness (Jasanoff 2001) explores the nuances of these ideas as they have played out in environmental politics.

Framing the Globe II: Discursive Conflict in International Negotiations

Since the 1972 Stockholm Convention, the dominant approach to global environmental management has remained the Framework Convention-Protocol model of international treaty negotiation (Porter et al. 2000). This slow, incrementalist and state-dominated approach to the development of international treaties and organizations is fundamentally technocratic and managerial—not transformative. Supported by most of the large Northern environmental NGOs, it steadfastly avoids addressing underlying economic, social and political causes for environmental degradation and unreflective consumption. Yet, the on-going negotiations over two recent international conventions have been particularly potent sites of conflict between discourses of transnational environmentalism: the Convention on Biodiversity (CBD), and the UN Framework Convention on Climate Change (UNFCC), both first signed in Rio in 1992. The CBD was originally conceived of by conservation biologists and the International Union for the Conservation of Nature (IUCN) as a way to bring together existing treaties on wilderness protection, World Heritage sites, and species conservation, to protect the world's heritage of biological diversity as a global commons. However, Southern opposition to this notion, and their desire to protect their own natural resources from exploitation by Northern economic interests, as well as not to see their areas of natural biodiversity turned into playgrounds for wealthy tourists and their human inhabitants turned out, led to a very different sort of convention. Instead of declaring biodiversity the "common heritage of mankind," the main Articles in the Convention asserted national sovereignty over biodiversity, and subsequent negotiations have focused on North–South trading of genetically modified organisms. Members of the international conservation community are still appalled by this change in direction (Guruswamy 1998).

The UNFCC has followed a different trajectory, and remains weaker. Conflicts in the negotiation of the Framework Convention and the subsequent Kyoto Protocol have been manifold; here we highlight the debate over the relative burdens of Northern and Southern countries in terms of greenhouse gas emissions. In its 1990–91 Report, the World Resources Institute published a study that placed Southern countries, in particular

India and Brazil, toward the top of the list of GHG emitters. Anil Agarwal and Sunita Narain, of India's Center for Science and Environment responded with a report that savagely indicted the underlying assumptions of the WRI report, in particular by differentiating between "luxury" and "survival" emissions (Agarwal and Narain 1991). This in turn helped pave the way for equity issues to take on a larger role in negotiations over combating climate change, as well as more studies on the differential responsibilities and impacts of climate change, and the scales at which these should be addressed (Athanasiou and Baer 2002).

These two examples represent punctuation points in a gradual process of response and reorientation of Western environmentalists in the light of accusations of arrogance. There is a good deal of evidence that these groups, or at least a high percentage of them, have been taking these critiques on board—perhaps overboard in a few instances. For example, horizontal networks of groups have begun to take precedence over vertical organizations, opening up new opportunities for concerted action at different scales. Table 9.1 (above) demonstrates the diversity of these groups. Northern groups are learning not to "educate" their southern partners (Fox and Brown 1998). Charges of the imperialism of Western scientific knowledge and methods are being challenged through work on local, or indigenous, knowledge (Long-Martello 2001). Western groups are paying far more attention to community-based resource management (e.g., Zimbabwe's CAMPFIRE wildlife management program). Finally, as the following section argues, the antiglobalization movement has helped crystallize the linkages between the concentration and globalization of economic power, the ideology of free-market capitalism, and global/local environmental degradation. On the other hand, some argue that by privileging "indigenous voices" and "local communities," without examining how these categories themselves are open to construction and strategic manipulation, may add little additional representation to international politics or to our collective understanding of the production of knowledge (Jasanoff and Long-Martello 2004).

Nevertheless, the climate change issue—the attention it receives and the resources expended on it—continues to illustrate the prioritization of Northern, science-driven environmental concerns over issues of more immediate concern for the South. Desertification, for example, already adversely affects millions of people (mostly in the South) and tens of millions of hectares of habitat around the world. As many local and national NGOs and grassroots groups in the South struggle to combat desertification and its implications, the attention and material resources dedicated to desertification issues by Northern NGOs, scientists and governments, continue to be vastly overwhelmed by those aimed at climate change (Corell 1999).

Seattle 1999: The Antiglobalization Movement Comes out, and the Global Justice Movement Takes off

The years leading up to the 1999 Seattle protests against the WTO were ones of learning for Western transnational environmental groups. The growth of the transnational antiglobalization protest movement helped crystallize an agenda for environmental groups that linked them firmly to global justice and against neoliberal globalization. It also represented a change in tactics and strategies for members of the movement. The attention the protests received provided an impetus for groups to broaden their repertoire—from the boardroom to the streets—and enhance their street credibility. The violence, directed almost wholly toward corporate property, accompanying many of the protests also encouraged the mainstream to distance themselves from anarchist and radical groups, and to adopt (and/or reemphasize) explicitly peaceful mission statements, goals and tactics. Finally, events during and after the Seattle protests enabled environmentalists to join the growing Global Justice movement, a movement that seeks to advocate positive alternatives to existing models of neoliberal globalization (and which prefers not to use the "antiglobalization" label, owing to its negative connotations).

Three overlapping issues areas have afforded the large international environmental NGOs opportunities to better link their concerns and their institutions with those of labor and human rights groups: trade-environment debates, genetically modified foods and crops, and the environmental and social impacts of multinational corporations and international financial institutions. In North America, the debates around the negotiations, ratification, and implementation of NAFTA have increased and maintained the attention of environmental and labor groups to these issues of the last decade (see e.g., Audley 1997).

Transnational networks and alliances had been in place for many years prior to the late 1990s, providing a focal point and outlet for generalized grievances against globalization. Fostered by the rapid expansion of Internet technology, real-time intergroup communication and alliance formation was growing at an exponential and much more affordable rate. People and organizations in different countries, especially those sharing common cause, were looking for reasons to ally together: the "50 Years Is Enough" campaign against the World Bank was one of the first examples of transnational advocacy coalition building (Fox and Brown 1998). However, linkages (at least in the north) between human rights, environmental and labor abuses, for example, were slower to emerge. Some early lessons connecting these issues were drawn by some NGOs about the near obsession in the United States with issues such as human population growth (in poor societies) and "saving the rainforest." These issues, while important from many perspectives, conveniently shifted the locus of action from North to South. Yet, the Seattle protests were distinguished by strong alliances between hitherto opposing interests, some of whom were in fact historically inimical, as in the case of U.S. labor and environmental organizations. Further, the protests brought out many different types of activists: not only the established groups across the "radical to professional" spectrum, but also students, "ordinary people," and more hardcore anarchists.

Yet, Seattle 1999 was not the first antiglobalization event of its kind. Protests had begun, for instance, against G-8 meetings in London earlier in 1999.[1] Most importantly, NGOs had begun to realize their clout in a campaign that drew nowhere near the same attention as Seattle, but that was probably more effective: against the OECD-sponsored Multilateral Agreement on Investments (MAI). The protests of 1998 were instrumental in the final stalling of negotiations around the agreement. The MAI would have provided a framework for the protection of foreign direct investment against all sorts of domestic regulations (Deibert 2000), and was bitterly opposed by transnational activists, both because of its substance and its closed-door negotiation process.

Word about the agreement spread from "insider" NGOs aware of the negotiations progressively outward, bringing in the wider environmental activist community, rather like the ripple effect of a stone dropped in a pool of water (Shittecatte 2000). There were certainly strong divisions among the negotiating countries. However, many ascribe the stalling of MAI talks in April 1998 to a concerted effort by public interest, environmental and labor groups, working via the Internet, to halt the talks (Taglieri 1999; Deibert 2000). This effort culminated in street protests, though on a far smaller scale than Seattle, and Internet-based lobbying. The MAI in that incarnation was declared dead on arrival in December 1998, when France pulled out of the agreement. The success of this multinational organizing effort provided the impetus for groups involved in the anti-MAI campaign to turn their focus to a bigger target: the World Trade Organization.

Holding its Third Ministerial meeting in Seattle in November 1999, the WTO had chosen a North American city known for its liberalism, and strong labor base, an ideal site for protest organizers who could deliver a large U.S. and Canadian constituency. According to early reports, around 300 groups began preparing early for the meeting, deciding tactics and training activists.[2] A couple of months beforehand, Seattle city administrators, police and business owners began preparing for the onslaught, yet had no idea what would confront them in November. In the event, around 50,000 demonstrators gathered in the Seattle streets. The disparate forces represented by the demonstrators, and their sheer numbers overwhelmed both the organizers of the meeting, and the city of Seattle. Disruptions outside the meeting were mirrored by disagreements within, especially between northern and southern countries, and the meeting broke up without reaching a conclusion. Since 1999, the movement has maintained much of its momentum, as, for example, antiglobalization protests provided a template for coordinated global protests against the 2003 U.S.-led war against Iraq.

One of the distinguishing features of the Seattle protests was their absence of clearly defined leadership, or hierarchy. However, among the key organizing groups were the International Forum on Globalization, the Third World Network, Ralph Nader's organization Public Citizen, and the AFL-CIO (Retallack, 2000). Another key factor in the success of organizing Seattle was the proliferation of websites that announced events, advertised accommodations, and generally brought the activist community together. The use of E-mail, cell phones, pagers, and messaging technology has become a key tool in organizing protests, and in getting publicity out about events. State officials know this well, as many such technological fora are regularly monitored (at the very least) by various security and law enforcement bodies in advance of protests and official meetings and declarations.

In addition to its lack of clear hierarchy, and extensive use of Internet organizing, the WTO protest movement had several other features that distinguish it both from other environmental movement actions in the recent past and from other mass protests. The first was its transnational character. Groups from both northern and southern countries attended, though of course there was a predomination of North American participants (and a concerted attempt on the part of immigration officials to keep foreign protestors out). Second, as already mentioned, the movement had a diversity of claims, but a unity of purpose. For once, groups normally on opposing sides of different arguments came together in a common cause (albeit one that at that point had not formulated a constructive set of future options).

Third was the impressive palette of tactics employed by activists. Certainly there were demonstrations, and riots, but also, there were extensive teach-ins attended by many of the demonstrators, held by people such as Martin Khor of Third World Network, and Vandana Shiva. Many who went made an effort before leaving to educate themselves on the issues and attended educational sessions held around the city. Protest organizers often use the bus rides on the way to events and sessions at the locations where attendees spend the nights to organize various teach-ins and protest training sessions. A very big part of the protests were performative. Giant puppets, colorful costumes and bold gestures were the order of the day—many cite the mix of Monarch butterflies, giant tomatoes, and bare-breasted women in the parades. Participants from different countries adopted national dress to demonstrate diversity. Such street theatricals lent credence to the term "travelling circus." Applied as an epithet by some of the press, in fact they are one of the movement's sources of strength (O'Neill 2004). Finally, the Seattle mobilization was also a youth mobilization; many participants were in their twenties or younger, thus giving established groups a chance to reach out to a younger generation for support.[3]

Although the transnational protest movement has had little significant impact (as yet) in changing policies and practices of major governments, it has been influential in other ways. First, the movement has continued to generate new ideas (Cavanagh and Mander 2002), organizational forums (Teivainen, this volume), and waves of protests. Seattle marked the "coming out" party for this movement. Beside all the attention generated, the Seattle protests created new opportunities and new challenges for transnational environmentalists. Among the opportunities were chances to develop the environmental agenda to encompass a sophisticated critique of globalization in its current form, and to advocate the development of a "global civil society." Established NGOs, by turning again to street protest, a practice many had left behind, were able to begin rebuilding their "street credibility." Yet, Seattle also generated challenges. One was the need to develop a constructive alternative to neoliberal globalization that would serve to unite the diverse groups present at the protest. Another has been the choice mainstream NGOs have faced in their continued interactions with international institutions. The WTO and its sister institutions have (unlike many national authorities) responded to the societal challenge by demonstrating at least a willingness to listen to and meet with movement representatives. This poses a dilemma for activists. Should they respond to these invitations, leading to possible accusations of "selling out" even as they (might) gain chances at greater influence, or should they maintain their opposition? Finally, the role of anarchist and radical groups received media and political attention far outweighing their numbers. The mainstream movement therefore has been developing tactics to distance themselves from any violence, and to deflect media attention away from the radicals.

Framing Pro-Environmental Nonviolence

The violence and disorder experienced by many NGOs and state participants inside and outside of the Seattle Ministerial meetings, and covered so extensively by the global media, prompted many staffers in the mainstream environmental NGOs to position their environmental interests and tactics more explicitly within the language of nonviolence. For some activists such moves may be primarily strategic, driven by their desire to separate their agendas from more violent and politically unpopular tactics. Others express a desire to distance their actions and agendas from violence for moral and ethical reasons. In general, three strategies have been employed within post-1999 transnational environmental activism. First, a number of the Northern groups worked to enhance their nonviolent messages. Organizations such as Greenpeace and Friends of the Earth (FoE) reiterated their commitment to peaceful protest and/or civil disobedience at their international meetings and on their websites, press releases and communication with organizational members and collaborators. Second, the major Northern groups accelerated their attempts to establish and maintain networking and coalition building activities across the North-South divide. This strategy enhanced a commitment made by many of the large mainstream environmental organizations in the 1990s. They worked harder to establish chapters in the global South and to bring more diverse sets of Southern actors—often as stakeholders—into their programming and strategizing. As a third, and related strategy, these groups attempted to enhance the economic and political justice themes and programs within their core environmental activities. The "environmental" organizations have gradually increased their attention to issues associated with human, labor and civil rights. In many ways, this may be the most important shift in the programmatic behavior, goals and rhetoric of the Northern environmental groups.

Numerous examples help to illustrate the subtle but important shifts in the concerns of the major environmental groups. For example, FoE and the Sierra Club have supported the "international right to know" campaign (see www.irtk.org). The campaign focuses on increasing access to information and public awareness regarding the labor rights, environmental practices and worker safety issues of major U.S. companies' activities in Southern countries. Similarly, many of the major groups have launched—or collaborated to support—programs designed to push "corporate social responsibility." Not coincidentally, the latter issue has also been of interest to a number of influential foundations in recent years. Environmental organizations have thus joined the growing number of campaigns designed to expand "transparency" of public and private sector organizations. In this cause, environmental, human rights and labor organizations have found common cause—and a common set of target organizations (states and corporations).

The events at the 1999 Seattle Ministerial also emboldened the growing "environment and trade" agenda of the large Northern environmental groups. By 2003, organizations such as Greenpeace, WWF, FoE, and the Sierra Club were expanding (and in many cases coordinating) their programs targeted at achieving a host of legal, procedural and programmatic reforms of the WTO, IMF, the World Bank and the major regional multi-lateral development banks, and a host of large private international financial institutions (IFIs) including international banks, export credit agencies, insurance companies and investment agencies. They have also helped to coordinate protests and the issuance of common demands at annual G-8 meetings. In particular, environmental groups have endorsed calls for increased foreign assistance for antipoverty efforts in the global South. Other examples of the "green" groups' growing interest in international justice issues includes their support of "Jubilee 2000" and other programs designed to expand debt forgiveness and restructuring for Southern states. Also, many "environmental" groups have taken up the issue of quality freshwater as a human right. An estimated 1.2 billion people do not have access to adequate, clean water for daily needs (Gleick 2002). Hence, this issue took a leading place on the agenda of the WSSD in Johannesburg, 2002. In turn, this move plays a part in the growing movement to link the environmental agenda with human rights campaigns.

Perhaps the set of issues that best captures the reframing and changing nature of the environmental groups' global agendas is resource extraction. In recent years, the traditional Northern environmental groups, together with a set of newer Southern and Northern groups founded in the 1990s, have used the human and ecological ramifications of large scale resource extraction practices, frequently by large, multinational corporations to better integrate their environmental agendas with greater concern for human and labor rights, corporate responsibility and the need to reduce political corruption in Northern and Southern states. Environmental groups have long tried to expose the environmental damages done by unregulated forestry, mining and oil extraction around the world. In recent years, however, they have reframed much of this work to highlight the frequently brutal labor and human rights situations surrounding resource extraction facilities and companies. Well established organizations such as Oxfam America and Friends of the Earth help to coordinate extractive industries campaigns involving dozens of Northern and Southern actors.[4] They have focused political (and at times economic) pressure on the World Bank and other international financial institutions as well as on large Northern retailers such as Tiffany & Company and Home Depot.

Furthermore, organizations such as Global Witness have detailed the connections between resource extraction and commodities trading—by actors and consumers perceived to be "legitimate"—to violent and corrupt government leaders, organized crime groups, paramilitary organizations and terrorists.[5] Global Witness seeks to raise awareness about the connections between resources, violent conflict, and corruption. To date, its main areas of concern have been the forestry, oil and diamond industries. Global Witness has had some successes. It was instrumental in the on-going processes to develop and implement a certification process for diamond trading and in the cancellation of a number of forest concessions given to companies engaged in illegal logging. Even *The Economist* (May 22, 2003) has taken note, arguing that if the international diamonds agreement brokered among government, UN, NGO, corporate actors "works," it might serve as a model for regulating some of the most inhumane and ecologically damaging practices in the forestry industry. Other organizations involved in this general area include two Berkeley, California-based groups: Project Underground, and the International Rivers Network.[6] Both organizations focus on the impact of large-scale development, energy and resource extraction projects on indigenous or tribal peoples.

These strategies address at least two perceived needs of the Northern dominated transnational environmental agenda. First, the mainstream organizations sought to distance themselves from the more violent and physically aggressive elements of the antiglobalization movement. International program coordinators from groups such as Friends of the Earth and Greenpeace complained bitterly that major media outlets—particularly television news coverage—were most interested in covering violence and looting. From the perspective of the environmental organizations, this obsession with the violent fringe of the "antiglobalization movement" buried the pro-environmental and pro-labor messages that the groups sought to send. Second, the three broadly shared strategies sought to "globalize" both the substantive concerns and the participants in the international environmental movement. In other words, the large Northern based organizations are attempting to span some of the North–South divisions regarding environmental protection—without making some of the more "arrogant mistakes" of their earlier forays into the politics of the less-developed world.

Transformative Capacities?

Does a transnational environmental movement that is generally dominated by a set of Northern NGOs have transformative capacities vis-à-vis the international system? The literature on the influence of NGOs suggests a number of NGO strategies that can shape political outcomes (O'Neill, Balsiger and VanDeveer 2004). Likely the most powerfully transformative aspect of transnational environmental activism is its discursive basis. Whether they are in localized areas, national capitals or UN sponsored global summits, environmental activists manifest desires to establish and disseminate norms of "appropriateness" for environmental policies and consumer choices. They seek to "reframe" particular issues and behaviors, in order to highlight the "noneconomic" costs of particular activities—especially on human health and well-being, and ecosystem health. As norms are articulated and promulgated, norm violators become the targets of "shaming" politics, as environmental activists attempt to use various media outlets to publicize inappropriate behaviors. The shifts articulated above, in the way Northern environmentalists approach their Southern counterparts, as well as how they have started incorporating "non-environmental" issues into their agendas may widen their legitimacy. It also signals a disillusionment with "international relations as usual," as social movement organizations shift to working "outside the system," networking with other civil society actors to change outcomes and behaviors on the ground, rather than inside the boardroom, or meeting room. Similarly, environmental NGOs have long relied on promise extraction in combination with shaming, or the threat of it, to engender state policy and behavioral change. While environmental activists once focused almost exclusively on states, they have expanded their targets to include an array of international organizations and corporate actors. The expanding scope of environmental activism, beyond the state, may also expand opportunities to exploit—or create—elite cleavages.

Two remaining strategies to enhance the influence of transnational environmental activists have received a great deal of academic attention: transnational network construction (Keck and Sikkink 1998; Fox and Brown 1998; Khagram et al. 2002) and participation inside and outside of interstate negotiations (Betsill and Corell 2001; Princen and Finger 1994; Clark et al. 1998). What appears to be changing here is that environmental activist organizations are now more likely to network beyond narrowly defined environmental issues: for example, support for anti-sweatshop campaigns and other labor and human rights issues; Southern debt reduction campaigns; and collaboration with Amnesty International to increase attention to the cause of protecting persecuted environmental activists around the world.

Lastly, the major international environmental groups have achieved greater coordination among themselves and the Internet is allowing them to expand their connections with smaller and/or more grassroots organizations and movements around the world. One recent example is the on-line site oneworld.net. It provides an on-line information clearinghouse for groups and organizations interested in enhancing human rights and sustainable development. Launched in 2000, it has hundreds of affiliates, which can be searched by thematic/programmatic areas and contacted via E-mail and Internet links.

Certainly, limits remain regarding the transformative capacities of environmental organizations and movements. Questions about the social and ecological ramifications of Northern consumption remain problematic, with few major groups really willing to take them on. Some continue to question the ability of Northern groups to work in genuine partnerships with Southern counterparts, especially as inequalities remain in terms of funding, access to target states and organizations, and other sorts of resources, although they acknowledge much learning has occurred (Fox and Brown 1998). Finally, the dilemma of the extent to which to participate in conventional intergovernmental channels, or to work around or even against them remains, especially as some organizations, including the WTO, are making steps to address environmental concerns on their own terms (Bernstein 2002). The agenda and outcome of the WSSD in 2002 is indicative: while it made steps in seriously addressing "southern" issues, such as freshwater availability, many felt it seemed marginalized and (perhaps) pointless in a world threatened by the "war against terrorism" and a UN divided within itself (VanDeveer 2003; Wapner 2003).

Transnational Environmental Activism in the Early Twenty-First Century

Environmental activism has taken on a leading role in transnational politics. Yet, the growing set of transnational movements and networks is not yet (nor is it likely to become) a coherent global movement. Within and among groups, there remains a continued (and vital) diversity of ideas, frames, organizational logics, and strategic choices. Some compete for resources, voice, access to policy and for discursive influence. The material and discursive spaces in which transnational environmental politics occurs have helped to construct and promulgate some general ideas—such as the notion that humans must learn to share a finite and degradable earth with each other and other organisms. Yet, beyond such generalities, debate flourishes. This chapter has outlined one of the deepest and oldest contradictions within transnational or "global" environmental activism: that between the "managerialist" North (or mainstream NGOs) and more emancipatory Southern positions and/or larger critiques of twentieth-century capitalism. We do not intend to essentialize the views of northern and southern groups. For example, community and grassroots movements in northern countries have more in common, in terms of organization and strategy, with counterparts in developing countries than the larger, professionalized

NGOs (Carmin 1999). Conversely, "NGOization" has been noted as a trend in developing countries, whereby groups adopt the language and behavior of northern professionalized groups, thus often losing touch with their base (Baviskar 2001), Yet, the notion that one small part of a movement that purports to be global could manage, and develop priorities for the rest, led to some justified accusations of arrogance from movement partners and counterparts.

In recent years, mainstream environmental organizations and networks have shifted some of their earlier discursive positions. Shared protest points or targets have helped to build transnational coherence and expand strategic coalitions and substantive demands. For example, common protest points include international organizations such as the WTO, IMF, World Bank (and the regional development banks), many multinational corporations, and many Northern and Southern States. In fact, the recent work of many environmental organizations appears to be returning to some of the environmental movement's roots, by placing a critique of unfettered capitalism at its center and focusing on notions of global justice and human rights that incorporate—rather than prioritize—the need for environmental protection. Groups are emphasizing the need for networks and coalitions, in part to target international organizations more effectively, but also as an end in itself.

Issues associated with the "erosion of consent" explored in this volume do not apply merely to transnational reactions to traditional centers of state and corporate power. The transnational environmental movement is being transformed by them as well. No longer can Northern environmental NGOs expect to act and be seen as the "standard bearers" of global environmental activism. Increasingly, many of the movements' most important NGOs engage in debates with others in the movement, rather than practice their own version of Northern hegemony. As a result, what "environmentalism" is and what it means to be an environmental organization may be changing as issues of human, civil and labor rights—issues of fundamental human dignity—take their place in the center of the "global environmental agenda."

However, this transformation is not complete—and it is easy to overstate. The large Northern groups, as compared with smaller and/or poorer groups in the South and the North, retain many of the instruments of hegemonic power within the arenas of transnational environmentalism: more funding, more voice, more access to state power, and so on. To state the obvious, environmental NGOs can practice their own kinds of hegemonic domination of agendas and discourses. They can make and believe in their own myths when, for example, they come to see themselves as the stewards of the earth.

In short, the growing discord and debate within and among transnational environmental groups and organizations can be seen as a growing strength, rather than a weakness—as an increase in their emancipatory potential. If global environmental networks and social movements are to yield a more emancipatory politics in a diverse and unequal world, they must be contested spaces—not just "greener" Northern hegemonies. Such spaces, like democracy, are unlikely to be characterized by global consensus. (When they are, we should look for the myths underlying them.) This view is somewhat different than Tarrow's (1994) notion that successful social movements "identify consensual issues" (p. 109). This suggests that such issues and their frames are preexisting and awaiting discovery. The experience of transnational environmental organizations, and the activist movements of which they are a part, suggests that consensus positions are constructed in dynamic and contested spaces. Transnational environmental activism in the early twenty-first century is increasingly a contested space, one in which the "traditional" goals and agendas of Northern environmental NGOs are changing to incorporate issues of social justice and the hints of a larger critique of political and economic structures.

NOTES

1. For the early history of the transnational protest movement, see Broad and Heckscher (2002).
2. "For Seattle, Triumph and Protest," *New York Times*, October 13, 1999, p. A14.
3. For available demographic data on participation at transnational protests, see Lichbach and Almeida (2001), Fisher (2002), and Podobnik (2003).
4. See these organizations websites at <www.oxfamamerica.org> and <www.foe.org>.
5. See <www.globalwitness.org> for a host of reports.
6. At <http://www.moles.org> and <www.irn.org,respectively>.

BIBLIOGRAPHY

Agarwal, Anil and Sunita Narain. 1991. *Global Warming in an Unequal World: A Case of Environmental Colonialism*. New Delhi: Centre for Science and Environment.

Athanasiou, Tom and Paul Baer. 2002. *Dead Heat: Global Justice and Global Warming*. New York: Seven Stories Press.

Audley, John. 1997. *Green Politics and Global Trade: NAFTA and the Future of Environmental Politics*. Washington, D.C.: Georgetown University Press.

Baviskar, Amita. 2001. "Written on the Body, Written on the Land: Violence and Environmental Struggles in Central India." Pp. 354–79 in *Violent*

Environments, ed. Nancy L. Peluso and Michael Watts. Berkeley: University of California Press.

Bernstein, Steven. 2002. *The Compromise of Liberal Environmentalism*. New York: Columbia University Press.

Betsill, Michele M. and Elisabeth Corell. 2001. "NGO Influence in International Environmental Negotiations: A Framework for Analysis." *Global Environmental Politics* 1, no. 4: 65–85.

Blowers, Andrew. 1997. "Environmental Policy: Ecological Modernization or the Risk Society?" *Urban Studies* 34, no. 5–6: 845–71.

Broad, Robin and Zahara Heckscher. 2003. "Before Seattle: The Historical Roots of the Current Movement against Corporate-Led Globalization." *Third World Quarterly* 24, no. 4: 713–28.

Buttel, Frederick H., Ann P. Hawkins, and Alison F. Power 1990. "From Limits to Growth to Global Change: Constraints and Contradiction in the Evolution of Environmental Science and Ideology." *Global Environmental Change* 1, no. 1: 57–66.

Carmin, JoAnn. 1999. "Voluntary Association, Professional Organizations and the Environmental Movement in the United States." Pp. 101–21 in *Environmental Movements: Local, National and Global*, ed. Chris Roots. London: Frank Cass.

Carson, Rachel. 1962. *Silent Spring*. Cambridge, Mass.: Riverside Press.

Cavanagh, John and Jerry Mander, eds. 2002. *Alternatives to Economic Globalization: A Better World Is Possible. A Report of the International Forum on Globalization*. San Francisco: Berrett-Koehler Publishers.

Chatterjee, Pratap and Matthias Finger. 1994. *The Earth Brokers: Power, Politics and World Development*. London: Routledge.

Clark, Ann Marie, Elizabeth J. Friedman, D. Kathryn Hochstetler 1998. "The Sovereign Limits of Global Civil Society: A Comparison of NGO Participation in UN World Conferences on the Environment, Human Rights and Women." *World Politics* 51, no. 1: 1–35.

Corell, Elisabeth. 1999. *The Negotiable Desert: Expert Knowledge in the Negotiations of the Convention to Combat Desertification*. Ph.D. Thesis. Department of Water and Environmental Studies, Linkoping University. Linkoping, Sweden.

Deibert, Ronald J. 2000. "International Plug 'n Play? Citizen Activism, the Internet, and Global Public Policy." *International Studies Perspectives* 1, no. 3: 255–72.

Easterbrook, Gregg. 1994. "Forget PCB's. Radon. Alar." *New York Times Magazine*.

Fisher, Dana R. 2002. "Civil Society Protest and Participation: Civic Engagement within the Multilateral Governance Regime." *Cornell University Workshop on Transnational Contention, Working Paper #2002–04*.

Fox, Jonathan A. and L. David Brown, eds. 1998. *The Struggle for Accountability: The World Bank, NGOs and Grassroots Movements*. Cambridge, Mass.: MIT Press.

Gleick, Peter H., ed. 2002. *The World's Water 2002–2003: The Biennial Report on Freshwater Resources*. Washington, D.C.: Island Press.

Gudynas, Eduardo. 1993. "The Fallacy of Ecomessianism: Observations from Latin America." Pp. 170–78 in *Global Ecology: A New Arena of Political Conflict*, ed. Wolfgang Sachs. London: Zed Books.

Guha, Ramachandra. 1997. "Radical American Environmentalism and Wilderness Preservation: a Third World Critique." Pp. 92–108 in *Varieties of Environmentalism: Essays North and South*, ed. Ramachandra Guha and Juan Martinez-Alier. London: Earthscan.

Guha, Ramachandra and Juan Martinez-Alier. 1997. *Varieties of Environmentalism: Essays North and South*. London: Earthscan.

Guruswamy, Lakshman D. 1998. "The Convention on Biological Diversity: A Polemic." Pp. 351–59 in *Protection of Global Biodiversity: Converging Strategies*, ed. L. D. Guruswamy and J. A. McNeely Durham. North Carolina: Duke University Press.

Hecht, Susanna B. and Alexander Cockburn. 1989. *The Fate of the Forest: Developers, Destroyers, and Defenders of the Amazon*. London: Verso.

Jasanoff, Sheila. 2001. "Image and Imagination: The Formation of Global Environmental Consciousness." Pp. 309–38 in *Changing the Atmosphere: Expert Knowledge and Environmental Governance*, ed. C. A. Miller and P. N. Edwards. Cambridge, Mass.: MIT Press.

Jasanoff, Sheila and Marybeth Long Martello, eds. 2004. *Earthly Politics: Local and Global in Environmental Governance*. Cambridge, Mass.: MIT Press.

Keck, Margaret E. and Kathryn Sikkink. 1998. *Activists Beyond Borders: Advocacy Networks in International Politics*. Ithaca, N.Y.: Cornell University Press.

Khagram, Sanjeev, James V. Riker, Bert Klanderman and Kathyrn Sikkink eds. 2002. *Restructuring World Politics: Transnational Social Movements, Networks, and Norms*. Minneapolis, Minn.: University of Minnesota Press.

Lichbach, Mark I. and Paul Almeida (2001). Global Order and Local Resistance: The Neoliberal Institutional Trilemma and the Battle of Seattle. Accessed May 23, 2004 <http://www.bsos.umd.edu/gvpt/lichbach/Page2a.htm>.

Long Martello, Marybeth. 2001. "A Paradox of Virtue?: 'Other' Knowledges and Environment-Development Politics." *Global Environmental Politics* 1, no. 3: 114–41.

Maniates, Michael F. 2002. "Individualization: Buy a Bike, Plant a Tree, Save the World?" Pp. 43–66 in *Confronting Consumption*, ed. T. Princen, M. F. Maniates and K. Conca. Cambridge: MIT Press.

Mol, Arthur P. J. 2002. "Ecological Modernization and the Global Economy." *Global Environmental Politics* 2, no. 2: 92–115.

O'Neill, Kate. 2004. "Transnational Protest: States, Circuses and Conflict at the Frontline of Global Politics." *International Studies Review* 6, no. 2: 233–51.

O'Neill, Kate, Jörg Balsiger, and Stacy D. VanDeveer. 2004. "Actors, Norms and Impact: Recent International Cooperation Theory and the Influence of the Agent-Structure Debate." *Annual Review of Political Science* 7: 149–75.

Peluso, Nancy Lee. 1993. "Coercing Conservation: The Politics of State Resource Control." *Global Environmental Change* 3, no. 3: 199–218.

———. 1994. *Rich Forests, Poor People: Resource Control and Resistance in Java*. Berkeley, Cal.: University of California Press.

Podobnik, Bruce. 2003. "Resistance to Globalization: Social Transformations in the Global Protest Movement." Paper presented at the Annual Meeting of the International Studies Association, Portland, Oregon.

Porter, Gareth, Janet Welsh Brown, and Pamela Chasek. 2000. *Global Environmental Politics.* Third edition. Boulder, Colo.: Westview Press.

Princen, Thomas and Matthias Finger. 1994. *Environmental NGOs in World Politics: Linking the Local and the Global.* London: Routledge.

Princen, Thomas, Michael F. Maniates, and Ken Conca, eds. 2002. *Confronting Consumption.* Cambridge, Mass.: MIT Press.

Retallack, Simon. 2000. "After Seattle: Where Next for the WTO?" *The Ecologist* 30, no. 2: 30–34.

Sachs, Wolfgang, ed. 1993. *Global Ecology: A New Arena of Political Conflict.* London: Zed Books.

Sachs, Wolfgang. 1999. *Planet Dialectics: Explorations in Environment and Development.* London: Zed Books.

Shiva, Vandana. 1993. The Greening of the Global Reach. Pp. 149–156 in *Global Ecology: A New Arena of Political Conflict,* ed. Wolfgang Sachs. London: Zed Books.

Taglieri, Joe. 1999. "Pressure from Citizens' Groups Kills Trade Treaty for Now." *National Catholic Reporter* January 29.

Taylor, Peter J. and Frederick H. Buttel. 1992. "How Do We Know We Have Global Environmental Problems? Science and the Globalization of Environmental Discourse." *Geoforum* 23, no. 3: 405–16.

VanDeveer, Stacy. 2003. "Green Fatigue" *Wilson Quarterly* 27, no. 4: 55–59.

Wapner, Paul. 2003. "World Summit on Sustainable Development: Toward a Post-Jo'burg Environmentalism." *Global Environmental Politics* 3, no. 1: 1–10.

Chapter 10

Global Movement to Ban Landmines: A Case Study in Transformative Politics

Jim L. Nelson

The global movement to ban landmines reflects collaboration among nation-states and non-state actors, among coalitions of indigenous grassroots organizations and international NGOs and transnational social movements. While the indiscriminant killing and terror by landmines exposes the arrogance of producers, traders, and users, the discriminating responses to the crisis reveal the layers of arrogance, and potential for transformative policies beyond global arrogance—the global movement to ban landmines shapes, and is shaped by, certain paradoxes of globalization, norm transformation and building capacity for civic democracy. Efforts in the past decade in particular have embodied the richness of multitrack approaches to engage multilayered goals. The process involved with these approaches matter to creating a lasting impact.

This chapter examines the global movement to ban landmines leading up to the December 1997 signing of the Ottawa "Convention on the Prohibition of the Use, Stockpiling, Production and Transfer of Anti-Personnel Mines and on their Destruction," and aspects of the global movement during the seven years since that milestone. Since the Crimean War and U.S. Civil War, landmines had become an integral part of arsenals of nation-states and non-state actors alike. The impact of landmine usage intensified in the 1980s as civilian communities increasingly suffered. Those maimed and killed were not so much on designated battlefields, but along pathways, peasant fields, and among other public-use lands. Whole communities felt terrorized. Landmines that pollute fields and pathways have been killing civilians during so-called low-intensity conflicts as well as eras of post-conflict community development.

In the process of changing a long-held international norm involving a specific type of weapon, the movement itself was transformed. Challenges initially centered on understanding the scope of the situation and a holistic analysis of socioeconomic impacts. The more voices that were heard, the more compelling the analysis became. Campaigners and career diplomats, through a blend of tactics involving confrontation and coalition building, emerged with convictions to prioritize health security, human rights and humanitarian assistance. This reflected a networking chemistry among individuals and organizations that reinforced the dominant dynamics, and resisted bullying by powers pushing for loopholes. The persistence became fueled by legitimacy drawn from first-person voices, benchmark research and ongoing analysis, and tools for transparency and accountability. To some extent, the movement's impact builds upon anti-apartheid and other movements and solidarity struggles, ceasefires for immunization campaigns, corporate compliance with World Health Organization and UNICEF standards for infant formula marketing, and treaty-centered efforts for nuclear test-bans. In turn, the global movement to ban landmines has affected approaches to other causes and coalitions that seek debt forgiveness among Global South democracies, ending conscription of child soldiers, abolition of nuclear weapons, seeking transparency of trade in "blood diamonds," and broadening treaty regimes concerning trafficking of small arms.

The chapter also addresses ways in which movement players have initiated responses to the myths of global arrogance. The global movement understands that national instruments of treaty ratification filed by the member states with the United Nations do not in themselves create human security. The difference is not in the paper, but is in the implementation process and security of health and human rights of development experienced among survivors and all people. Moreover, the global movement has documented that landmines not only perpetuate insecurity for communities, but also complicate security and indeed undermine protection for military troops. At one layer the interstate hegemon provides the context—that even the largest of the UN Security Council permanent members with the vexing history of landmine production and transfer of landmines would honor, albeit selectively, repeated UN General Assembly resolutions condemning landmines; and smaller states would provide effective leadership. Left alone without civil society monitoring, the ritual of self-disclosure reports might sound arrogantly hollow. Conversely, without utilizing the nation-state apparatus the global movement against landmines might sound like it is arrogantly taking the high-ground, and yet too narrowly focused. At other levels the learned relationships among Global North and South actors reveal intra-movement arrogance, which to some extent has been checked by landmine survivor voices that transcend organization lines and bring temporary or lasting bonds across project priorities and issue-sectors.

This chapter is informed by the Southern Africa context in particular, yet argues that interregional responses have magnified the impact the movement has made in response to global arrogance. The author taught in northeastern Namibia 1992–95 and participated in the International Campaign to Ban Landmines (ICBL) and Mines Action Canada meetings in 1997 and late 2002, and draws from personal notes as well as published and electronically posted documentation and analysis.

This chapter is organized into four sections: the introduction provides the historic context for the global movement and introduces the myths of arrogance. The second section highlights the ICBL goals and achievements since the treaty was signed. The third section underscores four groups critical for the universalization and implementation the treaty: non-state-actors; children and youth; mid-size states' coalition for human security; and landmine monitor researchers. The fourth section addresses challenges in reducing regional disparity of voice and vocation in the movement, and increasing adherence to survivor assistance and community development principles.

Background leading up to Ottawa Convention

The term "mine" does not necessarily bring about images of children with missing limbs, abandoned productive agricultural fields, or land polluted with hidden weapons. Until recent decades, the "mines" that one would associate with South Africa and its neighboring Southern Africa nations were precolonial iron mining and industrial era gold and diamond operations. In recent decades, however, the term "mine" has also meant a small, relatively cheap weapon. Assorted mines are used as weapons at sea and on land to target tanks and people. The group of weapons that target people are generally called "anti-personnel land mines (APL)" (hereinafter "landmines").

The region of the Southern Africa Development Community (SADC) members in 1997 (Angola, Botswana, Lesotho, Malawi, Mauritius, Mozambique, Namibia, South Africa, Swaziland, Tanzania, Zambia, and Zimbabwe, later joined by the Democratic Republic of Congo and

Seychelles) is home to some of the world's most landmine-affected countries, particularly Angola and Mozambique. Former governments of South Africa (before the 1994 all-race elections) and liberation movements used land-mines against each other. Moreover, South Africa and other world powers produced and supplied landmines to warring factions within independent Angola and Mozambique.

The larger effect of landmines, if not intention, was to destabilize the region; the direct effect has been to destroy infrastructure and terrorize selected villages. Although the weapon is usually intended to harm or deter combatants during conflicts, soldiers are not the ones usually injured. Reports on landmine patients, gathered since 1979 from Red Cross/Red Crescent hospitals and war surgeons, indicate that civilians are more likely than soldiers to be injured by landmines (International Red Cross and Red Crescent Movement 1997, 7). Individuals who trip detonation wires or whose human weight directly detonates a landmine left behind are usually maimed or killed. Because children's vital organs are closer to points of impact, they are more likely than adults to die instantly and never make it to a hospital. A worldwide estimate often cited during the mid-1990s by landmine opponents was that someone was maimed or killed by a landmine an average of once every 22 minutes. Moreover, previously unex-ploded landmines have been known to cause injury decades after a war has ceased. Thus, landmines have had their own impact in the area, and in their own way—like the industrial mines associated with mineral extraction—have shaped inter-group relations and developments among human communities.

Historic pacifist churches (Brethren, Mennonites, Quakers) and other peace groups have included landmines when generally protesting wars and war preparation; efforts by some groups date back more than a century. It was in the last quarter-century, however, that some humanitarian groups made a concerted effort to get the world community to take the impact of land-mines more seriously. By the late 1970s, as some governments were still clear-ing landmines left from World Wars I and II, additional civilian populations in Indochina were facing the legacy of more recent war-time landmines. In 1980, nation-states included landmines in an international protocol that regulated the use of landmines and other "indiscriminate weapons." Indiscriminate weapons are those that cannot discriminate between friend and foe, let alone between civilian and combatant populations.

In spite of the reform to the rules, the 1980s saw a proliferation of the supply and use of landmines. This was particularly true in Afghanistan and Cambodia in Asia, El Salvador and Nicaragua in Central America, Eritrea and Somalia in Eastern Africa, and Angola and Mozambique in Southern Africa. Some of these areas were in the midst of intense fighting; other areas were experiencing drawn out and destabilizing "low-intensity conflict." In any case, medical workers in the landmine-affected areas reported increased caseloads of landmine injuries, and documented the complexity of treating survivors (International Committee of the Red Cross, hereafter ICRC 1997a, 2). Landmine survivors became involved in helping to develop prosthetic devices to substitute for lost limbs. Relief agencies increased their presence, but could not keep pace with the growing number of victims. Indeed, local and international development workers found that their projects were hampered, even undermined, by the weapon and its effects on entire communities.

In the southwestern African nation of Angola alone, medical and development workers estimated there were at least as many landmines as there were Angolan children.[1] The country gained the reputation of having more civilian amputees per capita than any other country in the world, comparable to Cambodia. Although there is debate over the reliability of estimates, the point for this discussion is that the severity of the landmines situation, and the number of people impacted, has shaped the global movement to ban landmines. The socioeconomic impact of landmines led observers to rank the weapon as one of the greatest threats to human and animal health, environment and human development in landmine-affected areas.

By the early 1990s, international politics had changed, particularly following the declared end of the U.S.-U.S.S.R. "Cold War." A few U.S.- and European-based health and humanitarian groups with connections to landmine-affected areas understood especially well the seriousness and scope of the landmine problem, and appreciated the opportunities presented by changes in the global political climate. They felt the time was right to take action. So they invited concerned organizations and individuals to join their call for a worldwide ban on landmines. This was not a call to modify the 1980 Protocol rules and regulations concerning landmines, but to drastically change the do's and don'ts—international norms—concerning landmines. This call directly challenged military rationales for the weapon, arguing that whatever military utility the weapon had was overridden by the reality of landmine-related destruction to environmental and human health. The call was to forbid or totally ban the production, sale, export, transfer, stockpile, or use of landmines.

Months following that call, the International Campaign to Ban Landmines (ICBL) was formed. Within five years, the ICBL had grown to over 1,000 affiliated organizations from dozens of countries. This number includes organizations and campaigns that have specifically formed around landmine issues, as well as nongovernmental organizations with broader agendas. They are now affiliated through national campaigns, yet globally linked thru electronic documentation and Internet organizing as well as face-to-face conferences. Although the ICBL lists a large coalition of affiliated members, the "global movement to ban landmines" (hereinafter global movement) is a broader term that includes all efforts to ban landmines and support survivors. This includes coordinated as well as ad hoc efforts by individuals, governmental and intergovernmental entities, and NGOs. Some NGOs that have furthered the cause have policies of not formally endorsing campaigns. The ICRC is such an example. Although it is not a member of the ICBL, its contribution to the global movement is unparalleled. Other groups whose landmine-related work predates the formation of the ICBL have found it prudent to continue efforts without affiliation with the ICBL, yet join the ICBL and the International Movement of Red Cross/ Red Crescent Societies at international gatherings.

All together, the global movement to ban anti-personnel landmines has brought together researchers, practitioners, educators and activists with interlocking areas of interest: human rights, health, environmental sustainability, military security, disarmament, physical rehabilitation, human security, and participatory development. By December 1997, this movement of individuals, NGOs and pro-ban nation-states succeeded in drafting, and getting nations to sign, a humanitarian international law that fundamentally changed the longstanding international norm for landmine production and usage with relative disregard for trampling existing humanitarian law. Compared with the usual channels of diplomacy and treaty negotiations, this historic milestone was done in record-breaking time. The result, the 1997 "Convention on the Prohibition of the Use, Stockpiling, Production and Transfer of Anti-Personnel Mines and on their Destruction," is commonly known as the "Landmine Ban Treaty" or the "Ottawa Treaty."

The Ottawa Treaty process spans the drafting period October 1996–September 1997, ratification period of the first 40 nation-states December 1997–October 1998 and initial implementation period March 1999–2004. A five-year review conference took place in Nairobi in November–December 2004. This Ottawa Treaty process has been hailed as an important example of collaboration between governments and "civil society." The 1997 treaty is the product of the will of nation-states, represented by governmental representatives, and the will of people's organizations— with relevant expertise but less formal power, as represented by the ICBL and the International Movement of Red Cross and Red Crescent Societies. Moreover, the global movement recognized that the victory was not contained in pieces of treaty-paper which by 2004 has been signed and ratified by nearly three-fourths of the world's nation-states. Rather, the victory would be in changing conditions for landmine survivors and their communities. Even before the formal ceremonies for signing the Ottawa Treaty had begun, many of the same groups and countries were discussing development issues and citizen-based methods for monitoring implementation of the treaty.

State-Civil Society Coalition Building and the Landmine Treaty Process

The majority of global society has responded to the arrogance of landmine production, stockpile, use and transfer with persistence and creativity. While the successes reflected varied styles by various players, the chemistry of interaction among players and intersections of strategies did not consist of equal portions of factors. Some focused on documentation and experts meetings, and others focused on popular education through essays, art contests and public symbols (pyramids of shoes representing landmine victims, an oversized chair missing a leg symbolizing landmine survivors). The discussions among school youth and churches' global mission events and ecumenical action days complemented petition drives. Peer pressure among diplomats garnered timely attention to shift political capital, and consider alternative treaty processes. Community shame of hometown landmine manufacturers tied into international analysis of trafficking and stockpiling of the weapon. Legal scholars connected the dots among human rights and humanitarian conventions, and bilateral commitments. Survivors exemplified dignity through sharing their stories, providing education for action, while creating mixed-media mine awareness material to curtail future incidents. Such initiatives were further informed by countries' domestic politics, shifts in international rivalries, and aspirations by some for new politics. The interaction of factors galvanized momentum for a treaty without loopholes (Ottawa I process, particularly 1996–97), and for mines action implementation that embraced people-centered development paradigms (Ottawa II process, outlined in 1997 and increasingly emphasized since).

The Ottawa I process builds upon the efforts of the ICBL. The ICBL began when the Washington-based Vietnam Veterans of America Foundation (VVAF) and Frankfurt-based Medico International (MI) agreed in November 1991 to jointly launch an advocacy campaign to bring together NGO's in a coordinated effort to ban landmines. Handicap International, Human Rights Watch, MI, Mines Advisory Group, Physicians for Human Rights and VVAF met in October 1992 and agreed to coordinate campaigning efforts, with VVAF hosting and financially supporting the coordinators. These initial meetings had ripple effects that reached broader communities differently. For example, humanitarian and faith-based peace coalitions and other development and justice organizations mobilized around common goals interpreted from the respective strengths of their organizational missions. In addition, some embraced responsibility for specific tasks. For example, some campaign endorsers such as VVAF and Handicap International offered staff time and talents or ability to extend awareness; others, including governmental affairs offices of mainstream Protestant organizations, made this a staff priority in addition to existing priorities, and time and newsletter and website space spent on landmines was in competition with other global and domestic issues. Other organizations endorsed the campaign in name, but did not alter existing organizational priorities. Notably, groups with prior experience researching and campaigning laid the foundation for credibility: the arms project of the American Friends Service Committee built upon its literature on militarization; Vietnam Veterans of America Foundation and Handicap International built upon their field experience with survivors; faith-based advocacy groups and anti-apartheid organizations used skills and structures for listening to partner organizations to convey stories and critiques. The credibility from any one of these records became magnified by the synergy of ICBL-member organizations working together, comparing notes from various sources and pooling resources. These achievements took considerable commitment, and a learning curve to respect contributions by many kinds of organizations and experiences.

This learning curve continued as the global movement grew to include, and respect, more actors from the Global South. Some groups in the ICBL were transnational with North American/European hubs, and others were either multinational feeding into global associations, or yearning for such identity and relationships. While the initial member organizations that convened in 1992 had global field experience, they were Northern based groups armed with Southern reports. From the outset, core campaigners recognized the need to incorporate global grassroots. Throughout the movement's development, the value-added by alternative processes and additional voices was learned repeatedly. Newcomer organizations and national campaigns kept the challenge fresh. It was not enough to speak to the landmine issue.

To overcome a perceived North-centric chauvinism the voices of landmine-affected countries needed to lead. Expanding rings of efficacy and diversity of participants materialized with each annual international NGO conference held over a four-year period starting in 1993. This First International NGO Conference on Landmines, London, brought together 50 representatives from 40 NGOs. The following year, in May 1994, the Second International Conference on Landmines, Geneva, with logistical support of UNICEF Geneva, brought together more than 110 representatives from more than 75 NGOs. In June 1995, the Third International NGO Conference on Landmines, hosted by the Cambodian Campaign to Ban Landmines and the NGO forum on Cambodia, was attended by more than 400 people from 42 countries, representing NGOs, governments, the UN, de-mining organizations and landmine survivors. By February 1997, the Fourth International NGO Conference on Landmines was held in Maputo,

Mozambique. Convened under the banner, "Toward a Mine-Free Southern Africa," it gathered more than 450 participants from 60 countries.

In these meetings, consensus on strategy was less important than contextual strategies for mobilizing support. While efforts appeared more directed by ICBL core leaders in the earlier years of building relations, the ICBL yielded to regional planning by late 1997. Each region developed a campaign plan, connecting ICBL objectives to events and other opportunities, such as meetings in Africa of the Non-Aligned Movement, Southern Africa Development Community, Economic Community of West African States, and African Union. Campaigners cultivated regional rapport and shared information and strategies, thus preparing for national governmental resistance or hostility. What was learned in the sphere of international inter-governmental organizations was presented to the governmental diplomatic sphere. The force of credible information helped the South African Campaign convince the South Africa government to shift from qualified support of "smart landmines" to leadership for a total ban of all anti-personnel landmines. While the conventional diplomatic review of the 1980 Convention on Conventional Weapons (CCW) languished in Geneva in January 1996, the landmine survivors insisted on a new approach. Certain nation-state delegations such as Belgium, the Netherlands and Austria, worked with the ICBL to amplify the voices of landmine survivors. No longer would conventional diplomatic standard-bearers hold back the movement; a new fast-track was emerging. The pace was augmented with blocs of nations in Africa and Central America committing support for landmine-free zones in 1996 and 1997.

In October 1996, NGOs and government participants from 75 countries gathered in Ottawa to discuss landmines. It might have passed as another global issue conference and networking opportunity. Rather, it served as the stage for Canada to launch a 14-month challenge to governmental delegations and NGO observers. A final declaration from the 1996 Ottawa meeting recognized the urgent need for a ban on landmines; the Chairman's Agenda for Action outlined steps for reaching a ban quickly. Shortly before adjournment—after the U.S. government delegation had departed—Lloyd Axworthy, Canadian Minister of Foreign Affairs and International Trade, announced that Canada would welcome a treaty-signing conference in December 1997, for a total ban on landmines. The Canadian domestic and foreign policy dynamics, combined with the persistence of the advocates of a ban on mines, formed a moment that has molded the movement's "must do" spirit since. Few people (heads of ICBL, ICRC, Mines Action Canada, Canadian Department of Foreign Affairs and International Trade) had advance knowledge of the Canadian announcement. In some diplomatic circles, the pronouncement was treated as folly and disrespectful of established treaty-making procedures. Nonetheless, experts meetings and momentum led more nation-states to risk support for the Ottawa process. Canada's diplomatic courage and open respect for ICBL catalyzed a pro-ban state/civil society synergy in movement circles. This synergy had the ego of a superpower.

The streams of technical, regional, and special interest meetings in 1997 culminated in the diplomatic conference in Oslo in September, and treaty signing in Ottawa in December. The ICBL's privileged status provided civil society voice at key junctions of deliberation. The carefully coordinated consistency of this voice on treaty language was supplemented by multiple perspectives at the concurrent NGO symposium, where campaigners and visiting diplomats covered grassroots experiences and landmine survivors' challenges. The proximity of the diplomatic conference and NGO symposium also provided space for asserting Ottawa Treaty process expectations and holding national delegations to the standards of political will that had been building at the early 1997 preparatory sessions in Austria and Belgium, and technical meeting in Germany. This common commitment was particularly important as the Clinton Administration had decided after those preparatory sessions to attend the Oslo Diplomatic Conference. The U.S. delegation came with directives to water-down the treaty language, and demonstrated little spirit of compromise. The ICBL maintained momentum for "no loopholes, no exceptions, no excuses." Seasoned campaigners saw through maneuvers to change definitions, beg an exception for landmines in the Korean demilitarized zone, and exemption in time of war. Participants, led by delegates from landmine-affected countries, knew a partial ban would be a useless ban.

The arrogance of Washington's obstruction backfired. The untimely death of the Princess Diana of Wales, a couple days before her scheduled appearance in Oslo, affected not only the delegation from the United Kingdom, but generated tributes from Commonwealth delegations and others also. When Japan, Poland and Spain initially mirrored Washington's wishes, they became focused targets of international campaigners in Oslo and around the world. Concerted yet decentralized direct actions and media alerts by national campaigns forged alliances. Rather than yield to traditional state power, the movement created a new state-civil society alignment that was principled in cultures of peace and human security.

This resilience was preserved by Ambassador Selebi of South Africa during the Oslo proceedings. As Diplomatic Conference President, Selebi held steadfast to the Conference rule that there be no agreement on portions of the draft until the Conference was ready to vote on the whole. This proved effective. Despite high-levels calls from the U.S. government, the pro-ban states heard the voices of ICBL for "no loopholes, no exceptions, no excuses." The maneuvers enhanced the credibility of ICBL partners on micro-understandings such as the terrain in the Korean demilitarized zone and leveraging for making macro-demands such as country reporting mechanisms and donor pledges for mine action centers and assistance to survivors. These successes not only emboldened campaigns, but also transformed working relationships between diplomats and civil society.

The challenges of building a movement leading to Ottawa, and resisting arrogance by major diplomatic and economic powers, were met by using both thoughtful research and creative force, such as mass petitions, postcards and stickers, public art and publicly-built shoe pyramids, published photography (see Cahill and Roma 1995) and youth art contests. The momentum was augmented by face-to-face gatherings as well as electronic-mail coordinated actions. The role of youth magnified the voices of landmine survivors, through classroom projects in some countries, or raising money and awareness at benefit concerts. The Peoples Treaty, with summary language parallel to the treaty instrument and signed by ordinary citizens, connects grassroots, and instills a shared history and responsibility (Mines Action Canada 1997). Civil society pushed for a change in the landmine regime, yet also created the space for declaring civil society's responsibility for making it happen.

Making Safe Passages Real—The Ottawa II Process

Pieces of paper alone do not save lives, yet the commitments and processes they embody might. Even as the ICBL was intensifying efforts in the third quarter of 1997 to engage more countries to participate in the Convention signing and roundtable discussions in Ottawa, global movement participants were preparing for the medium- and long-term processes. The roundtable discussions in Ottawa bore fruit. The Action Plan presented to governmental delegations is mirrored by ICBL goals: universalization of the Convention, mines awareness, mine action programs, and victim assistance. Community development literature and Global South best practices are reflected in the prepared remarks at the 1997 Roundtable Discussions, and through the array of input through regional meetings.

Moreover, the regional coalitions of national campaigns devised timetables and measures of success, and developed space for conferring about strains and gains. The transnational nature of coalitions enabled neighboring countries to lend clout and pressure points when national governments slacked in responding to national campaign's inquiries and Ottawa Convention reporting requirements. Tools such as the implementation kits developed by legal staff of the International Committee for the Red Cross arguably primed the way for expedited review and ratification of treaty language in certain countries known for parliamentary and administrative delays.

The timeframe was augmented by ICBL momentum. The sooner the fortieth signatory nation deposited the instrument of ratification with the United Nations, the sooner the Ottawa Convention to Ban Landmines would take effect. Less than a year after the treaty-signing ceremony in Ottawa, Burkina Faso—notably one of the smaller states that has been landmine-affected—was that fortieth nation-state, triggering a March 1, 1999 treaty implementation date. Civil society generally, and the ICBL coordinating council in particular, has monitored compliance with subsequent Ottawa Convention compliance stages, and used its tailored methodology of shame and praise to sustain progress. The global movement has exposed certain states' arrogance of noncompliance and reinforced expected norms with annual research monitoring. In the process the global movement has moved beyond arrogance by mobilizing local and transnational actors to implement expectations, and lauding states for reaching milestones.

Five years following the convention signing, the annual figures documenting landmine-related injuries and deaths have dropped significantly, from an estimated 23,000 per year to 15,000–18,000 per year. Tens of millions of dollars have gone into de-mining activities. Mines awareness has been expanded. Whole communities have reclaimed land, and victim assistance is slowly gaining unprecedented attention. While the quantifiable trends such as hectares cleared and donor assistance is significant, the broader impact on community-based participation is mixed. ICBL urges institutionalizing active and substantive participation of landmine survivors.

Increasing Space for Emancipation

The global movement wanted to ensure that the measures called for on paper in the treaty were realized at the grassroots. Activists saw this global movement to ban landmines as an opportunity to broach discourses on development theory and case study. The 1997 and 1998 discussions in Bad Honnef concerning development paradigms (German Campaign to Ban Landmines 1997) inform nation-based Mines Action Centers, and donor conference discussions, but have not proven to permeate participatory policy-making. Campaigners indicate that more often than not, the project planning and policy directives flow through usual Ministerial channels. There tends to be a divide between international humanitarian de-mining actors and commercial de-miners with low-cost efficiency contracts. The Ottawa

Convention places concrete timetables for stockpile destruction and for de-mining, but benchmarks for participatory community development are less pronounced. Perhaps this reflects two paths of experience while moving beyond global arrogance—*universalizing* terms of the total ban of the weapon, yet respecting the *decentralized* adaptation of best practices for development.

Multidimensionality of the ICBL and Movement Resilience

Landmines have been labeled as "scourge of the earth," "hidden enemies," "hidden killers," "silent killers," "poacher's tool," "poor armies' weapon of choice," "the coward's weapon," "weapons of terror" and "field surgeons' number one enemy." The worldwide landmine situation has been termed a "cause of humanitarian and environmental disaster of massive proportions," a "deadly legacy," a "global health crisis" and even a "worldwide epidemic." These labels are far different from the image of the classical defensive use of landmines provided in traditional military doctrine: "sentries that never sleep." The range of negative labels reflects the scope of orientations that concerned people bring to the global movement to ban landmines: human security, environment, arms production and use, human rights and humanitarian law, health care, rehabilitation, de-mining, and development. The landmine context, understood from multiple perspectives, helps to clarify the reasons why diverse organizations—now numbering more than 1,400—have come together around landmines issues.

The Southern Africa context not only exhibits most of the landmines issues raised at international fora, but is also the origin of some of the reports and expertise that have been influential in broadening the campaign. The reports and actions of NGOs involved in Southern Africa converge to underscore the argument that landmines are a menace to *human security*. A UNICEF booklet that summarizes the terror faced by children in Southern Africa and other landmine-affected countries states that "if children try to sow seeds in the fields or irrigate the crops, or graze their flocks on the hillside, they are taking their lives in their hands. . . . Some mines are mistaken for toys, and children pick them up to play with them. Children's physical vulnerability means that appalling numbers of them pay the highest price" (UNICEF 1997, 8).

Environmental degradation is also used as a tactic of war, aimed at destabilizing civilian populations. The antipersonnel landmine is a weapon which causes enormous environmental damage (Newton 1997, 2). The relationship between arms production and use, underdevelopment, poverty, and environmental degradation has long been observed. Thus, as the momentum for the Ottawa Treaty process was building, several South Africa NGOs pointedly linked traditional environmental issues with the effects landmines, in particular, have on the environment. At least a dozen environmentally focused groups have been part of the South African Campaign. These groups, collaborating through the Group for Environmental Monitoring, produced *The Scourge of the Earth: The Impact of Landmines on the Environment* (Newton 1997).

South Africa and Zimbabwe were known producers and exporters of landmines, illustrating the political economy of landmines. Credit for documenting the scope of the arms-web is shared by Human Rights Watch Arms Project researcher Alex Vines and several South African organizations that compiled information about economic ties and key players. The major producer of South African landmines was the Armaments Corporation of South Africa, known as ARMSCOR. It was established in 1964. ARMSCOR's role, to decrease South Africa's reliance upon arms imports, was intensified when P.W. Botha became minister of defense in 1966 (Readers Digest 1994, 422 and 530). However, South Africa had also begun reviewing its landmine policies in the early 1990s, and observing a moratorium on export of landmines in late 1993. This was in response to UN General Assembly resolutions against landmines, and in the midst of the Fredrik DeKlerk Administration efforts to improve South Africa's inter-national image. For the remainder of the DeKlerk administration and during the first few years of the Nelson Mandela government, South Africa's policy mirrored the U.S. policy: they found "dumb" landmines abhorrent, but believed in the merits of self-destructing "smart" landmines. The South African Campaign to Ban Landmines reasoned with military officials, government policy-makers and parliament members. Consequently, a *unilateral, comprehensive* ban on the production of all types of landmines took effect in February 1997. Furthermore, South Africa began destroying its landmine stockpile on the eve of hosting the May 1997 African Union summit on landmines. Less than a half-year later, on October 30, 1997, South Africa boasted the success of the final phase of destroying its landmine stockpile.

Another significant player in the region's supply and use of landmines, particularly in the 1990s, had been the private firm of Executive Outcomes. They represent a migratory force, and transnational arrogance. Although officially registered in the United Kingdom, Executive Outcomes maintains offices in South Africa, and people in the region regard it as a South African entity. This is because Angolan and Namibian citizens who encounter

Executive Outcomes personnel often recognize individuals from past encounters with South African Defence Force operations. Executive Outcomes is regarded as a "soldiers of fortune" operation involving former British and South African officers—notably those who had been involved in some of the more brutal units. They recruit from Portugal, South Africa, United Kingdom, Belgium, Namibia, and Zimbabwe. Their "violence management" contracts promise that they will "keep the violence and banditry under control and provide stability". . . in return for large sums of money and mineral or oil concessions. During the 1990s they had contracts in Southern Africa nations of Angola, Malawi, and Mozambique, as well as in Sierra Leone, Somalia, Sudan, and Uganda. They have used landmines as part of their methods for executing their contractual promise (Adio 1997, 27).

The more prolific users of landmines, however, have been warring parties. Their use, as suggested in NGO reports, has been strategic. An ICRC analysis notes that since landmines are "often designed to maim rather than kill, mines force not only the victim to leave the battlefield but also those required to provide care for him, and carry him behind the lines for treatment" (ICRC 1997b, 5). Consequently, the global movement to ban landmines has appealed to human rights, including those that have grown out of a "third generation" of discourse that includes development rights and the expansion of children's rights. And the global movement has favored stronger humanitarian laws and more consistent compliance. International covenants that focus on rights of groups of people, such as children, build upon precedents from both human rights law and humanitarian law.

The global movement's advocacy for humanitarian law and rights of survivors to assistance is grounded in contexts of landmine-affected areas and the relationship of the ban on a class of weapon to the promotion of human security. UNICEF (1997 p. 2) notes that in addition to children being killed by landmines, there have been many more who have fallen to preventable disease or starvation because access to food, relief services, immunization and other forms of health care was blocked by mines: "the use of mines to target children and other civilians . . . is not only a violation of international humanitarian law, but is also an egregious violation of their right to life." The ICRC not only tracks the impact of landmines in terms of trauma treatment and medical care, but also in terms of disruption to health care delivery systems and community health. The combination of field reports and legal analysis has led the ICRC to critique the situation broadly. Landmines might not be a traditional health issue in same sense as sleeping sickness, river blindness, smallpox, malaria, and prenatal care. However, landmines have a profound impact on health care in affected areas. The number of landmine victims who are alone and in isolated places when injured reflects that the geography of the landmine crisis is different from the geographic history of injuries caused by other conventional weapons or weapons of mass destruction. Indeed, the wide scope of the crisis led the ICRC's leading authority, Dr. Robin Coupland, to describe the medical consequences as "a worldwide epidemic of injuries and a public health disaster" (ICRC 1997b, 6).

Because of the need, and in spite of these challenges, the health community has responded in Southern Africa. The same organizations involved with rehabilitation have been among those involved in health care in landmine-affected areas. Some, such as Norwegian Peoples Aid, have devised unconventional and controversial methods for attending to victims before they can be safely transported to a hospital. Notably, treatment does not reach all landmine victims. In addition to victims who die instantly from landmine injuries, some victims die before getting transportation to a hospital. In other instances, either the passage to the health center had been mined, or the health center was closed because of security problems. Such was the case in 1997 in UNITA-controlled Huambo, where ICRC's health services were thwarted because of security concerns and looting by armed gangs.

The most convincing expertise about these factors has come from landmine survivors and their communities. The global movement has provided a means for expressing their voice. As the International Centre for the Advancement of Community Based Rehabilitation (1997, 2) has argued:

> persons living with disabilities have the same needs and desires as others: to go to school, find rewarding work, raise a family. Yet their needs have often been ignored. . . . Governments, agencies and communities are seeking innovative programs to help persons live more independently, participate more fully in the community, and reduce their dependence on health and social systems. Community based rehabilitation is an internationally recognized strategy that addresses these needs.

Southern Africa nations have been living laboratories for developing community-based rehabilitation programs that are sensitive to disability issues. For example, Angola has more amputees per capita than almost any other nation in the world, second only to Cambodia. For decades, local and international groups have been engaged in fitting prosthetic devices, and assisting landmine survivors with rehabilitation. Between 1972 and 1993, ICRC limb-fitting centers in Angola produced 12,420 artificial limbs (ICRC 1997a, 22). Efforts reflect various levels of services and models for government-NGO partnerships.

Already before the signing of the 1997 Ottawa Treaty, some of the founding international NGOs of the ICBL had landmine survivor assistance and community development projects in landmine-affected countries.

Field workers reported, then argued, the futility of land-based agricultural extension work and community development when participants have to abandon those same areas that are found to be landmine-affected.

For example, OXFAM stated in 1994 that "landmines present a major block to development in the Third World and it is vital that aid workers in the field, development agencies, and all those with a responsibility for refugees have a comprehensive understanding of the problem of mines" (OXFAM 1994, documented in Handicap International 1997, A34). This might be obvious in war-zones. Whole villages and adjacent fields of Mozambique were abandoned because of landmines planted by fighting factions. Even the rumored or propagandized presence of landmines was enough to cause abandonment of the communities physically, and strain the displaced community psychologically.

The ongoing work of the ICBL Landmine Monitor project (ICBL Landmine Monitor Reports 1999–2004), with a deliberate effort to consult and involve a broader base of indigenous NGOs, has also increased the knowledge base and local capacity (skills, access, and courage) to monitor national entities and organize for informed action. The resulting network of researchers has been as transnational as the focus of another important dimension of inquiry: the political economy of small arms sales, trade, and smuggling.

As we can see from the multidimensionality of the global movement to ban land mines, there is a composite of organizations and individuals contributing a variety of perspectives to the reporting on the problems and working toward solutions. These are not competing perspectives, but overlapping sectors of a more complete circle of understanding. Collectively, they have proven to generate a synergy of greater influence, and greater network of mutual support and accountability. Indeed, certain groups emphasize the linkage of sectors; for example, the Physicians for Human Rights explicitly connect health and human rights. Whatever their collective impact might imply, they remain individual organizations with diverse histories and capacities, playing roles for reflecting and transforming power relationships.

Lessons Learned from the Global Movement

The dynamics of the global movement to ban landmines reflect a richness of peoples' stories, organizations' priorities, national contexts, and transnational realities. However, the achievements of the global movement were not arbitrary. While there may be some room for historical "flukes," the momentum was for the most part calculated and coordinated. Advocacy networks joined the campaigns, and campaigns employed information politics. Although member organizations were free to improvise and guide their respective national campaigns—indeed, they strengthened the global momentum by generating local research and popular mine-awareness materials—the global movement's priorities were guided by calculations and augmented by creativity. That combination of calculations and creativity provided the framework for a collective conviction; a total ban was essential and feasible.

The global movement centered around a common decision to ban a particular weapon, narrowly defined as antipersonnel landmines. By 1996, the Review Conference of the 1980 Protocol proved less and less satisfactory. Among the diverse voices that came to make up the global movement to ban landmines, the common decision was to pursue a fast-track approach. The ICBL had a special friend in Bob Lawson, who served as a mid-level bureaucrat in the Canadian Ministry of Foreign Affairs and International Trade who was pursuing an advanced educational degree, and understood the importance of the cause as well as the opportunity for a new diplomatic model. He thrived on the opportunity to help engineer this experiment in affecting the emergence of a new international norm. On one level he was a communication liaison to the ICBL, and on another level he conspired with other strategists who were likewise informed by history and theory, to make the fast-track approach diplomatically viable and politically irreversible. Among other campaigners within the ICBL inner circle, the common decision of goals led to delegation of roles: Steve Goose became the international humanitarian law wonk, Jody Williams became known as the persuasive pace-setter, Jill Bernstein served as the E-mail link with a human personality, and others codified goals into treaty language, generated schemes to involve school children through artwork and mobilize faith-based groups in petition-drives. The point is that a relatively few campaigners generated and facilitated the parameters for the early years of the global movement. This was not unlike the "20/80 Principle" whereby 20 percent of those involved are responsible for 80 percent of achievements. This leadership transformed the lone voices of the 1980s and turned the outrageous quest to change an international norm into a courageous bandwagon. The guiding principle was simple and nonnegotiable: if one supported a total ban, join the bandwagon; if one advocated loopholes or exceptions or delays, stay out of the way.

Sidney Tarrow discusses the political structuring of social movements relative to collective action as either cross-sectional and static structures of opportunity or as intrasystemic and dynamic political structures (Tarrow 1994, 41). Within "proximate opportunity structure" he describes policy-specific opportunities and group-specific opportunities. Often, these approaches are grounded in the subnational or group level. However, as social scientists have pursued comparative research on the increasingly trans-national dynamics of social movements, the state-centered opportunity structure has been increasingly questioned. Opportunities arise through national, transnational and global structures.

The global movement to ban land mines pursued elements of opportunity at all levels, from local to global, and created dynamics of opportunity. It worked the UN system, critiqued conventional methods, and created alliances to strengthen the UN capacity to monitor compliance with the treaty regime. The global movement was both a recipient of signals of encouragement and a catalyst for creating those signals that Tarrow considers key: (1) opening up of access to power, (2) shifting alignments, (3) the availability of influential allies, and (4) cleavages within and among elites (1994, 54). For example, the network of actors identified starting points. While Canada may have eventually championed the fast-track approach to the Ottawa Treaty, those doors opened only after a sequence of other doors of access had been opened. Likewise, the support from United Kingdom and France occurred only after changes in elected government. Influential allies were not born, but cultivated—sometimes with a direct phone call or office visit and sometimes through a directed rally. As the social movement's insights deepened and intelligence expanded, strategists learned how to work the cleavage within and among elites at one level, and build like-minded coalitions at another level. Friendly elites were enlisted to apply positive peer pressure on others; those not aligning with the global movement were stigmatized.

The most poignant grievances came from landmine survivors who expressed outrage at the Convention on Conventional Weapons review meetings in Geneva in 1996, and demonstrated leadership through their witness of petition drives, networking across nations, and constructing principles of survivor assistance. Second, the wider spectrum of global movement participants tackled the landmine issue with a vengeance to change an international norm. Their clear message was that landmines were wrong, and they enlisted military users to concur that strategic utility was dwarfed by the devastation of landmines. Third, the global movement's capacity to act collectively was exhibited through devising and implementing action plans. Notably, before the conclusion of international NGO conferences, the next wave of action plans were drafted, discussed and disseminated. Meeting venues themselves became integral to strategies of targeted momentum. The movement collectively approached key nation-states with problematic policies, and acted collectively to reinforce support and courage of other nation-states. The capacity was enhanced by an enabling spirit de corps, whereby national campaigns collaborated regionally—mobilizing awareness and providing logistical support. Fourth, the global movement seized political opportunity. The ICBL chronology is filled with events when members raised the landmines agenda before various bodies: whether or not the connection to the landmines issue was obvious, the ICBL presence created a connection. Whether the focus of a gathering was topic-specific or was the regular assembly of groups such as Commonwealth nations, the Non-Aligned Movement or the World Council of Churches, ICBL members were prepared with packets and mobilized with resource persons.

Within Southern Africa, political opportunity occurred on many levels, and different sectors built upon other campaigns' leads. The theory behind this activity was that resource mobilization emphasized activist success. While some of the field of actors among Southern Africa campaigns dealt more with stable aspects of political opportunity, other campaigners framed their opportunity in volatility, and navigation of "rhetoric of reaction." William Gamson and David Meyer identify the themes of this rhetoric as jeopardy, futility, and perverse effects (Gamson and Meyer 1996, 285). As did Martin Luther King, Jr., in Gamson and Meyer's example, the activists in the Global Movement to Ban Landmines countered the futility theme by arguing the time parameters of the opportunity. The time to act had arrived. Deadlines were attached to goals and objectives, and the bandwagon would be in town only so long. Much more could be researched and written about national campaigns and comparative exploits of political opportunity.

To be a force for social change, a social movement needs to reinforce commitment of campaigners and attract new recruits, cultivate credible documentation and generate media coverage, mobilize the support of various "bystander publics" and anticipate social control options of its opposition, and ultimately shape public policy and state action (McAdam, McCarthy and Zald 1996). All these hurdles were surmounted in the global movement to ban landmines. First, campaigns were popularized and newer recruits could get up to speed through browsing online resources. Additionally, ICBL archives were deposited for public access with the Canadian Archives in September 2004. Mines Action Canada, with government funding, fields and supports Youth Ambassadors, representing a new generation of informed and engaged campaigners.

Second, campaigns celebrated incremental successes, whether this was a country signature or ratification or stockpile destruction, or presence of unlikely actors at specialized meetings. These helped to cultivate the momentum. The working group on Non-State Actors has produced seminal discourse; building upon an understanding of humanitarian law among groups that moved from liberation movement to elected governing parties, and challenging current Non-State-Actors to minimally embrace the tenets of the Geneva Convention that guarantee rights of noncombatants and their environment. Developments reported by national campaigns were posted electronically. Individuals and national campaigns were not isolated, but could feel connected to regional and global breakthroughs. Third, persistent cultivation of backers yielded important meetings in nations not prepared to sign the treaty; the groups hosting such meetings enabled campaigners to draw more decision-makers and NGOs into the regime to ban landmines. This could then be used as leverage with campaigners' local efforts. Fourth, the ICBL distributed press releases about grassroots promotions and policy breakthroughs (and as necessary, critiques of policies). Fifth, the casual "bystander" publics were engaged through various activities. Sixth, the ICBL debunked myths espoused by those forces preferring business-as-usual. Finally, all these activities and strategies impacted formation of, or change in, nation-state policy, and monitoring of nation-state action.

The original core group of movement leaders and their respective home organizations were veterans of critiquing U.S. foreign policy. While foreign policy analysts were writing about the United States as the surviving hegemon, members in the core group knew there was a more inclusive community of people who could be mobilized into a different sort of superpower. As their numbers and networking capacity grew, they benefited from connections and access to the players of disarmament discussions among UN circles. They were gaining access to the "elites." The movement also benefited from the grassroots popular movement. While some nation-states such as Sweden and the New South Africa foster social movements within their institutions (Mines Action Southern Africa 1999, 1), other nation-states such as France or Zambia appear closed (Mwananyanda 1998, 1), leading social movements to be confrontational. Still others, such as the Japan Campaign Against Landmines, inspired foreign policy reversals while operating without a long history of a domestic civil society (Mekata 2000, 167–69). The global movement exercised strategies that were grassroots-based and played the games that were state-centered. The lessons drawn from the movement's success suggest that bold visions still require transitions from present paradigms. The transition employed by the global movement was to garner nation-states to sign and ratify the Ottawa Treaty, and while gathered together, interact with NGO delegations to push the agenda further. What began as a discussion about a narrow topic—a weapon—led to comprehensive analysis of the multifaceted impact that weapon had, and exposed the relative shallowness of the military doctrine behind its utility.

Note

1. Another UN estimate extended this to one landmine per Angolan (among a population of 10 million) (ICBL Landmine Monitor Working Group 1999, 117). By comparison, a worldwide estimate printed in a UNICEF mines awareness brochure suggests there is one landmine for every twelve children (1997, 1). It should be emphasized that landmine numbers have been rough estimates. Although there is debate over the reliability of such estimates, the point for this discussion is that the severity of the landmines situation, and the number of people impacted, has shaped the global movement to ban landmines.

Bibliography

Adio, Alfred. 1997. "Corporate Dogs of War." *African Topics* London (November–December).

Cahill, Kevin M. and Thomas Roma. 1995. *Silent Witnesses*. United Nations and The Center for International Health and Cooperation.

Coupland, Robin M. 1997. "Assistance for Victims of Anti-Personnel Mines: Needs, Constraints and Strategy." Geneva: ICRC.

Gamson, William and David Meyer. 1996. "Framing Political Opportunity." Pp. 275–90 in *Comparative Perspectives on Social Movements*, ed. Doug McAdam, John McCarthy, and Mayer Zald. New York: Cambridge University Press.

German Campaign to Ban Landmines. June 1997. "Guidelines for Mine Action Programmes from a Development-Oriented Point of View. Revised Version Integrating Proposals Made at the International NGO-Symposium from Bad Honnef, 23rd/24th June 1997." Frankfurt: Medico International.

Handicap International, ed. 1997. *An Explosion Every Twenty Minutes: Conference Report—Brussells International Conference for the Total Ban on Anti-Personnel Landmines, 24–27 June 1997*. Brussells: Handicap International (for the ICBL/Vietnam Veterans of America Foundation).

International Campaign to Ban Landmines. 1997. *Report on Activities: Diplomatic Conference on an International Total Ban on Anti-Personnel Landmines*. Washington: Vietnam Veterans of America Foundation.

———. 1996. *Report on Activities: Review Conference of the Convention on Conventional Weapons. Second Resumed Session, Geneva, Switzerland. 22 April–3 May 1996*. Brattleboro, Vermont: ICBL.

International Campaign to Ban Landmines-Chronology. 2004. "Ban Movement Chronology." Accessed at <http://www.icbl.org/chronology.html>.

International Campaign to Ban Landmines Landmine Monitor Core Group. 2002. *Landmine Monitor Report 2002: Toward a Mine-Free World*. New York: Human Rights Watch.

International Centre for the Advancement of Community Based Rehabilitation. 1997. "Community Based Rehabilitation: A Peace Building Opportunity." Kingston, Ontario: Queen's University.

International Committee of the Red Cross. 1997a. *Landmines Must Be Stopped.* Packet. Geneva: ICRC.

———. 1997b. "The Worldwide Epidemic of Landmine Injuries: The ICRC's Health Oriented Approach," in ICRC, *Landmines Must Be Stopped.* Geneva: ICRC.

International Red Cross and Red Crescent Movement. 1997. *Red Cross, Red Crescent.* Volume 1997: 2. Geneva: IRCRCM.

McAdam, Doug, John D. McCarthy, and Meyers N. Zald, eds. 1996. *Comparative Perspectives on Social Movements: Political Opportunities, Mobilizing Structures, and Cultural Framings.* Cambridge, U.K.: Cambridge University Press.

Mekata, Motoko. 2000. "Building Partnerships Toward a Common Goal: Experiences of the International Campaign to Ban Landmines." Pp. 143–76 in *The Third Force: The Rise of Transnational Civil Society,* ed. Ann Florini. Tokyo: Japan Center for International Exchange and the Carnegie Endowment for International Peace.

Mines Action Canada. December 1997. "The People's Treaty: Convention on the Prohibition of the Use, Stockpiling, Production and Transfer of Antipersonnel Mines and on Their Destruction" in ICBL and Mines Action Canada, *Media Information: Treaty Signing Conference and Action Forum on Anti-Personnel Mines. Ottawa, December, 1997.* Ottawa: Mines Action Canada.

Mwananyanda, Muleya. 1998. "The Zambian Campaign to Ban Landmines Response to ICBL Campaign Questionnaire." July. Lusaka: Zambian Campaign to Ban Landmines. ICBL. Document on file with author.

Newton, Monica. February 1997. *The Scourge of the Earth: The Impact of Landmines on the Environment.* Johannesburg: Group for Environmental Monitoring.

Norwegian People's Aid. April 1996. *Mines: The Silent Killers.* Oslo: Norwegian Peoples Aid.

Oxfam Press Office. May 1994. "OXFAM Calls for Ban on Anti-Personnel Mines." News release of May 12, 1994 reprinted in Handicap International, *Antipersonnel Landmines: For the Banning of Massacres of Civilians in Time of Peace. Facts and Chronologies,* second edition. Paris and Brussels: Handicap International.

Readers Digest. 1994. *Illustrated History of South Africa: The Real Story,* third edition. Cape Town: The Readers Digest Association Limited.

Tarrow, Sidney. 1994. *Power in Movement: Collective Action, Social Movements and Politics.* New York: Cambridge University Press.

United Nations Childrens Fund Office of Emergency Programs. 1997. *A Child Rights Guide to the 1996 Mines Protocol.* New York: UNICEF.

Vines, Alex. 1998. "The Crisis of Anti-Personnel Mines." Pp. 118–35 in *To Walk Without Fear,* ed. Maxwell Cameron, Robert Lawson, and Brian Tomlin. Toronto: Oxford University Press.

Part 4

Creating Democratic Alternatives

Chapter 11

The World Social Forum: Arena or Actor?

Teivo Teivainen

Introduction

The concentration of power in transnational and global institutions was one of the most significant social processes of the twentieth century. Nevertheless, democratic theory and practice have remained very nation-state-centered. Although there were some examples of cosmopolitan democratic thinking and transnational democratic practice throughout the century, most analysts and politicians simply ignored them. An example of a reasonably moderate attempt to democratize global power relations, especially as regards the North–South dimension, was the 1970s project of the New International Economic Order (NIEO). It did not, however, lead to any significant redistribution of power and was considered a failure by most commentators of the 1980s and 1990s.

At the very end of the century, the public perception of the issues at stake seemed to be changing. While, for example, designating the undemocratic nature of the International Monetary Fund as a significant political problem was generally not taken very seriously in the early 1990s, in the last years we have seen substantial crowds of people marching on the streets pointing out this problem. Global capitalism may have entered one of its most serious legitimacy crises.

The solidarity movements related to many of the earlier attempts to democratize global power, such as the NIEO project, tended to see the problem more in terms of interstate relations. Many of the movements in these first years of the new millenium are beginning to perceive the world in a less state-centric manner. Instead of asking that a particular Third World state be given more decision-making power in global affairs, today's activists may ask for more power to the civil society groups that confront both governmental and corporate power all over the world. This trend holds many promising aspects. In order to imagine and construct institutional features of alternative futures, however, we may need political structures that "civil society," as it is generally conceived, is unlikely to deliver.

The Battle in Seattle during the World Trade Organization meeting in 1999 boosted the local, transnational and global organizations and movements protesting against undemocratic sites of global power (Sader 2003, 19). In recent years, we have observed the emergence of an increasing number of arenas that attract civil society organizations and active citizens to express concern about capitalist globalization. The arenas are varied, in terms of both political orientation and organizational design. The spectacular demonstrations from Okinawa to Gothenburg and Genoa have received ample media coverage and become prominent models of critical civil society organizing. In most of them the main focus has been on defensive measures, being against something. While reactive protests may play an important role in democratic transformations, the concrete initiatives for the transformations are more likely to emerge from proactive meetings.

Many of the most visible civil society gatherings have been explicitly, and often antagonistically, related to events of the global elite. The principal meetings of the intergovernmental economic institutions such as the World Bank, International Monetary Fund, and World Trade Organization, including its predecessor GATT, have been facing counter-events quite regularly since the late 1980s, including the anti-Bretton Woods riots of Berlin in 1988 or the protests against the GATT meeting of 1990 in Brussels. The lack of democracy in these institutions has been an increasingly important motivation of the counter-events.

More significantly but with less media attention, organized protests around these issues have been taking place in the more peripheral parts of our world. Some Third World observers, such as Camilo Guevara, characterize Seattle and other similar media events in the United States and Europe as rather irrelevant for the great majorities of the world.[1] While I cannot fully agree with his observation, it is undoubtedly true that in the poorer regions of the world there has been a lot going on before and besides Seattle. Middle-class youth protesting in a European or North American city have been much more attractive to the global media networks than impoverished peasants campaigning against structural adjustment programs in the South.

From Anti-Davos to Porto Alegre

The meetings of the formally private elite organizations such as the Bilderberg Society, Trilateral Commission, and Mont Pelerin Society have tended to attract less public attention than those of the Bretton Woods institutions and other semipublic multilateral organs. Nevertheless, they constitute highly influential networks of transnational coordination in matters of global governance. One of the most influential and controversial of them is the World Economic Forum (WEF). The first informal business gathering in Davos, a Swiss mountain town, took place in January 1971 under the name of European Management Forum. Since 1982 the Davos meeting has focused on bringing world economic leaders to its annual meetings, and in 1987 it got its present name World Economic Forum.[2]

In January 1999, after various years of preparations, various organizations started organizing a counter-event in Switzerland under the banners of "another Davos" and "anti-Davos." Apart from the World Forum of Alternatives, these included the French journal *Le Monde Diplomatique* and ATTAC, founded in France in June 1998 (Amin and Founou-Tchuigoua 2002). In the first major anti-Davos event, organized simultaneously with the WEF 2000, various groups ranging from the World Women's March to the Brazilian Landless Rural Workers first had a seminar in Zurich and then marched to Davos to hold a press conference and, some 150 of them, to face cold weather and Robocop-like police in a demonstration.[3] The difficult geographical conditions and heavy police presence contributed to convincing some of the key organizers that it would be difficult to organize a huge anti-Davos gathering in Davos itself.[4]

In Brazil, the concrete initiative for a worldwide civil society event emerged in early 2000. Even if the emergence of the initiative needs to be understood and explained in the context of strategies of various collective actors, it also possible to point to some key individuals who played a role in formulating it. The first formulations of the idea are generally attributed to Oded Grajew, coordinator of the Brazilian Business Association for Citizenship (Associação Brasileira de Empresários pela Cidadania) CIVES (Sader 2003, 19).[5] In February 2000, Bernard Cassen, chair of ATTAC and director of *Le Monde Diplomatique*, met with Grajew and Francisco Whitaker, of the Brazilian Justice and Peace Commission (CBJP), in Paris to discuss the possibility to organize such a forum. Their discussion produced three central ideas for the forum. First of all, it should be held in the South, and more concretely in the Brazilian city of Porto Alegre. While the Brazilians had initially thought that the forum should be held in Europe, it was Cassen who pointed out the importance of holding it in the

South, and more particularly in Porto Alegre (Sader 2003, 19). Second, the name should be World Social Forum (WSF), changing only one key word from the adversary's name. And third, it should be organized during the same dates as the WEF, partially because this symbolism was considered attractive for the media (Cassen 2002).[6]

Soon after it was clear that apart from *Le Monde Diplomatique* and ATTAC many other organizations influential within transnational activist networks would support the initiative, eight Brazilian civil society organizations decided to form the Organizing Committee of the forum. In March 2000 they formally secured the support of the municipal government of Porto Alegre and the state government of Rio Grande do Sul, both controlled at the time by the Workers Party PT (Partido dos Trabalhadores) (Whitaker 2002). Initially it was especially the mayor of Porto Alegre, Raul Pont, who received the idea with great enthusiasm, but soon also the state government led by governor Olivio Dutra decided to dedicate plenty of time and effort into the WSF process.[7] The idea was presented internationally by Miguel Rossetto, vice-governor of Rio Grande do Sul, in June 2000 during an alternative UN meeting in Geneva.

Local Roots of a Global Event

Events conceived in transnational contexts may often have relatively weak roots in the locality where they are organized. In the WSF of Porto Alegre, this has not been the case. Porto Alegre, the capital of the Rio Grande do Sul state in southern Brazil, is one of the most important strongholds of the Workers Party PT. Already during Brazil's military rule, the city was a center of resistance with energetic neighborhood associations (Wainwright 2003). Founded in 1980, the PT has deep roots in these associations, trade unions, catholic organizations, women's movements and many other parts of the vibrant Brazilian civil society.[8] One of the most important strengths of the PT has always been its ability to gather support from and critically articulate with emancipatory civil society groups.

Porto Alegre was a smart choice for hosting the WSF also because both municipal and state governments were willing to allocate significant material and human resources to the event. The possibilities of autonomous state and municipal policies had been enhanced by the 1988 Federal Constitution that increased resource transfer to and taxation powers of the local authorities (Abers, n.d.). In 2002 the municipality provided approximately USD 300,000 and the state USD one million for the event. In 2003, there was some increase in the money invested by the municipal government and a substantial decrease in the investment by the state government. This was to a significant extent a consequence of the electoral defeat of the PT in the October 2002 governor elections. The new state government led by Germano Rigotto, from the center-right PMPD party, decided to cut the money the preceding PT government had budgeted for the 2003 forum (which had in dollar terms already been slightly less than the sum invested in 2002). Not surprisingly, the new federal government of Lula da Silva decided to compensate for the cuts of the state government.[9] Even though governor Rigotto repeated in many declarations that his new government remained very willing to host the WSF events, the relationship with the state government has clearly changed. A symbolic expression of this was the intense booing when the new governor left the congress hall during the opening ceremony of WSF 2003.

Fernando Henrique Cardoso, Brazil's president during the first two forums, repeatedly criticized the local authorities of misspending taxpayers' resources. According to most estimates the thousands of visitors filling local hotels, restaurants and other commercial establishments bring in much more money than what is spent by the local authorities in organizing the forum. This is also a major reason for the municipal and state governments of different political backgrounds to have a welcoming attitude toward the WSF.

Whereas in short-term commercial terms the WSF is considered a good deal by most locals, in ideological terms not everyone agrees. Two months after the WSF 2002, various business organizations and right-wing groups of Rio Grande do Sul organized a Forum of Liberties, with positions openly critical of the WSF.[10] During the WSF 2003, a bomb threat paralyzed some of the activities for a short moment. The local press speculated that the cardboard box containing sand, wires, a clock and a hand-written note stating that it was a bomb was probably a "joke of bad taste" by some participant of the forum.[11] Despite these marginal expressions of animosity, for many international participants who had been taking part in massive protests elsewhere, the welcoming attitude of the Porto Alegre residents was one of the most pleasant aspects of the event.

Who Governs?

Naomi Klein characterized the organizational structure of the first WSF as "so opaque that it was nearly impossible to figure out how decisions were made" (Klein 2001). Similar critical remarks have been raised by many others in all the annual editions of the WSF main event. Even if according to the WSF Charter of Principles the forum "does not constitute a locus of power to be disputed by the participants," disputes of power do exist.

In Brazil, the formal decision-making power of the WSF process has been mainly in the hands of the Organizing Committee, consisting since its founding of the Central Trade Union Confederation CUT (*Central Única dos Trabalhadores*), the Movement of Landless Rural Workers MST (*Movimento dos Trabalhadores Rurais Sem Terra*) and six smaller Brazilian civil society organizations.[12] In terms of sheer numbers of affiliates, there is a huge difference between the two big ones and the others. In the decision-making process within the Organizing Committee, the CUT and MST have generally acted "generously" toward the smaller organizations. In this sense, the disparity of resources has generally not translated into significant disparities in the decision-making power. The disparity in resources should, however, not be exaggerated. Even if much smaller, some of the participating NGOs may have better access to financial resources than especially the MST. The role of IBASE, a Rio-based socially engaged research institute, has been particularly important in fund-raising for the WSF.

The other main organ of the WSF, the International Council (IC), was founded in São Paulo in June 2001. According to Cândido Grzybowski, director of IBASE, the idea to create an international council emerged in Porto Alegre on the last day of the first WSF.[13] During the following months, the Organizing Committee made a list of organizations that were then invited to the founding meeting in São Paulo. As of February 2004 the Council nominally consists of 113 organizations, though in practice many of them have not actively participated in the process. This number also includes the eight members of the Organizing Committee. Most IC members come from the Americas and Western Europe though many have activities also in other parts of the world. Organizations based in Asia and Africa include the Asian Regional Exchange for New Alternatives (ARENA), Environnement et Développement du Tiers-Monde (ENDA) and Palestinian NGO Network. According to some definitions the IC member should be regional or global networks rather than purely national organizations, but this criterion has not been strictly followed. Apart from the proper members, there are 15 observer organizations, mostly the representatives of regional and thematic social forums in various parts of the world.

The division of labor between the IC and the Brazilian Organizing Committee has been ambiguous. During the first WSF the former did not exist. When founded, the IC was assigned an essentially advisory role. Before the founding meeting in São Paulo, the Organizing Committee had drafted its name as "International Advisory Council." The ambiguity of the relationship between the Organizing Committee and the IC was already present in the São Paulo meeting when some delegates of the invited organizations raised the question "advising whom?" During the meeting, it was decided that the term "advisory" be deleted from the name. The IC has gained increasing importance on paper and, to a lesser extent, also in practice. Even if some observers have characterized it as "barely a rubber stamp," it has certainly played a role (Albert 2003). For example, in at least two meetings the Organizing Committee suggested that the WSF main event should be held biannually rather than annually, and in both cases the IC decided to continue with the annual meetings. The role of the IC should not be exaggerated, either. It is fair to emphasize its role in giving international legitimacy to the Brazilian organizers (Waterman 2003), though this has not been its only role. Especially after it was decided that the main annual event of the WSF process in 2004 would take place in India, the linkage between the IC and the organizers both in Brazil and India became more complex.

A typical mechanism for making decisions in the meetings of the IC is that the Organization Committee, always present in the meetings, submits a proposal on an issue. Then the IC debates the issue. The debate has normally been presided by the Organization Committee, though other IC members have also been given responsibilities in the running of the council meetings.[14] In case no clear consensus emerges, the Organizing Committee will have a separate meeting and reconsider its original proposal. In some cases, it will then (typically on the second day of the two-day meeting) present a new proposal where the earlier discussion will have been taken into account. Normally, the new proposal will carry the day and almost everyone agrees, more or less. The underlying assumption in this working method is that the WSF is not a deliberative body or actor that would take political stands and thereby need rigorous decision-making procedures. Until now the system has worked relatively well, making decisions through what some of the Brazilian organizers call *construção*, constructing them in a critical debate and sometimes laborious consensus building. The IC is not supposed to have mechanisms for disputing representation, nor for voting.[15] The only time there has been a vote was when in its first meeting it had to be decided whether the following meeting would take place somewhere in Europe or in Dakar. The overwhelming majority voted for Dakar.

The most difficult decision of the IC thus far was made in January 2003 when the Council decided to organize the WSF 2004 in India. Even if there was formally a consensus, a small minority argued strongly against the decision until the very end. The strongest opposition was voiced by some delegates from Cuba. Their main argument was that Latin America is the traditional stronghold of radical movements, the greatest expression of which being the Cuban Revolution, and therefore, as representatives of that revolution, they categorically opposed moving the forum away from the continent, in this case from Porto Alegre.[16]

The composition of the IC and its working methods are likely to experience changes in the future. The selection of the founding members of the IC, mostly through invitations by the Organizing Committee, was reasonably easy when the overall process was still known to only relatively few networks. In the future, when there will be more groups interested in joining the IC, more explicit selection procedures will, I believe, have to be established. There are indications that the question of fair representation will become more controversial in the WSF process.

Following its own plan drafted in April 2002, the Brazilian Organizing Committee has been transformed into the Secretariat. The ambiguity of the relationship with the IC has, however, not been totally overcome. In some documents the renamed body is (self-) defined as "Secretariat of the International Council," whereas others refer to "Secretariat of the World Social Forum." The decision to organize the WSF 2004 in India implied new changes for the governing bodies, when Indian organizations assumed the local organizing responsibilities. After India, a new Brazilian Organizing Committee, consisting of 22 organizations, was formed to prepare the WSF 2005 in Porto Alegre.

The decision to organize the WSF 2004 in India was made simultaneously with the decision to organize the WSF 2005 back in Porto Alegre. It would probably have been impossible to reach the decision on going to India in 2004 without at the same time agreeing that the WSF 2005 will take place in Porto Alegre. Various IC members repeatedly expressed fears that if the WSF leaves Porto Alegre indefinitely, and the next venues do not meet the expectations, the whole process might die out. Already fixing the place of the 2005 forum can be considered a guarantee against the unlikely eventuality that the process to move the Forum to India were to result in a catastrophe. In that case, 2004 could later be seen as a year in which there was no "real" WSF. Some of the Brazilian organizers have in fact been arguing that the main global event should not be organized annually but perhaps every two years. In April 2004, the IC decided that the WSF 2007 would be organized in Africa.

One aspect of the decision-making that has been somewhat neglected in the WSF process is the possibilities information technology could imply. Of course, much of the informal decision-making and strategic planning of the forum takes place through E-mail. The organizers have, however, been reluctant to explore ways in which cyberspace could be used in organizing more formal decision-making processes. Peter Waterman has argued insightfully and provocatively that the WSF "*uses* the media, culture and cyberspace but it does not *think* of itself in primarily cultural/communicational terms, nor does it *live* fully within this increasingly central and infinitely expanding universe." He sees the WSF as "a shrine of the written and spoken word" (Waterman 2003).

In the new suggestions for rules and procedures of the IC that will be discussed and possibly decided on at the next IC meeting scheduled for June 2003, it is mentioned that the use of cyberspace in the decision-making should be at least considered. There are people who consider increasing cyberspace use only to play in the hands (and pockets) of Bill Gates and the like. Some feel that increased reliance on the Internet could marginalize groups that have limited or no access to the Internet. On the other hand, considering the costs for a poor organization in the Global South to fly someone into a meeting in another continent may certainly be higher than taking part in a cybermeeting through the Internet.[17]

From the Porto Alegre Events
Toward a Transnational Process

For many, the increasing numbers of participants have been one of the most important assets of the WSF. The numbers are often used in the press to indicate the success of the event. The first WSF in January 2001 attracted some 5,000 registered participants of 117 countries and thousands of Brazilian activists. For the second forum, the figures had grown significantly, rising to over 12,000 official delegates from 123 countries and tens of thousands of total participants, mostly from Brazil.[18] The third forum in January 2003 was even more massive. Over 20,000 official delegates and roughly 100,000 total participants made the WSF III a truly massive event. In Mumbai, the WSF 2004 also gathered over 100,000 participants.

Others, however, thought that the number of participants and parallel events has become too high for any strategically relevant debate on key issues. According to Roberto Savio, long-time director of the Inter Press Service, holding 1,714 panels and seminars in the WSF 2003 led to an atomization of dialogue (Savio 2003, 6). Correspondingly, Savio has proposed publicly that in future there should be severe restrictions to the number of people allowed to participate in the event. In his contribution, it has been left open who would decide who can and who cannot participate. Michael Albert has made a more concrete proposal on the issue. According to him, the main annual WSF gathering should be made a delegate event. In Albert's vision, the WSF event would be attended by

5,000–10,000 people "delegated to it from the major regional forums of the world" (2003).

It has become increasingly clear that the WSF is much more than a series of annual massive events. The main mechanism for the globalization of the WSF process has been the holding of regional and thematic forums in various parts of the world. Among the most visible events have been the thematic forum on neoliberalism organized in Argentina in August 2002, the European Social Forums in Florence, Paris, and London in 2002–04, the Asian Social Forum in Hyderabad in January 2003 and the Social Forum of the Americas organized in Quito in July 2004. These forums have formed part of the semiofficial forum calendar maintained and controlled by the Organizing Committee/Secretariat and the IC.

There have sometimes been tensions between the WSF governance bodies and the organizers of the other forums. For example, the Italian organizers of the European Social Forum 2002 wanted to use a declaration of social movements drafted by movements that participated in the WSF as the foundation of their regional forum. The Brazilian Organizing Committee, however, insisted in the Barcelona meeting of the IC in April 2002 that the Charter of Principles is the only official basis for such events that are organized within the WSF umbrella (Whitaker 2003b, 237–44). A further debate emerged in the IC meeting of Bangkok in August 2002 when the Brazilians were strongly opposed to the plans of the Italians to invite political parties to take officially part in the European Social Forum. According to the Charter of Principles, the WSF is a "nonparty context" and political parties are not supposed to directly take part in the activities. The Italian delegates present in the Bangkok meeting responded by accusing the Brazilian Organizing Committee of hypocrisy. The fact that the Workers Party PT has been visibly present in all Porto Alegre forums has often been considered to be problematic in terms of the Charter of Principles. The Italians claimed that the open violation of the Charter by the Brazilians had been always accepted by the participants in the WSF and therefore the Brazilians should not get upset if minor political parties play a small role in a regional forum.

Another controversy was related to the plans to organize a social forum event in Quito, Ecuador, in October 2002. The event was to focus on the Free Trade Area of the Americas (FTAA), coinciding with a FTAA ministerial meeting. During early 2002 the Quito event was in the semiofficial list of WSF events, but by mid-year it had been taken off the list. There was no public debate that I would be aware of on the issue, but one of the main reasons was the insistence of some IC members that the Quito event would be too focused on one particular issue (FTAA) and with too narrow organizational basis. The event was organized, and many of the slogans and other symbols made it in many ways part of the WSF process even if it was not in the semiofficial list. It was only in July 2004 that an "official" Social Forum of the Americas was held in Quito.

These controversies are examples of the organizational problems that the WSF encounters in its process of geographical and thematic expansion. On the one hand, there are reasons to maintain coherence and some underlying rules in the process so that the WSF brand does not simply evaporate. On the other hand, too much control by the IC and the Secretariat is bound to place limits to the creativity and motivation of those in charge of the decentralized events.

Apart from the semiofficial list of regional and thematic forums, a myriad of local events have been organized under the banners of the WSF. Many of these events have not received, nor asked for, any official recognition by the WSF governance bodies. Their proliferation is one of the most vital signs that the WSF process is indeed expanding. The fact that they are often beyond the control of any centralized WSF bodies also implies complications for attempts to see the WSF as a movement of movements with a more or less clearly defined political strategy.

How to Be and Not to Be Political

The WSF provides a space for actors that may construct projects in different contexts, both local and global. According to the organizers that emphasize this role, the WSF should avoid issuing declarations of support for any particular political processes. As stated by Cândido Grzybowski, "political action is the responsibility of each individual and the coalitions they form, not an attribute of the forum" (2003, 5). Relying on a more pronounced dichotomy between forum as a space and forum as a movement, Chico Whitaker has criticized the "self-nominated social movements" that "seek to put the forum inside their own mobilizing dynamics, to serve their own objectives" (Whitaker 2003a. See also 2003c).

Among the organizers and participants there have been different ways to emphasize the different identities of the WSF. For some they are by no means incompatible: it is possible to be an arena and an actor simultaneously. One of the expressions of this actor-identity is the term "movement of movements." My impression on the basis of various discussions both in the IC of the WSF and in the corridors of the forum sites is that there are increasing pressures to overcome the current reluctance to issue political statements. These demands often include a questioning of the way the WSF is officially governed.

One of the reasons for the reluctance to become an explicitly political actor is that the WSF does not have internal procedures for democratic collective will-formation. Therefore, no one can legitimately claim to represent the multitude of movements that constitute the WSF. Among those who share the view that the official decision-making bodies of the WSF do not have a democratic mandate to issue statements in the name of the WSF as a whole, there are different conclusions about this matter. Many in the governing bodies of the WSF tend to conclude that the WSF should therefore not even plan to become a political actor. More critical voices argue that the correct way forward is to create mechanisms for democratic participation within the political architecture of the forum. Once reasonably transparent and democratic mechanisms have been established, the WSF could more legitimately start to express itself as a collective movement.

The pressures for more explicit political will-formation are also expressed by and through the media. The press has tended to look at the WSF as a (potential) political actor in itself, while many of the organizers have wanted to downplay this role and argue that they simply provide a space for different groups to interact. These different conceptions of the event have clashed for example when the press has asked for "final declarations" and considered the lack of any such final document a proof of weakness in the organization. From the perspective of most organizers the idea has been not to produce any official final document of the event that would pretend to represent the views of the thousands of other organizations that have participated in the meetings.[19]

The unwillingness to formulate political statements, beyond the Charter of Principles drafted in 2001, is occasionally questioned among some organizers and related actors who would like to see the WSF as an organization expressing opinions on certain issues such as the crises in Argentina, Palestine, and Venezuela.[20] In two meetings of the WSF International Council there have been angry demands by some groups to issue a declaration on a particular topic. In the Bangkok meeting in August 2002, Walden Bello and others argued that the Council should produce a public statement that encourages movements around the world to take part in the protests to be organized during the WTO meeting in Cancún in 2003. In the Porto Alegre meeting of the Council in January 2003, various delegates argued strongly in favor of making a public statement against the imminent war in Iraq. In both cases, the apparently consensual decision of the council was not to issue any such statements. It is, however, likely that there will be more intense debates on this in the near future.

Some participants and observers analyze the WSF as an example of an emerging institution that may embody seeds of global democracy. For example, George Monbiot has suggested that it could form part of the process of building a "world parliament in exile" (Monbiot 2002). Some others who locate the WSF more explicitly in the historical traditions of socialist movements have visualized it as "opposition party" or "radical international" (e.g., Monereo 2002). From this perspective, it is particularly important to modify its organizational design and the way its decision-making structure functions. The fear of many is that these modifications could lead to such politicization that would destroy the forum as a relatively neutral space that facilitates encounters between different kinds of civil society organizations.

One way to avoid political silence without violating the Charter of Principles is to facilitate processes whereby organizations that take part in the WSF produce political declarations. Ideally, most of the participating organizations would sign such declarations and they could have powerful political impacts. Until now, the social movement declarations produced during the WSF events have not been circulated very widely and their impact has been relatively modest. Nevertheless, they have created controversies among the WSF organizers. Even if these declarations do not officially claim to represent the WSF as a whole, Chico Whitaker fears that the media may consider them as semiofficial conclusions. This can then lead to political disputes about whose concerns get to be expressed in the declarations.

Inclusions and Exclusions

One way the internal politics of the WSF have been played out is in how different groups have created or been given spaces during the main annual events. Racial tensions created some internal controversies, particularly in the first forum.[21] Even though during the Carnival and Soccer World Cup Brazil may show an image of racial harmony, racism is present in most walks of life, and it would be naïve to claim that it does not exist within progressive intellectuals' ranks. For many observers, both forums have been surprisingly "white" events (Hardt 2002). The perceived whiteness is not only due to the lack of large delegations from Africa, Asia, and other parts of Latin America, but also to the fact that the average Brazilian participating in the forum is clearly "whiter" than the average Brazilian. It has to be remembered, as well, that Rio Grande do Sul is one of the rare parts of Brazil, Latin America, and the whole Third World where many locals are light-skinned people of European, including Germanic, origin. This contrasted strongly with the WSF 2004 in Mumbai, where the poor sectors of India had high visibility.

Gender tensions have also been present in the WSF. Even though there exist no major gender differences in the numbers of overall participants, especially the original Brazilian Organizing Committee has consisted predominantly of middle-aged men. In the IC, representatives of feminist organizations and other women have played a more visible role and gender issues have been present in the program. Struggles for sexual preference rights have had an increasing, though still somewhat marginal, role in the events. There have also been other controversies on hierarchies and partial exclusions within the WSF, based for example on the celebrity status of some participants. During the first forum a group of young and angry participants raided the VIP room by one of the most transited corridors of the main forum venue. The room (with glass ceilings) had become the most visible symbol of the status differences within the forum.

The presence of representatives of the Cuban government and of the Armed Revolutionary Forces of Colombia (FARC) raised mixed feelings in 2001. Open disapproval of Cuba's presence came mostly from outside the meeting, particularly from the local press. In Rio Grande do Sul, during the electoral campaign of 2002 the opposition sometimes claimed that the PT state government wanted to transform the state into "another Cuba." For the electoral strategy of the PT it was important to create an image that would not dissuade potential moderate voters. It was therefore not surprising that the Cuban representatives no longer had a prominent official role in 2002, even though Cuba's delegation was more numerous than the year before. The island's political visibility has in the last two forums been clearest in the marches and the surroundings of the venue where one could observe plenty of Che Guevara paraphernalia displayed by participating organizations.

During the first WSF, the FARC guerrillas received a lot of sympathy from some participants. In Brazil, the relatively strong anti-U.S. sentiments are often reflected in solidarity attitudes toward Colombian rebels, and there were even extra-official recruitment efforts to create internationalist brigades to travel to Colombia. Not all the participants, however, were happy with the presence of a group accused of committing atrocities. For the second and third WSF, the FARC representatives were not officially allowed to register as participants. The WSF Charter of Principles, drafted between the first two forums and approved by the IC in June 2001, excludes the participation of armed organizations. Also the mistakenly approved registration of members of the Basque armed organizations was cancelled as soon as their identity was discovered in 2002.

Even if it is not determined whether the WSF will become a more active political entity with more explicit internal will-formation mechanisms, it is clear that until now the most important impact of the forum on democratic projects has consisted of the myriads of encounters between different groups and activists within its confines. Geographically, most participants have come from the Southern Cone of Latin America (especially Brasil, Uruguay, and Argentina) and Southern Europe (especially Italy, France, and Spain), but there has been a conscious effort to facilitate the participation of people from Asia, Africa, and other parts of Latin America.

Limits of Civil Society Purity: Connecting with and Distancing from Other Kinds of Actors

According to its Charter of Principles, the WSF is "a plural, diversified, non-confessional, non-governmental and non-party context." Even if the Brazilian media often portrays the events as almost directly organized by the Workers Party PT, the party does not formally belong to the Organizing Committee. Its importance stems from the fact that many or the key civil society organizations involved in the process are somehow related to or sympathetic toward it, and that it controls the hosting municipal government. During the first and second forums it also controlled the state government and after the elections of 2002 it now controls the federal government.

The participation of Lula da Silva in the WSF 2001 and 2002 was technically as representative of an NGO he had founded rather than as representative of his political party. Having become the president of Brazil his participation was of different status in the WSF 2003. As a response to the accusations of using different criteria for different governmental participation, the role of the hosting governments, from the municipal to federal levels, have been given a special status in recent semiofficial formulations of the WSF procedures.[22] Therefore as representative of a hosting country it was possible to include Lula in the official program, whereas the Venezuelan president Hugo Chávez who surprisingly arrived in Porto Alegre during the forum was not provided a space within the official venues of the forum.

The participation of various ministers of the government of France in the WSF 2002 was criticized by many delegates. During the same forum, the Belgian prime minister who had announced a visit was told by the Organizing Committee that he would not be welcome. The decisions on how to connect with governmental entities have suffered from a lack of coherence. The same is true of intergovernmental organizations. For example, certain

UN organs have been actively involved in organizing activities related to women's issues, but at the same time the official line has been that inter-governmental bodies cannot participate.

In order to at least partially overcome these dilemmas, a new form of participation was designed by the organizers. In the IC meetings of 2002 it was decided that the WSF would have a new category of events: round-tables of dialogue and controversy. Through these roundtables representatives of such institutions that are banned from the list of official delegates could be invited to debate and discuss. This institutional innovation was an attempt to combine two prima facie contradictory aims: to keep the WSF as a purely civil society arena or actor and not to become an inward-looking space for same-minded civil society organizations. These roundtables have not yet had an important weight in the WSF events, but it is possible that they will be relied on more in the future. The policy on who would be invited to these roundtables has not been clearly defined, but some key organizers think that representatives of some UN bodies could be invited, but for example the World Bank and IMF should be kept out.[23]

The question of how to relate to the original symbolic adversary has also been repeatedly debated and modified. One of the motivations for the naming and timing of the first WSF in Porto Alegre was to attract media attention. The oppositional stance toward the WEF in Davos was combined with a search for a critical dialogue. The televised debate between Davos and Porto Alegre reflected the desire of the WSF organizers to engage with the adversary.

The global media impact of the second and third Porto Alegre forum was significantly stronger than in 2001. Even though the event was in all three years organized simultaneously with the WEF, there were fewer attempts in the second and third year to interact with the WEF. This reflected a grow-ing self-confidence of the organizers, some of whom liked to repeat that "from now onwards Davos will be the shadow event of Porto Alegre."

In the WSF 2003 there was, however, one particular issue that made the activists in Porto Alegre focus on Davos in their debates, often passionately. The decision of Lula da Silva to travel to Davos immediately after the WSF 2003 in Porto Alegre raised plenty of criticism among the organizers. In his main public appearance in front of tens of thousands of admirers during WSF 2003 Lula compared his decision to travel to Davos to his decision over 25 years ago to get involved in trade unions. His friends had been opposed to his getting involved with "dirty trade union politics," but the fact that Brazil has a vibrant and progressive trade union movement today shows that he was right to act against his friends' advice. Lula was, however, not explicit about whether he believed the WEF could also be changed with equally progressive results. At least within the IC, many remained skeptical.

Despite the commotion caused by Lula's visit, the importance of the WEF for the WSF is actively being diminished. It does seem that within the WEF there is slightly more openness toward the issues discussed by critical social movements, in order to recover some of the lost legitimacy, but the movements are less willing to engage in a dialogue. The most important expression of this tendency is that in January 2003 time was finally ripe for the IC to decide that in the future the main event of the WSF process will no longer take place simultaneously with the WEF. In January 2004, however, the same Council decided that the WSF 2005 should again be organized during the WEF.

In sum, the enthusiasm the WSF has generated around the world will lead to various dilemmas. Conceived as a civil society initiative, the WSF will have increasing numbers of international organizations, governments, and even business organizations proposing it different forms of cooperation. Some organizers may emphasize the importance of clinging to strictly defined civil society partners, others are likely to have more pragmatic positions to obtain material and political support.

The question of connections with other kinds of organizations should also be analyzed in terms of financial help and dependence. The WSF events have received sizable funding from organizations such as Oxfam United Kingdom, Ford Foundation, and Heinrich Böll Foundation. This support has not created any significant debates on the possible conditionalities or relations of dependence it could generate. It should be taken into account, for example, that in order to get funding from the Ford Foundation, the organizers had to convince the foundation that the Workers Party is not involved in the process. Since the autonomy from the political parties has been important for the WSF organizers for various other reasons as well, the importance of the funding conditionality should not be exaggerated. The organization of the WSF 2004 in India, where the role of the Ford Foundation has been more controversial than in Brazil, implied more critical attitudes toward foreign funding (Teivainen, 2005).

From Anti to Alternative

Being anti-something can be politically useful, but only up to a point. The protesters of Seattle and similar events have been very effective in pointing out authoritarian aspects of the capitalist world-system. Even if various groups that have participated in these events do have programmatic statements for alternative futures, the way these events have been staged has not been very conducive in showing these futures to the world. The criticism of not being able to show a credible alternative, or any alternative at all, has become a problem for the legitimacy of the protest movements.

In most of the post-Seattle events, the protesters have often been labeled as "antiglobalization," and some of them have used the expression themselves.[24] It would, however, be analytically faulty and politically unwise to simply define the movements as being *against* globalization, if the term is understood as the increasing transgression of nation-state borders on a worldwide level. Many of them are, I would claim, looking for a *different kind of* globalization, though some may prefer to use the older term internationalism. From a democratic perspective, the problem in some antiglobalization rhetoric is that one easily ends up with rather strange bedfellows. Professing antiglobalization pure and simple is not very helpful in terms of making a distinction between regulating the cross-border movements of speculative capital and those of black immigrants.

Outra globalização (another globalization) is an expression that has been emphasized by some of the key organizers of the Porto Alegre meetings (Grzybowski 1998; de Souza Santos 2001). Despite their insistence, the mass media in many parts of Latin America often talks of antiglobalization activists when referring to both Porto Alegre and some of the events inspired by it. The February 2001 protests related to a WEF regional meeting in Mexico and the March 2001 marches around the Inter-American Development Bank meeting in Santiago de Chile were the first big globalization-related protest events in Latin America after the first WSF, and the media coverage of them often referred to the Porto Alegre event as an important moment in the antiglobalization struggles.[25]

For those who want to argue for the possibility of a different kind of globalization, the risk of ending up with strange bedfellows is by no means absent. It is not always easy to see the differences, if any, of the "alternative" globalization proposals with the idea of many business leaders that some democratization is necessary in order to make the global expansion of capitalism acceptable (Falk and Strauss 2001). Those who cling to antiglobalization discourse are often right when they claim that the alternative globalization strategies would only lead to very moderate changes. Often, but not always.

It is frequently assumed that in the anti/alternative divide of globalization debates, being "anti" represents more radical and revolutionary options, whereas the "alternatives" are on the side of more superficial reforms. In terms of thinking about how to democratize the world, this assumption is not very helpful. Within the alternative globalization specter, it is possible to find and even easier to imagine such political projects that strive for a globalization that radically transforms the world. While antiglobalization people can be pro-capitalist, pro-globalization people may be anticapitalist.

Some of the debate and divide between the "anti" and the "alternative" is due to confused semantics or distorted categorizations. In order to fundamentally democratize the world, people who have chosen to regard globalization as a term that has been too polluted by its dominant usage and those who think it can still be given more progressive meanings can often work together. In principle, the WSF offers many opportunities for this to happen.

Despite various references to the necessity of imagining and constructing a different world, the issue of democratic global order has not had a very high priority in the agenda of the WSF. There have been claims by intellectuals and groups working on issues of global democracy that the WSF process has been too much dominated by nationalists whose discourse is dominated by antiglobalization themes. As noted by Michael Hardt, those who "advocate strengthening national sovereignty as a solution to the ills of contemporary globalization" have dominated the representations of the Forum. More polemically, he also claims that while the "non-sovereign, alternative globalization position" has not obtained a prominent place in the Forum, it may well have been the position of the majority of the participants (Hardt 2002, Klein 2001). Be it as it may, one of the intellectual problems of the WSF has been the lack of open debates between different visions of how the world should concretely be reorganized if, as the main slogan of the WSF says, another world is to be possible (Teivainen 2003).[26]

Notes

1. In my September 2000 conversation in Helsinki with Camilo Guevara, whose status as the son of Che Guevara makes him some kind of politico-cultural ambassador of the Cuban government, he argued that the Battle of Seattle expressed the illusions of an alienated Western youth.
2. For a semiofficial historical overview of the WEF, see <http://www.weforum. org/site/homepublic.nsf/Content/Our+History> (13.4.2002).
3. Personal Communication with Susan George, April 15, 2002.
4. Ibid., April 16, 2002.
5. CIVES has sometimes been characterized as an association of business representatives that support the Workers Party PT. This connection became more explicit when Grajew started working as Luiz Inácio Lula da Silva's special advisor in January 2003.
6. Personal Communication with Bernard Cassen, April 16, 2002.
7. Personal communication with Jefferson Miola, April 20, 2002.
8. On the origins of the PT in Rio Grande do Sul, see Paulo Prestes (1999, 72–76).
9. The approximate 2003 figures were USD 500,000 by the state government, USD 450,000 by the municipal government and USD 370,000 by the federal

government. The federal contribution was allocated through the companies Petrobras and Banco do Brasil. See also "Governo Lula compensa corte de gastos com Fórum," *Zero Hora* 2003, p. 6; and oral presentation by Cândido Grzybowsky in the WSF International Council meeting, January 22, 2003, Porto Alegre. When comparing the dollar-based figures it has to be remembered that between the second and the third forum, the Brazilian currency real was heavily devalued.

10. See *Zero Hora* April 9, 2002.

11. Regarding the threat that led to a break of less than one hour in the forum activities at the Catholic University of Porto Alegre, see "Ameaça de bomba assusta o Fórum," *Zero Hora* January 28, 2003, p. 14.

12. Associação Brasileira de Organizações não-governamentais (ABONG); Ação pela Tributação das Transações financeiras em Apoio aos Cidadãos (ATTAC); Comissão Brasileira de Justiça e Paz (CBJP); Associação Brasileira de Empresários pela Cidadania (CIVES); Instituto Brasileiro de Análises Sociais e Econômicas (IBASE); and Rede Social de Justiça e Direitos Humanos.

13. Personal communication, March 23, 2003 Amsterdam.

14. It should be noted that the Brazilian Organizing Committee member organizations also have a membership in the IC.

15. See "International Council: Nature, Responsibilities, Composition and Functioning" accessed April 11, 2002, at <http://www.forumsocialmundial. org.br/eng/qconselho_1.asp>.

16. The role of the Cubans has also been pointed out by Zibechi (2003).

17. I am grateful to Peter Waterman for articulating this point.

18. These are the official 2002 figures, available at <http:// www.forumsocialmundial.org.br/eng/noticias_numeros_FSM2002_eng.asp>. Many commentators give higher figures.

19. For example, see the 2002 interview of Roberto Bissio in *Cadernos do Terceiro Mundo* 239.

20. The fact that in April 2002 representatives of groups related to the WSF International Council and Organizing Committee arranged an international observer mission to Israel/Palestine is an indication of the tendencies to increase the political protagonism of the WSF.

21. See "Grupo afro lamenta pouco espaço," *Correio do Povo*, January 30, 2001, p. 11.

22. In a meeting with the IC during the WSF 2003 Walden Bello asked Lula if he would accept an invitation to take part in the WSF 2004 in India. Lula responded positively, but at the same time expressed his view that the WSF should not be transformed into a "parade of presidents." He added—half-seriously, half-jokingly—that if the organizers in India should have problems in inviting a foreign president, they should remember that his comrades in the Brazilian trade union still consider him a trade union leader and he could always be invited as such.

23. This example was used by some Brazilian organizers in the WSF International Council meeting in Bangkok, August 12–15, 2002.

24. See Walden Bello, "2000: The Year of Global Protest against Globalization." This is a printed article distributed at the first WSF in Porto Alegre, January 2001.

25. In retrospective, *Financial Times* described the first Forum as a success. See "Free trade still rules in Mexico," *Financial Times* February 27, 2001, p. 6.
26. Also available at <www.worldsocialforum.org> (2.3.2002).

BIBLIOGRAPHY

Abers, Rebecca. n.d. "Overcoming the Dilemmas of Participatory Democracy: The Participatory Budget Policy in Porto Alegre, Brazil." Unpublished manuscript.

Albert, Michael. 2003. "WSF: Where To Now?" accessed February 17, 2003 <www.forumsocialmundial.org.br>.

Amin, Samin and B. Founou-Tchuigoua. 2002. *Integrated Programmes of Third World Forum For Calendar Years 2002, 2003 and 2004*. Document of Third World Forum: Dakar.

Cassen, Bernard. 2002. "Comment est né le Forum social mondial." Unpublished manuscript.

Falk, Richard and Andrew Strauss. 2001. "Toward Global Parliament." *Foreign Affairs* 80, no. 1: 212–20.

Grzybowski, Cândido. 2003. "Fórum Social Mundial: a construção de uma utopia," *Terraviva* (January 24): 5.

———. 1998. "Lógica econômica vs. lógica democrática." Pp. 6–34 in *Neoliberalismo: Alternativas?* ed. Cândido Grzybowski, J. M. Gomez and Pablo Gentili. Rio de Janeiro: Publicações Novamerica.

Hardt, Michael. 2002. "Porto Alegre: Today's Bandung?" *New Left Review* 14 (March–April), accessed April 13, 2002 <http://www.newleftreview.net/NLR24806.shtml>.

Klein, Naomi. 2001. "Farewell to 'End of History': Organization and Vision in Anti-Corporate Movements." Pp. 1–14 in *Socialist Register 2002: A World of Contradictions*, ed. Leo Panitch and Colin Leys. London: The Merlin Press.

Monbiot, George. 2002. "A Parliament for the Planet." *New Internationalist* 342 (January/February) <www.newint.org/issue342/planet.htm>.

Monereo, Manuel, Miguel Riera, and Pep Valenzuela eds. 2002. *Hacia el Partido de Oposición: Foro Social Mundial/Porto Alegre 2002*. España: El Viejo Topo.

Prestes, Paulo. 1999. *13 Leituras Petistas*. Porto Alegre, pp. 72–76.

Sader, Emir. 2003. "Porto Alegre, até logo," *Zero Hora* (January 28): 19.

———. 2001. "Antes e depois de Seattle." *Observatorio Social de América Latina* (January): 5–8.

Savio, Roberto. 2003. "Menor es mejor." *Terraviva* (January 28): 6.

de Souza Santos, B. 2001. "O principio do futuro," accessed April 4, 2001 <http://www.worldsocialforum.org>.

Teivainen, Teivo. Forthcoming. *Dilemmas of Democratization in the World Social Forum*. London: Routledge.

———. 2003. "Conference Synthesis of International Organizations and Architecture of World Power." Pp. 290–95 in *Another World Is Possible: Popular Alternatives to Globalization at the World Social Forum*, ed. William F. Fisher and Thomas Ponniah. London and New York: Zed Books.

Wainwright, Hillary. 2003. "Porto Alegre: Public Power beyond the State." Pp. 103–33 in *Politics Transformed: Lula and the Workers Party in Brazil*, ed. Sue Bradford and Bernardo Kucinski. London: Latin America Bureau.

Waterman, Peter. 2003. "From Comrades' Agreements to the Reinvention of Social Emancipation." Unpublished manuscript, February 2.

Whitaker, Chico. 2003a. "Notes about the World Social Forum." Accessed March 23, 2003 <www.worldsocialforum.org>.

————. 2003b. "O FSM como método de ação política." Pp. 237–44 in *O Espírito de Porto Alegre*, ed. Isabel Loureiro, Jose Correa and Maria Elisa Cevasco. São Paulo: Paz e Terra.

————. 2003c. "O que o Fórum Social Mundial traz de novo como modo de atuação política?" *Democracia Viva* 14 (January): 20–24.

Whitaker, Francisco. 2002. "Fórum Social Mundial: origens e objetivos." Accessed April 13, 2002 <http://www.forumsocialmundial.org.br/por/qorigem.asp>.

Zibechi, Raúl. 2003. "III Foro Social Mundial: La hora de estrategias." ALAI-AMLATINA (February 3).

Chapter 12

Making Space for Transnational Democracy

Janie Leatherman

Our survey of transnational social movements in this volume suggests the state system is losing its place of privilege. We are witnessing the dislocation of traditional politics and the reordering of global affairs. As new forms of globally networked civil and (uncivil) actors emerge, the interstate system and hegemonic structures of world order are being disrupted, dislocated, and increasingly, sidestepped. The rise of global civil society is giving way to new identities, ties and dialogues that lay outside the reach and control of states. The actors of global civil society are also pressuring global governance institutions to become more transparent and engage them directly. Indeed, much of the real implementation of the work of global institutions—as in peacemaking, de-mining, environmental monitoring, development, emergency humanitarian assistance—depends on NGO and social movement capacities to work the ground in local settings around the world, to network, and report back.

I develop these arguments below in terms of four claims that summarize the findings of our study on global arrogance. First, the discursive practices of global arrogance and its politics of mythmaking are being disrupted by a new awareness and by claims for new norms of social responsibility promoted by transnational social movements. Second, traditional governance is being dislocated by claims to democratic space in a transnational context. Social movements and organizations spanning the local to global context are transforming the ways we think about the politics of inclusion/exclusion, transnational solidarity, identity, and representation.

Third, transnational actors draw on new forms of information technology to promote their causes, but technology is no panacea. It can promote or thwart transnational democracy. Nevertheless, the Internet represents the ultimate vulnerability of the state system. It is a military–industrial–media–entertainment network designed to ensure economies of scale, which has now eclipsed economies of governance and control (Der Derian 2000). And fourth, the internal struggles in the spaces of transnational activity between oppositional and transformationalist voices provide a site of democratic instruction unlike any the sovereign nation-state, or global institutions can provide to date. Dialogue may not lead to consensus but it is educational. Learning is thus a key component of the democratic process. In particular, activists from the global South have challenged the North to reexamine their own discourse and practices of global arrogance. The Internet can facilitate this democratic exchange and amplify its effects, but it facilitates both protest and repression. Nevertheless, dialogue through networks of transnational activism is a new political methodology, mode of education and cultural experiment that is shaping participatory democracy.

Global Arrogance and the Risks of Replicating It

Global arrogance is about willful ignorance—an absence of critical thought and action about the structural conditions of inequality, violence and injustice in the world, and their daily manifestations. To this end, political elites engage in management strategies to define problems and elevate to the "crisis" level those issues on which they seek to focus attention (Edelman 1992). This self-serving approach serves to contain the realm of analysis, discovery or awareness of underlying structural causes (cf. Galtung 1969, 1990). It also limits the scope of possible solutions and the debate over them. Instead, explanations are sought in individual, cultural, ethnic, religious, and national or regional pathologies.

The end of the Cold War opened new possibilities for questioning the politics of global arrogance. However, sentiment about the Cold War's passing has varied around the world, as Parodi reminds us in his chapter. In the West, and the United States in particular, an air of triumphalism has predominated. We have arrived at the inevitable end station of history; the reign of democracy and neoliberal capitalism. The essence of such global arrogance is irresponsibility—the politics of not having to answer to the past, the present or the future.

In contrast to the historical amnesia of the United States and much of the West regarding colonial, neocolonial and imperialist adventures, elsewhere in the world the end of the Cold War signaled an opportunity for awareness-raising, recovery of memory, accountability, and restoration of democratic and just social and political relations. Truth commissions from Chile, Argentina, Peru, El Salvador, Guatemala, and South Africa all turned to self-criticism, reflection, inquiry, truth-telling, and reconciliation. Yet this recovery of history has typically unfolded in self-limiting parameters. Approached through a national framework, the truth commission methodology falls short of situating atrocities in the larger context of the Cold War or the still longer-running colonial histories that preceded it and often still determine local circumstances. Parodi's discussion of apologies by President Clinton also draws our attention to gestures that have more opportunistic appeal than commitment to truth-telling and reconciliation. Of what consequence is an apology that skips over listening, dialogue and compassion, and brings neither costs nor mechanisms of accountability with it?

Global arrogance is also about what is right in front of us in plain view, but we look past, or ignore. In their chapter, Zoelle and Josephson approach arrogance as political maneuvers that cast into the private realm and ascribe to individual pathologies the larger structural conditions of inequality that diminish life chances and choices. Such a maneuver was essential to the rhetoric of the Cold War in the West, where poverty could not be explained as the failure of capitalism. Instead, it had to be cast in terms of the lack of development, knowledge, sophistication, education, and advancement of society and their people—that is individual, not structural. Pretending poverty doesn't exist serves to reinforce the myth of inclusion and rekindle the hope that opportunity is spread equally and the gates to democracy are wide open. McDonald's golden arches symbolize to the world that all are entitled to the proverbial, if unobtainable "Happy Meal."

The politics of global arrogance is also about the lack of self-awareness and self-criticism within elite NGOs and social movements of the global North. Here we find the dangers of replicating global arrogance within progressive circles. As O'Neill and VanDeveer document, the transnational environmental movement has been patronizing and managerial. During much of the last twenty or thirty years, the movements became engaged with privileged and powerful actors, focusing their attention on the boardrooms and the meeting halls of the United Nations and its agencies, rather than on the grassroots base and their members' daily struggles. Northern environmental movements often claimed to represent the global South—a tendency that echoes the myth of familiarity: "We know what is best for you and how to solve your problems." As O'Neill explains, "the right technology and the right science can solve problems . . . . This reminds us of the close relationship between environmentalism and modernization, and the fact that the prescriptions for success through globalization are not so far removed from those of an earlier era." Central to the lack of self-reflection and perspective is the unwillingness of the global North to face the consumption issue. O'Neill argues there is a "strong element of 'anti-sacrifice' in the politics of global arrogance, despite the rhetoric of sacrifice."[1] Like Zoelle and Josephson argue with poverty, environmental devastation can be reduced to the individual. The causes are not structural, so they do not entail major changes in society.

The transition from communism to market-based democracies in Eastern Europe has not escaped the domination of managerialist views on environmental matters, either. Even though environmentalism provided one of the key areas for the emergence of civil society that helped lead to the overthrow of communism in many Eastern European states (Kaldor 2003), the linkage between Europeanization and the environmentally oriented civil society in East Central Europe has not been entirely positive. Hallström finds in his analysis of the Czech and Polish experiences in particular that the interaction has often been to the detriment of civil society. The early trend of the postcommunist decade in East Central Europe has been to move toward the top—down model of action that the global South has been critiquing the North about, too.

Much like the environmental movements in postcommunist Europe, the global movement against landmines gained momentum with the end of the Cold War, as humanitarian groups in the United States and Europe dealing with landmine-effected areas seized the political opening to call for drastic changes. As Nelson documents in his chapter, this movement sought and obtained new international norms, arguing the costs of landmine-related destruction to the environment and human health over-rides military utility. The global movement against landmines called for a total ban to reclaim safe social space. By networking with nation-states and international organizations, the movement has rolled back a conventional weapon widely used, while it has empowered survivors and drawn from their experiences to promote learning and new social relationships across health, development, environmental and security sectors. But even the international movement to ban landmines has not been without its own dangers of replicating the politics of global arrogance. We see this in the United States efforts to weaken the treaty provisions, and provide exceptions for its policies and use of landmines: the global standard bearer does not live up to the rules it imposes on others. The global will to challenge such arrogance was manifest in the rapid signing and ratification of the treaty despite U.S. pressures, and ultimately unwillingness to come on board.

While the demise of the Cold War was a watershed event in world politics, the myths of global arrogance that helped sustain it have persisted in its aftermath. The 1990s gave way to new justifications for this mythology. For example, the war on communism has been replaced with an even more desperate war on terrorism. The myths of sacrifice and protection are now cloaked with new, more unobtainable purposes. These developments have not escaped the attention of the growing transnational feminist movement. In her chapter, Hunt points to the usurping of women's rights by the West, especially by the Bush administration, in an attempt to legitimize the U.S. intervention in Afghanistan and the larger "war on terror."

We find dilemmas of reproducing global arrogance also in the transnational feminist efforts at solidarity (cf. Eschle 2001, 212–17). Not unlike their counterparts in the global environmental movement, Western feminists also presume to speak on behalf of their sisters in the global South. Hence, Hunt's charge that global feminisms have often been elite/Western feminisms in disguise and that the use of the Internet has tended to reinforce dominant myths plaguing global feminisms. Webber notes in her chapter a similar insensitivity and presumptive action on the part of Western feminists who mobilized on the Internet to protest the stoning to death of a Nigerian woman accused of having sex outside of marriage. Local Nigerians were frightened that this exposure could backfire on them. Women need to work together to promote a common cause by means that serve the local stakeholders, not just those in solidarity internationally. Eschle, for example, calls for a "transversal politics," so that "there is a politicized, rather than reified notion of identity at work." This requires a dialogue of " 'rooting' and 'shifting' according to each participant." As Eschle explains (2001, 207, citing Yuval-Davis), "each participant . . . brings with her a rooting in her own membership and identity, but at the same time tries to shift in order to put herself in a situation of exchange with women who have different membership and identity."

The myths of global arrogance are also a function of a lack of understanding, and access to information and knowledge. Tadros argues in her chapter on human rights in the Middle East that the flow of information is a crucial part of hegemony. One-way communication is a monologue that reinforces arrogance, but exchanges of information can challenge arrogance in its tracks, and affect change on multiple levels of awareness and identification. As Teivainen argues in his chapter, the World Social Forum disrupts arrogance by promoting transnational dialogue. The annual meetings, regional and local events officially sanctioned by the WSF or those related to it, are changing the terms of debate and redefining the issues. The sum of these activities is greater than the parts—even if the organizational form and rules structuring the WSF's search for transnational democracy are still in development.

Democratizing Transnational Spaces

Three different kinds of spatial dynamics pervade the politics of global arrogance and drive efforts to get beyond it. First, there are elements of enclosure. For example, Gill argues that the contradiction between big capital and democracy encloses democracy: neoliberalism privileges trade and investment, while closing down democratic control over policies in the economic, social and ecological spheres (2003, 214). Neoliberalism also intensifies discipline on labor while foreclosing alternative market opportunities. Unfair WTO trade practices threaten self-sufficiency—for example Senegalese chicken farmers are going out of business in the face of a deluge of subsized chickens from Europe and the West entering the local market under the WTO's Marrakesh agreements of 1994 that opened the door to free trade in agricultural products (Pigeaud 2003). The discipline of capital is linked to the intensifying crisis of social reproduction: a disproportionate burden of structural adjustment falls on women's shoulders (Rupert 2000, 87). The spread of neoliberalism also leads to the enclosure of sociocultural and biological diversity through their substitution by monocultures that increase health risks and lead to a loss of food security.

We also see the enclosure of social space with the use of heavily armed police and militia at "the Battle of Seattle" and at other protests, such as the G-8 meeting in Genoa, Italy, in 2001, where police shot an Italian activist to death. We see enclosures of social space for protest also in the change of venue of global elite to locales where the transnational civil society simply cannot gain access, such as the WTO meeting held in undemocratic Qatar, or the G-8 meeting in a remote Canadian mountain resort (Glasius and Kaldor 2002; Gill 2003, 216; O'Neill 2004). All these problems add up to a global or organic crisis that "links diverse forces across and within nations, specifically to oppose the ideas, institutions and material power of disciplinary neo-liberalism" (Gill 2003, 216).

A second spatial dynamic is social enclavization—in this case we are talking about privileged spheres being closed off from others (Gill 2003, 198). This happens when wealthy neighborhoods are physically removed from poor ones, or protected from them by high walls and gated communities. Other examples include the Israeli plan for a wall to keep out Palestinians (Zur 2002); U.S. fortifications along the U.S.-Mexican border (Nivins 2002); and Australia's "imprisonment" of immigrants, stateless persons, refugees and asylum seekers (Bowden 2003).

Resistance to the maneuvers of global arrogance involve a third spatial dynamic—the opening of democratic space. This is the liberating aspect of social movements that run the gambit from real/virtual/local/transnational.

One of the most striking features of these new spaces is their nonhierarchical forms of governance where politics does not depend on central leadership figures or bodies. Similarly, Gill suggests that these movements represent a kind of "post-modern transnational political party" that has no clear leadership structure, and cannot be easily decapitated—a fact that confounded the press at Seattle (Gill 2003, 219). These movements are more effective because of their ability to see particular struggles as part of a "more general set of interconnections between problems and movements worldwide" (220).

These liberating forms of transnational authority vary in organizational structure, spatial location, focus and outreach. Networks have both horizontal breadth and vertical ties to the local. Hence, we can look at them from the ground up—starting with social movements rooted in local contexts that network into the transnational arena to enhance their resources and influence. Alternatively, we can focus on the network as a whole. Keck and Sikkink (1998) argue that at the core of these relationships lie dense exchanges of information and services, principled action, common discourse, and shared values. Networks contribute to democratic processes at the transnational level. But groups use them to bring global norms and resources of governance to bear on their campaigns at home—a boomerang pattern of influence (Keck and Sikkink 1998).

In this global era, "local" is not local in the traditional sense. Most communities are no longer isolated. The Internet, fax machines, cells phones, satellite television, and other forms of communication have helped to erase differences imposed by time and space. Social movements are part of the network of relations that interpellate the local and global (Magnusson 1996, 72). Such dynamics are in play with the KWRU, the RAWA, the truth commissions, or the interaction of environmental movements in East Central Europe with local governments and the European Union. KWRU is an NGO operating out of Philadelphia with roots deep in the Kensington neighborhood. But KWRU has also formed transnational ties, participated in the WSF, and worked in solidarity with transnational campaigns including protesting against the Free Trade Area of the Americas (FTAA). These commitments emerge partly out of solidarity with others in the hemisphere and are an effort to bring pressure through global governance institutions, such as the OAS, to seek redress for local and national issues of poverty in the United States.

Truth commissions, not unlike the KWRU, also have deep ties to the local political context. However, the spread of truth commissions around the globe as a mechanism for political transformation, and the connections that are emerging among them, suggests a transnational dimension reinforced by an emergent norm to truth-telling and a right to know

(Forsberg and Teivainen 2004). Like truth commissions, RAWA's focus has been on the local context, documenting abuses, and promoting the participation of Afghan women in social and political activities to help achieve democracy and a secular society. While providing their own representation to the marginalized, isolated, forgotten women and children of their country, they have used the Internet to seek international support and resources to leverage change at home.

Tadros' analysis of the human rights movement in the Middle East encompasses both the regional breadth of organizations such as the Arab Organization for Human Rights—the oldest, formed 20 years ago outside the Arab world when no Arab state would host it—and others locally rooted. She shows us how these movements have claimed new space—mostly virtual—in a region of the world where activists are in a precarious position. Thus, the Internet has had a significant intermediary role. No longer do activists need to rely exclusively on diplomats or outside contacts as did dissidents in the former Soviet Union and in Eastern Europe monitoring the 1975 Helsinki Final Act during the Cold War; they risked their lives to pass reports of human rights violations out the communist bloc and into the hands of Western human rights groups and delegations to the Conferences on Security and Cooperation in Europe (Leatherman 2003). Now the Internet serves as a direct conduit stretching the horizon of the local into a virtual global context.

At the other end of the spectrum we see new forms of transnational political authority with more diffuse organizational forms. The movement to ban landmines, the global feminist movement, the human rights movement and its networks in the Middle East, the world peace movement and the environmental movement all operate through transnational advocacy networks. These agents of transnational authority operate at a global level, but are constituted and sustained by associations that tie them into the local and regional contexts. Cultivating these ties in these contexts moves us away from a politics of global arrogance where the global supersedes the local.

The global environmental movement, like the World Social Forum, is really a movement of movements, but lacks the more structured form of the World Social Forum. However, of the various types of environmental movements that O'Neill and VanDeveer analyze, they argue that diffuse networks of activist organizations are the ones at the vanguard of reshaping transnational environmental activism—not just with lobbying governments, but with their work in the civil sphere and with local actors, and because of their efforts outside of official channels. This lack of defined leadership or hierarchy has also become a template for other movements—most notably the protests against the U.S. invasion of Iraq in 2003. Then even a handful of activists working E-mail and the Internet, as Cortright's chapter shows us, could organize events to bring people out on the street simultaneously around the world.

As the global peace movement shows, in the end, it's the local action that counts. So, we have to be cautious about the global context. O'Neill and VanDeveer also warn against erasing the local from the environmental movement in favor of transnational and globalizing approaches. Globalizing tends to empower Northern institutions and their agendas, and detracts attention from finding solutions to pressing local problems pervasive in many parts of the world, like safe drinking water and desertification, and it discounts Southern approaches to environmentalism that focus on physical survival and overcoming poverty or environmental destruction caused by mega development projects. Hunt documents similar problems with representation in her chapter on the global feminist movement and its interaction with RAWA. Thus, social movements face the peril of reinventing global arrogance.

Despite these drawbacks, the trend toward transnationalizing governance through civil society brings with it some important new developments. Gradually, transnational engagement is creating the conditions for dialogue, and challenging the way issues are defined and solutions sought. The terms of the debate are being reframed, and the issues at stake are increasingly multifaceted. We see a system of learning and approaches to governance that are more complex and nuanced and informed by a diversity of circumstances and needs around the globe. Both the global environmental movement and the International Campaign to Ban Landmines provide an instructive window on such developments. The global environmental movement has forged linkages on labor, socioeconomic justice, health, and security issues—to name a few. The movement to ban landmines has undergone a similar transformation.

The Internet and Transnational Democracy

The burgeoning field of information technology provides many new avenues for redefining traditional spaces of political contestation, establishing new sites of authority, and democratization. The Internet has been one of the most dramatic applications of the new communications technology. There are several dimensions along which we can speak of its democratizing potential. It enhances the voice of the people, allowing them to be networked in virtual spaces, engaged, participate in the exchange of ideas and contribute to the flow of information. Thus, the Internet provides means for bypassing traditional gatekeepers of information and knowledge, in particular government officials, experts, and the media. The Internet provides a means for democratizing expertise. In doing so, the Internet subverts hierarchies of power, while promoting new (horizontal) forms of leadership. It gives new opportunities for bringing to light social values and claims for redress of marginalized and oppressed voices. Hence, the Internet has the potential to amplify voices calling for social justice, equality, peace, reconciliation, and truth (Naughton 2001).[2]

The Internet provides an avenue for like-minded individuals to discover each other, form new identifications and solidarities, and mobilize in joint causes. Tadros reminds us in her chapter that the Internet also provides a forum for serendipitous encounters; on the worldwide web we find like-minded individuals and causes, but also stumble into views and campaigns that we are against. Thus, the Internet has the potential at least to encourage awareness-raising, if not dialogue among groups of people with different interests.

The democratic potential of the Internet will not be realized if it exists merely as a virtual experience. Indeed, an important question is how movements get supporters to go from the virtual to the real. How does the Internet promote, mobilize, train and discipline members? It is clear that it gives movements the ability to react quickly over a global sphere. As Kidd (2001) (citing Wayne Sharpe) argues, the Internet has a stealth or enigma factor: the invisibility of the organizing and mobilization of opposition was a key factor in the success of the Seattle protests, the pro-democracy campaigns in Indonesia, or the recent antiwar protests that erupted simultaneously around the world in the winter of 2003 in opposition to the war against Iraq. Nevertheless, Kidd cautions that the surprise factor has not been long-lived. "Since the mid-1990s and the Rand Corporation publication on 'netwars,'" protest groups are closely monitored by the United States and other government intelligence networks (2001, 327).

We are reminded the Internet is a tool, not an end in itself. So, it can be used to pursue quite different goals than social justice and global transformation. Indeed, the Internet can reinscribe traditional hierarchies, rather than subvert them. Governments engage in various policing activities on the Net to accomplish just this, as Tadros shows in her chapter detailing entrapment of activists in the Middle East. The Internet also tends to reinforce already existing inequalities rather than challenge them. It does this in the gendered aspects of access to the Net, as well as in other types of power relationships (Ebo 2001). Thus, the Internet reproduces the North–South divide digitally, and the divide between the rich/poor in all societies. Ultimately, the Internet provides conservative forces with incentives to limit civil society access to it, and a new tool to police and monitor use of it (Gill 2003, 193).

Nevertheless, the Internet, as Tadros' chapter shows us, has been essential for the human rights movement in the Middle East to get its feet off the ground. The Internet has transformed the direction, flow and control of information. No longer are Arab governments solely in control of information and people relegated to the role of passive recipients. The Internet also reaches a new audience in the younger generations of users seeking to develop an identity in an increasingly globalized world. In fact, Tadros pins her hope for building transnational democracy on these youth. The Internet helps with this by creating conditions of interaction with the West that place Middle Easterners on the same intellectual level. Thus, the Internet may well facilitate a number of social transformations. It changes the relationship between the State and individual, as well as the civil society and the State. In addition, it helps to forge a global civil society, while creating more equal partnerships among its members and more diverse representation and stakeholders than previously. All this in turn changes the relationship of the state system to global civil society.

Like the human rights movements in the Middle East, the KWRU and the truth commissions direct most of their efforts to redressing issues within the local context. However, for all of them new forms of information technology are important, including the Internet. These tools of communication alter both information flows and power relationships. For example, the truth commissions subvert traditional power relationships by legitimizing the stories and life experiences of survivors of torture, their families, communities and witnesses. In addition, the presence of truth commission documentation and methodology on the Internet creates new flows of information in a transnational context. At the very least, the availability of such information has the potential to help mobilize other truth commissions and empower people in other parts of the world to take up similar causes. A norm for the right to truth can be a deterrent factor for governments that (might otherwise) act with impunity.

Indeed, Parodi argues that the Internet has improved the potential for the truth commissions, especially through the establishment of the National Security Archive in 1985, and the U.S. Institute of Peace, which has an online collection of 24 cases with links to several national reports. Other key sites include the Virtual Truth Commission and national truth commissions, such as Peru's and Chile's that have their own websites and update them regularly. In addition, there are methodologies and courses online with tool kits to implement truth commissions through such institutions as the University of Colorado, Conflict Research Consortium and Creative Associates International based in Washington, D.C.

The KWRU has used various forms of information technology, including video documentaries of their activities as part of their civil rights strategies for truth telling and accountability. These strategies are also designed to encourage mobilization to form new coalitions, and create publicity and public engagement. The KWRU uses its website to overcome the isolation of the poor Kensington neighborhood in the real world by bringing it to life through the virtual tours of the Internet. By making poor neighborhoods accessible in a virtual context, they break down ghetto barriers and help the local community reach out to connect with other communities of poverty and with social activists in the U.S. and around the world. The website challenges the economically privileged to come out of their "gated communities" at least online. As Zoelle and Josephson argue, the focus on Kensington helps to keep the organization "grounded in local conditions," and relevant to the constituency that is their concern. The website has amplifying effects in this context, too, so that the testimonies of those interviewed on tours are not just known to KWRU, but their voices can be heard globally. By claiming a democratic space not just on the ground but also on the web, KWRU is helping to forge the kinds of cross-national class identifications for which the group stands. Thus, the KWRU works to create more inclusive understandings of citizenship, democracy, and social responsibility, building these both in domestic and transnational contexts.

The Internet is an important tool that allows the diffuse, networked movements to stay grounded locally, and connect with small grassroots organizations and movements that do not have resources to operate outside their own locales. O'Neill and VanDeveer argue that the Internet has facilitated the expansion of these kinds of connections in the global environmental movement. The Internet has played a similar role in the global feminist movement. Hunt's chapter highlights the positive as well as the negative effects of feminists using the Internet to link women around the globe in the struggle for women's rights. On the positive front, the Internet helps to create a common space and a democratic site to challenge oppression and dominant myths against women, foster solidarity, exchange information, build coalitions around global issues, and strengthen local organizing. For example, the Internet gave voice in the virtual world to groups such as RAWA to counter the stereotypical images of voiceless, faceless victims with information instead about their courageous, active struggles for political change.

But the Internet is not without contradictions and shortcomings. As Tadros notes, these have to do partly with the structure and accessibility of the Internet itself. Even though the Internet is decentralized, it is still under governance from the United States, which creates a new "model of power structure." The Internet, therefore, provides new opportunities to inscribe

Western hegemony on the Middle East and the rest of the world. And as a product of the U.S. military, the Internet also reinforces the hegemony of English as a language of global communication, although this is slowly diminishing. Meanwhile the presence of English provides a mechanism for the dissemination of Western culture and values—a cultural invasion.

Questions of equality, access, and representation are also intertwined with the debate over how and to what extent the Internet is a useful tool to promote community among transnational movements. For participants in the WSF, these questions led to some caution about taking the WSF online. So far, person-to-person meetings, rather than less expensive virtual gatherings are preferred, thus eliminating questions about access issues, up-to-date technology, cultural issues of Western domination of the Internet, and so on. So while the WSF has struggled with the issue of representation, it has not seen the Internet as a means to reconcile these.

In her chapter Hunt also urges some caution about the way the Internet can distort efforts at inclusiveness and fair representation, rather than enhance them. She argues that some Western feminist groups, such as the Feminist Majority Foundation have failed to avoid colonial and hegemonic tendencies of the West in their attempts to speak for Afghan women. Thus, they turned to RAWA as the authentic voice of Afghan women in an effort to "save them." There is nothing inherently democratic or fair as far as the representation of voices and ideas are concerned when it comes to the web. So, there is a risk that people will use the Internet to become native informants for the West to get favors, funding, support, status, prestige, recognition, and so on. And there is also the risk that the West will focus its attention on such likeminded voices, either ignoring others online, or failing to take the extra effort to learn about others that lack access to it. These problems reinforce class/gender/urban/rural/literate/illiterate divisions both in the national and global contexts. Here again we find the pitfalls of replicating global arrogance instead of getting beyond it.

From Anti to Alternative Global Orders

Much of the literature on the emergence of transnational relations has focused on the oppositional character of activists and social movements (Smith and Johnston 2002; Gill 2003). "Antiglobalization" serves as the common designation of resistance. However, as Mittelman notes, this is "problematic since it defines a phenomenon solely as a negation. It impoverishes social criticism by mystifying what may be learned from the debates over globalization" (2002, 7). In practice, much of the resistance is against neoliberalism but in favor of globalization as long as it serves just social ends—such as institutional reforms. But others advocate abolishing institutions such as capitalism while some activists seek to give it a human face.

Creating alternatives is very different from just reacting to the negative aspects of globalization. A lot of energy is spent reacting. The protests against the U.S.-led war on Iraq illustrate the frustrations movements face pushing against the hegemon without budging it. The creative force of movements can be exhausted this way. In fact, it is in the hegemon's interest to keep movements engaged in a reactionary mode, since the lines of debate are well-defined, and the nature of the game, its boundaries, its possibilities, the expertise at stake, the players, and so on, are all predetermined and predictable to a large degree.

How do movements break free of hegemonic maneuvers to trap them in a reactionary mode? Where do they get their energy and vision for alternatives? How do they respond to authorities efforts to close new spaces? How do they keep from being co-opted, mainstreamed? Does turning conflictual relationships into cooperative ones risk cooptation? Becoming a functionary? Reproducing arrogance? What part of the new initiatives get captured in the old system?

In our study, the answers to these questions are mixed. For example, movements vary in terms of the emphasis they place on promoting alternatives versus opposing the political order that is in place. At the same time, they also vary in terms of the scope and level of political change they are aspiring to: Is it directed locally or globally or at some intermediate level? All of the movements, however, seek to leverage political change and mobilize support through transnational connections, either in the virtual or the real, and usually through a combination of both.

Teivainen suggests that the most important transformations are likely to emerge from proactive rather than reactive initiatives and meetings. The World Social Forum stands as perhaps the most important example of working toward a transformative vision. As Teivainen has documented, the group shifted quickly from protesting at Davos, to organizing an alternative forum, to distancing itself almost entirely from Davos to underscore the WSF's alternative character. The WSF has also cast a wide net in its efforts to challenge globalization. But how the WSF will channel debate among its participants is not yet clear. Teivainen gives us some sense of the incipient contours of debate. "Outra globalização" (another globalization) is a term that some key organizers emphasized at the Porto Alegre meetings. However, this approach doesn't take activists too far from the managerialist perspectives of international capitalism and its myths of inclusion. "Another globalization" can end up sounding a lot like democracy plus capitalism. Teivainen argues that the anti/alternative divide is often taken to mean that anti is radical while alternative is superficial reform. However, he argues this assumption breaks down in practice, as some antiglobalization people can be pro-capitalist, while the pro-globalization may be anti-capitalist.

The WSF experience is emblematic of the challenges faced across the spectrum of cases in this volume. Training in new skills, as well as consciousness-raising and new shifts in identification and solidarity are more evident across the cases than the outlines of an alternative global order. Still, these changes in themselves are significant. The myths of global arrogance are being contested at the same time that new norms and principles of interaction in the global civil society are emerging. The global North is coming under scrutiny as much as the South—since the disputed 2000 U.S. presidential election, even the United States has come under scrutiny with election observers from the Organization of Security and Cooperation in Europe (Curl 2004). We can see this scrutiny of the North in the campaigns of the environmental movement, the human rights movement, and the work of groups such as the KWRU. Not only are Northern states the target of criticism, but non-state actors, too, including corporations. The scrutiny is focused both on their action domestically and transnationally. Global institutions are also taking groups from global civil society more seriously. O'Neill and VanDeveer note that intergovernmental bodies, including the WTO and World Bank, are more willing to listen to and meet with representatives of movements, and more willing to address their concerns.

In some instances the Internet has made it possible for a greater diversity of voices to be heard. We see this in the global environmental movement. Over the last decade in particular, there has been a period of learning between North and South. Here we find a transformation within one sector of global civil society itself. Through such dialogue, the environmental movement has moved from a managerialist, incrementalist, science driven approach that was state-dominated, and non-transformative, to more awareness and appreciation of local, or indigenous knowledge, and more community-based resource management. These changes have been accompanied by the focus on new norms. O'Neill and VanDeveer also highlight Global Witness' efforts to raise awareness about the connection between resources, violent conflict and corruption, especially in commodities, brutal labor practices and human rights violations that surround this kind of extraction—for example, the diamond industry. Global Witness' groundbreaking work to certify diamond trading proves that consumers need not be passive participants of global injustice and oppression, but can find practical, workable methods that ensure accountability and transparency. Students Against Sweatshops provides another useful example.

Global change is unfolding through the actions of new political movements operating out of the local and networking into the global, as well as from the transnational to the local. KWRU is at the local end of the spectrum, while the environmental movement, the ICBL and the World Social Forum, for example, are at the other. Hallström's chapter shows us the intermediate range, with the environmental movements of East Central Europe working locally, yet trying to build coalitions with state officials and the European Union experts at the regional level—despite the disempowering tendencies of the latter.

Thus, we find many different kinds of organizational forms through which civil society actors are promoting participation in the transnational arena. As new spaces are claimed, and connections woven across state boundaries at multiple levels of society, the state-centeredness of international relations is being eclipsed. Traditional forms of authority and control as exercised through balance of power politics, state-centered coalitions, or even multilateral organizations such as the United Nations, World Bank, WTO, and so on, are being challenged. As Mittelman puts it, the

> nub of the problem is that the interstate system relies on national institutional forms at a level that does not correspond to an increasing portion of the world's political and economic activities. This incongruity between the cage of the nation-state and actual global flows is an invitation to use more fully the political imagination. Globalization, at bottom, involves a quest for an appropriate temporal and spatial scale for governance. (2002, 11)

The rise of global civil society is a response to these incongruities between the state and globalization. So, too, is the proliferation of international regimes, institutions and agreements. Social movements interact with them to contest authority over processes of globalization that threaten to spiral out of control. Some scholars suggest that "global NGOs have become influential simply because they possess a property that happens to be the peculiar hallmark of ethical political intervention: moral authority and legitimacy. And they possess moral authority because they claim to represent the public or the general interest against official interests of the state or the economy" (Chandhoke 2002, 41). But what we have sought to stress in this volume is that even the moral authority of NGOs has been subject to new scrutiny for replicating global arrogance.

The way past arrogance is rooted partly in movements' emphasis on dialogue more than consensus. As Webber suggests in her theory chapter, dialogue affords the expression of a *generic will* to keep the future open and pliable to the imagination. It stokes the desires of humanity against the reactionary and hegemonic projects that work to foreclose them. Meanwhile, networked movements remain fluid and unsettled in their pursuit of a generic will. For example, O'Neill and VanDeveer caution us that the transnational environmental movement is unlikely to ever be coherent. What we find instead is a diversity of ideas, frames, organizational logics, and strategic choices. Consensus, if it does exist, centers around the awareness that we live on a finite earth, but the debate flourishes on ways to deal with this reality. In the meantime, deep contradictions persist. In the environmental movement these lie between global environmental activism from the managerialist North, and the more emancipatory Southern positions and critiques of capitalism under globalization. But the debate has been opened, and the groundwork for a new awareness, and new norms are broached by creating space for transnational, democratic instruction and participation.

Movements that have gone beyond global arrogance, that are not only engaged in critique and resistance but also creating alternative sites of democratic engagement and action, are at the real vanguard of global change. Real power is the power to remove obstacles and create new realities. Engaging in global democracy must start with dismantling the obstacles of hegemonic hierarchies. We see this most prominently with the WSF—a novel attempt to establish horizontal relationships and engagement. There is no high fee to attend this meeting, unlike the World Economic Forum at Davos, which curries favor to the rich and famous of the global corporate world and cozy state interests. The multifaceted nature of the WSF's concerns is also instructive: it is not just discussing the economy but a range of issues embracing justice, inequality, and sustainable development.

Many other transnational movements are also discovering new and overlapping concerns: the movement to ban landmines encompasses a whole range of issues that in the final analysis are aimed at promoting security rooted in local-to-global cultures of peace and justice. Like the environmental movement, the movement to ban landmines is calling for norms that go beyond the Westphalian system of states. For example, the monopoly of control and use of landmines has been displaced from states' hands literally into the hands of the global community. This development follows on a growing list of prohibitions on the state that we saw earlier in human rights law and the convention outlawing torture. But now these prohibitions are moving into the military-security sector. So the larger question is to what extent do the new political agents of transnational democracy simply bypass the authority of states and traditional global institutions? To what extent do their actions render the Westphalia system less and less relevant? What forms of global order or orders are emergent? These questions are undoubtedly key for future research.

Conclusions

The activists of global civil society are defining new responsibilities that extend beyond national borders. The globally connected social movements raise the imperative to see issues in a multifaceted framework, rather than from narrow, sectoral, or national interests. But they call for keeping the local in focus, as does the Cardoso Report on UN—Civil Society Relations (*We the Peoples* 2004). Social movements are redefining social responsibility as a collective undertaking that can be realized through transnational spaces, virtually and on the ground. They have also demanded new norms and rights, especially the right to know and the right to the truth. This is an appeal to envision, engage in dialogue about, and begin to commit to an alternative future which dimensions are still only in the earliest stages of articulation and debate.

This is a politics of flows and connections, not enclosed spaces like the traditional state system (Magnusson 1996, 302; Appadurai 2001). This is not a utopia, not a deliverance from the disorders and disciplining madness of the (fading) inter-national system. What we have before us is a cacophony of voices calling for change and going about it, too. They may not be singing the same tune, but they are a new chorus all the same. They are practicing transnational democracy by forging new boundaries of community while searching for shared responses to the tasks at hand.

NOTES

1. E-mail correspondence with the author, May 26, 2003.
2. Of course, the Internet amplifies voices of terrorist groups and other illicit actors—like sex traffickers.

BIBLIOGRAPHY

Appadurai, Arjun, ed. 2001. *Globalization*. Durham: Duke University Press.

Bowden, Charles. 2003. "Outback Nightmares and Refugee Dreams." *Mother Jones* (March/April): 47–55.

Chandhoke, Neera. 2002. "The Limits of Global Civil Society." Pp. 35–53 in *Global Civil Society 2002*, ed. Mary Glasius, Mary Kaldor, and Helmut Anheier. New York: Oxford University Press.

Curl, Joseph. 2004. "Foreign Observers to Audit Election." *Washington Times*, August 7.

Der Derian, James. 2000. *Virtual War*. Boulder, Colo.: Westview.

Ebo, Bosah. 2001. *Cyberimperialism: Global Relations in the New Electronic Frontier*. Westport, Conn.: Praeger.

Edelman, Murray. 1992. "The Construction and Uses of Social Problems." Pp. 263–80 in *Jean Baudrillard: The Disappearance of Art and Politics*, ed. William Sterns and William Cholopka. New York: St. Martin's Press.

Eschle, Catherine. 2001. *Global Democracy, Social Movements and Feminism*. Boulder, Colo.: Westview.

Forsberg, Tuomas and Teivo Teivainen. 2004. *Past Injustice in World Politics: Prospects of Truth-Commission-Like-Global Institutions*. Crisis Management Initiative. Office of President Ahtisaari. Accessed at <http://www.ahtisaari.fi/files/Truth_Commission.pdf>.

Galtung, Johan. 1990. "Cultural Violence." *Journal of Peace Research* 27, no. 3: 291–305.

———. 1969. "Violence, Peace and Peace Research." *Journal of Peace Research* 6, no. 3: 167–91.

Gill, Stephen. 2003. *Power and Resistance in the New World Order*. New York: Palgrave Macmillan.

Glasius, Marlies and Mary Kaldor. 2002. "The State of Global Civil Society Before and After September 11." Pp. 3–33 in *Global Civil Society*, ed. Marlies Glasius, Mary Kaldor, and Helmut Anheier. New York: Oxford University Press.

Kaldor, Mary. 2003. *Global Civil Society: An Answer to War*. Cambridge, U.K.: Polity Press.

Keck, Margaret and Kathryn Sikkink, 1998. *Activists beyond Borders*. Ithaca, N.Y.: Cornell University Press.

Leatherman, Janie. 2003. *From Cold War to Democratic Peace: Third Parties, Peaceful Change and the OSCE*. Syrause, NY: Syracuse University Press.

Magnussen, Warren. 1996. *The Search for Political Space*. Toronto: University of Toronto Press.

Mittelman, James H. 2002. "Making Globalization work for the Have Nots." *International Journal on World Peace* 19, no. 2 (June): 3–25.

Naughton, John. 2001. "Contested Space: the Internet and Global Civil Society." Pp. 147–68 in *Global Civil Society 2001*, ed. Glasius, Marlies, Mary Kaldor, and Helmut Anheier. New York: Oxford Univeristy Press.

O'Neill, Kate. 2004. "Transnational Protest: States, Circuses, and Conflict at the Frontline of Global Politics." *International Studies Review* 6: 233–51.

Pigeaud, Fanny. 2003. "The Sengalese Chicken is Debated at the WTO." *La Liberation*. Accessed October 19, 2004 <http://www.truthout.org/docs_03/080703I.shtml>.

Rupert, Mark. 2000. *Ideologies of Globalization*. New York: Taylor and Francis.

Smith, Jackie, and Hank Johnston, eds. 2002. *Globalization and Resistance*. Lanham, Maryland: Rowman and Littlefield.

Zur, Ofer. 2002. "Time for a Wall." *Tikkun* 17, no. 3: 20–22.

Index